ISBN 978-1-330-04119-2
PIBN 10011040

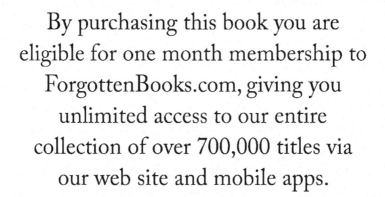

Similar Books Are Available from
www.forgottenbooks.com

COMPRISING

WITH A SPECIAL INTRODUCTION BY
EPIPHANIUS WILSON, A.M.

REVISED EDITION

SPECIAL INTRODUCTION

HEBREW literature contains some of the most profound and most influential productions of the human spirit. It constitutes a potent factor in modern civilization, and possesses merits which place it far above most other literatures of the world. The common salutation of the Hebrew is "Peace," while that of the Greeks is "Grace," and that of the Romans, "Safety." The Greek sought after grace, or intellectual and bodily perfection, and the power of artistic accomplishment. The Roman's ideal was strength and security of life and property. The Hebrew sought after peace, peace in the heart, as founded on a sense of Jehovah's good providence, and a moral conformity in conduct to His revealed will. While the Greek in art, literature, and even in morals, made beauty his standard, the Roman stood for power, domination and law, and the Hebrew for religion. The Hebrew, indeed, introduced into Europe the first clear conception of religion, as implied in monotheism, and a rigidly defined moral law, founded upon the will of Jehovah. The basis of morals among the Latins was political, among the Greeks æsthetic, and among the Hebrews it was the revealed will of Jehovah.

While the most important remains of Hebrew literature are comprised in the Scriptures known to us as the Bible, there exists also a voluminous mass of Hebrew writings which are not included in the sacred canon. These writings are of supreme importance and value, and the selections which we have made from them in the present volume give a good idea of their interest, beauty, and subtlety of thought.

From the very beginning of their history the Hebrews were a deeply poetic race. They were fully alive to the beauties of external nature, and no national poetry contains more vivid descriptions of the sea, sky, and the panorama of forest, stream and mountain, peopled by the varied activities of animated

iii

nature. The songs of Zion glow with poetic enthusiasm, but
their principal characteristic is their intense earnestness. They
are no idle lays of love and wine or warlike triumph. They
depict the joy of existence as dependent upon the smile and
favor of Jehovah, and all the happiness, plenty, victory and
success of life are attributed, without hesitation, to nothing else
but " the loving-kindness of the Lord." Yet this religious
fervor becomes the basis of sublimity, pathos, and picturesque-
ness, such as can seldom be approached even by the finest productions of the Attic muse.

But the Hebrews were also philosophers, and if they never
attained to what we may call the *netteté et clarté* of the Greek
metaphysician, they excelled all other thinkers in the boldness
and profound spirituality of their philosophical mysticism. In
proof of this assertion we may point to that body of writings
known as the Kabbalah.

The word " Kabbalah " means " doctrine received by oral
tradition," and is applied to these remains to distinguish them
from the canonical Hebrew Scriptures, which were written
by " the Finger of Jehovah." Hebrew speculation attempts in
the Kabbalah to give a philosophical or theosophistic basis to
Hebrew belief, while at the same time it supplements the doctrines of the Old Testament. For instance, it is a disputed point
whether the immortality of the soul is taught in the Hebrew
canon, but in the Kabbalah it is taken for granted, and a complete and consistent psychology is propounded, in which is
included the Oriental theory of metempsychosis. This account
of the human soul, as distinct from the human body, treats of
the origin and eternal destiny of man's immortal part. On the
other hand God and Nature, and the connection between the
Creator and the creation, are most exactly treated of in detail.
God is the *En-Soph*, the boundless One, as in modern philosophy
God is the Absolute. He manifests Himself in the ten *Sephiroth*,
or intelligences. It would be easy on this point to show Dante's
indebtedness to the Kabbalah in his description of the various
heavens of his Paradise. These intelligences control, in groups
of three, the three worlds of intellect, of soul, and of matter.
The tenth of the *Sephiroth* is called Kingdom, *i.e.*, the personal
Deity, as seen in the workings of Providence, with which conception we may compare Dante's description of Fortune, in the

seventh book of the "Inferno." This last of the *Sephiroth* is manifested visibly in the Shekinah. This is the barest and baldest outline of the main features in this famous system.

The rise of Kabbalism is not very clearly known as regards authorship and date; it is in turn, by different Jewish writers, ascribed to Adam, Abraham, Moses and Ezra; but doubtless the work is an aggregation of successive writings, and some critics believe that it was not compiled before the Middle Ages, *i.e.,* in the centuries between the conquest of Gaul by the Franks and the period following the death of Dante.

There can be no doubt that the Kabbalah contains the ripest fruit of spiritual and mystical speculation which the Jewish world produced on subjects which had hitherto been obscured by the gross anthropomorphism of such men as Maimonides and his school. We can understand the revolt of the devout Hebrew mind from traditions like those which represented Jehovah as wearing a phylactery, and as descending to earth for the purpose of taking a razor and shaving the head and beard of Sennacherib. The theory of the *Sephiroth* was at least a noble and truly reverent guess at the mode of God's immanence in nature. This conception won the favor of Christian philosophers in the Middle Ages, and, indeed, was adopted or adapted by the angelic Doctor Aquinas himself, the foremost of ecclesiastical and scholastic metaphysicians. The psychology of the Kabbalah, even its treatment of the soul's preëxistence before union with the body, found many advocates among Gentile and even Christian philosophers.

We are therefore led to the conclusion that the Kabbalah is by far the most exalted, the most profound and the most interesting of all that mass of traditional literature which comprises, among other writings, such remains as the Targums and the Talmud.

A study of Hebrew literature would indeed be incomplete unless it included the Talmud.

"Talmud" in Hebrew means "Doctrine," and this strange work must be looked upon as a practical handbook, intended for the Jews who, after the downfall of Jerusalem and the Dispersion, found that most of the Law had to be adjusted to new circumstances, in which the institution of sacrifices and propitiatory offerings had been practically abolished. The Talmud

contains the decisions of Jewish doctors of many generations
on almost every single question which might puzzle the con-
science of a punctilious Jew in keeping the Law under the
altered conditions of the nation. The basis of the Talmud is the
Mishna, *i.e.*, an explanation of the text of the Mosaic laws, and
their application to new cases and circumstances. The Mishna
has been well described by the illustrious Spanish Jew, Maimonides, who in the twelfth century published it at Cordova,
with a preface, in which he says: "From Moses, our teacher,
to our holy rabbi, no one has united in a single body of doctrine
what was publicly taught as the oral law; but in every generation, the chief of the tribunal, or the prophet of his day, made
memoranda of what he had heard from his predecessors and
instructors, and communicated it orally to the people. In like
manner each individual committed to writing, for his own use
and according to the degree of his ability, the oral laws and
the information he had received respecting the interpretation
of the Bible, with the various decisions that had been pronounced in every age and sanctified by the authority of the great
tribunal. Such was the form of proceeding until the coming
of our Rabbi the Holy, who first collected all the traditions, the
judgments, the sentences, and the expositions of the law,
heard by Moses, our master, and taught in each generation."

The Mishna itself in turn became the subject of a series of
comments and elucidations, which formed what was called the
Gemara. The text of the original Hebrew scripture was abandoned, and a new crop of casuistical quibbles, opinions and
decisions rose like mushrooms upon the text of the Mishna, and
from the combination of text and Gemaraic commentary was
formed that odd, rambling, and sometimes perplexing work,
"wonderful monument of human industry, human wisdom
and human folly," which we know as the Talmud. The book
is compounded of all materials, an encyclopædia of history, an-
tiquities and chronology, a story book, a code of laws and conduct, a manual of ethics, a treatise on astronomy, and a medical
handbook; sometimes indelicate, sometimes irreverent, but always completely and persistently in earnest. Its trifling frivol-
ity, its curious prying into topics which were better left alone,
the occasional beauty of its spiritual and imaginative fancies,
make it one of the most remarkable books that human wit and
human industry have ever compiled.

The selections which we print in this volume are from the Mishna, and form part of the Sedarim, or orders; in them are given minute directions as to the ceremonial practice of the Jewish religion.

The treatise on "Blessings" speaks of daily prayers and thanksgiving. It is most minute in prescribing the position of the body, and how the voice is to be used in prayer. It specifies the prayers to be said on seeing signs and wonders, on building a house, on entering or leaving a city; and how to speak the name of God in social salutations. That on the "Sabbatical Year" is a discourse on agriculture from a religious point of view. The Sabbatical year among the Hebrews was every seventh year, in which the land was to be left fallow and uncultivated, and all debts were to be remitted or outlawed. Provision is made in this section for doing certain necessary work, such as picking and using fruits which may have grown without cultivation during the Sabbatical year, with some notes on manuring the fields, pruning trees and pulling down walls. Very interesting is the section which deals with "The Sabbath Day." The most minute and exhaustive account is given of what may and what may not be done on the seventh day.

The treatise on "The Day of Atonement" deals with the preparation and deportment of the high-priest on that day. That on "The Passover" treats of the Lamb to be sacrificed, of the search for leaven, so that none be found in the house, and of all the details of the festival. "Measurements" is an interesting and valuable account of the dimensions of the Temple at Jerusalem. "The Tabernacle" deals with the ritual worship of the Jews under the new conditions of their exile from Palestine.

All of these treatises show the vitality of Jewish religion in Europe, under the most adverse circumstances, and illustrate the place which the Talmud must have occupied in Jewish history, as supplying a religious literature and a code of ritual and worship which kept Judaism united, even when it had become banished and dissociated from Palestine, Jerusalem, and the Temple.

Epiphanius Wilson. —

CONTENTS

CONTENTS

ILLUSTRATIONS

SELECTIONS FROM THE TALMUD

[*Translated by Joseph Barclay, LL.D.*]

TRANSLATOR'S INTRODUCTION

THE Talmud (teaching) comprises the Mishna and the Gemara. The Mishna (" learning " or " second law ") was, according to Jewish tradition, delivered to Moses on Mount Sinai. " Rabbi Levi, the son of Chama, says, Rabbi Simon, the son of Lakish, says, what is that which is written, ' I will give thee tables of stone, and a law and commandments which I have written, that thou mayest teach them '? [1] The Tables are the ten commandments; the Law is the written law; and the commandment is the Mishna; ' which I have written ' means the prophets and sacred writings; ' that thou mayest teach them ' means the Gemara. It teaches us that they were all given to Moses from Mount Sinai." From Moses the Mishna was transmitted by oral tradition through forty " Receivers," until the time of Rabbi Judah the Holy. These Receivers were qualified by ordination to hand it on from generation to generation. Abarbanel and Maimonides disagree as to the names of these Receivers. While the Temple still stood as a centre of unity to the nation, it was considered unlawful to reduce these traditions to writing. But when the Temple was burned, and the Jews were dispersed among other peoples, it was considered politic to form them into a written code, which should serve as a bond of union, and keep alive the spirit of patriotism. The Jewish leaders saw the effect of Constitutions and Pandects in consolidating nations—the advantage of written laws over arbitrary decisions. Numberless precedents of case law, answering to our common law, were already recorded: and the teachings of the Hebrew jurisconsults, or " *Responsa prudentium*," which were held to be binding on the people, had been preserved from former ages.

All these traditions Rabbi Judah the Holy undertook to

[1] Exod. xxiv. 12.

3

reduce into one digest. And this laborious work he completed about A.D. 190, or more than a century after the destruction of Jerusalem by Titus. Rabbi Judah was born on the day that Rabbi Akibah died. Solomon is said to have foretold the event: "One sun ariseth, and one sun goeth down." Akibah was the setting and Judah the rising sun. The Mishna of Rabbi Judah, afterward revised by Abba Areka in Sura, is the text of the Babylon Talmud. The commentaries written on this text by various Rabbis in the neighborhood of Babylon, until the close of the fifth century, are called the Gemara (completion), and are published in twelve folio volumes, called the Babylon Talmud—the Talmud most esteemed by the Jews. The Jerusalem Talmud contains commentaries written partly by Rabbis in Jamnia and partly in Tiberias, where they were completed by Rabbi Jochanan in the beginning of the fourth century. As now published it has only four out of the six orders or books of the Mishna, with the treatise Niddah from the sixth. In the time of Maimonides it contained five orders. On twenty-six treatises it has no Gemara, though in the treatise on shekels the Gemara of Jerusalem is used for the Babylon Talmud. The six books of the Mishna are subdivided into sixty-three treatises, in the following manner:

BOOK I

This book, called Order of Seeds, contains the following treatises:

1. "Blessings," together with prayers and thanksgivings, with the times and places in which they are to be used.

2. "A Corner of a Field" (Lev. xxiii. 22; Deut. xxiv. 19) treats of the corners of the field to be left for the poor to glean them—the forgotten sheaves, olives, and grapes—and of giving alms, etc.

3. "Doubtful" treats of the doubt about the tithes being paid, as the Jews were not allowed to use anything without its being first tithed.

4. "Diversities" (Lev. xix. 19; Deut. xxii. 9-11) treats of the unlawful mixing or joining together things of a different nature or kind—of sowing seeds of a different species in one

bed—grafting a scion on a stock of a different kind, suffering cattle of different kinds to come together.

5. "The Sabbatical Year" (Exod. xxiii. 11; Lev. xxv. 4) treats of the laws which regulated the land as it lay fallow and rested.

6. "Heave Offerings" (Num. xviii. 8) treats of separating the heave offering—who may eat it, and who may not eat of it—of its pollutions, etc.

7. "The First Tithes" (Lev. xxvii. 30; Num. xviii. 28) treats of the law of tithes for the priests.

8. "The Second Tithes" (Deut. xiv. 22; xxvi. 14) treats of those which were to be carried to Jerusalem and there eaten, or to be redeemed and the money spent in Jerusalem in peace offerings.

9. "Cake of Dough" (Num. xv. 20) treats of setting apart a cake of dough for the priests; also, from what kind of dough the cake must be separated.

10. "Uncircumcised Fruit" (Lev. xix. 23) treats of the unlawfulness of eating the fruit of any tree till the fifth year. The first three years it is uncircumcised; the fourth year it is holy to the Lord; the fifth year it may be eaten.

11. "First Fruits" (Exod. xxiii. 19; Deut. xxvi. 1) treats of what fruits were to be offered in the Temple, and in what manner; also of the baskets in which they were to be carried.

BOOK II

The Order of the Festivals

1. "Sabbath" treats of the laws relating to the seventh day.

2. "Mixtures," or combinations, treats of the extension of boundaries, whereby all the inhabitants of the court, or entry, where the mixture is made, are counted as one family inhabiting one domicile; and are therefore allowed to carry victuals from one house to another. It also treats of the mixtures for a Sabbath day's journey, whereby the distance may be extended for an additional 2,000 cubits.

3. "Passovers" treats of all rites and ceremonies relating to the Paschal Lamb.

4. "Shekels" (Exod. xxx. 13) treats of the half shekel, which every Jew, rich or poor, was obliged to pay every year to the daily sacrifice.

5. "Day of Atonement" treats of the solemnities peculiar to it.

6. "Tabernacles" teaches how they are to be built, and how to be used.

7. "The Egg Laid on a Festival" treats of the works which may or may not be done on any of the festivals, which are called days of holy convocation, on which no servile work may be done.

8. "New Year" treats of the laws and solemnities of the feast of the New Year, as also of the feasts of the New Moons.

9. "Fasts" treats of the various fasts throughout the year.

10. "The Roll" treats of the feast of Purim, and gives instructions how and in what manner the Book of Esther and other Lessons are to be read. The Gemara directs Jews to get so drunk on this feast, that they cannot discern the difference between "Blessed be Mordecai and cursed be Haman," and "Cursed be Mordecai and blessed be Haman."

11. "Minor Feasts" treats of the works that may and that may not be lawfully done on the 2d, 3d, 4th, 5th, and 6th days, when the first and seventh are holy; these intermediate days being lesser festivals.

12. "Sacrifices on Festivals" treats of the three great festivals, when all the males were obliged to appear before the Lord, and of the sacrifices which they were to bring. It also lays down rules for the dissolution of vows, which it says " are like mountains hanging on a hair, for the text is slender and the constitutions many."

BOOK III

On Women

1. "Brother's Widow" (Deut. xxv. 5-11) treats of the law obliging a brother to marry the relict of his deceased brother; also, when the obligation is to take place, and the ceremonies to be used at its performance.

2. "Marriage Settlements" treats of dowries and women

who happen to obtain estates, either real or personal. From this tract the baptism of infant proselytes can be proved.

3. " Vows " (Num. xxx. 4-16) shows when vows are binding and when null and void. When a married woman makes a vow the husband can confirm or annul it. This tract points out what vows fall under his cognizance and what do not.

4. " The Nazarite " (Num. vi. 21) treats of the laws relating to the different sorts of Nazarites.

5. " Trial of Jealousy " (Num. v. 11-31) treats of the mode of trial and punishment of criminals. Men may go home to their wives from voluntary wars, but not from wars of command. This tract shows the miserable state of the Jews at the destruction of the second Temple, and at the future advent of the Messiah.

6. " Divorces " treats of the laws relating to divorces, also the formalities to be observed both before and after they are given. A man may divorce his wife if she spoil his broth, or if he find another more handsome.

7. " Betrothing " treats of the laws of espousals and some other previous rites of marriage. It commands sons to be taught suitable trades. It states that all ass-drivers are wicked, camel-drivers are honest, sailors are pious, physicians are destined for hell, and butchers are company for Amalek.

BOOK IV

ON DAMAGES

1. " First Gate," so called because in the East law is often administered in the gateway of a city. It treats of all such damages as may be received from man or beast. It assesses damages done by a beast according to the benefit which the beast receives. If it eat a peck of dates its owner would be fined for a peck of barley, as dates are not more nourishing for a beast than barley.

2. " The Middle Gate " treats of laws of usury and trusts, of letting out on hire, of landlord and tenant, etc.

3. " Last Gate " treats of the laws of commerce and co-partnership, of buying and selling, of the laws of inheritance and the right of succession.

4. " Sanhedrin " treats of the great national senate.

5. " Stripes " treats of false witnesses, of the law of the forty stripes save one, of those who were bound to fly to the cities of refuge.

6. " Oaths " explains the laws for administering oaths; when an oath is to be admitted between contending parties who are qualified to take them. In Hilchoth Eduth. ix. 1 it is taught that ten sorts of persons are disqualified—women, slaves, children, idiots, deaf persons, the blind, the wicked, the despised, relations, and those interested in their evidence.

7. " Evidences " are a collection of many important decisions gathered from the testimonies of distinguished Rabbis. It is observable that the decisions of the School of Shammai are more rigorous than those of the School of Hillel, from whence it is inferred that the former adhered more closely to Scripture, the latter to tradition. The former were the Scribes, and are now represented by the Karaites, who reject the Talmud.

8. " Idolatry," or the worship of stars and meteors, treats of the way to avoid this grievous sin.

9. " The Fathers " contains a history of those who handed down the Oral Law, also many maxims and proverbs.

10. " Punishment " treats of the punishment of those disobedient to the Sanhedrin (Deut. xvii. 8-11).

BOOK V

ON HOLY THINGS

1. " Sacrifices " treats of the nature and quality of the offerings; the time, the place, and the persons, by whom they ought to be killed, prepared, and offered.

2. " Meat Offerings " treats of the flour, oil, and wine, and the wave loaves.

3. " Unconsecrated Things " treats of what is clean and unclean, of not eating the sinew that shrank, and not killing the dam and her young in one day (Deut. xxii. 6).

4. " First Born " treats of their redemption by money, and their being offered in sacrifice; also of the tithes of all manner of cattle.

5. " Estimations " (Lev. xxvii. 2) treats of the way in which things devoted to the Lord are to be valued in order to be redeemed for ordinary use; also, how a priest is to value a field which a person has sanctified.

7. " Cutting Off " treats of offenders being cut off from the Lord.

6. " Exchanges " (Lev. xxvii. 10, 33) treats of the way exchanges are to be effected between sacred things.

8. " Trespass " (Num. v. 6, 8) treats of things partaking of the nature of sacrilege. It asserts that if a man take away a consecrated stone or beam he commits no trespass. If he give it to his companion he commits a trespass, but his companion commits none. If he build it into his house he commits no trespass till he lives in the house long enough to gain the value of a half-farthing. If he take away a consecrated half-farthing he commits no trespass. If he give it to his companion he commits a trespass, but his companion commits none. If he give it to a bath-keeper he commits a trespass though be docs not bathe, because the bath-keeper says to him, " See, the bath is open, go in and bathe."

9. " The Daily Sacrifice " treats of the morning and evening offerings.

10. " The Measurements " treats of the measurements of the Temple.

11. " Birds' Nests " treats of the mistakes about doves and beasts brought into the Temple for sacrifice.

BOOK VI

ON PURIFICATIONS

1. " Vessels " treats of those which convey uncleanness (Lev. xi. 33).

2. " Tents " (Num. xix. 14) treats of tents and houses retaining uncleanness, how persons who enter them become unclean, and how they are to be cleansed.

3. " Plagues of Leprosy " treats of leprosy of men, garments, or dwellings, how their pollution is conveyed, and how they are to be purified.

4. " The Red Heifer " directs how she is to be burned, and how her ashes are to be used in purifying.

5. " Purifications " teaches how purifications are to be effected.

6. " Pools of Water " (Num. xxxi. 23) treats of their construction, and the quantity of water necessary for cleansing.

7. " Separation " of women.

8. " Liquors " that dispose seeds and fruits to receive pollution (Lev. xi. 38).

9. " Issues " that cause pollution.

10. " Baptism " on the day of uncleanness (Lev. xxii. 6).

11. " Hands " treats of the washing of hands before eating bread, though dry fruits are allowed to be eaten without such washing.

12. " Stalks of Fruit which convey Uncleanness " treats of fruits growing out of the earth, which have a stalk and no husk. They can be polluted and can pollute, but may not be compounded with anything that was unclean before. If they have neither stalks nor husks they neither can be polluted nor can they pollute. It also treats of the hair and wool that grows on some fruits, and the beards of barley, etc.

From the six books or " Orders " the Jews call the Babylon Talmud by the pet name of " *Shas* " (six). The language in which it is written is Hebrew intermingled with Aramaic, Chaldee, Syriac, Arabic, Greek, and Latin words. The Gemara was first begun by Rabban Judah's two sons, Rabbi Gamaliel and Rabbi Simeon. It was vigorously carried on by Rabbi Ashé in Sura, a town on the Euphrates, from 365 A.D. to 425. He divided the Mishna into its sixty-three treatises, and every half-year summoned his disciples and assigned to them two fresh portions of the Law and two of the Mishna. At each meeting their remarks on these portions were discussed, and if approved were incorporated into the Gemara. Rabbis Zabid, Gebbia Rychuma, and Semo of Pumbeditha ;[1] and Rabbis Marimer, Adda bar Abbin, Nachman bar Huno, and Touspho, presidents of the schools of Sura, labored for its advancement ; and it was finally completed by Rabbi Abino (Rabbina), and sealed by Rabbi José

[1] So named from its situation at the mouth (" Pum ") of the Bedaitha, a canal between the Tigris and the Euphrates.

about 498 A.D. He was the last of the " Dictators." Those who lived after him were called " Opinionists," as they did not dictate any doctrines; but only deduced opinions from what had already been settled in the canon of the Talmud. The Opinionists were succeeded by the Sublime Doctors, who were in turn replaced by the ordinary Rabbis. In addition to the Talmud there has been handed down a vast amount of Jewish learning, such as the Bereitha, the Tosephtoth or appendices, the Mechilta or traditions unknown to Rabbi Judah the Holy, and the commentaries Sifra and Sifre. Of these the Jews regard the Bereitha as second to the Mishna. " The mark of Bereitha is ' the sages learned,' or ' it is once learned,' or ' it is learned in another one.' And everything which is not disputed of all these things is an established decision. And whatever is disputed goes according to the concluded decision. What is disputed in the Bereitha, which is not questioned in the Mishna, the decision is according to the Mishna. What is disputed in the Mishna, and not questioned in the Bereitha, is not to be decided according to the Bereitha. And thus it is said, ' If Rabbi Judah the Holy did not teach it, whence could Rabbi Chayya know it?' The exception is, that when the decision of Rabbi Eliezer, the son of Jacob, is given, it is regarded as equal to the Mishna. In 102 questions the decision is always with him."

The period during which both the Jerusalem and Babylon Talmuds were compiled was a season of comparative peace for the Jews. From the death of Rabbi Judah the Holy until Constantine ascended the throne the schools in Tiberias were unmolested. Judah was succeeded in the Patriarchate by Gamaliel; and he in turn gave way to Judah the second. Being inferior in learning to some of his own Rabbis, the splendor of his Patriarchate was eclipsed by the superior talents of Simon Ben Laches and Rabbi Jochanan. From that time the Patriarchate gradually sank in estimation, till the struggles for unlimited power, and the rapacity of the Rabbis, brought the office into contempt, and caused the Emperor Honorius in one of his laws to brand them as " Devastators." Still, with a loyal affection to the race of Israel, the Jews, wherever scattered in the West, looked to Tiberias as their Zion, and willingly taxed themselves for the support of its

Rabbinical schools. The Jews in the East regarded the Prince of the Captivity or Patriarch of Babylon as their centre and chief. He rose to power between the abandonment of the Mesopotamian provinces by Hadrian and the rise of the Persian kingdom. He presided over his subjects with Viceregal power and a splendid court. Rabbis were his satraps, and the wise and learned his officers and councillors. Wealth flowed in upon his people, who were engaged in every kind of commerce. One of his merchants in Babylon was said to have had 1,000 vessels on sea and 1,000 cities on shore. There was for a time a spirit of rivalry between the spiritual courts of Tiberias and Babylon.

On one occasion there was an open schism about the calculation of the Paschal feast. The struggle for supremacy took place when Simon, son of Gamaliel, who claimed descent from Aaron, was Patriarch of Tiberias, and Ahia, who claimed descent from King David, was Prince of the Captivity. His two most learned men were Hananiah, the rector of Nahar-pakod, and Judah, son of Bethuriah. To humble these men was the aim of Simon. Accordingly he sent two legates with three letters to Babylon. The first letter was given to Hananiah. It was addressed, "To your holiness." Flattered by the title, he politely asked the reason of their visit. "To learn your system of instruction." Still more gratified, he paid them every attention. Availing themselves of their advantage, the legates used every effort to undermine his teaching and lessen his authority. Hananiah, enraged by their conduct, summoned an assembly, and denounced their treachery. The people cried out, "That which thou hast built, thou canst not so soon pull down; the hedge which thou hast planted, thou canst not pluck up without injury to thyself." Hananiah demanded their objections to his teaching. They answered, "Thou hast dared to fix intercalations and new moons, by which nonconformity has arisen between Babylon and Palestine." "So did Rabbi Akiba," said Hananiah, "when in Babylon." "Akiba," they replied, "left not his like in Palestine." "Neither," cried Hananiah, "have I left my equal in Palestine." The legates then produced their second letter, in which it was written, "That which thou hast left a kid is grown up a strong horned goat." Hananiah was struck dumb. Rabbi Isaac, one of the legates, ran, and mounted the reading desk. "These," said he, calling them' out aloud, "are the holy days of God, and these the holy days of Hananiah."

The people began to murmur. Rabbi Nathan, the second legate, arose, and read the verse of Isaiah, "Out of Zion shall go forth the Law, and the word of the Lord from Jerusalem." Then in a mocking voice, "Out of Babylon shall go forth the Law, and the Word of the Lord from Nahor-pakod." The congregation was in an uproar. "Alter not the word of God" was the universal shout. The legates then produced the third letter, threatening excommunication to all who would not obey their decrees. They further said, "The learned have sent us, and commanded us to say, if he will submit, well; if not, utter at once the Cherem.[2] Also set the choice before our brethren in foreign parts. If they will stand by us, well; if not, let them ascend their high places. Let Ahia build them an altar, and Hananiah (a Levite) sing at the sacrifice, and let them at once set themselves apart, and say, 'We have no portion in the God of Israel.'" From every side the cry arose, "Heaven preserve us from heresy; we have still a portion in the Israel of God." The authority of Tiberias was then recognized as supreme. But when Babylon was afterward politically severed from the Roman power in the West, and fell to the Persians, the Prince of the Captivity represented the Jews of the East as their independent head.

The canon of the Talmud was closed in a season of opulence and repose. This scene, however, speedily changed. Gloomy and dark days were followed by a storm of persecution from the Persian kings, Yesdigird and Firuz "the tyrant." When their schools were closed, the Jews clung more closely to the Talmud than before. Although never formally adopted by any general council, all orthodox Jews embraced it as supplying a want which they felt. And they have adhered to it

---

[2] The Cherem was most fearful. The excommunicate was cursed with the curse of Joshua against Jericho, and the curse of Elisha against those that mocked him, and the curse of fiends of deadly power: "Let nothing good come out of him, let his end be sudden, let all creatures become his enemy, let the whirlwind crush him, the fever and every other malady, and the edge of the sword smite him; let his death be unforeseen and drive him into outer darkness," etc. There were three degrees of excommunication. The first was "the casting out of the synagogue." The second "the delivering over to Satan." And the third was the anathema proclaimed by priests with the sounding of trumpets.

through long and dreary centuries, despite the rack and fire of the Inquisitor, and the contempt and scorn of a hostile world. The Talmud has been periodically banned, and often publicly burned, from the age of the Emperor Justinian till the time of Pope Clement VIII. In the year 1569 the famous Jewish library in Cremona was plundered, and 12,000 copies of the Talmud and other Jewish·writings were committed to the flames. The first to demand for it toleration and free inquiry was Reuchlin. He declared that he must oppose the destruction of "a book written by Christ's nearest relations." Before him, Haschim II, Caliph of Cordova in the close of the tenth century, had ordered it to be translated into Arabic. This was done by Rabbi Joseph, the son of Rabbi Moses, surnamed "clad in a sack," because he was thus meanly clad when his great talents were discovered.

The study of the Talmud has the most fascinating influence over the Jewish mind, and if the latter is to be comprehended, the teaching which moulds it must be clearly understood. "Everyone," say the Jews, "is bound to divide the time of his study into three parts—one-third is to be devoted to the written law, one-third to the Mishna, and one-third to Gemara." To understand it in accordance with the thirteen rules of interpretation, it takes a study of seven hours a day for seven years. They also say that it is lawful to rend a man ignorant of the Talmud "like a fish." Israelites are forbidden to marry the daughter of such a one, as "she is no better than a beast."

To obviate arguments furnished by its own statements against itself, its adherents make a distinction between its decisions, its directions, and its legendary or romance part,— a distinction fatal to its claim of equality with Holy Scripture. For this legendary part some of the ancient Rabbis had but little respect. Rabbi Joshua, son of Levi, says, "He who writes it down will have no part in the world to come; he who explains it will be scorched." Maimonides also says, "If one of the many foolish rabbis reads these histories and proverbs, he will find an explanation unnecessary, for to a fool everything is right, and he finds no difficulty anywhere. And if a really wise man reads them, there will be but two ways in which he will consider them. If he takes them in their literal sense and thinks them bad, he will say, This is foolishness, and in so doing he says nothing at all against the foundation of the faith." The School of Shammai, who lived before Christ, and the School of Hillel, who lived till eight [3] years after His birth, are brought forward as contradictory in their decisions. Like Christian leaders in later times, they strove to exceed each other in learning and pride. Hillel, called also the second Ezra, was born in Babylon. His thirst for learning drove him to Jerusalem. He was so poor he could not fee the porter of the college. So he used to listen at the window. One bitter winter's night he became insensible from cold, and the snow falling fast covered him up. The darkened window called the attention of those inside to his form without. He was then brought in, and soon restored to life. It is said that afterward " he had eighty scholars: thirty of them were fit that the divine glory should rest upon them, as it did upon Moses—thirty others were worthy that the sun should stand still for them, as it did for Joshua—and twenty were of a form between."

By a sort of legal fiction both schools are supposed to be of equal authority. A Bath Kol [4] or holy echo, supplying the place of departed Urim and Thummim, and of oracles long since silent, is related to have established it. " There came forth a divine voice at Jabneh and said, The words of the one and of the other are the words of the living God, but the certain determination of the thing is according to the School of Hillel, and whosoever transgresseth against the words of the School of Hillel deserves death." Both schools were Pharisees, but the School of Shammai was the straiter sect. Seven different shades of character have been attributed to the Pharisees of that age: there were those who served God

[3] Some think he died twelve years B.C.
[4] The Jews say that the Holy Spirit spake to the Israelites during the Tabernacle by Urim and Thummim, and under the first Temple by the Prophets, and under the second by Bath Kol. The Bath Kol, which signifies " daughter voice " or " daughter of a voice," was a kind of divine intimation, which was as inferior to the oracular voice proceeding from the Mercy Seat as a daughter is supposed to be inferior to her mother. It was said to be preceded by a clap of thunder. This, however, was not always the case. The Talmud relates that " Rabbis Jochanan and Simeon ben Lachish wished to see the face of Rabbi Samuel, a Babylon Rabbi. ' Let us follow,' said they, ' the hearing of Bath Kol.' They journeyed near a school, and as they were passing it they heard a boy reading from the book of Samuel the words, ' And Samuel died.' Observing this, they concluded that their friend was dead. And it so happened that news was soon brought to them that Rabbi Samuel of Babylon had died." The Bath Kol seems to have been a sort of divination practised with the words of Scripture, like the Sortes Virgilianæ among the heathen.

from selfishness—those who did it gradually—those who avoided the sight of women—saints in office—those who asked you to name some duty which they ought to perform—those who were pious from fear of God—and those who were pious from love of Him. Popular opinion differed with regard to them. Some said, " If only two men be saved, one must be a Pharisee "; while others defined a Pharisee to be " one who wished to play the part of Zimri, and to claim the reward of Phinehas." The great opponents of the Pharisees were the Sadducees, who arose B.C. 300, and were followers of Baithos and Sadok. Their rivals on the other side were the Mehestanites, who returned from the Captivity versed in the doctrines of Zoroaster—in astrology, and in the influences of good and bad spirits. To these might be added the Misraimites, who studied the Kabbala, specially in reference to the forms of letters. The letter Koph, for example, has its curved part severed from its stem, and thus teaches that " the door of mercy is always open to the penitent." The numerical value of the letters of Messiah and Nachash (serpent) is the same, and this teaches that " the Messiah will overcome the Serpent."

The Kabbalists believed nothing but what they " received." Their teachers received from the prophets—the prophets received from angels—David from the Angel Michael, Moses from Metatron, Isaac from Raphael, Shem from Yophiel—and the angels themselves from God. The Metatron is the connecting link between the Divine Spirit and the world of matter. It resembles the Demiurgos of the Gnostics. It is the mystical expression for the Being that forms a union between God and nature, or, as the Zohar puts it, between the " King and the Queen." There were also the Essenes, who allegorized the Law; the Hellenists, who mixed it up with Greek philosophy; the Therapeutists, who thought supreme happiness to be meditation; the political Herodians; the Zealots; and other petty sects who formed the great mass of the people, and held either with or against the two great schools. The decisions of both schools are remarkable for their concise brevity. A phrase suggests many thoughts—a single word awakes a whole train of reasoning. A German writer has said of the Mishna, that " it is a firmament of telescopic stars, containing many a cluster of light, which no un-aided eye has ever resolved." Some of its sayings are of touching beauty. Such are the words of Rabbi Tarphon, "The day is short—the labor vast;—but the laborers are slothful, though the reward is great, and the Master of the house presseth for despatch." Some of its sayings are ex-travagant—some are loathsome—and some are blasphemous. But mixed up as they are together, they form an extraordinary monument of "human industry, human wisdom, and human folly."

The Talmud contains a system of casuistry in reference to the doctrines of intention and legal uncleanness. It propor-tions responsibility to the amount of intention, and thereby hands over tender consciences to the control of the Rabbis. It proportions legal uncleanness to every degree of approach to the source, or, as it is called, "the father" of uncleanness; and this again renders necessary continual appeals to the decision of the Rabbis.

Predestination and free will are both taught. "Everything is in the hands of heaven, except the fear of heaven." "All things are ordained of God, but men's actions are their own." When men wish to sin they are enjoined to go to a place where they are unknown, and to clothe themselves in black so as not to dishonor God openly. Hereditary sin was denied by the early Kabbalists, but the later ones allow it. They be-lieve that all souls were created in Adam, and therefore par-take of his fall. Every kind of philosophy known at the time of its compilation is more or less introduced into the Talmud, and all more or less tinged with Magian superstition. From this superstition grew the mysticism of the Jewish schools. All the arts and sciences, under some form or other, are al-luded to, and references to historical events abound in its pages. When it is dangerous to speak of them openly they are veiled under some figure known only to the initiated. Some observations seem to anticipate future discoveries. The Antipodes are hinted at. And the Jerusalem Gemara says that Alexander the Great was represented as carrying a ball in his hand because he believed the figure of the earth to be a sphere. Astronomy is fully discussed. The planets are "moving stars." Mercury is "the star"; Venus, "splendor"; Mars,

2

"redness"; Jupiter, "rightness"; Saturn, "the Sabbath star." The signs of the Zodiac have the same names as are now used. The Galaxy is "the river of light." Comets are "burning arrows." And it is said that when a comet passes through Orion it will destroy the world. A certain Ishmaelite merchant is related to have invited Rabba to come and see where the heavens and the earth touched. Rabba took his bread basket and placed it on the window while he prayed. He afterward looked for it, but it was gone. He asked the Ishmaelite, "Are there thieves here?" "No," he replied, "but your basket has gone up in the revolving of the firmament. It will return if you wait till morning when the revolving of the firmament returns where it was before."

Astrology is treated as a science which governs the life of man. The stars make men wise. The stars make them rich. "A man born on the first day of the week will excel in only one quality. He that is born on the second day will be an angry man, because on that day the waters were divided. He that is born on the third day of the week will be rich and licentious, because on it the herbs were created. He that is born on the fourth day will be wise and of good memory, because on that day the lights were hung up. He that is born on the fifth day will be charitable, because on that day the fishes and fowls were created. He that is born on the Sabbath, on the Sabbath he also shall die, because on his account they profaned the great Sabbath day." Rabba bar Shila says, "He shall be eminently holy." Rabbi Chanina says, "The influence of the stars makes wise, the influence of the stars makes rich, and Israel is under the influence of the stars." Rabbi Jochanan says, "Israel is not under the influence of the stars. Whence is it proved? 'Thus saith the Lord, Learn not the way of the heathen, and be not dismayed at the signs of heaven, for the heathen are dismayed at them' (Jer. x. 2). The heathen, but not Israel." "An eclipse of the sun is an evil sign to the nations of the world; an eclipse of the moon is an evil sign to Israel, for Israel reckons by the moon, the nations of the world by the sun." It is also said that Saturn and Mars are the baleful stars, and whosoever begins a work, or walks in the way, when either of these two is in the ascendant, will come to sorrow. Astrology naturally leads to amulets and charms. Amulets are divided into two classes, approved and disapproved. An approved amulet is "one that has cured three persons, or has been made by a man who has cured three persons with other amulets."

Charms are abundantly provided against accidents. "For bleeding of the nose let a man be brought to a priest named Levi, and let the name Levi be written backward. If there be not a priest, get a layman, who is to write backward "Ana pipi Shila bar Sumki," or "Taam dli bemi ceseph, taam dli bemi pagam"; or let him take a root of grass, and the cord of an old bed, and paper, and saffron, and the red part of the inside of a palm tree, and let him burn them together, and let him take some wool, and twist two threads, and dip them in vinegar, and roll them in ashes, and put them into his nose; or let him look out for a stream of water which flows from east to west, and let him go and stand with one leg on each side of it, and let him take with his right hand some mud from under his left foot, and with his left hand from under his right foot, and let him twist two threads of wool, and dip them in the mud, and put them into his nose." If a man be bitten by a mad dog he must die, unless some remedy be found for him. "Abai says he must take the skin of a male adder, and write upon it, 'I, M, the son of the woman N, upon the skin of a male adder, write against thee, Kanti Kanti Klirus, but some say, Kandi Kandi Klurus, Lord of Hosts. Amen. Selah.' Let him also cast off his clothes, and bury them in a graveyard for twelve months of a year; then let him take them up, and burn them in a furnace, and let him strew the ashes at the parting of the roads. And during these twelve months let him only drink out of a brass tube, lest he see the phantom form of the demon, and he be endangered. This was done by Abba, the son of Martha—he is Abba, the son of Manjumi. His mother made him a tube of gold."

Magic naturally follows from such teaching. Abba Benjamin says, "If leave had been given to see the hurtful demons, no creature could stand before them." Abbai says, "They are more than we are, and stand against us, like the trench round a garden bed." Rav Huni says, "Everyone has a thousand on his left hand, and ten thousand on his right hand." Rabba says, "The want of room at the sermon is from them, the wearing out of the Rabbis' clothes is from their rubbing against them, bruised legs are from them." "Whosoever wishes to know their existence, let him take ashes passed through a sieve, and strew them in his bed, and in the morning he will see the marks of a cock's claws. Whosoever wishes to see them, let him take the inner covering of a black cat, the kitten of a first-born black cat, which is also the kitten of a first-born, and let him burn it in the fire, and powder it, and fill his eyes with it, and he will see them. And let him pour the powder into an iron tube, and seal it with an iron signet, lest they steal any of it, and let him seal the mouth of it, lest any harm ensue. Rav Bibi bar Abbai did thus, and he was harmed, but the Rabbis prayed for mercy, and he was healed." Arts, of sorcery are attributed to the Rabbis. They are represented as having the power to create both men and melons. One of them is said to have changed a woman into an ass, and ridden the ass to market, when another sorcerer changed the ass again into a woman.

This sorcery is traced to Abraham, who is said (Gen. xxv. 6) to have given his sons gifts. These gifts are stated to have been the arts of sorcery. Legends abound everywhere throughout the Talmud. Rabbi Judah said, Rav said, "Everything that God created in the world, He created male and female. And thus he did with leviathan, the piercing serpent, and leviathan the crooked serpent. He created them male and female; but if they had been joined together they would have desolated the whole world. What then did the Holy One do? He enervated the male leviathan, and slew the female, and salted her for the righteous in the time to come, for it is said, ' And He shall slay the dragon that is in the sea ' (Isa. xxvii. 1). Likewise, with regard to behemoth upon a thousand mountains, He created them male and female; but if they had been joined together they would have desolated the whole world. What then did the Holy One do? He enervated the male behemoth, and made the female barren, and preserved her for the righteous in the time to come." That period is to be a season of great feasting. The liquor to be drunk will be apple-wine of more than seventy years old. The cup of David alone will hold one hundred and twenty-one logs. It is related that a Rabbi once saw in a desert a flock of geese so fat that their feathers fell off, and the rivers flowed in fat. He said to them, " Shall we have part of you in the world to come? " One of them lifted up a wing and another a leg, to signify the parts we shall have. We should otherwise have had all parts of these geese, but that their sufferings are owing to us. It is our iniquities that have delayed the coming of the Messiah, and these geese suffer greatly by reason of their ex- cessive fat, which daily increases, and will increase till the Messiah comes."

Rabba bar Chama says that he once saw " a bird so tall, that its head reached to the sky and its legs to the bottom of the ocean." The water in which it stood was so deep that a carpenter's axe which had fallen in seven years before had not then reached the bottom. He also saw " a frog as large as a village containing sixty houses." This frog was swallowed up by a serpent, and this serpent in turn by a crow; this crow flew, and perched upon a cedar, and this cedar was as broad as sixteen wagons abreast. There is also an account of a fish which was killed by a worm. This fish, when driven ashore, destroyed sixty cities, and sixty cities ate of it, and sixty cities salted it, and with its bones the ruined cities were rebuilt. Stories are also told of fishes with eyes like the moon, and of horned fishes three hundred miles in length. These stories are intended to confirm the text, " They that go down to the sea in ships, that do business in great waters; these see the works of the Lord and his wonders in the deep " (Ps. cvii. 23, 24). To illustrate the statement of Amos (iii. 8), a story is told of a lion which one of the Cæsars wished to see. At 400 miles distance he roared, and the walls of Rome fell. At 300 miles he again roared, and all the people fell on their backs, and their teeth fell out, and Cæsar fell off his throne. Cæsar then prayed for his removal to a safer distance.

The Talmud informs us that " a young unicorn, one day old, is as large as Mount Tabor." Consequently Noah had great difficulty in saving an old one alive. He could not get it into the ark, so he bound it by its horn to the side of the ark. At the same time Og, King of Bashan (being one of the antediluvians), was saved by riding on its back. We are further informed that he was one of the giants who came from the intermarriage of angels with the daughters of men.

His footsteps were forty miles long, and one of his teeth served to make a couch for Abraham. When the Israelites came against him under the command of Moses, he inquired the size of their camp, and hearing that it was three miles in extent he tore up a mountain of that size, to hurl it upon them. Grasshoppers were, however, sent to bore holes in it, so that it fell over his head on to his neck. His teeth also grew and were entangled in the rocks, as the Psalmist says, "Thou hast broken the teeth of the ungodly" (Ps. iii. 7). He is also said to be identical with Eliezer the servant of Abraham, and to have been, like Enoch, translated to Paradise. This account, however, differs widely from the statements of the Jerusalem Targum on the Book of Numbers (xxi. 34).

The Talmud affirms that Adam was made from dust of all parts of the earth; and that he was created with two faces, as it is written, "Thou hast beset me behind and before" (Ps. cxxxix. 5). The Rabbis further state that he was formed in two parts, one male and one female. His height before his fall reached to the firmament, but after his fall God put his hand upon him, and compressed him small. In the tenth hour after he was made, he sinned; and in the twelfth he was driven out of Paradise. Abraham is said to have put Sarah into a box when he brought her into Egypt, that none should see her beauty. At the custom-house toll was demanded. Abraham said he was ready to pay. The custom-house officers said, "Thou bringest clothes." He said, "I will pay for clothes." They said, "Thou bringest gold." He said, "I will pay for gold." They said, "Thou bringest silk." He said, "I will pay for silk." They said, "Thou bringest pearls." He said, "I will pay for pearls." They said, "Thou must open the box," whereupon her splendor shone over the whole land of Egypt.

Abraham, it is also said, had a precious stone hung around his throat, on which when the sick looked they were healed. Some of the laws of Sodom are also recorded: "Whosoever cut off the ears of another's ass received the ass till his ears grew again." "Whosoever wounded another, the man wounded was obliged to pay him for letting his blood." When the judges of Sodom attempted to fine Eliezer, the servant of Abraham, because another man had wounded him, he took up a stone and flung it at the judge. He then bid the judge to pay the fine, which was now due to him for letting his blood, to the man who had first wounded him. There was a public bed in Sodom, and every stranger was obliged to lie in it. If his legs were too long for it, they were cut off; and if too short, they were racked out to the proper length. When a traveller came, each citizen, to show his hospitality, was obliged to give him a coin with his name written upon it. The traveller was then deprived of bread; and when he had died of starvation, the citizens came, and each one took back his own money. The Sodomites thus kept up their character for liberality.

At the giving of the Law the Israelites stood at the lower part of the mount (Exod. xix. 17). Rabbi Avidmi says, " these words teach us that the Holy One, blessed be He, turned the mountain over them like a tub, and said to them, ' If ye will receive the Law, well; but if not, there shall be your grave.'" Rabbi Joshua says, " As each commandment proceeded from the mouth of the Holy One, Israel retreated twelve miles, and the ministering angels led them back, as it is said, ' The angels of the host did flee apace ' [4] (Ps. lxviii. 13). Do not read ' they fled ' but ' they led.' " Rabbi Eliezer, the Modite, says, that Jethro " heard the giving of the Law; for when the Law was given to Israel His voice went from one end of the world to the other, and all the nations of the world were seized with trembling in their temples, and they repeated a hymn, as it is said, ' In His temple doth everyone speak of His glory '" (Ps. xxix. 9). The question is asked, " Why are the Gentiles defiled?" " Because they did not stand on Mount Sinai, for in the hour the serpent came to Eve he communicated defilement, which was removed from Israel when they stood on Mount Sinai." Rav Acha, the son of Rabbi, said to Rav Ashai, " How then is it with proselytes?" He answered, " Although they went not there, their lucky star was there, as it is written, ' With *him* that standeth here with us this day before the Lord our God, and also with *him* that *is* not here with us this day '" (Deut. xxix. 15).

---

[4] The Rabbis make two changes in this verse—they change " kings " into " angels," and " fled " into " led."

In the hour that Moses ascended up on high the ministering angels said before God, " O Lord of the world, what business has he that is born of woman amongst us?"   He answered, "He is come to receive the Law."   They replied,
" This desirable treasure, which has been treasured up from
the six days of creation, six hundred and seventy-four generations before the world was created, dost Thou now wish to
give it to flesh and blood? what is man that Thou art mindful
of him? and the son of man that Thou visitest him?   O Lord,
our Lord, how excellent is Thy name in all the earth, Who
hast set Thy glory above the heavens."   The Holy One said
to Moses, " Return them an answer."   He said, " O Lord of
the world, I fear, lest they burn me with the breath of their
mouth."   God said, " Lay hold on the throne of my glory, and
return them an answer; for it is said, ' He that holdeth the face
of His throne, He spreadeth His cloud over him ' " (Job xxvi.
9).   Rabbi Nahum says, " This means that the Almighty
spread some of the glory of the Shechinah and His cloud
over him."   He then said, " Lord of the world, what is written in the Law that Thou art about to give me? "   " I am the
Lord thy God, that brought thee out of Egypt."   He then
said, " Did ye (angels) ever go down into Egypt and serve
Pharaoh? why then should ye have the Law? "   Again,
" What is written therein? "   " Thou shalt have none other
God."   He then asked them, " Do ye then dwell among the
uncircumcised, that ye should commit idolatry? "   Again,
" What is written? "   " Remember the Sabbath day to sanctify
it."   " Do ye then do any work so as to need rest? "   Again,
" What is written? "   " Thou shalt not take the name of the
Lord in vain."   " Have ye then any work that would lead to
this sin? "   Again, " What is written? "   " Honor thy father
and mother."   " Have ye then got any father or mother? "
Again, " What is written? "   " Thou shalt do no murder."
" Thou shalt not commit adultery."   " Thou shalt not steal."
" Have ye then envy or the principle of evil amongst you? "
Immediately they praised the Holy One, " Blessed be He."

Wonderful stories are told of the manna.   The manna is
said to have fallen from heaven, accompanied by showers of
pearls and precious stones.   It tasted to everyone according
to his desire.   If one wished for fat fowl, so it tasted.   If an-

other wished for honey, so it tasted, as it is written, " Thou hast lacked nothing " (Deut. xi. 7). The Targum of Jonathan goes on to inform us, " At the fourth hour, when the sun had waxed hot upon it, it melted and became streams of water, which flowed away into the great sea, and wild animals that were clean, and cattle, came to drink of it, and the children of Israel hunted and ate them " (Exod. xvi. 21). It is further related that the Queen of Sheba (whom the Rabbis labor to prove to have been the King of Sheba) wished to test the knowledge of Solomon who had written on botany " from the cedar to the hyssop." She once stood at a distance from him with two exquisite wreaths of flowers—one artificial, one natural. They were so much alike that the King looked perplexed, and the courtiers looked melancholy. Observing a swarm of bees on the window, he commanded it to be opened. All the bees lighted on the natural and not one on the artificial wreath. Solomon is also said to have sent Benaiah, the son of Jehoiada, to bind Aschmedai, the king of the devils. After deceiving the devil with wine he made him reveal the secret of the Schamir, or little worm, which can cleave the hardest stone. And by the aid of this worm Solomon built the Temple. The devil afterward asked Solomon for his signet ring; and when he had given it to him the devil stretched one wing up to the firmament and the other to the earth, and jerked Solomon four hundred miles away. Then assuming the aspect of Solomon, he seated himself on his throne. After Solomon had again obtained it, he wrote, " What profit hath a man of all his labor which he taketh under the sun? " (Eccles. i. 3).

A story is told of Nebuzaradan, that he saw the blood of Zecharias bubbling in the court of the priests. When he asked what it meant, he was informed that it was the blood of bullocks and lambs. When he had ordered bullocks and lambs to be slain, the blood of Zecharias still bubbled and reeked above theirs. The priests then confessed that it was the blood of a priest and prophet and judge, whom they had slain. He then commanded eighty thousand priests to be put to death. The blood, however, still continued to bubble. God then said, " Is this man, who is but flesh and blood, filled with pity toward my children, and shall not I be much more? " So he gave a sign to the blood, and it was swallowed up in the place.

Of the eighty thousand priests slain none was left but Joshua the son of Jozedek, of whom it is written, "Is not this a brand plucked out of the fire?" (Zech. iii. 2). Of Titus it is said that he was unclean in the Temple, and with a blow of his sword rent the veil, which flowed with blood. To punish him a gnat was sent into his brain, which grew as large as a dove. When his skull was opened, the gnat was found to have a mouth of copper, and claws of iron.

The Talmud teaches that evil spirits, devils, and goblins are the offspring of Adam. They are said to fly about in all directions. They know from eavesdropping what is to come in the future. Like men, they eat, drink, and multiply. They are represented as playing men awkward tricks. One is stated to have broken a vessel of wine, and to have spilled it on the ground. The Rabbis, however, afterward compelled him to pay for it. People are forbidden to ride oxen fresh from the stall, as Satan dances between their horns. Men are forbidden to salute their companions by night, lest they may turn out to be devils. It is also commanded to shake out, before drinking, some water from the vessel, to get rid of what is sipped by the evil spirits. It is, however, permitted to consult Satan on week-days. He is considered identical with the Angel of Death. But he is described as having no power over those engaged in reading the law. Many of his devices are related in the Talmud, whereby he made learned men leave off reading, and then he snatched away their souls. A story is told of the attempt of Rabbi Joshua, the son of Levi, and Satan to deceive each other about the Rabbi's place in paradise. Finally, however, Satan managed to take away his life, whereupon the voice of Elijah is heard shouting in heaven, "Make room for the son of Levi,"—"Make room for the son of Levi." The Angel of Death is represented as standing at the head of the dying man. He has a drawn sword in his hand, on which is a drop of gall. When the dying man sees it, he shudders and opens his mouth. The Angel of Death then lets it fall into his mouth. The sick man dies, corrupts, and becomes pale. Three days the soul flies about the body, thinking to return to it, but after it sees the appearance of the face changed, it leaves it and goes away.

Rabbi Isaac moreover asserts, that a worm in a dead body

is as painful as a needle in a living one. The Talmud still further states that there are three voices continually heard— the voice of the sun as he rolls in his orbit—the voice of the multitudes of Rome—and the voice of the soul as it leaves the body. The Rabbis, however, prayed for mercy on the soul, and this voice has ceased. Instances are also given of men overhearing the conversations of the dead, and receiving profit from them. A man is said to have heard one girl tell another in the grave, that those who sowed their crops at a particular time would find their harvests fail. So he took care to sow at another time, and he had an abundant yield. It is also said that every Friday evening a second soul enters into the bodies of men, and that it remains to the end of the Sabbath, when it departs. The evidence of this second soul is shown by an increased appetite for eating and drinking.

Good angels are stated to be daily created out of the stream of glory which flows from the throne of God, and they sing a new song, and vanish; as it is said, "They are new every morning: great is thy faithfulness" (Lam. iii. 23). The Rabbis also say that angels are created out of every word which proceeds from the mouth of God; as it is said, "By the word of the LORD were the heavens made; and all the host of them by the breath of His mouth" (Ps. xxxiii. 6). The following story is also told: In the hour when Nimrod, the impious, cast Abraham into the midst of the fiery furnace, Gabriel said before the blessed God, "Lord of the world, I will go down and cool the flame, and deliver the righteous One from the furnace of fire." The blessed God said to him, "I am the ONE in this world, and he is the one in his world. It becomes the ONE to deliver the one." But as the blessed God deprives no one of his reward, He said, "Thou shalt be deemed worthy to deliver three of his posterity." Rabbi Simon, the Shilonite, taught, "In the hour that Nebuchadnezzar, the impious, cast Hananiah, Mishael, and Azariah into the midst of the fiery furnace, Jorkemo, the prince of hail, stood up before the blessed God, and said, ' I will go down and cool the flame, and deliver the righteous ones from the furnace of fire.' To him said Gabriel, 'The power of the blessed One is not so, since thou art the prince of hail, and everyone knows that waters quench fire; but I, the prince of fire, will go down and cool inwardly,

and heat outwardly, and I will make a wonder within a wonder.'" To him said the blessed God, "Go down." In the
same hour Gabriel began and said, "And the truth of the Lord
endureth for ever" (Ps. cxvii. 2).

Israelites are forbidden to pray in the Syriac language, as
the angels do not understand it, and consequently cannot carry
their petitions to God. Gabriel, however, is acquainted with it,
as he taught Joseph the seventy languages. The chief of all the
angels is said to be the Metatron, who once received fiery blows
from another angel called Ampiel. With regard to heaven, the
Rabbis teach that Egypt is four hundred miles long and broad,
the Morians' land is sixty times larger than Egypt, and the
world is sixty times larger than the Morians' land; heaven
is sixty times larger than the world, and hell is sixty times
larger than heaven. It follows that the "whole world is but
a pot-lid to hell." Yet some say that hell is immeasurable, and
some say heaven is immeasurable. It was a pearl amongst
the sayings of a Rabbi. "Heaven is not like this world, for in
it there is neither eating, nor drinking, nor marriage, nor increasing, nor trafficking, nor hate, nor envy, nor heart-burn-
ings; but the just shall sit with their crowns on their heads,
and enjoy the splendors of the Shechinah."

Hell is said to have three doors,—one in the wilderness, one
in the sea, and one in Jerusalem. In the wilderness, as it
is written, "They, and all that appertained to them, went down
alive into the pit" (Num. xvi. 33). In the sea, as it is written,
"Out of the belly of hell cried I, and thou heardest my voice"
(Jonah ii. 3). In Jerusalem, as it is written, "Saith the Lord
whose fire is in Zion, and His furnace in Jerusalem" (Is. xxxi.
9). The school of Rabbi Ishmael teaches that the "fire in
Zion" is hell and "His furnace in Jerusalem" is the gate of
hell. It is also taught that the fire of hell has no power over
the sinners in Israel, and that the fire of hell has no power over
the disciples of the wise. It is again, however, stated that the
Israelites who sin with their bodies, and the Gentiles who
sin with their bodies, go to hell, and are punished there twelve
months. After their body is wasted, and their soul is burned,
the wind scatters them beneath the soles of the righteous, as it
is said, "And ye shall tread down the wicked: for they shall
be ashes under the soles of your feet" (Mal. iv. 3). Here-

tics—deniers of the resurrection—Epicureans, and other sinners, shall be perpetually tormented "where their worm dieth
not and their fire is not quenched."

The doctrine of the resurrection is clearly taught in the Talmud. As for the last judgment, the following story is told:
"Said Antoninus to Rabbi, The body and soul can free themselves from judgment. How? The body can say, The soul
sinned from the time it separated from me, while I lay as a
stone in the grave. And the soul can say, The body sinned
from the time it separated from me, while I flew in the air as a
bird." He replied, "I will give you an example to which it
is like. It is like a king of flesh and blood, who has a beautiful garden, and in which are pleasant fruits, and he placed two
watchmen therein, of whom one was lame and the other was
blind. Said the lame to the blind, ' I see pleasant fruits in the
garden; come, and let me sit upon thee, and let us go and eat.' "
The lame sat upon the blind, and they went and ate. After
some days the lord of the garden came, and said, "Where are
my pleasant fruits?" The lame said, "I have no legs to go to
them." The blind said, "I have no eyes to see them." What
did he do? He set the lame upon the blind, and judged them
as one. So the blessed God will return the soul into the body,
and judge them as one, as it is said, "He shall call to the
heavens from above and to the earth, that he may judge his
people" (Ps. iv. 4). He shall call to the heavens from above,
that is the soul; and to the earth that he may judge his people,
that is, the body. After the resurrection men will live without
work or weariness of body, their houses shall be of precious
stones, and their beds of silk, and the rivers shall run with wine
and perfumed oil.

The Talmud often contradicts Holy Scripture. It says that
they are in error who believe the Bible account of the sons of
Reuben, of the sons of Eli, and of the sons of Samuel. It
allows usury, and the passing of children through the fire to
Moloch. It permits deceit, and supports it with the text,
"With the pure thou wilt show thyself pure, and with the
froward thou wilt show thyself unsavory" (2 Sam. xxii. 27).
The Rabbis teach hatred of Christians and Gentiles. Instead
of saying, "In the presence of the king," they are taught to
say, "In the presence of the dog." A Jew who bears witness

against another Jew before a Gentile is publicly cursed. A Jew is also released from any oath he may swear to a Gentile. It is only permitted a Jewish physician to heal Gentiles for the sake of the fee, or for the practice of medicine, but it is not allowed to save their lives in seasons of danger. Their marriage is no marriage; and their butchers' meat is only carrion. It is wrong to invite them into a Jewish house; and it is not needful to restore what they have lost. When the ox of a Jew gores the ox of a Gentile, the Jew is free; but if the ox of a Gentile gores the ox of a Jew, the Gentile must pay the full cost. A story is told of a Rabbi who sold a number of palm-trees to a Gentile, and afterward ordered his servant to cut off some pieces from them. "For," he said, "the Gentile knows their number, but he does not know whether they be thick or thin."

The precepts binding on the sons of Noah are stated to be seven: to do justice; to bless the name of God; to avoid idolatry; to flee from fornication and adultery; to abstain from blood-shedding; not to rob; and not to eat a member of a living animal. An account is given of the river Sambation, which flows with stones all the six days of the week, but rests on the Sabbath day. Examples are also furnished of gluttony and drunkenness. The paunches of some Rabbis grew so big, that, when put together, a pair of oxen might go between them. A story is also related of one Rabbi killing another in a drunken fit, and then working a miracle which restored him to life. In the following year he again invited the Rabbi to drink with him, but he declined, on the ground that "miracles are not wrought every day." Instances are also given of the anguish of Rabbis in the prospect of death. They express themselves as being without hope of salvation, and as having the fear of hell before them.

Proverbs everywhere abound in the Talmud, and they are generally replete with shrewd observation. "The world subsists through the breath of school children. Whosoever transgresses the words of the Scribes is guilty of death. Whosoever teaches a statute before his teachers ought to be bitten by a serpent. There is no likeness between him who has bread in his basket and him who has none. Rather be the head of foxes than the tail of lions." This, however, again appears as

"Rather be the tail of lions than the head of foxes." "The righteous in the city is its splendor, its profit, its glory: when he is departed, there is also departed the splendor, the profit, and the glory." "Licentiousness in a house is as a worm in a pumpkin." This reappears as "Violence in a house is as a worm in a pumpkin." "Thy friend has an acquaintance, and the acquaintance of thy friend has also an acquaintance; be discreet." The unworthy child of a good father is called "vinegar, the son of wine." "If the opportunity fails the thief, he deems himself honest. The cock and owl await together the morning dawn. Says the cock to the owl, 'Light profits me, but how does it profit thee?' Youth is a crown of roses, old age a crown of thorns. Many preach well, but do not practise well. It is the punishment of liars, that men don't listen to them when they speak truth. Every man who is proud is an idolater. To slander is to murder. Whosoever humbles himself, God exalts him; whosoever exalts himself, God humbles him. Men see every leprosy except their own. He who daily looks after his property finds a coin. The post does not honor the man; but the man the post. Every man is not so lucky as to have two tables. Not what thou sayest about thyself, but what thy companions say. The whole and broken tables of the Law lie in the ark. The salt of money is almsgiving. He who walks four cubits in the land of Israel is sure of being a child of the world to come. The plague lasted seven years, and no man died before his time. Let the drunkard only go, he will fall of himself. Be rather the one cursed than the one cursing. The world is like an inn, but the world to come is the real home. The child loves its mother more than its father: it fears its father more than its mother. Repent one day before thy death. If your God is a friend of the poor, why does He not support them? A wise man answered, 'Their case is left in our hands, that we may thereby acquire merits and forgiveness of sin.' The house that does not open to the poor shall open to the physician. He who visits the sick takes away one-sixtieth part of their pain. Descend a step in choosing a wife; mount a step in choosing a friend. An old woman in a house is a treasure. Whosoever does not persecute them that persecute him, whosoever takes an offence in silence, whosoever does good from love, whosoever is cheer-

ful under his sufferings, they are friends of God, and of them
says the Scripture, ' they shall shine forth as the sun at noon-
day.' " R. Phineas, son of Jair, said, " Industry brings purity
—purity, cleanness—cleanness, holiness—holiness, humbleness—humbleness, fear of sin—and fear of sin, partaking of
the Holy Ghost."

Ideas of God are gathered from the occupations which the
authors of the Talmud assign to him. " The day contains
twelve hours. The first three hours the Holy One, blessed be
He, sits and studies the Law. The second three hours He sits
and judges the whole world. When He sees that the world
deserves destruction, He stands up from the throne of judgment, and sits on the throne of mercy. The third three hours
He sits and feeds all the world, from the horns of the unicorns
to the eggs of the vermin. In the fourth three hours He sits
and plays with leviathan, for it is said, " The leviathan, whom
thou hast formed to play therein " (Ps. civ. 26). Rabbi Eliezer
says, " The night has three watches, and at every watch the
Holy One, blessed be He, sits and roars like a lion; for it is
said, ' The Lord shall roar from on high and uttter His voice
from His holy habitation; He shall mightily roar upon His
habitation ' " (Jer. xxv. 30). Rabbi Isaac, the son of Samuel,
says in the name of Rav, " The night has three watches, and
at every watch the Holy One, blessed be He, sits and roars
like a lion, and says, ' Woe is me, that I have laid desolate my
house, and burned my sanctuary, and sent my children into
captivity among the nations of the world!' " He is described
as praying, and wearing phylacteries, and as having a special
place for weeping. " Before the destruction of the Temple the
Holy One played with leviathan, but since the destruction of
the Temple, He plays with it no more. In the hour that the
Holy One remembers His children who are dwelling with
suffering among the nations, He lets two tears fall into the
Great Ocean, the noise of which is heard from one end of the
world to the other, and this is an earthquake." It is further
said that He " braided the hair of Eve," and " shaved the
head of Sennacherib." He is represented as keeping school,
and teaching the sages. To this school the devils come, especially Aschmedai, the king of the devils. In the discussions
that take place, God is said to be sometimes overcome by the
wiser Rabbis.

The question of the Messiah is often brought forward. " The tradition of the school of Elijah is, that the world is to stand six thousand years, two thousand years confusion, two thousand years the Law, and two thousand years the days of the Messiah." It is further said that the time for the coming of the Messiah is expired. " Rav says the appointed times are long since past." The Jerusalem Talmud relates that "it happened once to a Jew, who was standing ploughing, that his ox lowed before him. An Arab was passing, and heard its voice. He said ' O Jew! O Jew! unyoke thine ox, and loose thy ploughshare, for the Temple is desolate.' It lowed a second time, and he said, ' O Jew! O Jew! yoke thine ox and bind thy ploughshare, for King Messiah is born.' The Jew said, ' What is His name?' He answered ' Menachem.' He asked again, ' What is His father's name?' He said, ' Hezekiah.' He asked, ' From whence is He?' He replied, ' From the royal palace of Bethlehem Judah.' The Jew then went and saw him; but when he went again, the mother told him ' that the winds had borne the child away.' " The Babylon Talmud further states that " Rabbi Joshua, the son of Levi, found Elijah standing at the door of the cave of Rabbi Simeon ben Yochai, and said to him, ' Shall I reach the world to come?' He answered, ' If this Lord will.' Rabbi Joshua, the son of Levi, said, ' I see two, but I hear the voice of three.' He also asked, ' When will Messiah come?' Elijah answered, ' Go and ask Himself.' Rabbi Joshua then said, ' Where does he sit?' ' At the gate of Rome.' ' And how is he known?' ' He is sitting among the poor and sick, and they open their wounds, and bind them up again all at once: but he opens only one, and then he opens another, for he thinks, Perhaps I may be wanted, and then I must not be delayed.' Rabbi Joshua went to him, and said, ' Peace be upon thee, my Master, and my Lord.' He answered, ' Peace be upon thee, son of Levi.' The Rabbi then asked him, ' When will my Lord come?' He answered, ' To-day ' " (Ps. xcv. 7). It is said that " the bones of those who reckon the appointed time of the Messiah must burst assunder." Again, however, it is said that " Elias told Rabbi Judah, the brother of the pious Rabbi Salah, that the world would not stand less than eighty-five years of Jubilee, and in the last year of Jubilee the son of David will come." It is further stated that there

3

are first to be the wars of the Dragon, and of Gog and Magog; and that God will not renew the earth until seven thousand years are completed. The Rabbis also say that when the Messiah comes to fulfil the prophecy of riding upon an ass (Zech. ix. 9), the ass shall be one of "an hundred colors." As for the return of the ten tribes to their own land, the Talmud in some places asserts it, and in some places denies it. But it is said that in the days of the Messiah all the Gentiles shall become proselytes to the Jewish faith. The Rabbis are divided as to the continuance of the Messiah; some say forty years, some seventy years, some three generations, and some say that He will continue as long as from the creation of the world or the time of Noah "up to the present time." Others say that the kingdom of the Messiah will endure for thousands of years, as "when there is a good government it is not quickly dissolved." It is also said that He shall die, and His kingdom descend to His son and grandson. In proof of this opinion Isaiah xlii. 4 is quoted: "He shall not fail, nor be discouraged, till He have set judgment in the earth." The lives of men will be prolonged for centuries: "He will swallow up death in victory" (Is. xxv. 8); and "the child shall die an hundred years old" (Is. lxv. 20). The Talmud applies the former verse to Israel, the latter verse to the Gentiles. The men of that time will be two hundred ells high. This is said to be proved by the word "upright" (Lev. xxvi. 13), "upright" being applied to the supposed height of man before the fall. "Moreover the light of the moon shall be as the light of the sun; and the light of the sun shall be sevenfold, as the light of seven days" (Is. xxx. 26). The land of Israel will produce cakes and clothes of the finest wool. The wheat will grow on Lebanon as high as palm-trees; and a wind will be sent from God to reduce it to fine flour for the support of those who gather it; as it is said "with the fat of kidneys of wheat" (Deut. xxxii. 14). Each kidney will be as large as "the kidneys of the fattest oxen." To prove that this is nothing wonderful, an account is given of a rape seed in which a fox once brought forth young. These young ones were weighed, and found to be as heavy as sixty pounds of Cyprus weight. Lest these statements should be thought a contradiction of the verse "*There* is no new *thing* under the sun" (Eccles. i. 9), the

Rabbis say that it is just like the growth of mushrooms, toad-stools, and the delicate mosses on the branches of trees. Grapes will also grow most luxuriantly; and in every cluster there will be thirty jars of wine. Jerusalem will be built three miles high; as it is written, " It shall be lifted up " (Zech. xiv. 10). The gates of the city will be made of pearls and precious stones, thirty ells high and thirty ells broad. A disciple of the Rabbis once doubted whether precious stones could be found so large; and shortly afterward, he saw an angel with similar stones, as he was out at sea. On his return to land he related what he had seen to Rabbi Jochanan. Whereupon the Rabbi said, " Thou fool, if thou hadst not seen, thou hadst not believed; thou mockest the words of the wise." He then " lifted up his eyes upon him, and he was made an heap of bones."

Said R. Samuel, the son of Nachman, R. Jochanan said, " Three shall be called by the name of the Holy One; blessed be He." And these are the Righteous, the Messiah, and Jeru-salem. The Righteous, as is said (Is. xliii. 7). The Messiah, as it is written (Jer. xxiii. 6): " And this is His name whereby he shall be called, THE LORD OUR RIGHTEOUSNESS." Jerusalem, as it is written (Ezek. xlviii. 35): " It was round about eighteen thousand measures: and the name of the city from that day shall be The LORD is THERE." ·

In the later editions of the Talmud the allusions to Christ and Christianity are few and cautious, compared with the earlier or unexpurgated copies. The last of these was pub-lished at Amsterdam in 1645. In them our Lord and Saviour is " that one," " such an one," " a fool," " the leper," " the deceiver of Israel," etc. Efforts are made to prove that He is the son of Joseph Pandira before his marriage with Mary. His miracles are attributed to sorcery, the secret of which He brought in a slit in His flesh out of Egypt. His teacher is said to have been Joshua, the son of Perachiah. This Joshua is said to have afterward excommunicated him to the blast of 400 rams' horns, though he must have lived seventy years be-fore His time. Forty days before the death of Jesus a witness was summoned by public proclamation to attest His innocence, but none appeared. He is said to have been first stoned, and then hanged on the eve of the Passover. His disciples are called heretics, and opprobrious names. They are accused of immoral practices; and the New Testament is called a sinful book. The references to these subjects manifest the most bitter aversion and hatred.

The Rabbis have laid down thirteen rules for the interpretation of the Talmud. These rules form their system of logic. They are as follows:

(1.) "Light and heavy," an argument from the less to the greater. An example is furnished in the case of Miriam (Num. xii. 14). "If her father had but spit in her face, should she not be ashamed seven days? let her be shut out from the camp seven days, and after that let her be received in again." The argument is here drawn from the conduct of man, the less, to that of God, the greater. The owner of an ox is also fined more for his beast if it gores his neighbor's beast than if it eats his neighbor's corn; since the tooth only means sustenance for the stomach, but the horn means mischief.

(2.) "Equality," an argument from the similarity or identity of words and impressions. An example is furnished in Deut. xv. 12: "If thy brother, an Hebrew man, or an Hebrew woman, be sold unto thee, and serve thee six years, then in the seventh year thou shalt let him free from thee." In the 18th verse, when this law is again referred to, the man only is mentioned; but as the woman was mentioned in the former verse, it is concluded that the law applies equally to both.

(3.) "The building of the father," an argument from the statements in (a) one place in the Law to other passages, which are similar. An example is furnished in Exod. xii. 16, where servile work is forbidden during the feast of unleavened bread, and the conclusion is drawn that servile work is equally forbidden in all festivals of the same nature. This mode of argument is also applied to (b) two places in the Law, where one place refers to the general proposition, and another to particulars arising out of it. An example is furnished in Lev. xv. 1, where a man with an issue is unclean, but in the 4th verse this uncleanness is limited to his bed and his seat.

(4.) "Universal and particular." Where there is a general and a special statement, the special binds the general. An example is furnished in Lev. i. 2: "If any man of you bring an offering unto the Lord, ye shall bring your offering of the

cattle, even of the herd and of the flock." Cattle (in the Hebrew Behemah) includes both wild and tame. The special
terms "herd" and "flock" limit the offering to domesticated
animals.

(5.) "Particular and universal," or argument from the
special to the general. An example is furnished in Deut. xxii.
1: "Thou shalt not see thy brother's ox or his sheep go
astray: thou shalt in any case bring them again unto thy
brother." In the 3d verse, it is further commanded to restore
"all lost things of thy brother's." Hence it is concluded, not
only his ox or his sheep, but that everything, which he has lost
is to be restored to him.

(6.) "Universal, particular and universal." Where there are
two universal statements with a particular statement between,
the particular limits the universals. An example is furnished
in Deut. xiv. 26, where, speaking of the application of the
second tithe, it is said, "Thou shalt bestow that money for
whatsoever thy soul lusteth after; for oxen, or for sheep, or
for wine, or for strong drink, or for whatsoever thy soul desireth." The special limitation, between the two universal
permissions, is to productions of the land of Canaan.

(7.) "The general that requires the special, and the special
that requires the general." An example is furnished in Lev.
xvii. 13: "Whatsoever man . . . hunteth and catcheth
any beast or fowl that may be eaten, he shall even pour out the
blood thereof, and cover it with dust." The word "cover"
or "hide" is again used in Gen. xviii. 17: "Shall I hide from
Abraham that thing which I shall do?" The conclusion is
drawn, that cover is restricted to the blood being hidden under
dust, and not put in any vessel. Again (Exod. xiii. 2):
"Sanctify unto me all the first-born; whatever openeth the
womb among the children of Israel, both of man and beast,
it is mine." From this verse females might be included with
males. Reference is made to Deut. xv. 19, where it is found
"All the firstling males." Still it is obscure, when there are
firstling females, about the males born afterward. Reference
is made to Exod. xxxiv. 19: "All that openeth the matrix is
mine." Here all first-born are allowed. This, however, is too
general, and it is again restricted by the word males. And as
this is too general, it is again restricted by "all that openeth
the matrix."

(8.) " Whatsoever is taught in general and something special is mentioned—it is mentioned to strengthen the general rule." An example is furnished in Lev. xx. 2, where the worship of Moloch is forbidden, and the penalty for the sin is death. The conclusion drawn is, that such mention of a special form of idolatry confirms the prohibition of all idolatry.

(9.) " When there is a general rule and also an exception— the exception lightens and does not aggravate." An example is furnished in the command (Exod. xxi. 12), " He that smiteth a man so that he die, he shall surely be put to death." The exception is, " Whoso killeth his neighbor ignorantly " (Deut. xix. 4, 5), "he can flee to one of the cities of refuge."

(10.) " When there is a general rule, and an exception not agreeing with the general rule, the exception both lightens and aggravates." An example is furnished from the plague of leprosy (Lev. xiii. 3) when the hair is turned white. Tho head and beard are excepted (29th verse) lest there be gray hairs —this lightens. But if on the head and beard there be "yel- low thin hair," it is a dry scall—this aggravates.

(11.) " When there is an exception from a general rule to establish a new matter—the new matter cannot be brought under the general rule again, unless it be mentioned in the text." An example is furnished from the eating of holy things (Lev. xxii. 10-13). The priest, any soul bought with his money, and he that is born in his house, may eat of it. This is the general rule. If the priest's daughter be married to a stranger, she may not eat of them. This is the exception. This exception would have remained if she continued married to a stranger, or had a child, or had not returned to her father's house. Therefore a new law is provided, that in the event of none of these things happening, she may again eat of the holy things.

(12.) " Things that teach from the subject, and things that teach from the end." An example is furnished from the eighth commandment, " Thou shalt not steal." This law, if applied to man-stealing or kidnapping, implies capital punish- ment. The reason given is from its following " Thou shalt do no murder," and " Thou shalt not commit adultery "—two laws which, if violated, entailed death. The second part of this rule applies to things that teach from the end. What is meant by the end is a matter of dispute. Some say it means the final cause of logicians. Others say it means something in the end or conclusion of the law itself. If it be the latter, an example is furnished from the case of the leprous house (Lev. xiv. 45): "And he shall break down the house, the stones of it, and the timber thereof, and all the mortar of the house." These directions teach that houses made of mud are excepted.

(13.) "When two texts contradict each other, until a third be found to decide between them." An example is furnished in Gen. i. 1: "In the beginning God created the heaven and the earth." It is again written, Gen. ii. 4, "In the day that the Lord made the earth and the heavens." The question now arises, Which did He make first? The answer is found in Isaiah xlviii. 13: "Mine hand also hath laid the foundation of the earth, and My right hand hath spanned the heavens." The conclusion is drawn that He made both at once. Another instance is the discrepancy in the census of Israel. In 2 Sam. xxiv. 9, the number stated is eight hundred thousand. In 1 Chron. xxi. 5, the number is said to have been " eleven hundred thousand." The difference of three hundred thousand is accounted for by referring to 1 Chron. xxvii. 1, where it is said that twenty-four thousand served the king every month. These men, when multiplied by the months, make two hundred and eighty-eight thousand. And the twelve thousand which waited upon the twelve captains raise the number to three hundred thousand, the amount required to reconcile the two statements.

In reading the following tracts it should be borne in mind that the meaning in many places is more implied than expressed.[5] Often an idea is taken for granted, which patient continuance in reading can alone bring to light. The subjects to which these tracts refer should first be studied in the Bible; because after such study the restless subtlety of the Rabbis in "binding heavy burdens on men's shoulders" can be more fully discerned. It is desirable to look on these writings from this point of observation; just as on some mountain top one

[5] The expression " they " is often used in the phraseology of the Talmud to denote either certain officials or else the sages and men of authority. The exact reference can only be gathered from the context. So again with the use of " he." In such cases the expression " he " generally refers to the decision on a particular occasion.

looks not only at the gold which the morning sun pours on grass and flower, but also on the deep valley where the shadows still rest, that one may the more sensibly feel how glorious the sun is. The whole theory of this second, or Oral Law, has arisen from inattention to the express statement of Moses: " These words (the ten commandments) the Lord spake unto all your assembly in the mount out of the midst of the fire, of the cloud, and of the thick darkness, with a great voice: AND HE ADDED NO MORE " (Deut. v. 22). And it tends to nullify the declaration of the Targum of Jonathan Ben Uzziel, " For unto us a child is born, unto us a son is given; and he has taken the law upon himself to keep it " (Isaiah ix. 6).

In concluding this introduction it is perhaps well to glance briefly at the age in which the Talmud grew to its present state. It was a period of great activity and thought. Old systems of debasing superstition were breaking up and passing away. A new faith had arisen to regenerate man. The five centuries which followed the appearing of our Saviour in this world were filled with religious and political events which still make their vibrations felt. From the destruction of Jerusalem and the overthrow of the Jewish polity, an impulse was given to those political changes which have since gone on without intermission among the nations of the earth. From the overthrow of the Jewish Temple an impulse was given to religious earnestness which, often from wrong, often from right motives, has increased, and will increase, as the great consummation draws nigh.

While the Rabbis were laboring at their gigantic mental structure, while generation after generation of their wisest and most patriotic men were accumulating materials to build the tower which became a beacon to their countrymen for all time, the Christian Church was not idle. By their writings and eloquence the Fathers were gathering the treasures of patristic lore which have descended to us. While Rabbis were discoursing in the synagogues of Tiberias and Babylon, Christian orators were preaching in the basilicas of Constantinople and Rome. They have all gone from this mortal scene. But their thoughts are handed down, so that we may converse with them, though they are no longer on earth. We can hear their wisdom—we can see their errors—we can almost fancy we behold their forms—so that, being dead, they yet speak. Since they ceased from their labors empires have risen and fallen, countless millions of our race have vanished into eternity, and left their bodies to moulder into dust. But their teachings still live on, to influence immortal souls for weal or woe. Doubtless their departures from the Word of God prepared a way and furnished matter for the numerous heresies and lawless deeds which form a great portion of the history of mankind. From their errors sprang at least in part the Koran. This and kindred themes, however, open up an interminable vista, leading us away from the Talmud itself. It is better now to conclude this introduction. And with what more suitable words can I close than with those drawn from the wisdom of the Fathers? "It is not incumbent upon thee to complete the work: neither art thou free to cease from it. If thou hast studied the law, great shall be thy reward; for the Master of thy work is faithful to pay the reward of thy labor: but know that the reward of the righteous is in the world to come."

SELECTIONS FROM THE TALMUD

ON BLESSINGS

Recitation of the Shemah—Blessings—Rabbi Gamaliel—Exemptions from the Recitation—Prayers—Differences Between the Schools of Shammai and Hillel—Reverence for the Temple.

CHAPTER I

1. "From what time do we recite the Shemah[1] in the evening?" "From the hour the priests[2] enter (the temple) to eat their heave offerings, until the end of the first watch."[3] The words of R. Eleazar; but the Sages say "until midnight." Rabban Gamaliel says, "until the pillar of the morn ascend." It happened that his sons came from a banquet. They said to him, "we have not yet said the Shemah." He said to them, "if the pillar of the morn be not yet ascended, you are bound to say it; and not only this, but all that the Sages say, 'till midnight,' they command till the pillar of the morn ascend." The burning of the fat and members they command "till the pillar of the morn ascend." And all offerings, which must be eaten the same day, they command "till the pillar of the morn ascend." If so, why do the Sages say "until midnight"? "To withhold man from transgression."

---

[1] "Hear, O Israel, the Lord our God is one Lord," etc. (Deut. vi. 4-9, xi. 13-21; Num. xv. 37-41). Evening prayer might be said after 12.30 P.M. (Acts x. 9.) It is abundantly evident from the Zohar that the ancient Jews understood that in the Shemah there was a confession of the doctrine of the Trinity in unity — three Persons in One God. "Hear, O Israel: Jehovah our God is one Jehovah. By the first name in this sentence, Jehovah, is signified God the Father, the Head of all things. By the next words, our God, is signified God the Son, the fountain of all knowledge; and by the second Jehovah, is signified God the Holy Ghost, proceeding of them both; to all which is added the word One, to signify that these three are Indivisible. But this mystery shall not be revealed until the coming of Messiah." The Zohar gives also an imperfect illustration of this great Truth, by saying that the Trinity in unity is like "the human voice, which is composed of three elements—warmth, air, and vapor."

[2] Priests who were legally unclean. (Lev. xxii. 7.)

[3] The Mishna begins the night at 6 P.M., and divides it into three watches of four hours each.

43

2. " From what time do we recite the Shemah in the morning?" When one can discern betwixt " blue and white," R.
Eleazar says " betwixt blue and leek green." And it may be
finished "until the sun shine forth." R. Joshua says "until
the third hour." [4] For such is the way of royal princes to
rise at the third hour. He who recites Shemah afterward
loses nothing. He is like a man reading the Law.

3. The school of Shammai say that in the evening all men
are to recline when they recite the Shemah; and in the morning they are to stand up; for it is said, "when thou liest down
and when thou risest up." [5] But the school of Hillel say, that
every man is to recite it in his own way; for it is said, " when
thou walkest by the way." [6] If so, why is it said, " when thou
liest down and when thou risest up"? " When mankind
usually lie down, and when mankind usually rise up." R. Tarphon said, "I came on the road, and reclined to recite the
Shemah according to the words of the school of Shammai,
and I was in danger of robbers." The Sages said to him,
"thou wast guilty against thyself, because thou didst transgress the words of the school of Hillel."

4. In the morning two blessings are said before (the
Shemah), and one after it; and in the evening two blessings
before and two after it, one long and one short. [7] Where the
(Sages) have said to lengthen, none is allowed to shorten; and
to shorten none is allowed to lengthen: to close, none is allowed not to close; not to close, none is allowed to close.

5. We commemorate the departure from Egypt at night;
said R. Eleazar, son of Azariah, " truly I am a son of seventy
years, and was not clear that thou shouldst say the departure
from Egypt at night until the son of Zoma expounded, ' that
thou mayest remember the day when thou camest forth out
of the land of Egypt all the days of thy life;' [8] the days of thy
life (are) days; all the days of thy life (include) the nights."
But the Sages say, " the days of thy life (are) this world; all
the days of thy life (include) the days of the Messiah."

---

[4] The Mishna begins the day at 6 A.M.
The third hour is 9 A.M.
[5] Deut. vi. 7.
[6] Ibid.
[7] A long blessing begins and ends

with " Blessed art Thou, O Lord "; a
short blessing only ends with these
words.
[8] Deut. xvi. 3.

CHAPTER II

1. "If one who is reading in the Law when the time comes for praying intends it in his heart?" "He is free." "But if not?" "He is not free." "At the end of the sections one salutes out of respect, and responds; but in the middle of a section he salutes from fear, and responds." Such are the words of R. Mair. R. Judah says, "in the middle he salutes from fear, and responds out of respect; at the end he salutes out of respect, and repeats peace to every man."

2. The intervals of the sections are between the first blessing and the second—between the second and "Hear, O Israel;" between "Hear" and "it shall come to pass;"[1] between "and it shall come to pass" and "and he said;"[2] between "and he said" and "it is true and certain."[3] Said R. Judah, "between 'and he said' and 'it is true and certain,' none is to pause." R. Joshua, the son of Korcha, said, "Why does the (section) 'Hear,' etc., precede 'and it shall come to pass'? 'That one may take on himself the kingdom of heaven, before he take on himself the yoke of the commandments.' Why does (the section) 'and it shall come to pass' precede 'and he said'? Because 'and it shall come to pass' may be practised by day and by night;[4] but 'and he said,' etc., only by day."[5]

3. He who recites the Shemah so as not to be audible to his own ears, is legally free.[6] R. José says "he is not legally free." "If he has said it without grammar and pronunciation?" R. José says "he is legally free." R. Judah says "he is not legally free." "If he said it irregularly?" "He is not legally free." "In recitation he mistook?" "He must recommence from the place where he mistook."

4. Laborers may recite the Shemah on the top of a tree, or of a wall, but they are not allowed to do so with the prayer.[7]

5. A bridegroom is exempted from reciting the Shemah on the first night of marriage, and, even until the expiration

[1] Deut. xi. 13-21.
[2] Num. xv. 37-41.
[3] Because in Jer. x. 10 it is written, "But the Lord is the true God," etc.
[4] Deut. xi. 19.
[5] Because it says, "that ye may look upon it," i.e., the fringe. Num. xv. 39.
[6] When the expressions "free" or "not free" are used, they refer to the decisions of the Levitical Law. So also is it with the expressions "clean" or "unclean."
[7] I.e., the eighteen blessings called "Amidah."

of the Sabbath if the marriage be not complete. It happened that Rabban Gamaliel recited on the first night. His disciples said to him, " hast thou not taught us, our master, that a bridegroom is exempted from reciting Shemah on the first night? " He said to them, " I will not hear you, to deprive myself of the yoke of the kingdom of heaven even one hour."

6. He (R. Gamaliel) bathed on the first night of his wife's death. His disciples said to him, " hast thou not taught us, our master, that a mourner is forbidden to bathe? " He said to them, " I am not like all other men; I am infirm."

7. When his slave Tabbi died, he received visits of condolence. His disciples said to him, " hast thou not taught us, our master, that visits of condolence are not to be received for slaves? " He said to them, " my slave Tabbi was not like all other slaves, he was upright."

8. The bridegroom who wishes to recite the Shemah on the first night may recite it. R. Simeon, the son of Gamaliel, said, " not every one who wishes to affect the pious reputation can affect it."

CHAPTER III

1. He whose dead lies before him is exempted from reciting the Shemah,—from the prayer,—and from the phylacteries.[1] Those who carry the bier, and those who relieve them, and those who relieve the relief,—those who go before the bier, and those who follow it, who are required for the bier, are exempted from reciting the Shemah. But those not required for the bier are bound to recite it. Both (parties) are exempted from the prayer.

2. When they have buried the dead, and return, if they have time to begin and end (the Shemah) before they reach the rows (of mourners), they must begin: if not, they must not begin. Of those standing in the rows the inner (mourners) are exempt, but the outer ones are bound to recite the Shemah.

3. Women, slaves, and children, are exempt from reciting the Shemah, and also from the phylacteries; but they are

[1] Phylacteries consist of texts of Scripture (Exod. xiii. 2-10, 11-17; Deut. vi. 4-9, 13-22) written on parchment and inclosed in a leather box. They are bound by thongs round the left arm and forehead.

bound in the prayer, the sign on the door-post, and the bless
ing after food.

4. A man in his legal uncleanness is to meditate in his
heart on the (Shemah), but he is not to bless before, or after
it. After his food he blesses, but not before it. R. Judah
says " he blesses both before and after it."

If one stand in prayer, and recollect that he is in his uncleanness, he is not to pause, but to shorten (the prayer). If
he has gone down into the water (to bathe),[2] and can go up,
dress, and recite the Shemah before the sun shines forth, he
is to go up, dress, and recite it. But he is not to cover himself
with foul water or with water holding matter in solution unless he has poured clean water to it. " How far is he to keep
from foul water, or excrement?" " Four cubits."

6. A man in his uncleanness with a running issue, a woman
in her uncleanness, during separation, and she who perceives
the need of separation, require the bath. But R. Judah " ex-
empts them."

CHAPTER IV

1. The morning prayer may be said till noon. R. Judah
says " until the fourth hour." The afternoon prayer until
the evening. R. Judah says " until half the afternoon." The
evening prayer has no limit, and the additional prayers may
be said all day. R. Judah says " until the seventh hour."

2. R. Nechooniah, son of Hakanah, used to pray when he
entered the lecture-room, and when he went out he said a
short prayer. The (Sages) said to him, " what occasion is
there for this prayer?" He said to them, " when I enter I
pray that no cause of offence may arise through me ; and when
I go out I give thanks for my lot."

3. Rabban Gamaliel said, " one must daily say the eighteen
prayers." R. Joshua said " a summary of the eighteen." R.
Akivah said, " if his prayer be fluent in his mouth, he says the
eighteen ; if not, a summary of the eighteen."

4. R. Eleazar said, " if one make his prayer fixed, his
prayer is not supplications." R. Joshua said, " if a man travel
in dangerous places, let him use this short prayer : ' Save, O

² Lev. xv. 16.

Lord, thy people, the remnant of Israel; at every stage of their journey [1] let their wants be before thee. Blessed art thou, O Lord, who hearest prayers.'"

5. If one ride on an ass, he must dismount: if he cannot dismount, he must turn his face; and if he cannot turn his face, he must direct his heart toward the Holy of Holies.

6. If one be seated in a ship, or in a carriage, or on a raft, he must direct his mind toward the Holy of Holies.

7. R. Eleazar, the son of Azariah, said "the additional [2] prayers are only to be said in a public congregation." But the Sages say, "if there be a public congregation, or no public congregation." R. Judah said in his name, "in every place, where there is a public congregation, individuals are exempted from additional prayers."

CHAPTER V

1. Men should not stand up to pray, except with reverential head. The pious of ancient days used to pause one hour before they began to pray, that they might direct their hearts to God. Though the king salute, one must not respond; and though a serpent wind itself round his heel, one must not pause.

2. Men should mention the heavy rain in praying for the resurrection of the dead; and entreat for rain in the blessing for the year, and "the distinction between the Sabbath and week-day" [1] is to be said in the prayer "who graciously bestows knowledge." [2] R. Akivah said, "the distinction between the Sabbath and week-day is to be said in a fourth prayer by itself." R. Eleazar said, "in the thanksgivings."

3. He who says, "Thy mercies extend to a bird's nest," or, "for goodness be Thy name remembered," or he who says, "we give thanks, we give thanks," [3] is to be silenced. If a man pass up to the ark (where the rolls of the Law are kept) and make a mistake, another must pass up in his stead; nor may he in such a moment refuse. "Where does he begin?" "From the beginning of the prayer in which the other made the mistake."

[1] Or transgression.
[2] Called Musaph.
[1] Prayer called "Habdelah."
[3] Called "Chonen hada'ath."
[4] As if there were two gods.

4. He who passes up to the ark is not to answer " Amen " after the priests, lest his attention be distracted. If no other priest be present but himself, he is not to lift up his hands (to bless the congregation). But if he be confident that he can lift up his hands, and then resume, he is at liberty.

5. If a man pray, and make a mistake, it is a bad sign for him. If he be a representative of a congregation, it is a bad sign for his constituents, for a man's representative is like himself. They say of R. Hanina, son of Dosa, that when he prayed for the sick, he used to say, " this one will live," or " this one will die." The (Sages) said to him, " how do you know? " He said to them, " if my prayer be fluent in my mouth, I know that he is accepted; but if not, I know that he is lost."

CHAPTER VI

1. " How do we bless for fruit? "   " For fruit of a tree say, ' Who createst the fruit of the wood,' excepting the wine. For wine say, ' Who createst the fruit of the vine.' For fruits of the earth say, ' Who createst the fruit of the ground,' excepting the morsel. For the morsel say, ' Who bringest forth bread from the earth.' For vegetables say, ' Who createst the fruit of the ground.' R. Judah says, ' Who createst various kinds of herbs.' "

2. He who blessed the fruits of the tree (thus), " Who createst the fruits of the ground? " " He is free." And for the fruits of ground (said), " Who createst the fruits of the wood? " " He is not free." But, in general, if one say, " (Who createst) everything? " " He is free."

3. For the thing which groweth not from the earth, say, " (Who createst) everything." For vinegar, unripe fruit, and locusts, say " everything." For milk, cheese, and eggs, say " everything." R. Judah says, "whatever it be, which had its origin in a curse, is not to be blessed."

4. If a man have before him many kinds of fruits? R. Judah says, " if there be among them of the seven [1] kinds, he

---

[1] Mentioned Deut. viii. 8. The Jews make a distinction between Biccurim, the fruits of the soil in their natural state, and Therumoth, the fruits in a prepared state, such as oil, flour, and wine. The first fruits were always brought to Jerusalem with great pomp and display. The Talmud says that all the cities which were of the same course of priests gathered together into one of

is to bless them." But the Sages say "he may bless which-ever of them he pleases."

5. "If one blessed the wine before food?" "The blessing frees the wine after food." "If he blessed the titbit before food?" "It frees the titbit after food." "If he blessed the bread?" "It frees the titbit." But the blessing on the titbit does not free the bread. The school of Shammai say, "neither does it free the cookery."

6. "If several persons sit down to eat?" "Each blesses for himself." "But if they recline together?" "One blesses for all." "If wine come to them during food?" "Each blesses for himself." "But if after food?" "One blesses for all." He also blesses for the incense, even though they have not brought it till after the repast.

7. "If they first set salt food before a man and bread with it?" "He blesses the salt food, which frees the bread, as the bread is only an appendage." The rule is, whenever there is principal and with it appendage,—the blessing on the principal frees the appendage.

8. "If one have eaten figs, grapes, and pomegranates?" "He must say after them three blessings." The words of Rabban Gamaliel. But the Sages say, "one blessing—a summary of the three." R. Akivah says, "if one have eaten

---

the cities which was a priestly station, and they lodged in the streets. In the morning he who was chief among them said, "Arise, let us go up to Zion to the House of the Lord our God." An ox went before them with gilded horns, and an olive crown was on his head. This ox was intended for a peace offer-ing to be eaten by the priests in the court of the sanctuary. The pipe played before the procession until it ap-proached Jerusalem. When they drew near to the holy city, the first fruits were "crowned" and exposed to view with great ostentation. Then the chief men and the high officers and the treas-urers of the temple came out to meet them and receive them with honor. And all the workmen in Jerusalem rose up in their shops, and thus they saluted them: "O our brethren, inhabitants of such a city, ye are welcome." The pipe played before them till they came to the Temple Mount. Everyone, even King Agrippa himself, took his basket upon his shoulder, and went forward till he came to the court. Then the Levites sang, "I will exalt thee, O Lord, be-cause thou hast lifted me up, and hast not made my foes to rejoice over me" (Ps. xxx. 1). While the basket is still on his shoulder, he says, "I profess this day to the Lord my God." And when he repeats the passage, "A Syrian ready to perish was my father" (Deut. xxvi. 3-5), he casts the basket down from his shoulder, and keeps silent while the priest waves it hither and thither at the southwest corner of the altar. The whole passage of Scripture being then recited as far as the tenth verse, he places the basket before the altar—he worships—and goes out. The baskets of the rich were of gold or silver. The baskets of the poor were of peeled wil-low. These latter, together with their contents, were presented to the priests in service. The more valuable baskets were returned to their owners. They used to hang turtle doves and young pigeons round their baskets, which were adorned with flowers. These were sacri-ficed for burnt offerings. The parties who brought the first fruits were obliged to lodge in Jerusalem all the night after they brought them, and the next morning they were allowed to re-turn home. The first fruits were forbid-den to be offered before the feast of Pentecost, and after the feast of Dedi-cation.

boiled (pulse); and it is his meal, he must say after it three blessings." Whoever drinks water for his thirst, says, "By whose word everything is," etc. R. Tarphon says, "Who createst many souls," etc.

CHAPTER VII

1. Three men who have eaten together are bound to bless after food. " If a person have eaten of that which is doubtful, whether it has paid tithe or not; or of first tithe from which the heave offering has been taken; or of second tithe or conse- crated things, which have been redeemed; also, if the waiter have eaten the size of an olive; or a Samaritan be of the party?" "The blessing must be said." "But if one have eaten the untithed—or first tithes from which the heave offering has not been taken—or consecrated things which are unredeemed; or if the waiter have eaten less than the size of an olive, or a stranger be of the party?" "The blessing is not to be said."

2. There is no blessing at food for women, slaves, and chil- dren. What quantity is required for the blessing at food? The size of an olive. R. Judah says "the size of an egg."

3. "How do we bless at food?" "If there be three, one says, 'Let us bless,' etc.; if three and himself, he says, 'Bless ye,' etc.: if ten, he says, 'Let us bless our God,' etc.; if ten and himself, he says, 'Bless ye,' etc.; (so) if there be ten or ten myriads. If there be an hundred, he says, 'Let us bless the Lord our God,' etc.; if there be an hundred and himself, he says, 'Bless ye,' etc.: if there be a thousand, he says, 'Let us bless the Lord our God, the God of Israel;' if there be a thousand and himself, he says, 'Bless ye,' etc.: if there be a myriad, he says, 'Let us bless the Lord our God, the God of Israel, the God of Hosts, who sitteth between the Cherubim,' etc.; if there be a myriad and himself, he says, 'Bless ye,' etc. As he pronounces the blessing, so they respond after him, 'Blessed be the Lord our God, the God of Israel, the God of Hosts, who sitteth between the Cherubim, for the food we have eaten.'" R. José the Galilean says they should bless according to the number of the assembly; for it is written, "Bless ye God in the congregations; (even) the Lord from the fountain of

Israel." [1] Said R. Akivah, " What do we find in the syna-gogue? whether many or few the minister says, ' Bless ye the Lord,' " etc. R. Ishmael says, " Bless ye the Lord, who is ever blessed."

4. When three have eaten together, they are not permitted to separate without blessing; nor four or five. But six may divide into two parties, and so may any number up to ten. But ten may not separate without blessing, nor any number less than twenty (who can divide into two parties).

5. If two companies have eaten in one house, and some of each company be able to see some of the other company, they may join in the blessing; but if not, each company blesses for itself   " They should not bless the wine till it has been mixed with water." The words of R. Eleazar. But the Sages say " they may bless it unmixed."

CHAPTER VIII

1. These are the controversies relating to meals between the schools of Shammai and Hillel. The school of Shammai say, " one must say the blessing of the day, and then bless the wine; " but the school of Hillel say, " one must say the bless-ing on the wine, and then bless the day."

2. The school of Shammai say, " men must pour water on the hands, and then mix the goblet; " but the school of Hillel say, " the goblet must be mixed, and then water poured on the hands."

3. The school of Shammai say, " one is to wipe his hands on the napkin, and lay it on the table; " but the school of Hillel say, " on the cushion."

4. The school of Shammai bless " the light, the food, the spices, and the distinction of the day; " but the school of Hillel bless " the light, the spices, the food, and the distinction of the day." The school of Shammai say, " who created the light of fire; " but the school of Hillel say, " Creator of the lights of fire."

6. Men must not bless light and spices of idolatrous Gen-tiles, nor light and spices of corpses, nor light and spices be-

[1] Ps. lxviii. 26.

fore an idol. They must not bless the light until they have enjoyed the light.

7. "If one have eaten, and forgotten, and not blessed?" The school of Shammai say, "he must return to his place and bless." But the school of Hillel say, "he may bless in the place where he recollects." "How long is one obliged to bless?" "Until the food in his stomach be digested."

8. "If wine came to the company, and there is but one goblet?" The school of Shammai say "that one must bless the wine and then bless the food." But the school of Hillel say "that one must bless the food and then bless the wine." Men must answer "Amen" when an Israelite blesses; but they must not answer "Amen" when a Samaritan blesses, until the whole [1] blessing be heard.

CHAPTER IX

1. He who sees a place where signs were wrought for Israel, says, "Blessed be He who wrought signs for our fathers in this place;" a place where idolatry has been rooted out,— says, "Blessed be He who hath rooted idolatry out of our land."

2. On comets, earthquakes, lightnings, thunder, and tempests, say, "Blessed be He whose strength and might fill the world." On mountains, hills, seas, rivers, and deserts, say, "Blessed be He who made the creation." R. Judah says, when a man sees the great sea he is to say, "Blessed be He who made the great sea,"—when he sees it at intervals. On rains, and on good news say, "Blessed be He who is good and beneficent." On bad news say, "Blessed be the true Judge."

3. He who has built a new house, or bought new furniture, says, "Blessed be He who has kept us alive," etc. One must bless for evil the source of good; and for good the source of evil. "He who supplicates for what is past?" "Such prayer is vain." "How?" His wife is pregnant, and he says, "God grant that my wife may bring forth a male child." Such prayer is vain. Or if one on the road hear the voice of lamentation in the city, and say, "God grant that it may not be my son, my house," etc., such prayer is vain.

[1] Lest it be a blessing used on Mount Gerizzim.

4. Whoever enters a fortified town must say two prayers, one at his entrance, and one at his departure. Ben Azai says, "four, two at his entrance, and two at his departure; he returns thanks for the past, and supplicates for the future."

5. Man is bound to bless God for evil, as he is bound to bless Him for good. For it is said, " And thou shalt love the Lord thy God with all thy heart, and with all thy soul, and with all thy might." [2] " With all thy heart " means, with both thy inclinations, the evil as well as the good. " With all thy soul " means, even should He deprive thee of life ; and " with all thy might " means with all thy wealth. Another opinion is, that " with all thy might " means whatever measure He metes out unto thee, do thou thank Him with thy entire might. No man is to be irreverent opposite the eastern gate of the Temple, for it is opposite the Holy of Holies. No man is to go on the mountain of the house with his staff, shoes, or purse, nor with dust on his feet, nor is he to make it a short cut, nor is he to spit at all. All the seals of the blessings in the sanctuary used to say, " from eternity." But since the Epicureans perversely taught there is but one world, it was directed that man should say, " from eternity to eternity." It was also directed that every man should greet his friend in THE NAME, as it is said, " And behold Boaz came from Bethlehem, and said unto the reapers, The Lord (be) with you: and they answered him, The Lord bless thee." [3] And it is also said, " The Lord is with thee, thou mighty man of valor." [4] And it is said, " Despise not thy mother when she is old." [5] And it is also said, " (It is) time for (thee), Lord, to work, for they have made void thy law." [6] R. Nathan says, " They have made void thy law because (it is) time for (thee), Lord, to work."

[2] Deut. vi. 5.
[3] Ruth ii. 4.
[4] Judges vi. 12.
[5] Prov. xxiii. 22.
[6] Psalm cxix. 126.

ON THE SABBATICAL YEAR

Ploughing—Gardening—Dunging—Removing Stones—Sowing—Cutting Down Trees—Fruits—Buying and Selling—Territory Included in the Sabbatical Year—Produce Governed by Its Laws—Debts and Payments.

CHAPTER I

1. " How long do men plough in a field with trees on the eve of the Sabbatical year? "[1] The school of Shammai say, " so long as it is useful for the fruit; " but the school of Hillel say, " till Pentecost," and the words of the one are near to the words of the other.

2. " What is a field with trees? " " Three trees to every fifty cubits square, if they be fit to produce a heap of figs worth sixty Italian minas;[2] on their account men can legally plough the earth for the whole fifty cubits square around them. Less than for these they may not legally plough, save the extent of the gatherer of fruit with his basket outward.

3. "Whether they be fruitless or fruitful? " " Men may regard them as though they were fig-trees." " If they be fit to produce a heap of figs worth sixty Italian minas? " " On their account they may legally plough the whole fifty cubits square around them. Less than for these they may not plough, save what is absolutely needful."

4. " One tree produced a heap of figs, and two trees did not produce it; or two trees produced it, and one did not produce it? " " Men may not plough save what is absolutely needful for them, till they be from three to nine in number." " If they be ten? " " On their account men may legally plough around them the whole fifty cubits square; and also from ten trees and upward, whether they produce or do not pro-

---

[1] It has been a subject of dispute when the Sabbatical year began—whether in Nisan or Tishri. The weight of evidence is, however, in favor of the civil New Year's Day, which fell in Tishri (September).

[2] An Italian mina perbaps; a denarius. If so, the heap would be worth about £1 17s. 6d.

duce it." As is said, " in caring-time and in harvest thou shalt rest."[3] There is no need to say caring-time and harvest in the Sabbatical year, but earing-time on the eve of the Sabbatical year, when it is just entering on the Sabbatical year; and harvest of the Sabbatical year, which is proceeding toward the close of the Sabbatical year. Rabbi Ishmael said, " as the earing-time (mentioned Exod. xxxiv. 21) is voluntary, so the harvest is voluntary, except the harvest of the (omer) sheaf."[4]

5. " If the three trees belong to three owners?" " They are reckoned as one, and on their account they may legally plough the whole fifty cubits square around them." " And how much space must be between them?" Rabban Simon, the son of Gamaliel, said, " that a bullock with his ploughing instruments may pass."

6. " If there be ten saplings dispersed in the fifty cubits square?" " On their account men may plough the whole fifty cubits square around them till new year's day." " If they be placed in a row, or rounded like a crown?" " Men may not plough save what is absolutely needful for them."

7. The saplings and the gourds are reckoned alike in the fifty cubits square. Rabban Simon, the son of Gamaliel, said, " for every ten cucumbers in the fifty cubits square, men may plough the fifty cubits square around them till new year's day."

8. " How long are they called saplings?" Rabbi Eleazar, the son of Azariah, said,[5] " till they can be used." R. Joshua said, " till the age of seven years." R. Akiba said, " a sapling, as commonly named." " A tree decays and sprouts afresh; when less than a handbreadth, it is a sapling; when more than a handbreadth, it is a tree." The words of Rabbi Simon.

CHAPTER II

1. " How long may men plough in a white[1] field on the eve of the Sabbatical year?" " Till the productiveness ceases; so long as men usually plough to plant cucumbers and gourds." Said R. Simon, " thou hast put the law in every man's hand.

---

[3] Exod. xxxiv. 21.
[4] Lev. xxiii. 10. The omer or " wave sheaf " at the Passover, and the two wave loaves, at Pentecost, were to be made from grain grown in the field during the Sabbatical year. It was also allowed to till sufficient land to pay taxes.
[5] Lev. xix. 23-25.
[1] Grain or corn field.

But men may plough in a grain field till the Passover, and in a field of trees till Pentecost."

2. Men may dung and dig among cucumbers and gourds till new year's day, and they may also do so in a parched-up field. They may prune them, remove their leaves, cover them with earth, and fumigate them, till new year's day. R. Simon said, " one may even remove the leaf from the bunch of grapes in the Sabbatical year."

3. Men may remove stones till new year's day. They may gather the ears, they may break off branches, they may cut off the withered part till new year's day. R. Joshua said, " as they may break off branches and cut off the withered part of the fifth year, so also they may do it in the sixth year." Rabbi Simon said, " every time I am permitted to work among the trees, I am permitted to cut off the withered part."

4. Men may smear the saplings, and bind them, and cut them down, and make sheds for them, and water them, till new year's day. R. Eleazar, the son of Zadok, said, " one may even water the top of the branch in the Sabbatical year, but not the root."

5. Men may anoint unripe fruits, and puncture [2] them, till new year's day. Unripe fruit of the eve of the Sabbatical year which is just entering on the Sabbatical year, and unripe fruit of the Sabbatical year which is proceeding to the close of the Sabbatical year, they may neither anoint nor puncture. Rabbi Jehudah said, " the place where it is customary to anoint them, they may not anoint them, because that is work. The place where it is not customary to anoint them, they may anoint them." R. Simon " permitted it in trees because it is allowable in the usual culture of the trees."

6. Men may not plant trees, make layers, or engraft them, on the eve of the Sabbatical year, less than thirty days before new year's day. And if one plant them, or make layers, or engraft them, they must be rooted out. Rabbi Judah said, " every graft which does not cohere in three days has no more cohesion." Rabbi José and R. Simon said " in two weeks."

7. Rice, and millet, and poppy, and simsim,[3] which have taken root before new year's day, must be tithed for the past year, and are allowed for use in the Sabbatical year ; otherwise

[2] With a pointed instrument covered with oil.   [3] Linseed(?).

they are forbidden in the Sabbatical year, and must pay tithes
for the following year.

8. R. Simon of Shezur said, " Egyptian beans which are
sown at first for seed are reckoned like them."   R. Simon said,
" the large lentils are reckoned like them."   R. Eliezer said,
" the large lentils which put forth pods before new year's day
are also reckoned like them."

9. " Onions, not for seed, and Egyptian beans, from which
water is withheld thirty days before new year's day, must pay
tithes for the past year, and they are allowed for use in the
Sabbatical year.   Otherwise they are forbidden in the Sabbatical year, and must be tithed for the coming year, and so also
(the produce) of a rain-field [4] from which the water of irriga-
tion is withheld on two occasions."   The words of R. Maier.
But the Sages say " three."

10. " The gourds which stand over for seed? "   " If they
dry up before new year's day and are unfit for human food, it
is lawful to let them remain on the Sabbatical year.   Otherwise it is forbidden to let them stand over on the Sabbatical
year.   Their buds are forbidden in the Sabbatical year.   But
they may be sprinkled with white dust." [5]   The words of R.
Simon.   Rabbi Eliezer, the son of Jacob, " forbade them."
Men may irrigate rice in the Sabbatical year.   Rabbi Simon
said, " but they must not cut its leaves."

CHAPTER III

1. " How long may men bring out dung to the heap? "
" Till the time comes for stopping work."   The words of R.
Maier.   R. Judah said, " till its fertility [1] dry out."   R. José
said, " till it hardens into a lump."

2. " How much may men manure? "   " As much as three
times three heaps for fifty cubits square of ten times ten ass
panniers, each containing a letech. [2]   They may increase the

----

[4] Rain-field means a field irrigated
with rain water.
[5] Some suppose the meaning to be,
the permission to sprinkle with water a
" white " or corn field in which the
gourds are growing.
[1] The word translated " fertility "
means literally " sweetness." Some apply these words to the dung out of

which the moisture has " dried out,"
and it is then only reckoned as earth.
Others apply them to the ground which
has lost its fertility (sweetness) for want
of rain (Job xxi. 33). The meaning is
that no advantage must be gained from
it in the approaching Sabbatical year.
[2] About thirty-six and one-half gallons.

panniers, but they must not increase the heaps." Rabbi Simon said, " also the heaps."

3. A man may make for his field three times three heaps to the fifty cubits square. "For more than these he must excavate the earth." The words of R. Simon. But the Sages " forbid it, till he sink the heaps three handbreadths, or till he raise them three above the earth." A man may keep his manure in store. Rabbi Maier " forbade it till he sink it three handbreadths, or till he raise it three." If he have only a little, he may increase it and proceed in his work. Rabbi Eleazar, the son of Azariah, " forbade it till he sink the manure three handbreadths, or raise it three, or till he place it on a rock."

4. " He who stables his cattle in his field? " " He may make a pen twice fifty cubits square. He may remove three sides and leave the middle one. It follows that he has a stable four times fifty cubits square." Rabbi Simon, the son of Gamaliel, said " eight times fifty cubits square." " If his whole field were four times fifty square cubits? " " He should leave a little space because of the observant eye, and he may remove the manure of his cattle from the pen and put it into the middle of his field, as men usually manure."

5. A man may not open a quarry in the beginning of the Sabbatical year in his field, unless there be already in it three heaps of stones measuring three cubits by three cubits, and in height three cubits, counting twenty-seven stones in each heap.

6. A fence composed of ten stones each, of weight sufficient for two men, may be removed. " If the fence measure ten handbreadths? " " Less than this he may clear off, but he must leave it a handbreadth high over the ground." These words only speak of his own field. But from his neighbor's field he may take away what he pleases. These words speak of the time when one did not begin the work on the eve of the Sabbatical year. " But if one begin on the eve of the Sabbatical year? " " He may take away what he pleases."

7. Stones shaken by the plough, or those covered and afterward exposed, if there be among them two of a burden for two men, may be removed. He who removes stones from his field may remove the upper (ones),[3] but he must leave those touching the earth. And so also from a heap of rubbish, or a

---

[3] I.e., Stones lying on the top of other stones.

heap of stones, one may take away the upper part, but must leave that which touches [4] the earth.   If there be beneath them a rock, or stubble, they may be removed.

8. Men must not build terraces on the face of the hills on the eve of the Sabbatical year, when the rains have ceased, because that is preparation for the Sabbatical year.   But one may build them in the Sabbatical year, when the rains have ceased, because that is preparation for the close of the Sabbatical year.   And men must not strengthen them with mortar, but they may make a slight wall.   Every stone which they can reach [5] with their hands and remove, they may remove.

9. " Shoulder stones may come from every place, and the contractor may bring them from every place.   And these are shoulder stones, every one which cannot be carried in one hand."   The words of R. Maier.   Rabbi José said, " shoulder stones, commonly so named, all that can be carried, two, three, upon the shoulder."

10. He who builds a fence between his own and public property may sink it down to the rock   " What shall he do with the dust?"   " He may heap it up on the public property, and benefit it."   The words of R. Joshua.   R. Akiba said, " as we have no right to injure public property, so we have no right to benefit it."   " What shall he do with the dust?"   " He may heap it up in his own field like manure, and so also when he digs a well, or a cistern, or a cave."

CHAPTER IV

1. In olden times they used to say a man may gather wood, stones, and grass in his own (field), just as he may gather that which is greater out of his neighbor's field.   When transgressors increased, a rule was made that this one should gather from that one, and that one from this one, without benefit ; and it is unnecessary to say that one could not promise victuals to those who gathered.

2. A field cleared of thorns may be sown in the close of the Sabbatical year.   If it be tilled or manured by cattle, it must

---

[4] The removal of stones " touching " the earth might loosen it, and become a kind of cultivation.

[5] I.e., From the outside of the boundary wall, as in like manner his ears of corn might be plucked. An answer to envious remarks that he was preparing for cultivation (Jer. Tal.).

not be sown in the close of the Sabbatical year. " If a field be twice ploughed? "[1] The school of Shammai say, " its fruit must not be eaten in the Sabbatical year." But the school of Hillel say, " it may be eaten." The school of Shammai say, " they must not eat its fruit on the Sabbatical year, if (the owner of it have) benefit therefrom." But the school of Hillel say, " men may eat it whether there be or be not benefit." R. Judah said, " the words are contrary; that which is permitted by the school of Shammai is restricted by the school of Hillel.

3. Men may contract for cultivated fields from Gentiles on the Sabbatical year, but not from Israelites. And they may strengthen the hands of the Gentiles on the Sabbatical year, but not the hands of Israelites. And in saluting Gentiles they may ask after their peace for the sake of peace.[2]

4. " If one thins olive trees? " The school of Shammai say, " only cut them down," and the school of Hillel say, " one may root them out "; but they both agree that for smoothing the earth the trees must be cut down. " What is meant by thinning? " " Removing one or two." " What is meant by smoothing the earth? " " Removing three trees each by the side of the other." " How is this understood? " " That one may root them out not only of his own field, but also when smoothing down the field of his neighbor."

5. " He who cleaves olive trees must not fill in the vacuum with earth; but he may cover it over with stones or stubble. He who cuts down trunks of sycamore must not fill in the vacuum with earth, but he may cover it over with stones or stubble. Men must not cut down a young sycamore in the Sabbatical year, because that is labor. R. Judah said, " if as it is usually done it is forbidden: but one may allow it to be ten handbreadths high, or cut it just above the ground." " He who lops off vine tendrils, and cuts reeds? " R. José the Galilean said, " he must leave them an handbreadth high." Rabbi Akiba said, " he may cut them as it is usual with an axe, or sickle, or saw, or with whatever he pleases." " A tree that is split? " " Men may bind it round in the Sabbatical year, not that it may cohere, but that its fissure may not extend."

---

[1] Twice ploughed implies the payment of tribute when the land was under foreign rule. Its cultivation was allowed for this purpose during the Sabbatical year. So long as a foe could be resisted, it was not cultivated (1 Mac. vi. 49).

[2] Jer. xxix. 7.

7. "From what time may the fruits of trees in the Sabbatical year be eaten?" "Unripe fruits, when they are becoming transparent, may be eaten with a piece of bread in the field. When they are mellow, they may be gathered into the house; and so also with all like them." During the remainder of the seven years their tithes must be paid.

8. The sour grapes in which there is juice may be eaten with a piece of bread in the field. Before they rot they may be gathered into the house, and so also with all like them. During the remainder of the seven years their tithes must be paid.

9. "Olives from which men have collected the fourth of a log [3] of oil to the seah?" [4] "They may be crushed and eaten in the field." When men can collect from them half a log, they may be pounded and used for anointing in the field. When those have been collected which have attained a third of their size they may be pounded in the field, and gathered into the house, and so also with all like them. During the remainder of the seven years their tithes must be paid. But for the rest of all fruits of trees, as are their seasons for the laws of tithes, so are their seasons for the laws of the Sabbatical year.

10. "From what time may men not cut trees in the Sabbatical year?" The school of Shammai say, "every tree when it shoots forth." The school of Hillel say, "the locust trees when they put forth their curling tendrils, and the vines when they form berries, and the olives when they flower. And the rest of the trees when they shoot forth." But it is permitted to cut all trees, when they come to the season, for tithes. "How much fruit should be in the olive tree to prevent its being cut down?" "A quarter cab." Rabban Gamaliel said, "the whole depends on the size."

---

[3] A log held the contents of six egg-shells.

[4] A seah held about the third of a bushel.

CHAPTER V

1. The Sabbatical year of white figs [1] is the second after the Sabbatical year, because they produce in three years. Rabbi Judah said, " The Sabbatical year of the Persian figs is the close of the Sabbatical year, because they produce in two years." The Sages replied to him, "they only said white figs."

2. "If one store eschalots in the Sabbatical year?" R. Maier said, " there must be not less than two seahs,[2] in height three handbreadths, and over them an handbreadth of dust." But the Sages say, "not less than four cabs, in height an handbreadth, and an handbreadth of dust over them, and they must be stored in a place where men tread." [3]

3. " Eschalots over which the Sabbatical year has passed? " Rabbi Eleazar said, " if the poor have gathered the leaves they are theirs; but if not, the owner must reckon with the poor." R. Joshua said, " if the poor have gathered the leaves, they are theirs; but if not, the poor cannot reckon with the owner."

4. " Eschalots of the eve of the Sabbatical year which have entered on the Sabbatical year, and summer onions, and also dye [4] plants of the best ground? " The school of Shammai say, "they are to be rooted out with wooden spades." But the school of Hillel say, "with metal axes." But they both agree with regard to dye plants on rocky ground, that they are to be rooted out with metal axes.

5. " From what time is it allowed to buy eschalots on the departure of the Sabbatical year? " R. Judah said, " off hand "; but the Sages say, "when the new ones become plenty."

6. These are the implements which the farmer is not permitted to sell in the Sabbatical year—the plough with all its implements, the yoke, the shovel, and the goad. But he may sell the hand-sickle, and the harvest-sickle, and the wagon, with all its implements. This is the rule: " all implements,

[1] Literally, " daughters of the pit." "Adam's apples," (Jer. Tal.). Supposed to be the fruit which tempted Eve. The decision in the text assumes that the trees began to bud in the Sabbatical year, and that the fruit would not be ripe for three years.
[2] Twelve cabs.
[3] To prevent their growth.
[4] " Puah, for dyeing red "(?).

the use of which may be misapplied for transgression, are forbidden; but if they be (partly for things) forbidden and (partly for things) allowed, they are permitted."

7. The potter may sell five oil-jugs, and fifteen wine-jugs, because it is usual to collect fruits from the free property. And if one bring more than these, it is allowed, and he may sell them to idolaters in the land, and to Israelites out of the land.

8. The school of Shammai say, "a man must not sell a ploughing heifer on the Sabbatical year"; but the school of Hillel allow it, "because the buyer may slaughter her." He may sell fruits in the time of sowing, and may lend another man his measure, even if he know that the other man have a threshing-floor, and he may change money for him, even if he know that he have laborers. But if it be openly declared, all is forbidden.

9. A woman may lend to her companion on the Sabbatical year, even when she is suspicious, a flour-sieve or a grain-sieve, and a hand-mill and an oven; but she is neither to pick the wheat nor grind it with her. A woman of a special religious society may lend to the wife [5] of an ordinary man a flour-sieve, or a grain-sieve, and may pick wheat, or grind it, or sift it, with her. But when she (the wife of an ordinary man) pours in the water, she (a woman of a special religious society) must not touch the flour (to knead it) with her, lest she strengthen the hands of a transgressor. And all these things were not said save for the sake of peace. And we may strengthen the hands of idolaters in the Sabbatical year, but not the hands of Israel; and in salutation we may ask after their peace, for the sake of peace.

CHAPTER VI

1. Three countries (are included) in the laws of the Sabbatical year. In all the possessions of those who returned from Babylon—from the (border) of the land of Israel and to Cezib,[1] we may not eat cultivated fruit, and we may not cultivate the ground. And in all the possessions of those who

[5] This permission has reference to certain laws with regard to legal cleanness.
[1] Achzib; Ecdippa, near Acca.

came up from Egypt from Cezib, and to the river of Egypt, and to the Amana,[2] we may eat cultivated fruits, but we may not cultivate the ground. From the river of Egypt, and from the Amana to the interior, we may eat the fruits and cultivate the ground.

2. Men may labor in that which is separated from the ground in Syria, but not in that which is attached to the ground. They may thresh, and shovel, and tread out, and make sheaves, but they must not reap the grain nor glean the grapes, nor beat the olives. This is the rule; said Rabbi Akiba, "all things similar to that which is allowed in the land of Israel, men may do in Syria."

3. "Onions upon which fell rain and they sprouted?" "If the leaves on them be dark, they are forbidden; if green, they are allowed." Rabbi Chanina, the son of Antigonus, said, "if they can be pulled up by their leaves they are forbidden; and contrariwise if it happened so in the close of the Sabbatical year, they are allowed."

4. "From what time may men buy greens at the close of the Sabbatical year?" "From the time that similar young ones are produced. If the earlier ones are prematurely ripened, then the later ones are allowed." Rabbi [3] allowed greens to be bought off-hand at the close of the Sabbatical year.

5. Men must not export oil [4] which is only to be burned, nor fruits of the Sabbatical year, from the land to lands abroad. Said Rabbi Simon, "I expressly heard that they may be exported to Syria, but that they must not be exported to lands abroad."

6. Men must not import a heave-offering from abroad into the land. Said Rabbi Simon, "I expressly heard that they may import it from Syria, but that they must not import it from lands abroad."

---

[2] Some consider this to be the Abana: others read Amnum, and try to identify it with Mount Hor.

[3] Rabbi Judah the Holy, called only Rabbi by way of eminence.
[4] I.e., Defiled oil of the heave-offering, etc.

CHAPTER VII

1. The Sages stated an important rule: "In the Sabbatical year, everything eaten by man and eaten by beast, and a kind of dye-stuff, and whatever cannot remain in the ground, to them the laws of the Sabbatical year apply, and to their value the laws of the Sabbatical year apply. They are to be cleared off from being private property, and their price is to be cleared off from being private property." [1] "And which are these?" "The leaves of the deceitful scallion, and the leaves of mint, succory, and cresses, and the leek, and the milk-flower." [2] "And what is eaten by beasts?" "Thorns and thistles and a kind of dye-stuff, sprouts of indigo and madder. To them the laws of the Sabbatical year apply, and to their price the laws of the Sabbatical year apply. They are to be cleared off from being private property, and their price is to be cleared off from being private property."

2. And again, the Sages stated another rule: "All which is not eaten by man nor eaten by beasts, and a kind of dye-stuff, and whatever remains in the ground, to them the laws of the Sabbatical year apply, and to their price the laws of the Sabbatical year apply, but they are not to be cleared off from being private property, nor is their price to be cleared off from being private property." "And which are these?" "The root of the deceitful scallion, and the root of the mint, and scorpion grass, [3] and the bulbs of the milk-flower, and the spikenard, and a kind of dye-stuff, the dye-plant, and the wormwood,—to them the laws of the Sabbatical year apply, and to their price the laws of the Sabbatical year apply. They are not to be cleared off from being private property, nor is their price to be cleared off from being private property." Rabbi Maier said, "their prices are to be cleared off from being private property till New Year's Day." The Sages said to him, "if they are not to be cleared off from being private property, it is immaterial about their prices."

3. "The peelings and flower of the pomegranate, the shells and kernels of nuts?" "To them the laws of the Sabbatical

---

[1] I.e., They become common property, and are to be depastured by cattle (Lev. xxv. 7).

[2] Perhaps "the star of Bethlehem."

[3] A spiral grass growing on the palm tree(?).

year apply, and to their prices the laws of the Sabbatical year apply." The dyer may dye for himself, but he must not dye for pay, because men must not trade in fruits of the Sabbatical year, nor in the first-born, nor in heave-offerings, nor in carcasses, nor in that which is torn, nor in abominations, nor in creeping things. And one must not buy greens of the field and sell them in the market. But one may gather them, and his son may sell them on his account. He may, however, buy for himself, and he is allowed to sell what is superfluous.

"He bought a first-born animal for a feast for his son, or for a holiday, and has no need of it?" "He is allowed to sell it."

4. "Hunters of wild animals—birds and fishes—who chanced to find sorts that are unclean?" "It is allowed to sell them." R. Judah said, "if a man become possessed of them in his ordinary way, he may buy and sell them, excepting that such shall not be his practice." But the Sages "disallow them."

5. "The shoots of vines and of the locust-trees?" "To them the laws of the Sabbatical year apply, and to their prices the laws of the Sabbatical year apply." They are to be cleared off from being private property, and their prices are to be cleared off from being private property. "The shoots of the oak, and the nuts,[4] and the blackberries?" "To them the laws of the Sabbatical year apply, and to their prices the laws of the Sabbatical year apply." They are not to be cleared off from being private property, and their prices are not to be cleared off from being private property. But their leaves must be cleared away to become public property, as they fall down from their stems."[5]

6. "The rose and the carnation and the balsam and the chestnut?" "To them the laws of the Sabbatical year apply, and to their prices the laws of the Sabbatical year apply." R. Simon said, "there is no Sabbatical year for the balsam, because it has no fruit."

7. "A new Sabbatical rose which one steeped in old oil?" "One may pick out the rose." "But an old rose in new oil?" "One is bound to clear it off from being private property." "New locust fruit which one steeped in old wine, and old

(fruit) in new (wine)?" "Men are bound to clear them off
from being private property." This is the rule: everything
which produces taste one is bound to clear off from being private property, sorts that are different and sorts that are the
same, however little they be. The laws of the Sabbatical year
disallow however little of its own sort, and in different sorts
that which produces taste.[6]

CHAPTER VIII

1. The Sages stated an important rule for the Sabbatical
year: "Of all that is only fit for man's food a plaster may
not be made for man, and it is needless to say for beast. And
of all that is not fit for man's food a plaster may be made for
man, but not for beast." And all that is not fit either for man's
food or beast's food, if one consider it as food for man or food
for beasts, the Sages impose on it the inconveniences of the
laws relating to man and the inconveniences of the laws relating to beast. If one, however, consider it as wood, it is
reckoned as wood; for example, the savory and the hyssop
and the laurel.

2. Produce of the Sabbatical year is given for food, for
drink, and for anointing, to eat the thing which it is usual to
eat, and to anoint with what it is usual to anoint with. One
may not anoint with wine or vinegar. But one may anoint
with oil. And so is it likewise with the heave-offering and
second tithe. The laws of the Sabbatical year are more con-
venient for them, because it is permitted to light a candle made
from them.

3. Men must not sell the fruits of the Sabbatical year,
neither by measure, nor by weight, nor by count. Neither
may they sell figs by counting, nor greens by weight. The
school of Shammai say, "nor in bunches." But the school
of Hillel say, "that which it is usual to make in bunches in
the house men may make in bunches in the market; for example, cresses and the milk-flower."

4. If one said to a laborer, "Here! take this aisar[1] and

---

[6] This refers to the examples already given of a rose in oil, or locust fruit in
wine.　　　　　　　　[1] Aisar, a coin worth 3$\frac{1}{8}$ farthings.

gather greens for me to-day?" "His hire is allowed."
"Gather me for it greens to-day?" "His hire is forbidden."
If one take from the baker a cake for a pundion [2] (saying),
"when I will gather greens of the field I will bring them to
you?" "It is allowed." "If one take bread from the baker
in silence?" "He must not pay him from money of the Sabbatical year, because men must not pay a debt with money of
the Sabbatical year."

5. Men must not give money of the Sabbatical year to a
well-digger, nor to a bath-keeper, nor to a barber, nor to a
skipper, but one may give it to a well-digger for drink, and
to all persons one may give a gratuitous present.

6. Men may not dry figs of the Sabbatical year in the usual
place, but one may dry them in a waste place. They must not
tread grapes in a wine-press, but they may tread them in a
kneading-trough. And they must not put olives into the oil-
press with the stone over them, but they may pound them and
put them into a small press. Rabbi Simon said, "one may
also grind them in the house of the oil-press and put them into
the small press."

7. Men must not boil greens of the Sabbatical year in oil
of the heave-offering, lest they take it for uses that are forbidden. R. Simon "allowed it." And the very last thing (in
a series of exchanges) partakes of the laws of the Sabbatical
year; but the fruit itself (first exchanged) is forbidden.

8. Men must not buy servants, ground, or an unclean beast,
with money of the Sabbatical year; but if they buy them, they
must eat [3] as much as their value. They must not bring for
an offering the two pigeons of one with an issue, or the two
pigeons after childbirth bought with money of the Sabbatical
year. And if they bring them, they must eat [3] as much as
their value. They must not anoint vessels with oil of the Sabbatical year. But if they anoint them, they must eat [3] as much
as their value.

9. "A skin which one anointed with oil of the Sabbatical
year?" Rabbi Eleazar said, "it must be burned." But the
Sages say, "one must eat [3] as much as its value." The Sages
said before Rabbi Akiba it was a saying of Rabbi Eleazar, "a
skin smeared with oil of the Sabbatical year must be burned."

[2] Pundion, a coin worth 1½d.　　　[3] Of the fruits of the Sabbatical year.

He said to them, " Hush! I cannot tell you what Rabbi Eleazar said about it."

10. And again, the Sages said in his presence, it was a saying of Rabbi Eleazar,[4] " he who eats the bread of Samaritans is as one who eats swine-flesh." He said to them, " Hush! I cannot tell you what Rabbi Eleazar said about it."

11. " A bath which was heated with stubble or straw of the Sabbatical year?" " It is allowed to wash in it." " But if one confer honor (on the bath)?" " He should not wash in it."

CHAPTER IX

1. The rue, and the sorrel with spreading leaves, and the wild savory, the coriander of the mountains, and the parsley of the marshes, and the rocket of the desert, are free from tithes; and they may be bought from all men in the Sabbatical year, because nothing like them is legally guarded. Rabbi Judah said, " the sprouts of the mustard are allowed, because transgressors are not suspected for taking them from a guarded place" Rabbi Simon said, " all vegetables that sprout again are allowed, excepting the sprouts of cabbage, because there is not their like among the greens of the field." But the Sages say, " whatever sprouts again is forbidden."

2. There are three countries to be public property in the Sabbatical year: Judah and beyond Jordan and Galilee; and each is divided into three parts: Upper Galilee, Lower Galilee, and the Vale. From the village of Hananiah and upward, every part in which the sycamore tree does not grow is Upper Galilee. And from the village of Hananiah and lower down, where any sycamore tree grows, is Lower Galilee. And the neighborhood of Tiberias is the Vale. And in Judah, the mountains, the plain, and the vale, and the plain of Lydda is as the plain of the south. And its mountains are as the King's mountain.[1] From Bethhorn and to the sea is one province.

3. " And wherefore did the Sages say three countries?" " That men might eat during the Sabbatical year in every

[4] There are various Rabbis of this name, spelled in different ways, mentioned in the Talmud.
[1] The king's mountain is perhaps Mount Ephraim, or the mountain range over the plain of Sharon. It is also suggested that it might have been the mountains round Kirjathjearim (Abu Goosh?). It contained Cephar Bish, Cephar Sheclaim, Cephar Dikraia, etc.

one of them, till the last fruits be finished in it." R. Simon said, "they did not say three countries, they said only in Judah." And all the other countries are reckoned as the King's mountain; and all countries are reckoned the same for olives and dates.

4. Men may eat so long as there is any fruit legally free, but they must not eat of that which is legally guarded. Rabbi José "allowed it, even when guarded." They may eat fruit so long as it is found in birds' nests, and such fruit as is twice produced in each year, but they must not eat of winter fruit. R. Judah "allowed it at all times, if it ripened before the summer ended."

5. "If men pressed three sorts of fruit in one barrel?" R. Eliezer said, "they may eat of the first." R. Joshua said, "even of the last." Rabban Gamaliel said, "everything, the species of which is finished growing in the field, its species is to be removed from the barrel."[2] Rabbi Simon said, "all greens are reckoned as one. They are to be cleared away from the house." They may eat of the leeks till the teasels have ceased growing in the valley of Beth-Netopha.

6. "He who gathers fresh herbs?" "He may use them till their sap dry out" "And he who binds the dry in bundles?" "He may use them till the second rain descends."[3] "The leaves of reeds and the leaves of vines?" "They may be used till they fall from their stems." "And he who binds the dry in bundles?" "He may use them till the second rain descends." Rabbi Akiba said, "they may be used by all persons till the second rain descends."

7. "Like to this rule is his case who rented a house to his neighbor till the rains?" "This means till the second rain descends." "He who by his vow cannot get assistance from his neighbor till the rains?" "This means till the second rain descends." "When may the poor enter into the gardens?"[4] "When the second rain descends." "When may they use and burn the stubble and straw of the Sabbatical year?" "When the second rain descends."

8. "A man had fruit of the Sabbatical year, and the time

[2] Others read " and the decision is as his word."
[3] The second or the " latter " rain (Joel ii. 23), called Malkosh, falls in spring chiefly during the months of March and April.
[4] Lev. xxiii. 22; Deut. xxiv. 19.

came for clearing it out from his house?" "He may divide
to everyone victuals for three meals; and the poor may eat
the fruit after the clearing of it out, but not the rich." The
words of Rabbi Judah. Rabbi José said, "the poor and the
rich are alike, they may eat it after it is cleared out."

9. "A man had fruits of the Sabbatical year, whether they
fell to him by inheritance, or were given to him by gift?"
R. Eliezer said, "let them be given to those who may eat
them." But the Sages say, "the transgressor must not profit,
but let them be sold to those who may eat them, and let their
price be divided to every man." "He who eats dough of the
Sabbatical year before the heave-offering be separated from
it?" "He is guilty of death."

CHAPTER X

1. The Sabbatical year releases [1] a loan, whether it be with
or without a bill. The credit of a shop is not released. But
if one made it as a loan, it is released. Rabbi Judah said, "all
the first credit is released, the wages of an hireling is not released." "But if one made it as a loan?" "It is released."
Rabbi José said, "every work which ceases on the Sabbatical
year is released; but that which does not cease on the Sabbatical year is not released from payment."

2. The butcher who slaughtered a heifer (at the end of the
Sabbatical year), and divided her head (for sale on the first
of the two feast days of the new year), remains a debtor; but
if he did so in an intercalary month,[2] he is released (Deut. xv.
1). But if it be not an intercalary month, he is not released.
He who forced, or enticed, or uttered a slander, and every act
of the tribunal, have no release. "He who lent on security, or
delivered his bills to the tribunal?" "There is no release for
him."

3. The Defence [3] (for the poor) has no release. This is one
of the things which the old Hillel ruled. When he saw that

---

[1] Deut. xv. 1.

[2] This decision supposes the case of
the month Elul having thirty days, and
the last day to be in the Sabbatical
year; consequently it would not be one
of the two feast days of the new year,
which it should have been if the month
had been the usual lunar month.

[3] "The defence," called Pruzbul, was
a legal document constituted to encourage loans to the poor, and to protect the
interests of the lender.

the people refrained from mutual loans, and transgressed what is written in the law, " Beware that there be not a thought in thy wicked heart," [4] etc., Hillel ruled the Defence.

4. This is the substance of the Defence, " I hand over to you judges such and such men in such a place, that every debt which belongs to me I may collect, whenever I please." And the judges or witnesses sealed it below.

5. The Defence written before the Sabbatical year is valid, but afterward it is disallowed. Bills written before the Sabbatical year are disallowed, but afterward they are valid. He who borrows from five persons must write a Defence for each of them. If five persons borrow from one, he writes but one Defence for all of them.

6. Men must not write a Defence save only on ground. " If he have none?" " The lender may present him with however little from his own field " " If he had a field in pledge in a city?" " He may write on it the Defence." Rabbi Huzpith said, " a man may write it on the property of his wife; and for orphans on the property of their guardians."

7. " Beehives?" R. Eliezer said, " they are as ground, and men may write on them a Defence, and they contract no legal uncleanness in their proper place, but he who takes honey out of them on the Sabbath is liable (for a sin-offering). The Sages, however, say they are not as ground, and men must not write on them a Defence, and they do contract legal defilement in their place, and he who takes honey out of them on the Sabbath is free."

8. " He who paid his debt on the Sabbatical year?" " The lender must say to him, ' I release thee.'" " When he said it to him?" " Even so, he may receive it from him, as is said, and this is the manner of the release." [5] It is like the slayer who was banished to the city of refuge, and the men of the city wished to honor him. He must say to them, " I am a murderer." They say to him, " Even so." He may receive the honor from them, as is said, " and this is the case of the slayer." [6]

9. " He who pays a debt in the Sabbatical year?" " The spirit of the Sages reposes on him." [7] " He who borrowed

---

[4] Deut. xv. 9.
[5] Deut. xv. 2.
[6] Deut. xix. 4.
[7] I.e., They are well pleased with him.

from a proselyte, when his children [8] became proselytes with him?" "He need not repay his children." "But if he repay them?" "The spirit of the Sages reposes on him." All movables become property by acquisition; but everyone who keeps his word,

THE SPIRIT
OF THE SAGES
REPOSES
ON
HIM.

[8] Money owing to Jewish proselytes was generally repaid, but it was not obligatory to pay it to their heirs, as the persons from whom the proselytes came were no longer in a religious sense their next of kin.

NOTE.—At the Feast of Tabernacles in the Sabbatical year, the following portions of Scripture were appointed to be read: Deut. i. 1-6; vi. 4-8; xi. 13-22; xiv. 22; xv. 23; xvii. 14; xxvi. 12-19; xxvii.; xxviii. These portions were read by the king or high priest from a wooden platform erected in the Temple. The king or the high priest usually read them sitting. King Agrippa, however, read them standing, and when he came to the words "Thou mayst not set a stranger over thee, which is not thy brother" (Deut. xvii. 15), "tears dropped from his eyes." The people then cried out to encourage him, "Thou art our brother—thou art our brother" (Sotah, vii. 8).

ON THE SABBATH

Removals—Work to be Avoided—Discussion Between the Schools of
Shammai and Hillel as to What Constitutes Work—Work Allowed
Lighting—Eve of the Sabbath—Cooking and Hot Water—Retention
of Heat—Burdens—Ornaments—Principal and Secondary Work.

CHAPTER I

1. Removals [1] on the Sabbath are two. Of these removals
four are inside a place. And there are two other removals,
of which four are outside a place. "How?" "A beggar
stands without, and the master of the house within. The beggar reached his hand within, and gave something into the
hand of the master of the house, or took something from it
and brought it out?" "The beggar is guilty,[2] and the master
of the house is free." "The master of the house reached his
hand outside and gave something into the hand of the beggar, or took something from it and brought it in?" "The
master of the house is guilty, but the beggar is free." "The
beggar reached his hand within, and the master of the house
took something from it, or gave something into it, and the
beggar brought it out?" "Both are free." "The master of
the house reached his hand without, and the beggar took
something from it, or gave something into it, and the master
brought it in?" "Both are free."

2. A man must not sit before the barber near to evening
prayer,[3] until he has prayed. He must not enter a bath, nor a
tannery, nor eat, nor judge. "But if they began?" "They
need not cease." They may cease to read the "Hear,"[4] etc.,
but they must not cease to pray.

3. A tailor must not go out with his needle near dusk,[5] lest
he forget and go (afterward). Nor a scribe go out with his

[1] From private to public property. [5] On Friday evening.
[2] Of death. [4] Deut. vi. 4.

75

pen. Nor may one search his garments. Nor shall one read at the light of the lamp. In truth they said, "the teacher may overlook when children are reading, but he himself shall not read." Similar to him, one with an issue shall not eat with her who has an issue, because of the custom of transgression.

4. And these following are from the decisions which they mentioned of the upper chamber of Hananiah, the son of Hezekiah, the son of Gorion, when the Sages went up to visit him. The school of Shammai was counted, and was more numerous than the school of Hillel. And eighteen matters were determined on that day.

5. The school of Shammai said, "they must not soak ink, nor paints, nor vetches, unless they be sufficiently soaked while it is yet day." But the school of Hillel allow it.

6. The school of Shammai said, "they must not put bundles of flax inside the oven, except it be sufficiently steamed while it is yet day, nor wool into the boiler except it imbibe sufficient dye in the eye of day." But the school of Hillel allow it. The school of Shammai said, "they must not spread nets for beasts, nor birds, nor fishes, except they be netted while it is yet day." But the school of Hillel allow it.

7. The school of Shammai said, "they must not sell to a stranger, and they must not lade his ass with him, and they must not load on him, except they have sufficient time to reach a near place before the Sabbath." But the school of Hillel allow it.

8. The school of Shammai said, "they must not give skins to a tanner, nor articles to a strange laundress; except they can be sufficiently done while it is yet day." But all of them the school of Hillel allow "with the sun."

9. Said Rabbi Simon, the son of Gamaliel, "the house of my father used to give white articles to a strange laundress three days before the Sabbath." But both schools agree that "they may carry⁵ beams to the oil-press and logs to the wine-press."

10. "They must not fry flesh, onions, and eggs; except they be sufficiently fried while it is yet day. They must not put bread in the oven at dusk, nor a cake on coals, except its face

---

⁵ Though by their weight they continue to press out oil or wine on the Sabbath.

be sufficiently crusted while it is yet day." Rabbi Eliezer said, " that its under side be sufficiently crusted."

11. " They may hang up the passover [6] offering in an oven at dusk. And they may take a light from the wood pile in the house of burning.[7] And in the suburbs " when the fire has sufficiently lighted the greater part." Rabbi Judah says, " from the coals however little " (kindled before the Sabbath).

CHAPTER II

1. " With what may they light (lamps) on the Sabbath? " " And with what may they not light? " " They may not light with cedar moss, nor with unhackled flax, nor with floss silk, nor with a wick of willow, nor with a wick of nettles, nor with weeds from the surface of water, nor with pitch, nor with wax, nor with castor oil, nor with the defiled oil of heave-offering, nor with the tail, nor with the fat." Nahum the Median said, " they may light with cooked fat." But the Sages say, " whether cooked or uncooked, they must not light with it."

2. They must not light with the defiled oil of the heave-offering on a holiday. Rabbi Ishmael said, " they must not light with pitch dregs for the honor of the Sabbath." But the Sages allow all oils, " with sesame oil, with nut oil, with radish oil, with fish oil, with colocynth oil, with pitch dregs and naphtha." Rabbi Tarphon said, " they must only light with olive oil."

3. " They must not light with anything that grows from wood, except flax. And all that grows from wood does not contract the uncleanness of tents,[1] except flax. " A wick of cloth folded but not singed? " Rabbi Eliezer says, " it contracts uncleanness, and they must not light it." Rabbi Akiba says, " it is clean, and they may light it."

4. A man must not perforate an eggshell, and fill it with oil, and put it on the mouth of the lamp, because it drops, even though it be of pottery. But Rabbi Judah " allows it." " But if the potter joined it at first? " " It is allowed, since it is one

---

[6] When the eve of the passover and the eve of the Sabbath coincided.

[7] In the Temple. See tract Measurements, c. 1.

[1] Num. xix. 18.

vessel." A man must not fill a bowl of oil, and put it by the side of the lamp, and put the end of the wick into it because it imbibes. But Rabbi Judah " allows it."

5. " Whoever extinguishes the lamp because he fears the Gentiles, or robbers, or a bad spirit, or that the sick may sleep? " " He is free." " He spares the lamp? " " He spares the oil? " " He spares the wick? " " He is guilty." But Rabbi José frees in all cases except the wick, because " it makes coal."

6. For three transgressions women die in the hour of child-birth: when they neglect times, and the dough offering,[2] and lighting the Sabbath lamp.

7. Three things are necessary for a man to say in his house on the eve of the Sabbath at dusk. " Have you taken tithes? " " Have you prepared erub? "[3] " Light the lamp." " It is doubtful if it be dark or not? "[4] " They must not tithe that which is certainly untithed, and they must not baptize vessels, and they must not light the lamps. But they may take tithes of the doubtful heave-offering, and prepare erub, and cover up hot water."

CHAPTER III

1. " A cooking oven which was heated with stubble or brushwood? " " They may place on it cookery." " With oil-dregs and with wood? " " They must not place it, till the coals are raked out, or ashes put in." The school of Shammai say, " hot water, but not cookery." But the school of Hillel say, " hot water and cookery." The school of Shammai say, " they may take it off, but not place it back." But the school of Hillel say, " they may place it back."

2. " A cooking stove, which was heated with stubble or brushwood? " " They must not place anything either inside or upon it." " A bake oven, which was heated with stubble or brushwood? " " It is as a cooking oven." " With oil-dregs or with wood? " " It is as a cooking stove."

3. They must not put an egg beside a boiler, lest it be boiled. And they must not wrap it in towels. But Rabbi José allows

---

[2] Num. xv. 20.
[3] I.e., Have you so joined houses that are apart that they may be counted as one on the Sabbath for carrying ar-

ticles, etc. It is done by persons bless-ing a piece of dough which is common property.
[4] When three stars are seen, it is dark.

it. And they must not hide it in sand, or in the dust of the
roads, lest it be roasted.

4. It happened that the men of Tiberias arranged, and introduced a pipe of cold water into a canal of the hot springs.
The Sages said to them, " if it be Sabbath, it is as if hot waters
were heated on Sabbath, they are forbidden for washing and
drinking. But if on a holiday, as if hot waters were heated on
a holiday, they are forbidden for washing but allowed for
drinking." " A skillet with attached brazier? " " If one rake
out the coals (on Friday evening), persons may drink its hot
waters on Sabbath." " A pan with double bottom? " " Even
though the coals are raked out, they must not drink of it."

5. " The boiler which is set aside (from the fire) ? " " They
must not put into it cold water to be warmed; but they may
put into it—or into a cup—cold water to make it lukewarm."
" A saucepan or an earthen pot, which they took off boiling? "
" They must not put into it spices, but they may put them into
a bowl or into a plate." Rabbi Judah says, " they may put them
into all vessels, excepting a thing in which there is vinegar or
fish-brine."

6. They must not put vessels under a lamp to catch the oil.
" But if they place them, while it is still day? " " It is allowed." But they must not use it, because it is not purposely
prepared (for Sabbath use). They may remove a new lamp,
but not an old one. Rabbi Simon says, " all lamps may be removed, except the lamp lighted for the Sabbath." They may
put a vessel under the lamp to catch sparks, but they must
not put water into it, as it quenches.

CHAPTER IV

1. " With what may they cover up (pots to retain the
heat)? " " And with what may they not cover them up? "
" They may not cover them up with oil-dregs, or dung, or
salt, or lime, or sand either fresh or dry, or straw, or grapeskins, or woollen, or herbs when they are fresh, but they may
cover up with them when they are dry. They may cover up
with garments, and fruits, with doves' wings, with carpenters'
sawdust, and with tow of fine flax." Rabbi Judah forbids
" fine," but allows " coarse."

2. They may cover up with hides, and remove them—with woollen fleeces, but they must not remove them. " How does one do?" " He takes off the cover, and they fall down." Rabbi Eleazar, the son of Azariah, says " the vessel is inclined on its side, and he takes them away." " Perhaps he took them away and cannot return them?"[1] But the Sages say " he may take them away, and return them." " He does not cover it, while it is yet day?" " He must not cover it, when it begins to be dark." " He covered it, and it opened?" " It is allowed to cover it again." A man may fill the goblet, and put it under the pillow or under the bolster (to warm it).

CHAPTER V

1. " With what is a beast led forth, and with what is it not led forth?"[1] One may lead forth the camel with a head-stall, and the she-camel with a nose-ring, and the Lydda,[2] asses with a bridle, and a horse with a halter, and all animals that wear a halter they may lead forth with a halter, and they are held with a halter, and, if unclean, they may sprinkle water upon them, and baptize them in their places.

2. The ass one may lead forth with a pack-saddle when it is bound on it. Rams go forth tied up. Ewes go forth with tails bound back, doubled down, or put in a bag. The goats go forth bound tightly. Rabbi José " forbids all, excepting ewes, to have their tails in a bag." Rabbi Judah says " the goats go forth bound tightly to dry up their udders, but not to guard the milk."

3. " And with what must they not go forth?" " A camel must not go forth with a rag bound as a mark to its tail, nor fettered, nor with fore-foot tied doubled up, and so with the rest of all beasts; a man must not bind camels one to another, and lead them, but he may take their ropes into his hand, and hold them, guarding that they be not twisted.[3]

4. One must not bring forth an ass with a pack-saddle, when it is not tied upon him before the Sabbath; nor with a bell, even though it be muffled, nor with a ladder[4] on its throat, nor

---

[1] As that would involve "labor."
[1] The point to be decided is the difference between what is necessary and what is a burden.
[2] Others think " Lybian " asses.

[3] Through fear of linen and woollen being mixed. Deut. xxii. 11.
[4] Ladder-shaped piece of wood to prevent it rubbing its throat if it have a sore.

with a strap on its leg; nor may cocks and hens be led forth
with twine or straps on their legs. Nor may rams be led forth
with a gocart under their tails, nor ewes with John wood.[5]
And the calf must not be led forth with a muzzle, nor a cow with
the skin of the hedgehog,[6] nor with a strap between her horns.
The cow [7] of Rabbi Eleazar, the son of Azariah, used to go
out with a strap between her horns, but not with the will of the
Sages.

CHAPTER VI

1. "With what may a woman go out?" And "with what
may she not go out?" "A woman may not go out with laces
of wool, nor with laces of flax, nor with straps on her head,
and she cannot baptize herself in them till she unloose them;
nor with frontlets, nor temple fillets, unless sewn to her cap,
nor with a headband, into the public street, nor with a golden
crown in the form of Jerusalem, nor with a necklace, nor with
nose-rings, nor with a ring without a seal, nor with a needle
without an eye; but, if she go out, she is not guilty of a sin-
offering."

2. A man must not go out with hobnailed sandals,[1] nor with
one sandal when there is no sore on his other foot, nor with
phylacteries, nor with an amulet unless it be of an expert, nor
with a coat of mail, nor with a helmet, nor with greaves; but,
if he go out, he is not guilty of a sin-offering.

3. "A woman must not go out with an eyed needle, nor
with a signet ring, nor with a spiral head-dress, nor with a
scent-box, nor with a bottle of musk; and if she go out she is
guilty of a sin-offering." The words of Rabbi Meier. But the
Sages "absolve the scent-box and the bottle of musk."

4. The man must not go out with sword, nor bow, nor shield,
nor sling, nor lance; and if he go out he is guilty of a sin-
offering. Rabbi Eleazar said, "they are his ornaments." But
the Sages say, "they are only for shame, as is said, 'And they
shall beat their swords into ploughshares, and their spears

[5] Wood discovered by one John, which when put into sheep's nostrils, caused them to sneeze and the maggots to fall off.

[6] To prevent her being sucked by reptiles.

[7] The Gemara says, the cow was his neighbor's, but as he did not object, the blame was laid on him.

[1] Once a number of Jews took refuge in a cave, and hearing some persons pass, whom they supposed to be ene-mies, they fell on each other with their hobnailed sandals, and beat each other to death.

into pruning hooks: nation shall not lift up sword against
nation, neither shall they learn war any more.' " [2] Garters are
clean, and they may go forth in them on Sabbath. Anklets [3]
contract uncleanness, and they must not go out in them on Sabbath.

5. A woman may go out with plaits of hair whether they
be her own, or her companion's, or a beast's hair, with frontlets
and temple fillets, when they are sewn to her cap, with a headband or a stranger's curl into the courtyard, with wool in her
ear, and wool in her shoe, and wool prepared for her separation,
with pepper, or with a grain of salt, [4] or with anything which
she will put inside her mouth, except that she shall not put it
in for the first time on the Sabbath, and if it fall out she must
not put it back. " A false tooth or a tooth of gold? " Rabbi
" allows it." But the Sages " forbid it."

6. A woman may go out with a coin on a sore foot. Little
girls may go out with plaits and even splinters in their ears.
Arab women go out veiled, and Median women with mantillas;
and so may any one, but, as the Sages have said, " according
to their custom."

7. A mantilla may be folded over a stone, or a nut, or money,
save only that it be not expressly folded·for the Sabbath.

8. " The cripple may go out on his wooden leg." The words
of Rabbi Meier. But Rabbi José forbids it. " But if it have a
place for receiving rags? " " It is unclean." His crutches
cause uncleanness by treading. But they may go out with them
on the Sabbath, and they may enter with them into the Temple
court. The chair and crutches (of a paralytic) cause uncleanness by treading, and they must not go out with them
on the Sabbath, and they must not enter with them into the
Temple court. Stilts [5] are clean, but they must not go out with
them.

9. The sons may go out with their (father's) girdles. And
sons of kings with little bells; and so may anyone, but,
as the Sages have said, " according to their custom."

10. " They may go out with an egg of a locust, [6] and a tooth
of a fox, [7] and a nail of one crucified, as medicine." [8] The words

[2] Isaiah xi. 4; Micah iv. 3.
[3] These anklets were a kind of chain
used to prevent members of certain
families in Jerusalem taking too wide
strides in walking.
[4] To cure toothache.
[5] Others translate " masks."

[6] To cure ear-ache.
[7] To cure one who did not sleep
enough they used a tooth of a dead
fox. For one who slept too much, they
used a tooth of a living fox.
[8] To cure ague.

of Rabbi Meier. But the Sages say (others read the words of Rabbi José and Rabbi Meier) "it is forbidden even on a week day, because of the ways of the Amorites." [9]

CHAPTER VII

1. The Sages laid down a great rule for the Sabbath: "Everyone who forgets the principle of Sabbath, and did many works on many Sabbaths, is only responsible for one sin-offering. Everyone who knows the principle of Sabbath, and did many works on many Sabbaths, is responsible for every Sabbath. Everyone who knows that there is Sabbath, and did many works on many Sabbaths, is responsible for every principal work.[1] Everyone who has done many works, springing from one principal work, is only responsible for one sin-offering."

2. The principal works are forty, less one—sowing, ploughing, reaping, binding sheaves, threshing, winnowing, sifting, grinding, riddling, kneading, baking, shearing wool, whitening, carding, dyeing, spinning, warping, making two spools, weaving two threads, taking out two threads, twisting, loosing, sewing two stitches, tearing thread for two sewings, hunting the gazelle, slaughtering, skinning, salting, curing its skin, tanning, cutting up, writing two letters, erasing to write two letters, building, demolishing, quenching, kindling, hammering, carrying from private to public property. Lo, these are principal works—forty, less one.

3. And another rule the Sages laid down: "All that is worthy of reservation, and they reserve its like—if they carry it out on the Sabbath, they are responsible for a sin-offering; and everything which is not worthy of reservation, and they do not reserve its like—if they carry it out on the Sabbath, none is responsible but the reserver."

4. Whoever brings out straw—a heifer's mouthful; hay—a camel's mouthful; chaff—a lamb's mouthful; herbs—a kid's mouthful; garlic leaves and onion leaves—if fresh, the size of

[9] Lev. xviii. 3.
[1] Works are divided into principal and secondary, or in Rabbinic language fathers and children. And if a man does one principal work and twenty secondary works, they regarded them as one sin, and consequently deserving one punishment.

a dried fig—if dry, a kid's mouthful; but they must not add one with the other, for they are not equal in their measures. Whoever carries out food the size of a dried fig, is guilty of death. And victuals, they may add one to another as they are equal in their measures, excepting their peels and their kernels, and their stalks and the fine and coarse bran. Rabbi Judah says, "excepting the peels of lentils, as they may cook them with them."

CHAPTER VIII

1. One may bring out wine sufficient for the cup,[1] milk sufficient for a gulp, honey sufficient for a bruise, oil sufficient to anoint a small member, water sufficient to moisten the eye-salve, and the rest of all beverages a quarter of a log, and whatever can be poured out[2] a quarter of a log. Rabbi Simeon says, "all of them by the quarter log." And they did not mention these measures save for those who reserve them.

2. "Whoever brings out cord sufficient to make an ear for a tub, bulrush sufficient to hang the sieve and the riddle?" Rabbi Judah said, "sufficient to take from it the measure of a child's shoe; paper sufficient to write on it the signature of the taxgatherers; erased paper sufficient to wrap round a small bottle of balm—is guilty" (of death).

3. Leather sufficient for an amulet; parchment polished on both sides, sufficient to write a sign for a door-post; vellum sufficient to write on it a small portion, which is in phylacteries, that is, "Hear, O Israel;" ink sufficient to write two letters; kohl[3] sufficient to paint one eye.

4. Bird-lime sufficient to put on the top of a perch; pitch or sulphur to fill a hole; wax sufficient to fill the mouth of a small hole; brick-clay sufficient to make a mouth of a crucible bellows for goldsmiths—Rabbi Judah says, "sufficient to make a crucible stand;" bran sufficient to put on the mouth of a crucible blow-pipe for goldsmiths; ointment sufficient to anoint the little finger of girls—Rabbi Judah savs, "sufficient to make the hair grow;" Rabbi Nehemiah says, "to freshen the temple."

[1] I.e., one part wine and three parts water.
[2] E.g., foul water.
[3] Henna dust for women's eyes.

5. Red earth " as the seal of merchants "—the words of R. Akiba; but the Sages say, " as the seal of letters; " dung and fine sand, " sufficient to manure a cabbage stalk,"—the words of Rabbi Akiba; but the Sages say, " sufficient to manure a leek; " coarse sand sufficient to put on a full lime-hod; a reed sufficient to make a pen. " But if it be thick or split? " " sufficient to boil with it a hen's egg easy (to be cooked) among eggs, mixed with oil and put in a pan."

6. A bone sufficient to make a spoon,—Rabbi Judah said, " sufficient to make the ward of a key; " glass sufficient to scrape the top of a shuttle; a lump of earth or a stone sufficient to fling at a bird; Rabbi Eliezer said, " sufficient to fling at a beast."

7. " A potsherd? " " Sufficient to put between two beans," —the words of Rabbi Judah; Rabbi Meier says, " sufficient to take away fire with it; " Rabbi José says, " sufficient to receive in it the fourth of a log." Said Rabbi Meier, " Although there is no visible proof of the matter, there is an indication of the matter, as is said, " there shall not be found in the bursting of it a sherd to take fire from the hearth." [4] Rabbi José said to him, " thence is the visible proof, ' or to take water out of the pit.' " [4]

[4] Isaiah xxx. 14.

ON THE PASSOVER

Searching for Leaven—How Leaven Is to be Put Away—Restrictions with Regard to It—What Things Make Leaven—Leavening—Work on the Eve of the Passover—Trades Allowed—Men of Jericho—Hezekiah—The Daily Offering—Intention—Slaughter of Passover Offering—Mode of Proceeding—The Passover on a Sabbath—Discussion Between R. Akiba and R. Eleazar—Roasting the Passover—Various Contingencies—Hinderances—Rules and Directions—How the Passover Is to be Eaten—Praise and Thanksgiving.

CHAPTER I

1. On the eve of the fourteenth day of Nisan [1] men search for leaven by candlelight. Every place where men do not bring in leaven, there is no need of search. "And wherefore do they say, two lines of barrels in the wine cellar?" "The place is meant into which persons bring leaven." The school of Shammai say, "two rows in front of the whole cellar." But the school of Hillel say, "the two outer lines on the top."

2. People need not suspect, lest perchance the weasel have slipped (with leaven) from house to house or from place to place. If so, from court to court, from city to city, there is no end to the matter.

3. Rabbi Judah said, "men search on the eve of the fourteenth and on the morning of the fourteenth day, and at the time of burning it." But the Sages say, "if one did not search on the eve of the fourteenth, he must search on the fourteenth; if he did not search on the fourteenth, he must search during the feast; if he did not search during the feast, he must search after the feast; and whatever remains, he shall leave well concealed, that there be no further need of search after it."

4. Rabbi Meier said, "men may eat it till five o'clock,[2] and

---

[1] Nisan nearly corresponds with the month of March.
[2] I.e., 11 o'clock A.M. To obtain our computation of time, six must be added to the hours mentioned in the Mishna.

burn it at the beginning of six." Rabbi Judah said, "thev may eat it till four, and they are in suspense about five, but they burn it at the beginning of six."

5. And again said R. Judah, "two loaves of the disallowed praise-offering were placed on the portico of the Temple inclosure; whilst they were placed there, all the people might eat leaven. If one were taken down they were in suspense; they neither ate nor burned it. When both were taken down they began to burn it." Rabban Gamaliel said, "men may eat ordinary food till four o'clock, and the heave-offering till five o'clock, but they burned the leaven at six o'clock."

6. Rabbi Chanina, the deputy of the priesthood, said, "from the (first) days of the priesthood the priests did not object to burn the flesh rendered legally unclean [3] with the second degree of uncleanness, with the flesh rendered legally unclean with the first degree of uncleanness. Even though they should add legal uncleanness to legal uncleanness." Rabbi Akiba went further and said, "from the (first) days of the priesthood the priests did not object to light the oil which was disallowed on the day of a man's baptism (who had been legally unclean), with a candle which was unclean with the uncleanness of the dead, even though they should add legal uncleanness to legal uncleanness."

7. Said R. Meier, "from their words we learn that men may burn the clean heave-offering of leaven, with that which is unclean, on account of the passover." To him replied Rabbi José, "this is not the conclusion." But Rabbi Eliezer and Rabbi Joshua confess "that men should burn each by itself." And the contention is with regard to what is doubtful, and what is unclean. Because Rabbi Eliezer said, "thou shalt burn each by itself." But R. Joshua said, "both at once."

CHAPTER II

1. The whole time that it is allowed to eat leaven, men may feed beasts with it, and wild animals and fowls, and they may sell it to a stranger. And they are allowed to enjoy it in every way. When that season has passed over its enjoyment is disallowed, and they must not heat with it an oven or a stove.

---

[3] When uncleanness is mentioned, it is to be understood of legal uncleanness.

Rabbi Judah said, " there is no riddance of leaven but by burning." But the Sages say, " also by powdering and scattering
it to the wind, or casting it into the sea."

2. " The leaven of a stranger, over which the passover has
passed?" " Its enjoyment is allowed " " But of an Israelite?" " Its enjoyment is disallowed," as is said,[1] " And there
shall no leavened bread be seen with thee."

3. " The stranger who has lent money to an Israelite on his
leaven?" " After passover its enjoyment is allowed." " And
an Israelite who lent money to the stranger on his leaven?"
" Its enjoyment after passover is disallowed." " Leaven over
which a building fell?" " It is as though it was cleared away."
Rabban Simon, son of Gamaliel, said, " all after which the dog
cannot snuff."

4. " He who has eaten a leavened heave-offering during the
passover in error?" " He must pay its value and a fifth
more." " In presumption?" " He is free from the payment,
and from its value even for fuel."[2]

5. These are the things by which one can discharge his
obligation to eat unleavened bread during the passover; with
cakes made of wheat, and barley, and rye, and oats, and spelt;
and they discharge their obligation in that of which the tithing was doubtful, and in the first tithe after the heave-offering was separated from it, and in second tithes and holy things
after their redemption. And the priests discharge their obligation with cakes of dough-offering and heave-offering, but
not with that which owes first tithes, or before the heave-offering was separated from it, nor with that which owes second
tithes or holy things before their redemption. " The loaves
of the praise-offering and the cakes of the Nazarite?" " If
made for themselves, they do not discharge the obligation: if
made for sale in the market, they discharge the obligation."

6. And these are the herbs with which one discharges his
obligation to eat bitter herbs in the passover: lettuce, endives,
horse-radish, liquorice, and coriander. The obligation can be
discharged whether they be moist or dry, but not if they be
pickled, or much boiled, or even a little boiled. And they may
be united to form the size of an olive. And the obligation may
be discharged with their roots; and also if their tithes be in

---

[1] Exod. xiii. 7.   [2] I.e., he is to be put to death forthwith.

doubt; and with their first tithing, when the heave-offering has been taken from them; and with their second tithe, and with holy things which are redeemed.

7. Persons must not moisten bran during the passover for chickens, but they may scald it. A woman must not moisten bran in her hand when she goes to the bath. But she may rub it dry on her flesh. A man should not chew wheat and leave it on a wound during Passover, because it becomes leavened.

8. People must not put flour into the charoseth [3] or into the mustard. "But if one puts it?" "He must eat it off-hand." But Rabbi Meier forbids it. They must not boil the passover offering in liquids nor in fruit juice. But one may smear it (after it is roasted), or dip it into them. Water used by the baker must be poured away because it becomes leavened.

CHAPTER III

1. These cause transgression during passover: the Babylonian cutback,[1] and the Median beer, and the Edomite vinegar, and the Egyptian zithum,[2] and the purifying dough of the dyer,[3] and the clarifying grain of the cooks, and the paste of the bookbinders. Rabbi Eleazar said, "even the cosmetics of women." This is the rule. All kinds of grain whatever may cause transgression during the passover. These are negative commands, and they are not visited by cutting off.

2. "Dough in a split of a kneading trough?" "If there be the size of an olive in a single place one is bound to clear it out." Less than this is worthless from its minuteness. And so is it with the question of uncleanness. Particularity causes division. "But if one wish it to remain?" "It is reckoned as the trough." "Dough dried up?"[4] "If it be like that which can become leavened it is forbidden."

3. "How do persons separate the dough-offering when it becomes unclean on a holiday?" Rabbi Eleazar said, "you cannot call it a dough-offering till it be baked." Rabbi Judah,

---

[3] Fruit-sauce; a mixture of dates, raisins, and other fruits, to recall the memory of the mortar from which the bricks in Egypt were made.
[1] Fragments of chickens and dough left to ferment.
[2] A compound of barley, wild saffron, and salt, one-third of each.

[3] A dough or unripe grain lid put over the liquid to absorb the dregs from the foam of fermentation.
[4] Literally, "deaf"; that is, dough which does not rise, or that sounds dull when it is struck.

the son of Bethira, said, " you must put it in cold water." Said
R. Joshua, " it is not leaven so as to transgress the negative
command ' It shall not be seen nor found,' [5] but it must be
separated and left till the evening. But if it become leavened
it is leavened."

4. Rabban Gamaliel said, " three women may knead at once,
and bake in one oven, each after the other." But the Sages say,
" three women may be busied with the dough, one kneads, and
one prepares, and one bakes." Rabbi Akiba said, " all women,
and all wood, and all ovens, are not alike." This is the rule.
" If it ferment it must be smoothed down with cold water."

5. Dough which begins to leaven must be burned, but he
who eats it is free. When it begins to crack it must be burned,
and he who eats it must be cut off. " What is leavening? "
" Like the horns of locusts." " Cracking? " " When the
cracks intermingle." The words of R. Judah. But the Sages
say, " if either of them be eaten, the eater must be cut off."
" And what is leavening? " " All which changed its appearance, as when a man's hairs stand on end through fright."

6. " If the fourteenth day of Nisan happened on the Sabbath? " " They must clear off all the leaven before the Sabbath
begins." The words of R. Meier. But the Sages say, " in the
proper season." Rabbi Eleazar, the son of Zaduk, said, " the
heave-offering before the Sabbath, and ordinary things in the
proper season."

7. " If one went to kill his passover, or circumcise his son,
or to eat the marriage-feast in the house of his father-in-law,
and he remembered that there was leaven in his house? " " If
he can he must return and clear it out, and return to his duties.
He must return and clear it away. But if not, he can esteem
it as nothing in his heart." " (If one went) to save a person
from the militia, or from a river, or from robbers, or from
burning, or from the fall of buildings? " " He may esteem
it as nothing in his heart." " But if he is reposing at his ease? "
" He must return off-hand."

8. And so also when one went forth from Jerusalem and
remembered that he had holy flesh in his hand. If he passed
Zophim [6] he must burn it on the spot. But if not he must return and burn it in front of the temple with the wood of the

[5] Exod. xi. 19.   [6] An eminence from which there was a clear view of the temple.

altar. " And for how much flesh or leaven must men return? "
Rabbi Meier said, " both of them the size of an egg." Rabbi
Judah said, " both the size of an olive." But the Sages say,
" Holy flesh the size of an olive, and leaven the size of an
egg."

CHAPTER IV

1. " A place in which men are accustomed to do work on the
eve of the passover? " " For half a day they may work." " A
place in which they are not accustomed to work? " " They
must not work." " If one goes from a place where they work
to a place where they do not work; or from a place where they
do not work to a place where they do work? " "The Sages put
on him the burden [1] of the place from which he went, or the
burden of the place to which he came; but a man should not
change the customs of a place, as it causes quarrels."

2. Like to him is he who carried fruits of the Sabbatical
year from a place where they were finished growing to a place
where they were not finished growing; or from a place where
they were not finished to a place where they were finished.
He is bound to remove them. Rabbi Judah said, " they can
say to him, go and bring them for yourself from the field." [2]

3. " A place in which men are accustomed to sell small
cattle to Gentiles? " " They may sell them." " A place in
which they are not accustomed to sell them? " " They may
not sell them." But in no place may they sell working cattle
—calves, ass-foals, either unblemished or broken down. [3]
Rabbi Judah " allowed the broken down." The son of Bethira
" allowed a horse."

4. " A place where men are accustomed to eat roast meat
on the night of the passover? " " They may eat it." " A place
in which they are not accustomed to eat it? " " They may not
eat it." " A place in which they are accustomed to light a
candle on the night of the Day of Atonement? " " They may
light it " " A place in which they are not accustomed to light
it? " " They may not light it." But men may light candles
in the synagogues, and in the schools, and in the dark streets,
and for the sick.

[1] The burden means that the man is
forbidden to work.
[2] See treatise on the Sabbatical year,
ix. 5, etc.
[3] Lest the Gentiles should set them to
work on the Sabbath.

5. "A place in which men are accustomed to do work on the ninth of Ab;"[4] "They may work." "A place in which they are not accustomed to work?." "They may not work." But everywhere the disciples of the Sages are idle. Rabban Simon, the son of Gamaliel, said, "a man may always make himself a disciple of the Sages." But the Sages say, "in Judah they did work on the eves of the passovers for half a day, and in Galilee they did nothing." And work in the night before the passover the school of Shammai disallowed; but the school of Hillel "allowed it till sunrise."

6. Rabbi Meier said, "every work which was begun before the fourteenth day of Nisan may be finished on the fourteenth; but it must not be commenced on the fourteenth, even though it can be finished." And the Sages say, "three trades can carry on business on the eves of the passovers for half a day; and these are they—the tailors, and the barbers, and the washers." Rabbi José, the son of Judah, said, "also shoe-makers."

7. Persons may set hens on their nests on the fourteenth. "But if the hen ran off?" "They may return her to her place." "And if she died?" "They may set another instead of her." They may clear away from beneath the feet of beasts on the fourteenth. But on the holiday (or middle-days) they put it aside. They may carry to and bring vessels from the house of the trader, even though they be not necessary for the holiday.

8. The men of Jericho did six things, in three they were prohibited, and in three they were allowed. And these are they in which they were allowed: they engrafted dates the whole fourteenth day of Nisan, and they shortened the "Hear,"[5] and they reaped and stacked new corn before "the sheaf"[6] was offered; and they were allowed. And in these they were prohibited: they used the produce of what was consecrated, and they ate on the Sabbath the fruit that had fallen down from the trees, and they gave[7] (to the poor) the corners of the fields of vegetables. And the Sages prohibited them from these things.[8]

[4] Part of July and August. The ninth of Ab is the anniversary of the threefold destruction of the Temple.
[5] Deut. vi. 4.
[6] Lev. xxiii. 15.
[7] Lev. xix. 9, 10.
[8] Because the poor might eat them un-tithed, thinking they were Peah.

9. BEREITHA—EXTERNAL TRADITION.—Hezekiah the king did six things; to three the Sages consented, and to three they did not consent. He carried the bones of his father (Ahaz) on a rope bed,[9] and they consented. He powdered the brazen serpent,[10] and they consented. He concealed the book of medicines,[1] and they consented. And to three they did not consent: he cut off (the gold from) the doors of the temple[2] and sent it to the Assyrian king, and they did not consent. He stopped the waters of the upper Gihon,[3] and they did not consent. He introduced an intercalary Nisan, and they did not consent.

CHAPTER V

1. The daily offering was slaughtered at half-past eight,[1] and offered at half-past nine. On the eve of the passover it was slaughtered at half-past seven and offered at half-past eight, whether the passover fell on a week-day or on the Sabbath. When the eve of the passover began on the eve of the Sabbath (Friday), it was slaughtered at half-past six, and offered at half-past seven, and the passover followed after it.

2. "The passover offering, which was slaughtered without intention—and the priest took its blood, and he went and sprinkled it without intention?" or "with intention, and without intention?" or "without intention and with intention?" "It is disallowed." "How can it be with intention and without intention?" "With intention partly for the passover, and with intention partly for peace-offerings." "Without intention and with intention?" "With intention partly for peace-offerings, and with intention partly for the passover-offering."

3. "If he slaughtered the passover for those who may not legally eat it—for those who are not reckoned in one company—for the uncircumcised, and for the unclean?" "It is disallowed." "For those who may eat, and for those who may not eat it?" "For those who are reckoned in one company, and for those who are not so reckoned?" "For circumcised, and for uncircumcised?" "For unclean, and for clean?" "It

---

[9] To show his abhorrence of his father's idolatry.
[10] 2 Kings xviii. 4.
[1] Lest the people should substitute medicine for God.

[2] 2 Kings xviii. 16.
[3] 2 Chron. xxxii. 4.
[1] I.e., 2.30 P.M.

is allowed." "If he slaughtered it before noon?" "It is disallowed." Because it is said "between the evenings." [2] "If he slaughtered it before the daily offering?" "It is allowed." Except that one must keep stirring [3] its blood, till the blood of the daily offering be sprinkled. "But if it be *even* sprinkled (before?)" "It is lawful."

4. "He who slaughtered the passover-offering possessing leaven?" "He transgressed a negative command." [4] Rabbi Judah said, "this applies even to the daily offering (of that evening)." Rabbi Simon said, "the slaughter of the passover on the fourteenth with intention for the passover makes (a man possessing leaven) guilty; but if it be slaughtered without intention for the passover he is free" "And in all other sacrifices during the feast, whether one sacrifice with or without the proper intention?" "He is free." "When one thus offers in the feast itself with proper intention?" "He is free." "Without proper intention?" "He is guilty." "And in all the other sacrifices, when one possessing leaven offers either with or without intention?" "He is guilty, only excepting the sin-offering, which was slaughtered without intention."

5. The passover was slaughtered [5] for three bands in succession, as is said, "The whole assembly of the congregation of Israel" [6]—assembly, congregation, Israel. The first band entered, the court was filled, the doors of the court were locked. The trumpeters blew with the trumpets, blew an alarm, and blew. The priests stood in rows, and in their hands were bowls of silver and bowls of gold. All the silver row was entirely silver, and all the golden row was entirely gold. They were not mingled. And the bowls were not flat-bottomed, lest they should lay them down, and the blood be coagulated.

6. When an Israelite slaughtered, and a priest caught the blood, he gave it to his companion, and his companion to his companion, and he took the full, and returned the empty bowl. The priest nearest the altar poured it out at once in front of the foundation of the altar.

[2] Exod. xii. 6.
[3] To prevent its coagulating.
[4] Exod. xxiii. 18.
[5] Josephus mentions the number of lambs slain at a particular passover to have been numbered by the high priest, and they were found to have been 256,-

500. Allowing not less than ten persons to the eating of each lamb, he computes those present at the feast to have been 2,700,200 persons. — Josephus' "Wars," vi. 9, 3.
[6] Exod. xii. 6.

7. The first band went out, the second band entered; the second went out, the third entered. As was the proceeding of the first, so was the proceeding of the second and the third. They read the praise.[7] When they finished they repeated it, and after repeating it they read it a third time, even though they did not complete it thrice in their time. R. Judah said, "during the time of the third band they did not reach to 'I love the Lord, for He hath heard,' because the people were few."

8. As was the proceeding in ordinary days, so was the proceeding on the Sabbath, save that the priests washed out the court,[8] though not with the will of the Sages. R. Judah said, "a cup was filled with mixed-up blood,[9] and poured out at once upon the altar;" but the Sages "did not admit it."

9. "How did they hang up and skin the passover sacrifices?" "Iron hooks were fixed in the walls and pillars, and on them they hung them, and skinned them." "And every one who had not a place to hang them up and skin them?" "Thin smooth rods were there, and he rested one on his shoulder and on the shoulder of his companion, and hung it up and skinned it." Rabbi Eliezer said, "when the fourteenth began on a Sabbath, he rested his hand on the shoulder of his companion, and the hand of his companion on his shoulder, and he hung it up and skinned it."

10. He cut it open, and took out its entrails. He put them on a dish and incensed them on the altar. The first party went out, and sat down on the Mountain of the House. The second party were in the Chel,[10] and the third party remained in their place. When it grew dark they went out and roasted their passovers.

CHAPTER VI

1. These things in the passover abrogate the command against work on the Sabbath: its slaughtering, and the sprinkling of its blood, and purging its inwards, and incensing its fat. But its roasting and the rinsing of its inwards do not abrogate the Sabbath. But to carry it, and to bring it beyond a Sabbath

[7] Psalms cxiii.-cxviii.
[8] They washed the court indirectly by stopping a canal of water which overflowed the court; they afterward opened it, when all flowed off again.
[9] Taken from the intermingled blood of the many offerings.
[10] See "Measurements," ii. 3.

day's journey, and to cut off its wen, do not abrogate the Sabbath. Rabbi Eleazar said, "they abrogate it."

2. Said Rabbi Eleazar, "and is not this the teaching? when slaughtering is work it abrogates the Sabbath. Things which are for 'resting' do not abrogate the Sabbath."[1] To him said Rabbi Joshua, "a holiday will give the proof; the Sages permitted that which is work, and they forbade that which is resting." Rabbi Eleazar said to him, "what do you mean, Joshua? what comparison is there between a command and that which is voluntary?" Rabbi Akiba answered and said, "sprinkling[2] will give the proof, because it is a positive command, and it is for 'resting,' and does not abrogate the Sabbath; but you should not wonder at this, even though it be a command, as it is for 'resting,' and does not abrogate the Sabbath." Rabbi Eleazar said to him, "and on that I form my judgment, when slaughtering is work it abrogates the Sabbath; sprinkling, which is for 'resting,' does it not teach that it abrogates the Sabbath?" Rabbi Akiba said to him, "on the contrary, if sprinkling, which is for 'resting,' does not abrogate the Sabbath, slaughtering, which is for work, is it not the teaching? should not abrogate the Sabbath." Rabbi Eleazar said to him, "Akiba, thou hast annulled what is written in the Law, 'between the evenings,' 'in its appointed time,' whether it be a week-day or a Sabbath." He said to him, "My teacher, give me proof of an appointed time for these things, like the appointed time for slaughtering the passover-offering?" The rule is, said R. Akiba, "all work for the passover which it is possible to do on the eve of the Sabbath does not abrogate the Sabbath; slaughtering, which it is impossible to do on the eve of the passover which falls on a Sabbath, abrogates the Sabbath."

3. "When do men bring with the passover a feast-offering?" "When the passover falls on a week-day, when those who offer it are legally clean, and when the lamb is too small for the eaters. But when the passover falls on a Sabbath, when the lamb is too much for the eaters, and there is legal uncleanness, they should not bring with it a feast-offering."

4. The feast-offering[3] came from flocks, from herds, from

[1] The following subtle discussion arises out of the distinction between "work" forbidden by the law of God and "resting from work" enjoined by tradition.

[2] The sprinkling of a person unclean from touching a dead body when the passover fell on a Sabbath.

[3] This refers to the second chagigah —the feast-offering of individuals on the

sheep and goats, from rams and ewes, and it may be eaten during a period of two days and one night.

5. "The passover which was slaughtered without the proper intention on a Sabbath?" "The offerer of it is indebted for a sin-offering." "And all the other sacrifices which he slaughtered for the passover?" "If they be not suitable for it he is guilty." "And if they be suitable?" Rabbi Eleazar declares him "indebted for a sin-offering." But R. Joshua "frees him." Said Rabbi Eleazar, "what! if the passover which was allowed for proper intention when the offerer changed its intention, makes him guilty; is it not the teaching that sacrifices, which are disallowed for want of proper intention when the offerer changed their intention, make him also guilty?" Rabbi Joshua said to him, "no; if thou saidst in the passover when he changed its intention it is changed to a thing disallowed, thou wilt say in the other sacrifices when he changed their intention they are changed to a thing allowed." Rabbi Eleazar said to him, "the congregational offerings will give the proof, because they are rendered lawful on the Sabbath by intention, but whoever slaughtered (another) sacrifice with their intention is guilty." Rabbi Joshua said to him, "no; if thou sayest so in the congregational offerings, which are a determined number, thou wilt also say so in the passover sacrifice which has no determined number. Rabbi Meier said, "even he who slaughtered other offerings on the Sabbath, with the intention of the congregational offerings, is free."

6. "When one slaughtered the passover, but not for its eaters, or not for those numbered to eat it, for uncircumcised and for unclean persons?" "He is guilty." "For its eaters and not for its eaters? For its reckoning and not for its reckoning? For circumcised and uncircumcised? For clean and unclean?" "He is free." "He slaughtered it, and it was found blemished?" "He is guilty." "He slaughtered it and it was found torn in secret?" "He is free." "He slaughtered it, and it became known that its owners retired from it, or died, or became legally unclean?" "He is free, because he slaughtered it with lawful permission."

15th of Nisan. It is called by the general name passover, John xviii. 28. Want of acquaintance with this subject has led some commentators to suppose that there is a discrepancy between the account of the last passover of our Lord as related in the Synoptical Gospels, and as recorded by St. John.

CHAPTER VII

1. " How do men roast the passover? "   " They bring a
stick of pomegranate and thrust it through its mouth to its
tail.   And they put its legs and intestines inside it."   The words
of R. José, the Galilean.   Rabbi Akiba said, " that is a kind of
boiling, therefore they hang them outside of it."

2. Men must not roast the passover on a spit or a girdiron.
Said R. Zaduk, " it happened to Rabban Gamaliel that he said
to Zabi, his servant, ' go and roast for us the passover on the
gridiron.' "   " If it touch the side of the oven? "   " That part
must be peeled off."   " If its gravy drop on the side of the
oven, and again return on it? "   " That part must be taken
out."   " If the gravy drop on the fine flour? "   " That part
must be pulled out " (and burned).

3. " If men anointed (basted) it with oil of the heave-offering? "   " If it be a company of priests, they may eat it."   " If
it be a company of Israelites? "   " If it be raw they can wash
it away."   " But if roast? "   " They must peel off the surface."
" If it was anointed with oil of the second tithe? "   " Its value
in money must not be charged to the members of the company,
because they cannot redeem [1] the second tithes in Jerusalem."

4. Five things may be brought during legal uncleanness,
but they must not be eaten in legal uncleanness: the sheaf,[2]
the two wave loaves,[3] and the shewbread,[4] sacrifices of peace-
offerings of the congregation,[5] and the kids[6] on the feast of
the New Moon.   The passover which was brought during legal
uncleanness, may be eaten in uncleanness, because in the beginning the command came only for eating.

5. " If the flesh be legally unclean and the fat unpolluted? "
" The priest must not sprinkle its blood on the altar."   " If
the fat be unclean and the flesh unpolluted? "   " The priest
may sprinkle its blood."   But with other holy offerings it is
not so, for though their flesh be unclean, and their fat remains
unpolluted, the priest may sprinkle their blood on the altar.

6. " If the congregation be legally unclean, or its majority,
or the priests be legally unclean, and the congregation legally

[1] Jer. Tal. reads " sell."
[2] Lev. xxiii. 11.
[3] Lev. xxiii. 17.
[4] Exod. xxv. 30.
[5] Lev. xxiii. 19.
    Num. xxviii. 15.

clean?" "The passover may be kept in legal uncleanness."
"If the minority of the congregation be legally unclean?"
"The clean majority can keep the first, and the unclean
minority the second passover" (on the fourteenth day of the
following month).

7. When the blood of the passover-offering was poured on
the altar, and it was afterward known that it was unclean, the
(golden)[7] plate of the High Priest makes it accepted. When
the body of the paschal sacrifice was unclean, "the plate"
cannot make it accepted, as they say the Nazarite and the
celebrant of the passover have the uncleanness of the blood accepted with "the plate." But "the plate" does not make the
legal uncleanness of the body of the paschal lamb accepted.
If it be legally unclean with an unknown uncleanness, the
plate makes it accepted.

8. "If it be legally unclean in whole or in most part?"
"The passover must be burned in front of 'the palace'[8] with
the wood of the altar." "A little which is unclean, and that
which is left over?" "The owners may burn it in their own
courts, or on their roofs with their own wood." The stingy
ones burnt it in front of the palace, that they might use the
wood of the altar.

9. "The passover which was carried out of the city, or became unclean?" "The owner must burn it off-hand." "Its
masters became unclean or died?" "Let its appearance
change, and let it be burned on the sixteenth."[9] Rabbi
Jochanan, the son of Beruka, said, "even it must be burned
off-hand, because it has no one to eat it."

10. "Bones and tendons and what is left over?" They
must be burned on the sixteenth. "If the sixteenth happened
on a Sabbath?" "They must be burned on the seventeenth,
because they cannot abrogate either the laws of the Sabbath
or the holiday."

11. All that is eaten in a great ox may be eaten in a tender
kid, and the tops of the shoulder-blades, and the gristle.
"Whoever broke any bone in a clean passover?" "He must
receive forty stripes." "But for what is left over in the clean,

[7] Exod. xxviii. 36-38.
[8] 1 Chron. xxix. 19.
[9] It remained uneaten overnight, and therefore must be burned, in accordance with Exod. xii. 10.

and broken in an unclean passover?" "He does not receive
the forty."

12. "A member partly displaced?" "One must cut in till
he reach the bone, and he must peel off the flesh till he reach
the joint, and he cuts it off. But in other holy offerings one
may cleave the displaced members with an axe, since there
does not exist any (prohibition of) breaking the bone for
them." (For example), from the door-post and inwards is inside. From the door-post and outwards is outside. The windows and thickness of the wall are reckoned as inside.

13. "Two companies which eat the passover in one house?"
"These turn their faces to this side and eat; and those turn
their faces to that side and eat. And the boiler [10] is between
the companies. The servant stands to mix wine. The servant must shut his mouth till he serve the other company. He
afterward turns his face till he reach his own company, and
then he may eat. And she who is newly married can turn her
face aside and eat it."

CHAPTER VIII

1. "The married woman, while she is in the house of her
husband?" "Her husband slaughtered on her account, and
her father slaughtered on her account?" "She must eat the
passover with her husband." "She went to spend the first
feast after her marriage in the house of her father—her father
slaughtered on her account, and her husband slaughtered on
her account?" "She may eat in the place which she wishes."
"An orphan on whose account the guardians slaughtered?"
"He may eat in the place which he wishes." "A slave of two
partners?" "He must not eat with both." "A slave who is
half free?" "He must not eat with his master."

2. One said to his slave, "go and slaughter for me the
passover." "He slaughtered a kid?" "He may eat it." "He
slaughtered a lamb?" "He may eat it." "He slaughtered
a kid and a lamb?" "He may eat of the first." "He forgot
what his master said to him—what shall he do?" "He must
slaughter a lamb and a kid, and shall say, 'If my master said

[10] From the need of a boiler it appears   mixed with hot water. The wine itself
that the wine used at the passover was   was always red.

to me—a kid, the kid is on his account, and the lamb is on my account; and if my master said to me—a lamb, the lamb is for him, and the kid is for me.'" "If his master forgot what he said to him?" "Both animals must go forth to the house of burning; and they are free from keeping the second passover."

3. One said to his sons, "I am ready to slaughter the passover for you who shall first go up to Jerusalem." As soon as one of them entered with his head and the greater part of his body inside the city gate, he gained his own share of the passover, and gained it for his brothers with him. They may always be reckoned in one company, when each one obtains the size of an olive. They may first be reckoned, and afterward withdraw from a company till the passover be slaughtered. Rabbi Simon said, "until its blood be poured out on their account."

4. "He who reckoned others with himself in his portion of the lamb?" "The members of the company are allowed to give to him his share, and he may eat of it with his own guests; and they may eat their portion with their own guests."

5. "If one observed an issue twice?" "They may slaughter the lamb on his account on the seventh day of the issue if it be the fourteenth day of Nisan." "If he observed it thrice?"[1] "They may only slaughter on his account on the eighth day of the issue" (if it be the fourteenth day of Nisan).

6. "The mourner and the person who opened a heap,[2] and also the person who has the promise of release from prison, and the sick, and the aged, who are able to eat the size of an olive?" "They may slaughter the passover for them." For all of them they must not slaughter the lamb on their own account alone, lest they bring the passover into contempt,[3] because there might happen to them some abomination. They are freed from keeping a second passover—excepting him who in opening the heap was unclean from the beginning.

7. "They must not slaughter the passover for one person."

---

[1] If one observed the issue three times on the same day, he could not be considered clean before he brought a sacrifice.
[2] In which there is a dead body.

[3] The mourner might be too sorrowful to eat, the sick too ill to eat, and the prisoner might be detained in prison, etc.

The words of Rabbi Judah; but Rabbi José "allowed it."
Even for a company of a hundred, when they cannot eat the
size of an olive, they must not slaughter the passover; and
they must not form a company of women, of slaves, and of little ones.

8. A mourner may be baptized, and eat his passover in the
evening, but not other holy things. "He who heard of a death,
or had the bones of his relations collected?" "He may be
baptized and eat holy things." "A stranger who was
proselytized on the eve of the passover?" The school of
Shammai say, "He may be baptized and eat his passover in
the evening"; but the school of Hillel say, "he who just departed from the foreskin is as legally unclean as he who just
departs from the grave."

CHAPTER IX

1. He who was legally unclean, or in a journey afar off, and
did not keep the first, must keep the second (passover). "He
mistook it, or was constrained by force, and did not keep the
first?" "He must keep the second." "If so, why is it said
unclean [1] or in a journey afar off?" "Because such persons
are free from being cut off, but those bound to observe it are
to be cut off if they neglect it."

2. What is a "journey afar off?" "From Modiim [2] and
outward; and so is the measure from Jerusalem on every side."
The words of Rabbi Akiba; Rabbi Eleazar said, "from the
threshold of the temple-court and outward." Said R. José,
"for this reason there is a dot on the 'he,' to explain not that
it is really afar off, but that one is afar off from the threshold
of the temple-court and outward."

3. "What is the difference between the first and second
passover?" "The first passover forbids leaven to be seen or
found; but the second allows unleavened and leavened bread
in one's house." The first passover requires hallel [3] during
eating, but the second does not require hallel during eating.

---

[1] Numbers ix. 10.
[2] About fifteen miles from Jerusalem.
Modiim or Modin was the city of the
Maccabees.
[3] Psalms cxiii.-cxviii.

Both require hallel in their preparations, and the paschal sacrifices must be eaten roasted on unleavened bread with bitter herbs, and they both abrogate the Sabbath."

4. "The passover-offering which was brought during legal uncleanness?" "The man or woman with an issue may not eat of it, nor she in separation or in childbirth. But if they eat they are free from being cut off." Rabbi Eleazar "frees them even in going into the sanctuary."

5. "What is the difference between the passover of Egypt and the passover of succeeding generations?" "The passover of Egypt was taken on the tenth day,[4] and required the sprinkling with a bunch of hyssop on the lintel and the two side posts, and was eaten with haste in one night; but the passover of succeeding generations exists the whole seven days."

6. Said R. Joshua, "I once heard that the substitute[5] of the passover-offering san be sacrificed, and that the substitute of the passover-offering cannot be sacrificed, I have no one to explain." Said R. Akiba, "I will explain: the passover-offering, which was found (after being lost) before the time for slaughtering its substitute, may be pastured till it be blemished, and it can be sold, and the owner can take for its price peace-offerings, and so also for its substitute. After the time for slaughtering the passover-offering its substitute may be offered for a peace-offering, and so can also its substitute."

7. "He who set apart a ewe for his passover, or a male of two years?" "He may pasture it till it be blemished. And he can sell it, and its price may be used for a free-will offering." "He who selected his passover, and afterward died?" "His son must not offer it after him with the intention of a passover, but he may offer it with the intention of a peace-offering."

8. "The passover-offering which was mixed up with other sacrifices?" "All must be pastured till they be blemished, and they must be sold, and the offerer must bring the price of the best of this kind and the price of the best of that kind, and the loss he must make up from his private means." "The passover-offering which was mixed up with first-borns?"

[4] Exod. xii. 3.
[5] The substitute refers to one animal changed for another, which had been intended for the passover-offering.

Rabbi Simon said, " if there be companies of priests they may eat it."

9. " A company [6] which lost its passover-offering, and said to someone, ' go and seek it and slaughter it for us '; and he went and found it and slaughtered it, and they meanwhile also took one and slaughtered it,—if his be first slaughtered? " " He may eat of his and they may eat with him of his." " But if theirs be first slaughtered? " " They may eat of theirs, and he may eat of his." " But if it be not known which of them was first slaughtered, or both were slaughtered at once? " " He must eat of his passover, but they cannot eat with him, and their passover must go forth to the house of burning; and they are freed from keeping a second passover." " He said to them, ' if I be too late, go and slaughter for me '; he went, and meanwhile found (the lost) one and slaughtered it, and they took and also slaughtered one. If theirs be first slaughtered? " " They may eat of theirs, and he may eat with them." " But if his were first slaughtered? " " He shall eat of his, and they shall eat of theirs." " But if it be not known which of them was first slaughtered or both of them were slaughtered at once? " " They shall eat of theirs, but he must not eat with them, and his lamb must go forth to the house of burning, and he is freed from keeping a second (passover)." " If he said to them ' slaughter for me,' and they also said to him ' slaughter for us? ' " " All shall eat of that one first slaughtered." " But if it be not known which of them was first slaughtered? " " Both must go forth to the house of burning." " If he did not say it to them, nor they say it to him? " " They are not sureties one for the other " (and they must eat apart from each other).

10. " Two companies had their passover-offerings mixed: this company drew out one for themselves, and that company drew out one for themselves. One of these comes to those, and one of those comes to these, and thus they say, ' if this passover be ours, let our hands be withdrawn from yours and be counted with ours; but if this passover be yours, let our hands be withdrawn from ours and be counted with yours.'

---

[6] The following rules are founded on two principles; firstly, that every lamb must have its own numbered company of eaters; and secondly, that no person could be numbered with two companies.

And so with five companies of five each, and ten of ten each, they may draw out and join one from every company, and say so."

11. "Two persons who had their passover-offerings mixed?" "One draws out one for himself, and the other draws out one for himself. This one can count with himself a person invited from the market. And that one can count with himself a person invited from the market. This individual comes to that one, and that one comes to this one, and so they say, 'if this passover be mine, let thy hands be withdrawn from thine, and be counted with mine; and if this passover be thine, let my hands be withdrawn from mine, and be counted with thine.'"

CHAPTER X

1. On the eves of the passovers near to the time of evening prayer a man must not eat till it be dark. And even the poorest in Israel must not eat till he can recline at ease, and they must not withhold from him the four cups of wine, even though he receives the weekly alms.

2. When they mix for him the first cup of wine,[1] the school of Shammai say, "he shall repeat the blessing for the day, and after that the blessing for the wine." But the school of Hillel say, "he shall repeat the blessing for the wine, and after that the blessing for the day."

3. The attendants bring before him greens and lettuce. He dips the lettuce in its sauce till he come to the time for the seasoning of the bread. They bring before him unleavened bread, and lettuce, and the fruit sauce, on two dishes, even though the fruit sauce is not a command. Rabbi Eleazar, the son of Zadok, said (it is) "a command, and in the time of the sanctuary they used to bring before him the body of the passover offering."

4. The attendants mixed for him the second cup, and here the son asks his father, and if the son have no knowledge his father teaches him, "in what is this night different from all other nights?" "Because in all other nights we eat leavened

---

[1] It was after the first cup of wine was drunk that our Lord washed the disciples' feet (John xiii. 5; Luke xxii. 17).

and unleavened bread. In this night all is unleavened. Because in all other nights we eat every herb, in this night bitter herbs. Because in all other nights we eat flesh roasted, well boiled, and boiled. In this night all is roasted. Because in all other nights we dip what we eat once, in this night twice " (*i.e.*, in the sauce and in the seasoning). And according to the knowledge of the son his father teaches him. He begins in shame and he ends in praise. And he expounds from " a Syrian ready to perish was my father," [2] till he end the whole passage.

5. Rabban Gamaliel used to say, " everyone who did not speak of these three things in the passover did not discharge his duty, and these are they: the passover, the unleavened bread, and bitter herbs. Passover, because OMNIPRESENCE passed over the houses of our fathers in Egypt. Unleavened, because our fathers were redeemed from Egypt. Bitter, because the Egyptians made the lives of our fathers bitter in Egypt." In every generation man is bound to look to himself as though he in person went out from Egypt, as is said,[3] " And thou shalt show thy son in that day, saying, This is done because of that which the Lord did unto me when I came forth out of Egypt." For this reason we are bound to acknowledge, to thank, to praise, to glorify, to exalt, to magnify, to bless, to elevate, without limit, HIM who has done for our fathers and us all these miracles. He brought us from slavery to freedom, from sorrow to joy, and from mourning to festivity, and from thick darkness to great light, and from servitude to redemption, and let us say before Him Hallelujah.

6. " How far does he repeat? " The school of Shammai say, till " a joyful mother of children." [4] But the school of Hillel say, till " the flint into a fountain of waters," [5] and he finished with a " blessing for redemption." Rabbi Tarphon said, " ' Who redeemed us and redeemed our fathers from Egypt,' and he does not end with any other blessing." Rabbi Akiba adds, " So the Lord our God and the God of our fathers shall bring us to holidays and other feast-days yet to come to us in peace, rejoicing in the building of THY city, and delighting in THY service; and we shall eat there the sacrifices

[2] Deut. xxvi. 5-11.   [3] Exod. xiii. 8.   [4] Psalm cxiii. 9.   [5] Psalm cxiv. 8.

and the passovers, etc., until ' Blessed be Thou, Lord, the Redeemer of Israel.' "

7. When the attendants mixed for him the third cup [6] he says the blessing for his food, with the fourth cup he finished the hallel, and said over it the blessing of the Song.[7] Between the first and second cups if he wish to drink, he may drink as much as he likes. Between the third and fourth he must not drink.

8. Persons are not free after the passover to ask for more food. "If some fall asleep during the passover?"[8] "They may afterward eat of it" "All?" "They must not eat of it." Rabbi José says, "If they dozed?" "They may eat of it." "If they slept?" "They must not eat of it."

9. The passover after midnight renders hands legally unclean. False intention and the remains of the feast render hands legally unclean.[9] "When one repeated the passover-blessing?" "He is free from the sacrifice-blessing, but the sacrifice-blessing does not free him from that of the passover." The words of R. Ishmael. Rabbi Akiba said, "this does not free from that, nor that from this."

---

[6] The third cup was called the "cup of blessing" (1 Cor. x. 16). It was the one used by our Lord for the institution of the holy sacrament.

[7] Psalm cxxxvi.

[8] They may have been overcome with wine (1 Cor. xi. 21).

[9] This is explained in the treatise "Hands."

ON THE DAY OF ATONEMENT

Preparations of the High Priest—Cleansing the Altar—Casting Lots—
Daybreak — Offerings — Dress—Prayer—The Goats—Monobazus—
Helena—Azazel—The Golden Censer—The Vail—Holy of Holies—
" Foundation "—Sprinkling the Blood—Sending Forth the Goat into
the Wilderness—High Priest Burning the Bullock and Goat—Reading—Ceremonial—Rules and Exceptions—Repentance and Atonement.

CHAPTER I

1. Seven days before the Day of Atonement the High
Priest was removed from his house to the chamber [1] Par-
bedrin, and the council prepared for him another priest,[2] lest
there happen to him any defilement. R. Judah said, "they
prepared also another wife, lest his wife die"; as is said,[3]
"And he shall atone for himself and for his house"; for his
house, *i.e.*, for his wife. The Sages said to him, "if so, there
is no end to the matter."

2. All these seven days, he (the high priest) sprinkled the
blood, burned the incense, and trimmed the lamps, and offered
the head and the foot. On the remainder of all the days, if he
wished to offer, he offered; since the high priest first offered
part, and first took part (in the sacrifices).

3. The elders from the elders of the great Sanhedrin delivered to him, and read before him, the ceremonial of the day;
and they said to him, "My Lord High Priest, read with thy
mouth, perchance thou hast forgotten, or perchance thou hast
not learned"[4] On the eve of the day of atonement, toward
dawn, they placed him in the eastern gate (of the Temple),
and they caused to pass before him bullocks, rams, and lambs,
that he might be skilled and expert in his ministry.

[1] Where the counsellors sat.
[2] Called Sagan (suffragan) (2 Kings
xxv. 18; Jer. lii. 24).
[3] Lev. xvi. 6.
[4] As might occur from the frequent
changes during the second Temple.

4. All the seven days they did not withhold from him food and drink; the eve of the day of atonement, with the beginning of darkness, they did not permit him to eat much, since food induces sleep.

5. The elders of the great Sanhedrin delivered him to the elders of the priesthood, who brought him to the upper chamber of the house Abtinas. And they administered to him the oath,[5] and they left him and departed. And they said to him, " My Lord High Priest, we are ambassadors of the great Sanhedrin, and thou art our ambassador, and the ambassador of the great Sanhedrin. We adjure thee by Him, whose Name dwells in this house, that thou wilt not change aught of all which we have said to thee." He went apart and wept. They went apart and wept.[6]

6. If he were a learned man, he expounded; but if not, the disciples of the learned expounded before him. If he were skilled in reading, he read; but if not, they read before him. " And in what did they read before him?" " In Job, and in Ezra, and in Chronicles." Zachariah, the son of Kebutal, said, " I often read before him in Daniel."

7. If he desired to sleep, the young priests filliped with the first finger [7] before him, and said to him, " My Lord High Priest, stand up and refresh thyself [8] once on the pavement," and they kept him occupied [9] until the time approached for slaying (the victims).

8. Every day they cleansed the altar at cockcrow, or at its approach, intermediate before or after it; and on the day of atonement [10] at midnight; and in the three great feasts, at the first watch. And before cockcrow the court was crowded with Israel.

---

[5] That he would incense " within " the vail (Lev. xvi. 12, 13), in opposition to the Sadducees, who maintained that the incense should be burned " without."

[6] That such an oath was necessary.

[7] Or the " index " finger; other trans. the " middle " finger.

[8] Or change thyself.

[9] Singing to him " Unless the Lord build the house, they labor but in vain that build it," etc. (Psalm cxxvii.).

[10] The Jews think that the day of atonement was the day on which Adam sinned, on which Abraham was circumcised, and on which Moses offered atonement for the sin of the golden calf.

CHAPTER II

1. At first everyone who wished to (cleanse) the altar, cleansed it. When they were many, they ran and mounted the ascent, and each one, who at the middle outstripped his companion by four cubits, won it. If two were equal the president said to them, " lift your fingers." [1] " And what is that? " " They lifted one or two fingers, but no one lifted the thumb in the Sanctuary."

2. It happened that two were equal, and running and mounting the ascent, one of them thrust his companion, so that he fell, and his leg was broken. And when the great Sanhedrin saw that they were getting into danger, they decreed that they should not cleanse the altar save by lot. There were four lots, and this was the first lot.

3. The second lot was: Who should slay? Who sprinkle? Who should take the ashes from the inner altar? and who should take the ashes from the candlestick? and who should carry the members to the ascent? the head and the right foot, and the hind feet, the tail, and the left foot, the breast, and the throat, and the two sides, and the inwards, and the fine flour, and the pancakes, and the wine. Thirteen priests discharged this lot. Said Ben Asai in the presence of R. Akiba from the mouth of Rabbi Joshua, " like to its way of motion " (when alive).

4. The third lot [2] was for new men who came to offer incense, and they cast the lots. The fourth lot was for new men with the old, who should carry the members from the ascent to the altar.

5. The daily offering was with nine, ten, eleven, twelve, priests; not less and not more " How? " " Itself with nine: at the feast of Tabernacles in the hand of one, a glass of water there is ten. The evening offering with eleven, itself with nine, and in the hands of two, two fagots of wood. On Sab-

[1] I.e., cast lots, which was done by placing the priests in a row, and bidding them to hold up their fingers. After fixing on a certain number, the cap of one of them was taken off. With this priest the reckoning began, and proceeded till the prearranged number fell on some one of them; and his was the lot. Particular care was taken to count the fingers which were held up, and not to number their persons, as this was considered unlawful. (1 Chron. xxi. 1.)

[2] The third lot for burning incense was the most important. It was always done by a fresh man, so that a priest might burn incense only once during his lifetime. (Luke i. 9; Rev. viii. 3, 4.)

bath, eleven; itself with nine, and two, in their hands two
fragments of incense of the showbread. And on the Sabbath
in the feast of Tabernacles in the hand of one a glass of
water."

6. The ram was offered with eleven; the flesh with five, the
inner part, and the fine flour and the wine, to each two and
two.

7. The bullock was offered with twenty-four priests. "The
head and the right foot?" "The head with one, and the
foot with two." "The chine and the left foot?" "The tail
with two, and the left foot with two." "The breast and
the throat?" "The breast with one, and the throat with
three, the two hind feet with two, and the two sides with two,
the inner parts and the fine flour, and the wine, each with three
and three." "Of which is that said?" "Of the offering for
the whole congregation." "But for the offerings of an individual?" "If he wished to offer, he might offer" "For
the skinning and cutting up?" "For these all were equal."

CHAPTER III

1. The overseer said to them, "go and look if the time for
slaughter is come." If it came, the watchman said, "it is
brightening."[1] Matthew the son of Samuel said, "is the
whole east light as far as Hebron?" and he said "yes."

2. "And why was that necessary?" "Because it once
happened that the light of the moon came up, and they
deemed it the light from the east." And they slaughtered
the daily offering, and they brought it to the house of burning. And they brought down the High Priest to the house
of Baptism. This was the rule in the Sanctuary that everyone who covered his feet (was required) to wash; and everyone retiring was required to sanctify his hands and feet.

3. No one entered the court for service, however clean, until
he washed. The High Priest made five washings and ten
purifications in this day, and all were in the Holy place above
the house of Parva,[2] with the exception of the first one alone.

---

[1] Or, as your wish.
[2] The Gemara says it was so called
because Parva, a magician, built this
room and digged through from it to see
the service of the High Priest on the
day of atonement; or else because it
was used for storing "bullock-hides."

4. They made a screen of linen between him and the people. He undressed, descended, and washed. He came up and wiped himself. They brought to him robes of gold, and he dressed, and he sanctified his hands and feet. They brought to him the daily offering. He cut (its throat), and another finished the slaughter at his hand. He received the blood and sprinkled it. He entered to offer the morning incense and to trim the lights, and to offer the head and the members, and the things fried in the pan, and the wine.

5. The morning incense was offered between the blood and the members. That of the evening[3] between the members and the libations. If the High Priest were old, or delicate, they heated for him (iron), and they put it into the cold water, that its temperature should be changed.

6. They brought him to the house of Parva, and it was in the Sanctuary. They divided with the screen of linen between him and the people. He sanctified his hands and feet and undressed. R. Meier said, he undressed and sanctified his hands and feet, he descended and washed, he came up and he wiped himself. They brought to him white robes, he dressed and sanctified his hands and feet.

7. "In the morning he was dressed with Pelusian linen worth twelve minas,[4] and in the evening with Indian linen worth 800 zuz."[5] The words of R. Meier. But the Sages say, "that in the morning his dress was worth eighteen minas, and in the evening twelve minas"; all these thirty minas were from the congregation, and if he wished to add to them he might add of himself.

8. He came to the side of his bullock, and the bullock was standing between the porch and the altar; his head to the North, and his face to the West; and the Priest stood in the East, and his face Westward, and he placed both hands upon him and made confession, and thus he spake, "I beseech thee, O Name, I have committed iniquity. I have sinned before Thee—I, and my house—I beseech thee, O Name, pardon[6] now the iniquities and the transgressions and the sins which I have perversely committed, and transgressed, and sinned

---

[3] Literally, between the evenings.
[4] The mina of the sanctuary was worth about £5 14s., consequently the morning dress cost about £68 8s.
[5] The zuz was worth about 6½d., con- sequently the evening dress cost about £21 13s. 4d.
[6] Literally, "cover over"; i.e., "atone for."

before thee, I, and my house, as is written in the law of Moses thy servant, that in this day ' He will atone for you,' etc. And they answered after him, 'BLESSED BE THE NAME. THE HONOR OF HIS KINGDOM FOREVER AND EVER.' "

9. He came to the east of the court to the north of the altar. The Sagan was at his right hand, and the chief of the fathers at his left. And there were the two goats; and the urn was there, and in it were two lots of boxwood, and Ben Gamla made them of gold, and they commemorated him as praise-worthy.

10. The son of Katin made twelve pipes to the laver, where before there were but two; and also he made a wheel for the laver, lest its water should be polluted by night. Monobazus [7] the king made all the handles of the vessels, of gold for the day of atonement. Helena, his mother, made a chandelier of gold near the door of the Sanctuary, and she also made a tablet of gold upon which the section of the Sota [8] was written. Wonders were wrought for the doors of Nicanor,[9] and they were commemorated as praiseworthy.

11. And these were in ignominy: The family of Garmu, who were unwilling to instruct in the preparation of the show-bread. The family of Abtinas, who were unwilling to instruct in the preparation of incense. Hogrus, the son of Levi, knew a tune in the chant, and was unwilling to instruct. The son of Kamzar was unwilling to instruct in the art of writing. Concerning the former it is said, " The memory of the just is blessed "; and concerning the latter it is said, " but the name of the wicked shall rot " (Prov. x. 7).

CHAPTER IV

1. He shook the urn and brought up two lots; one was written " for the Name," and the other was written " for Azazel." [1] The Sagan stood at his right hand, and the Chief of the Fathers at his left. If " for the Name " came up in his right hand the Sagan said to him, " My Lord High Priest, lift

---

[7] King of Adiabene, a proselyte to Judaism about A.D. 45.
[8] The accused woman.

[9] See Treatise on " Measurements," ii. 3, note.
[1] A. V. " Scapegoat," or for the

8

up thy right hand "; and if " for the Name " came up in his left the Chief of the Fathers said to him, " My Lord High Priest, lift up thy left hand." He placed them upon the two goats, and said, " for the Lord is the sin-offering." R. Ismael said, " it was not necessary to mention the sin-offering " but " for the Lord." And they answered after him, " BLESSED BE THE NAME. THE HONOR OF HIS KINGDOM FOREVER AND EVER."

2. He twisted a tongue[2] of brightness on the head of the goat to be sent away, and he placed him opposite the gate from whence he should be sent. And the one for slaughter he placed opposite the slaughter-house. He himself came beside his bullock the second time, and laid his two hands upon him and made confession, and thus he spake: " I beseech Thee, O Name, I have committed iniquity, I have transgressed, I have sinned before Thee. I, and my house, and the sons of Aaron, Thy holy people. I beseech Thee, O Name, pardon iniquities, transgressions, and sins which I have perversely committed, and transgressed, and sinned before Thee, I, and my house, and the sons of Aaron, Thy holy people, as is written in the law of Moses, Thy servant, saying, that in this day he will atone for you to purify you from all your sins ' Before the LORD. Ye shall be pure.' " And they answered after him, " BLESSED BE THE NAME. THE HONOR OF HIS KINGDOM FOREVER AND EVER."

3. He slaughtered him and caught his blood in a bowl, and he gave it to him who mixed it upon the fourth platform of the Sanctuary, that it might not congeal. He took the censer, and went up to the top of the altar, and raked the live coals here and there, and gathered out from the inner embers. And went down and placed it upon the fourth platform in the court.

4. Every day he gathered out the coals with one of silver and poured them out into one of gold, but to-day he gathered them with one of gold and he entered with it. Every day he

---

" devil." Others translate " wholly put away " in reference to the sins of the people, or for " the hard mountain," and others the " demon of dry places." Some, however, think Azazel to be the fallen angel mentioned in the Book of Enoch, and identical with Sammael, the angel of death. Symmachus translates

" the goat that departs." Theodotion translates " the goat sent away." Aquila, " the goat set free." The LXX. and Josephus understand by the term " the averter of ills," and the Vulgate " caper emissarius."

[2] A tongue-shaped piece of scarlet wool.

gathered them out with one of four cabs [3] and poured them into one of three cabs. But to-day he gathered them out with one of three cabs, and with it he entered. Rabbi Joseph said, " every day he gathered out with one containing a seah,[4] and poured it into one of three cabs. But to-day he gathered out with one of three cabs, and with it he entered. Every day it was heavy, but to-day it was light. Every day its handle was short, but to-day long. Every day it was green gold; to-day red." The words of Rabbi Menachem. " Every day he offered half a pound in the morning, and half a pound in the evening, but to-day he added his handful. Every day it was fine; but to-day the finest of the fine."

5. Every day the priests went up the ascent (to the altar) in the east and descended in the west. But to-day the High Priest went up in the middle and descended in the middle. R. Judah said, " The High Priest ever went up in the middle and descended in the middle." Every day the High Priest sanctified his hands and his feet from the laver; but to-day from the golden basin. R. Judah said, " The High Priest ever sanctified his hands and his feet from the golden basin."

6. " Every day there were there four rows [5] of hearths; but to-day five," the words of R. Meier. Rabbi Joseph said, " every day three; but to-day four." Rabbi Judah said, " every day two; but to-day three."

CHAPTER V

1. They brought out for him the cup and the censer, and filled his hand full (of incense), and put it into the cup, the large according to his largeness,[1] and the smaller according to his smallness, and so was its measure. He took the censer in his right hand, and the spoon in his left. He proceeded in the Sanctuary until he came between the two vails dividing between the holy and the holy of holies, and intermediate was a cubit. R. Joseph said, " there was one vail only," as He said, " the vail is the division for you between the Holy and the Holy of Holies " (Exod. xxvi. 33). Outside it was looped

---

[3] A cab contained 2.8333 pints.
[4] A seah contained one peck and one pint.

[5] On the altar.
[1] The size of the priest's hands was proportionate to his stature.

up southward, inside northward. He proceeded between them till he reached the north. When he reached the north his face was turned southward. He proceeded leftward near the vail till he came to the ark. When he came to the ark, he put the censer between its two staves, he heaped the incense on the live coals, and the whole house was entirely filled with smoke. He went out, and returned by the way of his entrance, and he offered a short prayer in the outer house, and he did not prolong his prayer, lest he should excite terror [2] in Israel.

2. When the ark was removed, a stone was there from the days of the first prophets, and it was called " FOUNDATION." [3] It was three digits high above the earth, and upon it he put the censer.

3. He took the blood from the mixer.[4] With it he entered to the place where he entered, and stood in the place where he stood. He sprinkled of it once on high, and seven times below, and he did not purpose to sprinkle neither on high nor below, but unintentionally,[5] and so he counted, " one, one and one, one and two, one and three, one and four, one and five, one and six, one and seven." He went out and placed it on the golden pedestal, which was in the Sanctuary.

4. They brought to him the goat, he slaughtered it and caught his blood in a bowl. He entered to the place where he entered, and stood in the place where he stood, and sprinkled of it once on high and seven times below, and he did not purpose to sprinkle neither on high nor below, but unintentionally; [5] and so he counted, " one, one and one, one and two," etc. He went out, and placed it on the second pedestal, which was in the Sanctuary. R. Judah said " there was but one pedestal only." He took the blood of the bullock and laid down the blood of the goat, and sprinkled of it on the vail opposite the ark, on the outside, once on high, seven times below, and he did not purpose, etc., and so he counted. He took the blood of the goat and laid down the blood of the bullock, and sprinkled of it on the vail opposite the ark, on

---

[2] That he had been struck dead.

[3] Supposed by some to be the SUKH-RAH in the present Mosque of OMAR. From its position, however, it seems more probably to have been the foundation of the altar of burnt-offerings. This sacred rock is sixty feet across and five feet high. It is pierced quite through, to allow, as some think, the blood of the sacrifices to flow off into the " Noble Cave " and the canals beneath it.

[4] A priest continued to stir the blood to prevent its coagulation.

[5] Or, " as a thrasher."

the outside, once on high and seven times below, etc. He poured the blood of the bullock into the blood of the goat, and infused the full into the empty.

5. And he went out to the altar which is before the LORD. This was the golden altar. He began cleansing it, and went down. "From what place did he begin?" "From the Northeastern corner, the Northwestern, Southwestern, and Southeastern, the place where he began with the sin-offering of the outer altar, at the same place he finished upon the inner altar." R. Eliezer said, "he stood in his place and cleansed, and in general he operated from below upward, excepting that which was before him, on that he operated from above downward."

6. He sprinkled on the middle [6] of the altar seven times, and the remainder of the blood he poured out on the western foundation of the outer altar, and the blood from the outer altar he poured out on the southern foundation. This and that commingled in the channel, and flowed out to the Kidron Valley, and they were sold to the gardeners for manure, and they became guilty [7] in themselves.

7. All work of the day of atonement is described in order. If the High Priest performed one before the other, he did nothing. If the blood of tne goat be sprinkled before the blood of the bullock, he must return, and sprinkle from the blood of the goat after the blood of the bullock. And if he had not finished the performances within, the blood was spilled. He must bring other blood, and return to sprinkle first from within. And so in the Sanctuary, and so in the golden altar, because all are an atonement in themselves. R. Eleazar and R. Simon say, "from the place where he stopped there he began."

CHAPTER VI

1. Both he-goats for the day of atonement are commanded to be alike in color, and in stature, and in price, and to be selected at the same time, and although they be not equal, yet are they lawful. "If one be selected to-day and the other to-morrow?" "They are lawful." "If one of them died?"

---

[6] Or, "the clean place."
[7] I.e., the gardeners became liable for a trespass-offering.

"If he died before the lot be cast, the priest shall take a pair for the second; and if after the lot be cast he die, the priest shall fetch another pair, and cast the lot over them anew. And he shall say, " if that for the Name die, this over which this lot comes will be a substitute for the Name; and if that for Azazel die, this over which this lot comes will be a substitute for Azazel." And the second shall go to pasture, until he become blemished, and he shall be sold, and his price must be put into the offertory. Since the sin-offering of the congregation dies not. R. Judah said, " thou shalt die ";[1] and again said R. Judah, " is his blood shed?" " The one to be sent forth shall die." " Has the one to be sent forth died?" " His blood shall be shed."

2. The high priest came to the side of the goat to be sent forth, and he placed his two hands[2] on him and made confession, and thus he spake: " I beseech Thee, O Name, Thy people, the house of Israel, have done perversely, have transgressed and sinned before Thee. I beseech Thee, O Name, pardon now their perverse doings, and their transgressions, and their sins, which they have perversely committed, and transgressed, and sinned before thee. Thy people the house of Israel, as is written in the law of Moses Thy servant, saying, ' For on that day shall he make an atonement for you to cleanse you from all your sins; before the LORD ye shall be pure.'[3] And the priests and the people who stood in the court, on hearing the Name clearly pronounced by the mouth of the High Priest, knelt and worshipped, and fell on their faces and said, ' BLESSED BE THE NAME. THE HONOR OF HIS KINGDOM FOREVER AND EVER.' "

3. They delivered (the goat) to his conductor. All were eligible for conducting him. But the great priests made a rule, and they did not permit Israel to lead him forth. Said R. Joseph, " it occurred that Arsela of Zippori led him forth, and he was an Israelite."

4. And they made steps[4] for him by reason of the Babylonians,[5] who plucked off his hair and said to him, " take and go,

---

[1] R. Judah addresses in imagination the goat.
[2] It seems, according to the Talmud, that there was no " laying on of hands " on either the morning or evening sacrifice; or on any other public sacrifice, excepting the scapegoat and the bul-

lock, when the congregation had sinned through ignorance.
[3] Lev. xvi. 30.
[4] Or viaduct, or causeway.
[5] Supposed to be Alexandrine Jews, so called from hatred to the Babylonians.

take and go." The nobles of Jerusalem escorted him to the first booth. There were ten booths from Jerusalem to Zuk,[6] —ninety stadia—seven and a half to every mile.

5. At every booth they said to him, " there is food, there is water," and they escorted him from booth to booth, except the last. For they came not with him to Zuk, but stood afar off and saw his acts.

6. " What did he do?" "His conductor divided the tongue of brightness (iv. 2). Half he twisted on the rock, and half he twisted between his horns. And he thrust him backward, and the goat rolled, and descended, and he had not reached to the half of the mountain, till his members were made members.[7] He returned and sat under the last booth until darkness set in." "And when did he render garments unclean?"[8] " From his exit from the wall of Jerusalem." R. Simon said, " from the time of his thrusting at Zuk."

7. The High Priest came beside the bullock and he-goat which were to be burned. He cleft them, and brought out their entrails. He put them on a dish, and caused them to smoke upon the altar. He folded them in their skins, and caused them to be carried to the place of burning. " And when did he render garments unclean?" " From his proceeding without the wall of the court." R. Simon said, " when the fire kindled on the greatest part " (of the sacrifice).

8. They said to the High Priest, " the he-goat has arrived in the wilderness." " And whence knew they that the he-goat had arrived in the wilderness?" " They set watchmen, who waved handkerchiefs, and they knew that the he-goat had arrived in the wilderness." Said R. Judah, " and was not this a great sign to them? from Jerusalem to Bethhoron[9] there were three miles. They went a mile and returned, and rested the time of a mile, and they knew that the he-goat arrived in the desert." R. Ishmael [10] said, " and was there not another sign to them?

---

[6] Zuk is supposed by Lieutenant Conder of the Palestine Exploration Fund to be the modern el Mûntâr, about six and a half miles east of Jerusalem in the direction of the Dead Sea, and on the way to the ruins of Mird (Mons Mardes). A well near the place is still called Bir es Sûk.

[7] I.e., broken to pieces.

[8] Maimonides says that those connected with the red heifer and scapegoat were rendered unclean because these animals were " sin-bearing " animals. All that Israelites now have to offer on the day of atonement is for males a white cock (because gever in Hebrew signifies a man and a cock), and for females a hen. And they pray, " Let this be my substitute—this my atonement. This cock goeth to death, but may I be gathered and enter into a long and happy life, and into peace."

[9] " Place of the hollow."

[10] Bereitha, or External Traditions.

a tongue of brightness was twisted on the door of the Sanctuary, and when the he-goat arrived in the wilderness the tongue blanched, as is said, "Though your sins be as scarlet, they shall be white as snow." [1]

CHAPTER VII

1. The High Priest came to read. If he wished to read in linen garments, he read. If not, he read in his own white stole. The public Minister of the congregation took out the roll of the Law, and delivered it to the Chief of the congregation, and the Chief of the congregation gave it to the Sagan, and the Sagan gave it to the High Priest. And the High Priest stood and received it and read. He stood and read "after the death" [1] and "also on the tenth day." [2] And he rolled up the book of the Law, and put it into his bosom, and said, "More than what I have read before you is written here." And "on the tenth" [3] in the Pentateuch of overseers he recited, and pronounced upon it eight blessings; upon the Law, and upon the Service, and upon the confession, and upon the forgiveness of sins, and upon the Sanctuary separately, and upon Israel separately, and upon Jerusalem separately, and upon the Priests separately, and upon the remainder of the prayer.

2. He who saw the High Priest, when he read, could not see the bullock and the he-goat, when they were burning. And he who saw the bullock and the he-goat, when they were burning, could not see the High Priest, when he read. Not because it was forbidden, but because the way was far, and the work of both was proceeding at once.

3. If he read in linen garments, he sanctified his hands and his feet, he undressed, he descended and bathed. He came up, and wiped himself. They brought him golden garments, and he dressed, and he sanctified his hands and his feet, and went forth and offered the ram for himself, and the ram for the people, and seven lambs without blemish of a year old. The words of R. Eleazar. R. Akiba said, "with the morning sacrifice they were offered." And the bullock of burnt-offering and the he-goat, [4] which was prepared without, were offered with the evening sacrifice.

[1] Isaiah i. 18.   [1] Lev. xvi.   [3] Lev. xxiii. 27.
[3] Num. xxix. 7.   [4] Num. xxix. 7.

4. He purified his hands and his feet, and undressed, and washed, and he came up, and wiped himself. They brought to him white garments, and he dressed, and sanctified his hands and his feet. He entered to bring forth the spoon and the censer, he sanctified his hands and his feet, and undressed, and he descended, and washed. He came up, and wiped himself. They brought to him garments of gold, and he dressed, and sanctified his hands and his feet. And he entered to offer the evening incense, and to trim the lights; and he sanctified his hands and his feet, and he dressed. They brought to him his own garments, and he dressed. And they escorted him to his house. And he made a feast-day for his friends, when he went out in peace from the Sanctuary.

5. The High Priest ministered in eight vestments. And the ordinary priest in four, in the tunic, and drawers, and bonnet, and girdle. To these, the High Priest added the breast-plate, and ephod, and robe, and (golden) plate. In these they inquired by Urim and Thummim.[5] And they did not inquire in them for a private person; only for the King and the great Sanhedrin, and for whomsoever the congregation is necessary.

CHAPTER VIII

1. On the day of atonement, food, and drink, and washing, and anointing, and the sandal latchet,[1] and marriage duties, are restricted. "But the king and bride are allowed to wash their face, and the woman after childbirth may wear sandals." The words of R. Eleazar, but the Sages forbid them.

2. The person who eats the size of a big date and its grain, and drinks a jawful, is liable to punishment. All edible things are united for the measure of the date, and all drinkable things are united for the measure of the jawful. Eating and drinking are not united.

3. He who eats and drinks unwittingly, is only liable for one sin-offering. If he eat and work, he is liable for two sin-offerings. He who eats what is disagreeable for food, and

---

[5] Urim and Thummim (lights and perfections), the Jews think, gave answer by the divine illumination of the suitable letters composing the names of the tribes which were graven on the breast-plate of the High Priest.

[1] Sandals were, however, allowed where there was fear of serpents and scorpions. Woollen socks might be used.

drinks what is disagreeable for drinking, and he who drinks fish brine, or salt gravy, is free.

4. They do not afflict young children in the day of atonement, but they coax them one or two years before, that they may be accustomed to the commandments.

5. If the pregnant woman be affected by the odor, they give her food, till her strength return. To the sick person they give food by order from the physicians. If there be no physicians, they give him food at his own demand until he say, "it is enough."

6. Him who is affected with blindness, they fed even with unclean things, till his eyes got the power of vision. Him who is bitten by a mad dog, they fed not with the caul of his liver. But R. Mathia Ben Charash said, "it is allowed"; and again said R. Mathia Ben Charash, "to him who had throat complaint they administered medicine in his mouth on the Sabbath day, since there is uncertainty of life, and all uncertainty of life abrogates the Sabbath."

7. "On whomsoever an old ruin falls, if there be a doubt, whether one be under it or not; if there be doubt, whether he be alive or dead; if there be a doubt, whether he be a foreigner or an Israelite?" "They open over him the heap. If they find him alive, they open fully, but if dead, they leave him."

8. The sin-offering, and the offering for known transgression make atonement. Death and the day of atonement with repentance make atonement. Repentance atones for light transgressions, for commands positive and negative. But grave offences are suspended, till the day of atonement come, and it will atone.

9. He who said, "I will sin and repent—I will sin and repent?" "They did not give him the opportunity of repentance" "I will sin, and the day of atonement shall atone?" "The day of atonement makes no atonement." Transgressions between man and The Place [2] the day of atonement ex-

---

[2] I.e., God omnipresent. The Jews in a spirit of reverence use the words "Place" and the "Name" to denote God. In reading they do not now pronounce the word Jehovah, but substitute Adonai for it; and when Jehovah is followed by the word Adonai they then use the word Elohim. The true pronunciation of the Name has been a subject of much contention. It has been variously given, as Yeheveh, Yehveh, Yahveh, Yahavah, Yahaveh, and Yehovah. When it was uttered on the Day of Atonement the worshippers "fell on their faces" in reverence for it (vi. 2). It was spoken for the last time in the Temple by the mouth of Simon the Just. Henceforward, the Gemara says whoever attempts to pronounce it shall have no part in the world to come.

piates. Transgressions between man and his neighbor, the day of atonement does not expiate, until his companion be reconciled. This R. Eleazar Ben Azariah explained " From all thy sins before the LORD thou shalt be cleansed." Transgressions between man and The Place, the day of atonement expiated. Transgressions between man and his companion, the day of atonement did not expiate, until his companion be reconciled. Said R. Akiba, " Happy are ye, Israel! before whom are ye to be pure? Who will purify you? Your Father in heaven, as is said, ' I will sprinkle clean water upon you, and ye shall be clean.' " Then said the Fountain of Israel, the LORD, " As the fountain purifies the defiled, so the Holy One, blessed be He, purifies Israel."

ON TABERNACLES [1]

CHAPTER I

1. 'A booth which is above twenty cubits high is disallowed. R. Judah allows it. One which is not ten hands high, one which has not three walls, or which has more sun than shade, is disallowed. "An old booth?" "The school of Shammai disallow it; but the school of Hillel allow it." "What is an old booth?" "One that was made thirty days before the feast: but if it were made with intention for the feast, even from the beginning of the year, it is allowed."

2. "If a man make his booth beneath a tree?" "It is as though he made it in the house." "If one booth be above another?" "The upper one is allowed; but the lower one is disallowed." R. Judah says, "if they cannot inhabit the upper one, the lower one is allowed."

3. "If one spread a cloth over (its roof) [2] on account of the sun; or under (its roof) on account of the falling leaves; or if one spread a canopy over his bed?" "It is disallowed. But he may spread a cloth over two bedposts."

4. "If one have trained a vine, or a gourd, or ivy, and covered it over?" "It is disallowed. But if the covering be larger than these, or if they have been trimmed, it is allowed." The rule is, everything which contracts uncleanness, and does not grow from the ground, must not be used for a covering;

---

[1] According to Maimonides, we have in this treatise proof that it is coeval with the laws of Moses on the same subject.

[2] The cloth would change it into a tent.

but everything which does not contract uncleanness, and grows from the ground, may be used for a covering.

5. Bundles of straw, and bundles of wood, and bundles of twigs, must not be used for covering. But all of them, if untied, are allowed. And all of them are allowed for side walls.

6. " They may cover it with laths." The words of R. Judah; but R. Meier forbids it. " If one put a board four hands wide over it?" " It is allowed, provided he do not sleep under it."

7. " Rafters over which there is no ceiling?" R. Judah says, " the school of Shammai say, ' let him loosen them, and remove the middle one out of three.' But the school of Hillel say, ' he may either loosen them, or remove the middle one out of every three.' " R. Meier says, " he must remove the middle one out of every three, but he need not loosen them."

8. " If one roof in his booth with spits, or bed-boards?" " If the intermediate spaces be equal to them, it is allowed." " If one pile up loose sheaves to make a booth?" " It is no booth."

9. " If one interweave the side walls from above downwards?" " If they be three hand-breadths high from the ground, it is disallowed." " If from the ground upwards they be ten hand-breadths high?" " It is allowed." R. José says, " even as from the ground upward ten hand-breadths (are required), so likewise from the roof downward, ten hand-breadths (are required)." " If the covering be three hand breadths above the side walls?" " It is disallowed."

10. " If a house be unroofed and covered over?" " If there be a space of four cubits between the wall and the covering, it is disallowed: also a court, in which there is an enclosed passage." " If the large booth be enclosed with covering, which must not be used, and if there be below it a space of four cubits?" " It is disallowed."

11. " If one make his booth like a pyramid; or lean it against a wall?" R. Eleazar " disallows it, because it has no roof "; but the Sages " allow it." " A large reed mat, which has been made for sleeping purposes?" " It contracts uncleanness, and they must not cover with it." " If made for covering purposes?" " They may use it; and it contracts no uncleanness." R. Eleazar says, " whether large or small, if made for sleeping, it contracts uncleanness, and must not be used for covering;

but if made for covering, they may cover with it, and it contracts no uncleanness."

CHAPTER II

1. "If one sleep under a bed in the booth?" "He has not discharged his duty." R. Judah said, "we used to sleep under a bed before the elders, and they said nothing to us." R. Simon said, "it happened that Tabbi, the slave of R. Gamaliel, used to sleep under a bed, and R. Gamaliel said to the elders, 'you have seen my slave Tabbi, he is a disciple of the Sages, and knows that slaves are exempted from the booth, therefore he sleeps under a bedstead.' From this we in our way infer that he who sleeps under a bed has not discharged his duty."

2. "If a man support his booth with the posts of his bed?" "It is allowed." R. Judah says, "a booth which cannot stand by itself, is disallowed." A booth, which is unequally covered, and its shade greater than its sunlight, is allowed. If the covering be thick like a house roof, even though the stars are not seen through it, it is allowed.

3. "If one make his booth on the top of a wagon, or on a boat?" "It is allowed; and he may go up to it on the festival." "If one make it on the top of a tree, or on the back of a camel?" "It is allowed, but he must not go up to it on the festival."[1] "If two sides (be formed) by a tree, and one by the hands of man, or two by the hands of man and one by a tree?" "The booth is allowed, but he must not go up to it on the festival." "If three (sides be formed) by hands of man and the fourth by a tree?" "The booth is allowed, and he may go up to it on the festival." This is the rule—when, on the removal of the tree, it can stand by itself, the booth is allowed, and one may go up to it on the festival.

4. "If one make his booth between trees, and the trees form side walls?" "The booth is allowed." Messengers on a pious errand are exempted from the booth. The sick and their attendants are exempted from the booth. Persons may occasionally eat or drink outside the booth.

5. It happened that they brought to R. Jochanan, son of

[1] But he may go up on the middle days of the feast.

Zachai, a dish to taste, and to Rabban Gamaliel two dates and a jar of water, and they said, " bring them to the booth." But when they brought to R. Zadok food smaller than an egg, he took it in the napkin [2] and ate it outside the booth, but he did not say a blessing after it.

6. R. Eleazar says, " a man is bound to eat fourteen meals in the booth, one by day and one by night "; but the Sages say the matter is not determined, except on the first night of the festival. Moreover R. Eleazar said, " he who has not taken his meal on the first night of the festival, may complete it on the last night of the festival; but the Sages say that he must not complete it, and for this it is said, ' (That which is) crooked cannot be made straight, and that which is wanting, cannot be numbered.' " [3]

7. " If anyone's head, and the greater part of his body, be in the booth, and his table in the house?" The school of Shammai " disallow it "; but the school of Hillel " allow it." The school of Hillel said to the school of Shammai, " did it not happen that the elders of the school of Shammai, and those of the school of Hillel, went to visit R. Jochanan, son of Hachorni, and they found him sitting with his head and the greater part of his body in the booth while his table was in the house, and they said nothing to him?" The school of Shammai said to them, " Is that a proof? Even the elders did say to him, " if such has been thy custom, thou hast never in thy life fulfilled the commandment of the booth.' "

8. Women, slaves, and children, are exempted from the booth. A boy who no longer needs his mother is bound to the booth. It happened that the daughter-in-law of Shammai, the elder,[4] gave birth to a son, and Shammai removed the ceiling and covered over her bed on account of the little one.

9. During the whole seven days a man is to make the booth his regular dwelling, and (to use) his house only occasionally. " If rain fall, when is it permitted to remove from it?" " When the porridge is spoiled." The elders illustrate this by an example: " To what is the matter like?" " It is as if a servant pour out a cup for his master, who in return dashes a bowlful in his face."

[2] Lest he should render the food legally unclean with his unwashen hands. Mark vii. 2, 5.

[3] Eccles. i. 15.
[4] He lived about eighty years before the destruction of the Temple.

CHAPTER III

1. A palm branch stolen or withered is disallowed. One from an idolatrous grove, or from a city withdrawn to idolatry,[1] is disallowed. If the point be broken off, or the leaves torn off, it is disallowed. If they be only parted, it is allowed. R. Judah says, "it must be tied together at the top." Short-leaved palms from the Iron Mount[2] are allowed. A palm branch measuring three hands, sufficient to shake it by, is allowed.

2. A myrtle bough stolen, or withered, is disallowed. One from an idolatrous grove, or from a city withdrawn to idolatry, is disallowed. If the point be broken off, or the leaves torn off, or if it have more berries than leaves, it is disallowed. But if the berries be lessened it is allowed; but they must not diminish them on the festival.

3. A willow of the brook stolen, or withered. is disallowed. One from an idolatrous grove, or from a town withdrawn to idolatry, is disallowed. If the point be broken off, or the leaves torn off, or if it be a mountain willow, it is disallowed. One faded, or from which some leaves have dropped off, or which has grown on dry ground, is allowed.

4. R. Ishmael says, "three myrtle boughs, two willows, one palm branch, and one citron, even if two out of the three myrtle boughs have their points broken off." R. Tarphon says, "even if three have their points broken off." R. Akivah says, "even as there is one citron and one palm branch, so there is one myrtle bough and one willow."

5. A citron stolen or withered is disallowed. One from an idolatrous grove, or from a city withdrawn to idolatry, is disallowed. One off an uncircumcised tree[3] is disallowed. One from an unclean heave-offering[4] is disallowed. From the clean heave-offering one is not to take a citron, but if it be taken, it is allowed. "One from what is doubtful as to payment of tithe?" The school of Shammai "disallow it," but the school of Hillel "allow it." One is not to take a citron from the second tithe in Jerusalem, but if it be taken it is allowed.

---

[1] Deut. xiii. 13.
[2] Supposed to be the mountain east of the Dead Sea, above Callirrhoe.
[3] Lev. xix. 23.
[4] Num. xviii. 11, 12.

6. If a stain spread over the greater part (of the citron), if it have lost its crown, or its rind be peeled off, or if it be split, or bored, or if ever so little be wanting, it is disallowed. If a stain be spread over the smaller part of it, if it have lost its stalk, or if it be bored so that no part however small be wanting, it is allowed. A dusky citron is disallowed. A leek green one R. Meier "allows," but R. Judah "disallows it."

7. "What is the (legal) size of a small citron?" R. Meier says "like a nut." R. Judah says "like an egg." "And of a large citron?" "That one can hold two in his hand," the words of R. Judah. But R. José says, "One if (it must be held) in two hands."

8. "They must only tie the palm-branch with its own kind," the words of R. Judah. But R. Meier says, "even with twine." R. Meier said, "it happened that the men of Jerusalem tied their palm-branches with gold thread." The Sages said to him, "underneath they tied them with their own kind."

9. "When did they shake the palm-branch?" At the beginning and ending of "Oh, give thanks unto the Lord,"[5] and at "Save now, I beseech Thee, O Lord,"[6] the words of the school of Hillel. But the school of Shammai say, "also at ' O Lord, I beseech Thee,' send now prosperity."[7] R. Akivah said, "I watched Rabban Gamaliel and R. Joshua; and when all the people shook their palm-branches, they only shook theirs at ' Save now, I beseech Thee.'" If one be on the road, and have no palm-branch with him, he must, when he gets home, shake it at his table. If he have not done it in the morning, he must do it toward evening, as the whole day is allowed for the palm-branch.

10. If the hymns[8] be read to a man by a slave, or a woman, or a child,[9] he must repeat after them what they read, but it is a disgrace[10] to him. If a grown-up man read it to him, he must repeat after him, Hallelujah.

11. In a place where it is the custom to repeat,[1] a man must repeat; to simply read, a man must simply read; to bless after the palm-branch, a man must bless. In every case according to the custom of the country. If a person buy a

[5] Ps. cxviii. 1.
[6] Ps. cxviii. 25.
[7] Ps. cxviii. 25.
[8] Ps. cxiii. to cxviii. inclusive.
[9] These not being legally bound to this duty cannot act as deputies for another.
[10] His ignorance of reading.
[1] " I will praise thee," etc.—Ps. cxviii. 21 to end.

palm-branch from his neighbor during the Sabbatical year, he must give him a citron as a gift, for it is not permitted to buy a citron during the Sabbatical year.

12. At first the palm-branch was used in the Sanctuary seven days, and in the country one day. But after the Sanctuary was destroyed, R. Jochanan, the son of Zachai, decreed, "that in the country the palm-branch should be used seven days, in memory of the Sanctuary." He at the same time also decreed, "that on the day of the wave-sheaf [2] it should be unlawful to eat new grain."

13. If the first day of the feast fall on a Sabbath, all the people are to bring their palm-branches (beforehand) to the Synagogue. In the morning they come early, and each man must distinguish his own palm-branch, and take it, for the Sages say, "that a man cannot discharge his duty on the first day of the feast by means of his neighbor's palm-branch, but on the other days of the feast he may discharge his duty by means of his neighbor's palm-branch."

14. R. José says, "if the first day of the feast fall on the Sabbath, and a man forget, and carry his palm-branch out on the public common, he is absolved, because he carried it out with permission." [3]

15. A woman may receive the palm-branch from the hand of her son, or of her husband, and put it back into water on the Sabbath. R. Judah says, "on the Sabbath they may put it back; on the feast they may add water; and on the middle days they may change the water." A child who knows how to shake, is bound to shake the palm-branch.

CHAPTER IV

1. The palm-branch and the willow (were used) for six days and for seven. The hymn, and the rejoicings, for eight days. The booth and the pouring out of water for seven days; and the musical pipes for five and for six days.

2. The palm-branch (was used) for seven days. " How? " " When the first day of the feast fell on a Sabbath, the palm-branch (was used) for seven days. Otherwise all the days were six."

[2] Lev. xxiii. 10, 11.   [3] Permission arising out of his intention to fulfil the law.

3. The willow (was used) for seven days. "How?" "When the seventh day of the willow happened to fall on a Sabbath, the willow (was used) for seven days. Otherwise all the days were six."

4. "How was the command for the palm-branch when the first day of the feast fell on a Sabbath?" "They used to bring their palm-branches to the mountain of the House, and the inspectors received them, and arranged them on a bench. But the elders placed theirs in a chamber. And the people were taught to say, "Whoever takes my palm-branch in his hand, be it his as a gift." On the morrow they came early, and the inspectors spread them before them. And they used to snatch them and hurt each other. When the Sanhedrin saw that persons were endangered, it was decreed that every man should take them home."

5. "How was the command for the willow?" "There was a place below Jerusalem called Moza;[1] thither the people went down and gathered drooping willow-branches. And they came and erected them at the side of the altar, with their tops bending over the altar. They blew the trumpet, and sounded an alarm, and blew a blast. Every day they made one circuit round the altar, and said, "Save now, I beseech Thee, O Lord! O Lord, I beseech Thee, send now prosperity." Rabbi Judah said, "I and HE save now, I beseech thee."[2] On the day itself[3] they made seven circuits round the altar. "As they withdrew what did they say?" "Beauty is thine, O Altar!" "Beauty is thine, O Altar!" R. Eleazar said, "To the LORD and to thee, O Altar!" "To the LORD, and to thee, O Altar!"

6. As they did on the week-days, so they did on the Sabbath, save that they gathered the willow-boughs on the Sabbath-eve, and put them into vases of gold, that they might not fade. R. Joshua, son of Beroka, says, "they brought date-branches, and thrashed them on the ground at the sides of the altar" (others say "on the altar"). And the day itself was called "the day for thrashing the branches."

7. Immediately the children threw down their palm-branches, and ate their citrons.

---

[1] Means a place exempt from taxation called Colonin, perhaps the modern Colonia. Some, however, say it was a place in the Kedron Valley.

[2] Deut. xxxii. 39.
[3] The seventh day on which they used the willows.

8. The hymn and rejoicings were for eight days. " How? "
" It is taught, that a man is bound to the hymn, and the rejoicings in honor of the last day of the feast, even as on its
other days." " How is the booth for seven days? " " When
a man has completed his eating, he is not to pull down his
booth; but after the evening sacrifice he may remove his furniture in honor of the last day of the feast."

9. " How was the pouring out of the water? " " A golden
pitcher holding three logs [4] was filled from Siloam. When
they came (with it) to the water-gate they blew the trumpet,
an alarm, and a blast. The priest then went up the ascent to
the altar, and turned to his left. Two silver basins were there.
R. Judah says, " they were of lime, but their look was dark
from the wine." And they were bored with two narrow nostrils, one wider, the other narrower, that both might get empty
at once. " The one to the west was for the water; the other
to the east was for the wine; but if the water was poured into
the wine basin, or the wine into the water basin, it was allowed."
R. Judah said, " they poured out one log on each of the eight
days." To him, who poured out, they said, " lift your hand ":
for once it happened, that one poured over his feet,[5] and all
the people pelted him to death with their citrons.

10. As they did on the week-days, so they did on the Sabbath; save that on the Sabbath eve an unconsecrated golden
cask was filled from Siloam, and placed in a chamber. If it
were spilt or uncovered, it was refilled from the laver, as water
and wine which had been uncovered were disallowed on the
altar.

CHAPTER V

1. The musical pipes were (played) for five and (sometimes)
six days. That is to say, the pipes of the water-drawing,
which supersedes neither the Sabbath day nor the feast. The
(Sages) said, " he who has not seen the joy [1] of the water-
drawing, has never seen joy in his life."

2. With the departure of the first day of the feast, they went

---

[4] A log is about half a pint.
[5] He is said to have been a Sadducee
who rejected tradition. Alexander Jan-
næus, to show his contempt for the
Pharisees, poured the water on the
ground. The people became excited,
and pelted him with their ethrogs or
citrons till his body-guard interfered,
and, as fighting took place, some six
thousand Jews were killed in the Temple. Josephus, " Antiq.," book xiii.
chap. xiii. 5.
[1] Isa. xii. 3; John vii. 37, 38.

down into the women's court, and made great preparations.[2]
Four golden candlesticks were there, and four golden basins
on their tops, and four ladders to each candlestick, and four
lads from the young priests, and in their hands were jars of
oil containing 120 logs, with which they replenished each basin.

3. The cast-off breeches and belts of the priests were torn to
wicks, which they lighted. And there was not a court in Jerusalem that was not lit up by the lights of the water-drawing.

4. Pious and experienced men danced with lighted torches
in their hands, singing hymns and lauds before them. And
the Levites accompanied them with harps, psalteries, cymbals,
trumpets, and numberless musical instruments. On the fifteen
steps which went down from the court of Israel into the
women's court, corresponding with the fifteen songs of degrees,[3] stood the Levites with their musical instruments, and
sang. And at the upper gate, which went down from the
court of Israel to the court of the women, stood two priests
with trumpets in their hands. When the cock crew, they blew
a blast, an alarm, and a blast.[4] When they reached the tenth
step, they blew a blast, an alarm, and a blast. And when they
got into the court, they blew a blast, an alarm, and a blast.
They went on blowing as they went, until they reached the
gate, that leads out to the east. When they reached the gate,
that leads out to the east, they turned their faces westward,[5]
and said,

> " Our fathers, who were in this place,
> Turned their backs upon the Temple;
> And their faces toward the east,
> And worshipped the sun eastward."[6]

R. Judah says, they repeated again and again,

> " But we unto the LORD;
> To the LORD are our eyes."[7]

5. In the sanctuary they did not blow the trumpet less than
twenty-one times, nor oftener than forty-eight times. Every

---

[2] Galleries were erected for the wom-
en, and the men stood below them.
[3] Ps. cxx. to cxxxiv. inclusive.
[4] The signal for drawing water.
[5] The orthodox worshippers in the
Temple looked toward the west, or
Holy of Holies. The Baal or Sun worship ers turned toward the east, and
used the eastward position. Under the

Christian dispensation believers are directed to look to Jesus, who promises
to be in their midst (Matt. xviii. 20).
[6] Ezek. viii. 16.
[7] This is one of the very few speci-
mens of Hebrew poetry, apart from
Scripture (dating prior to the destruction of the temple), which have come
down to us.

day they blew the trumpet twenty-one times, thrice at opening he gates, nine times at the daily offering of the morning,
and nine times at the daily offering of the evening. When
there were additional offerings they blew nine times more.
On the eve of the Sabbath they again blew six times; thrice
to interdict the people from work, and thrice to separate the
holy from the ordinary day. But on the eve of the Sabbath
during the feast they blew forty-eight times: thrice at the
opening of the gates, thrice at the upper gate, thrice at the
lower gate, thrice at the water-drawing, thrice over the altar,
nine times at the daily offering of the morning, nine times
at the daily offering of the evening, nine times at the additional
offerings, thrice to interdict the people from work, and thrice
to separate the holy from the ordinary day.

6. On the first day of the feast there were thirteen bullocks,
two rams, and one goat. There then remained fourteen lambs
for eight courses of priests.[8] On the first day six courses
offered two lambs each, and the other (two) courses one lamb
each. On the second day five courses offered two lambs each,
and the remaining (four) courses one lamb each. On the
third day four courses offered two lambs each, and the remaining six one lamb each. On the fourth day three courses
offered two lambs each, and the remaining eight one lamb
each. On the fifth day two courses offered two lambs each,
and the remaining ten one lamb each. On the sixth day one
course offered two lambs, and the remaining twelve one lamb
each. On the seventh day they were all equal. On the eighth
day they cast lots, as on other feasts. They said, "that the
order which offered bullocks to-day, was not permitted to offer
bullocks to-morrow." But they changed in rotation.

7. Three times in the year all the courses shared alike in
the offerings of the great feasts, and in the distribution of the
showbread. In the Solemn Assembly [9] they say to each priest,
"Here is unleavened bread for thee, and here is leavened
for thee." The course in regular succession offered the daily
sacrifices, vows, and free-will offerings, and all the other sacrifices and services of the congregation. If a feast be next to

---

[8] The priesthood was divided into
twenty-four courses (1 Chron. xxiv. 7-
19). During the feast all the courses
ministered, and, as each day the number
of bullocks was decreased by one, the
lambs were redistributed so as to supply
an offering for every course.
[9] In the feast of weeks there were two
leavened wave loaves (Lev. xxiii. 17).

the Sabbath, either before or after it, all the courses shared alike in the distribution of the showbread.

8. "But if a day intervene between the two?" "The course in regular succession took ten loaves, and the loiterers [10] took two." At other times of the year, the course entering on duty took six loaves, and the course going off duty took six. R. Judah says, " the course entering took seven, and that going off took five." Those entering shared them on the north side (of the temple court), and those going out on the south side. The course Bilgah always shared theirs on the south side. But their slaughter-ring was fastened down, and the window of their closet was shut up.[1]

[10] Those priests who were slow in attendance, as they were obliged to share their perquisites with the whole priesthood.

[1] The course Bilgah was fifteenth (1 Chron. xxiv. 14). Each course had a ring to which the heads of the victims were tied, and also a closet for stores. These were taken from the course Bilgah as a mark of disgrace. During the persecution of Antiochus, Miriam, a daughter of Bilgah, married a Syro-Grecian husband. When the Greeks took the Temple, she struck the altar with her shoe, exclaiming, " O wolf, wolf, how long art thou to consume the wealth of Israel, and canst not preserve them in their hour of need! " It was supposed that she must have learned something evil in her father's house, and the whole course was therefore degraded. The Rabbis say that the courses of the priests were first ordained by Moses, and that he established eight of them. Four courses he assigned to the line of Eleazar, and four he assigned to the line of Ithamar. Samuel is said to have added eight courses more, and the remaining eight were added by David. The Scriptures, however, assert that David arranged the whole twenty-four courses. This arrangement continued till the captivity. After the captivity only four courses returned—namely Jedaiah, Harim, Pashur, and Immer. The Babylon Talmud mentions Jojarib instead of Harim. To restore again the number of courses, twenty-four lots were cast into a box, and each head of the four courses, which returned, drew six lots—one for himself, and five for the courses which they wished to revive. The restored order of courses continued as of old, except in the case of Jojarib, who yielded the first rank to Jedaiah, as Jedaiah was of the family of the High-priest Joshua, the son of Jozedek. They soon increased in numbers, and we read that each course kept a station of 2,400 priests at Jerusalem, and half a station at Jericho. The lesser number was stationed at Jericho to give honor to Jerusalem.

THE NEW YEAR

Four New Years—Judgments—New Moon—Witnesses—Evidence
Samaritans—Spreading the News—Beth Yangzek—Examining Wit-
nesses—Rabban Gamaliel's Plan of the Phases of the Moon—Rabbi
Joshua—Sanhedrin—Cornets and Trumpets—Intention—The Ser-
pent of Brass—Jerusalem and Jamnia—Blessings—Texts of Scripture
—How the Trumpets are to be Blown.

CHAPTER I

1. There are four new years. The first of Nisan[1] is a new
year for kings and for festivals.[2] The first of Elul[3] is a new
year for the tithing of cattle; but R. Eleazar and R. Simeon
say, " it is on the first of Tishri "[4] The first of Tishri is a
new year for civil years, for years of release, and for jubilees,
also for planting of trees[5] and herbs. The first of Sebat[6] is
a new year for (the tithing of) trees according to the school of
Shammai, but the school of Hillel say, " on its fifteenth."

2. The world is judged at four periods: at the passover,
for the growth of corn; at Pentecost, for the fruit of trees; at
new year's day, when all human beings pass before Him like
lambs, as is said, " He fashioneth their hearts alike; He con-
sidereth all their works ";[7] and at the feast of tabernacles,
judgment is given for the rains.

3. Messengers went forth (from Jerusalem) in six months:
in Nisan for the passover; in Ab[8] for the fast; in Elul for the
new year; in Tishri for the regulation of the feasts; in Kislev[9]
for the dedication; in Adar[10] for the feast of lots; and also in
Iyar[1] during the existence of the Temple for the little passover.

---

[1] Nisan answered to part of March
and April. The reign of kings was
counted from this month, so that if a
king began to reign in Adar (February
and March), in the following Nisan he
would be reckoned to have reigned two
years.
[2] The passover was the first of the
three feasts, beyond which one could
not neglect a vow.

[3] Part of August and September.
[4] Part of September and October.
[5] Lev. xix. 23-25.
[6] Part of January and February.
[7] Ps. xxxiii. 15.
[8] Part of July and August.
[9] Part of November and December.
[10] Part of February and March.
[1] Part of April and May.

4. For two months[2] they may profane the Sabbath, for Nisan and for Tishri, because in them the messengers went forth to Syria, and in them they regulated the feasts. And during the existence of the Temple they might profane it in all the months for the regulation of the offerings.

5. If the moon[3] appeared high and clear, or did not appear high and clear, the witnesses may profane the Sabbath on account of it. R. José says, "if it appeared high and clear, they may not profane the Sabbath on account of it."

6. It happened that more than forty pairs of witnesses were passing through, when R. Akivah detained them in Lydda. Rabban Gamaliel sent to him, "if thou thus detainest the people, it will be a stumbling-block in the future."

7. When father and son have seen the new moon, they must go (before the Sanhedrin), not that they may be combined together, but in order that, should the evidence of either of them be disallowed, the other may be combined with another witness. R. Simeon says, "father, and son, and relatives in every degree, may be allowed as competent witnesses for the new moon." R. José says, "it happened that Tobias, the physician, his son, and his freed slave, saw the new moon in Jerusalem, and the priests accepted his evidence, and that of his son, but disallowed his slave; but when they came before the Sanhedrin, they accepted him and his slave, but disallowed his son."

8. These witnesses are disallowed—gamblers with dice, usurers,[4] pigeon-breeders,[5] traders in produce of the Sabbatical year, and slaves. This is the rule: all evidence that cannot be received from a woman cannot be received from any of these.

9. "He who has seen the new moon but cannot walk?" "They must bring him on an ass or even in a bed." Those afraid of being waylaid may take sticks in their hands, and if they have a long way to go, they may take provisions. If

---

[2] That is, for the new moon observances.

[3] The Talmud states that when the sun and moon were first created they were of equal size. The moon became jealous of the sun and she was reduced in bulk. The moon then appealed to God, and she was consoled by the promise that Jacob, Samuel, and David were to be likewise small. As, however, some injustice seemed to have been committed, God ordained "a sin-offering" on every new moon, because the moon had become less than the sun!

[4] The Sanhedrin treated gamblers and usurers as thieves.

[5] Those who bred pigeons, to bet on their quickness of flight, or to entice their neighbors' pigeons to their dovecotes.

they must be a day and a night on the road, they may profane the Sabbath in travelling to testify for the new moon; as is said, " These are the feasts of the LORD, which ye shall proclaim in their seasons." [6]

CHAPTER II

1. If a witness were unknown, another was sent to testify to him. At first they received evidence of the new moon from anyone; but when the heretics [1] bribed (the witnesses), they ordained that evidence should only be received from those who were known.

2. At first high flames were lighted, but when the Samaritans mimicked them, it was ordained that messengers should be sent forth.

3. " How were these high flames lighted?" " They brought long staves of cedarwood, canes, and branches of the olive tree, and the tow of flax, which was tied with twine. And one went to the top of the mountain and lighted them, and waved the flame to and fro, up and down, till he could perceive his companion doing so on the second mountain, and so on the third mountain," etc.

4. " And where were these high flames lighted?" " From the Mount of Olives to Sartaba; from Sartaba to Grophinah; from Grophinah to Hoveran; from Hoveran to Bethbaltin; there they did not cease to wave them to and fro, up and down, till the whole country of the captivity [2] looked like torches of fire."

5. There was a large court in Jerusalem called Beth Yangzek,[3] there all the witnesses met, and there the Sanhedrin examined them. And they made great feasts for them, that they might come often. At first they did not stir from thence all day.[4] Rabban Gamaliel the elder ordained, that they might go 2,000 cubits on every side. And not only they, but the midwife going to a birth; and they who go to rescue from fire, or from enemies, or from inundation, or from fallen

[6] Lev. xxiii. 4.
[1] Literally, Bithosin, the followers of Biothos, who, with Zadok, the founder of the Sadducees, was a scholar of Antigonus of Socho.
[2] Babylon.

[3] So called in the Mishna. It means " the place fenced in." The Gemara reads, Beth Yazak, " the place of chains."
[4] I.e., the Sabbath, when they could only go four cubits.

buildings. These are as inhabitants of the place, and they have 2,000 cubits on every side.

6. " How did they examine the witnesses? " " The first pair which came were examined first, and they brought in the eldest of them, and they said to him, ' Tell us how you saw the moon—(her horns) toward the sun, or away from the sun? To the north, or to the south? What was her altitude? Toward where her declination? And what was her breath? ' If he said ' toward the sun,' he said nothing. Afterward they brought in the second and examined; if the evidence was found to agree, the evidence stood. The remaining pairs of witnesses were then superficially examined, not because there was necessity for their evidence, but not to discourage them, that they might be willing to come again."

7. The chief of the Sanhedrin said, ("the feast) is sanctified"; and all the people answered after him, "Sanctified, sanctified." Whether the new moon had been seen in its season, or not, they sanctified it. R. Eleazar, son of Zadok, said, "if it were not seen in its season, they did not sanctify it, for heaven had already sanctified it."

8. Rabban Gamaliel had on a tablet and on the wall of his chamber figures and phases of the moon which he showed to ignorant witnesses, and said, "was it like this you saw her, or like that?" It happened once that two witnesses came, and said, "we saw the moon in the morning in the east, and in the evening in the west"; said R. Johanan, son of Nourrie, "they are false witnesses," but when they came to Jamnia, Rabban Gamaliel received their evidence. Two other witnesses came, and said, "we saw the moon in her season, but on the next evening of the intercalary day she was invisible," and R. Gamaliel received them. Said R. Dosah, son of Arkenaz, "they are false witnesses, for how can they testify of a woman being delivered, and on the morrow she is still pregnant?" To him said R. Joshua, "I approve thy words."

9. Rabban Gamaliel sent to (R. Joshua), "I order thee to come to me with thy staff and money on the day of atonement, according to thy reckoning." [5] R. Akivah went to (R. Joshua), and found him sorrowing. He said to him, "I can

---

[5] To carry money on the day of atonement was unlawful, but according to R. Joshua's reckoning it would have been a day too late.

prove that all Rabban Gamaliel has done is well done, for it is said, ' These are the feasts of the Lord, even holy convocations, which ye shall proclaim in their seasons,' [6] or out of their seasons; I have no other feasts but these." R. Joshua came to R. Dose, son of Arkenaz. He said to him, " if we are to judge the tribunal of Rabban Gamaliel, we must also judge the tribunals which have existed from the days of Moses till now," for it is said, " Then went up Moses and Aaron, Nadab and Abihu, and seventy of the elders of Israel." [7] " And why were not the names of the elders mentioned, but to inform us that every three men in Israel who compose a tribunal, are as a tribunal of Moses?" R. Joshua took his staff and money in his hand, and went to Jamnia to Rabban Gamaliel on the day when the atonement began, according to his reckoning. Rabban Gamaliel stood up and kissed him on his head, saying to him, " come in peace, my master and disciple—my master in wisdom, my disciple in obeying my words."

CHAPTER III

1. " The Sanhedrin and all Israel saw (the new moon); the witnesses were examined, but it became dark before they could say, ' Sanctified '?" " The mouth is intercalary. " The Sanhedrin alone saw it?" " Two members must stand up and testify before them, and they shall say, ' Sanctified, sanctified." " Three composing a Sanhedrin saw it?" " Two of them must stand up, and their assessors must be seated with the single member, and before them they shall testify, and say, ' Sanctified, sanctified,' because an individual cannot be trusted by himself alone."

2. All cornets are allowed, except (horns) of a heifer,[1] because it is (written) horn.[2] Said Rabbi José, "are not all cornets called horn? for it is said, ' When they shall make a long (blast) with the ram's horn.' " [3]

3. The cornet of the New Year was a straight horn of a wild goat; and its mouthpiece was plated with gold. And the two trumpets [4] were stationed on each side. The cornet pro-

[6] Lev. xxiii. 4.
[7] Exod. xxiv. 9.
[1] Not to remind God of the sin of the golden calf.
[2] Deut. xxxiii. 17.
[3] Josh. vi. 5.
[4] Num. x.

longed its note when the trumpets ceased, because the obligation of the day was for the cornet.

4. On fast days (there were) crooked rams' horns; and their mouthpieces were plated with silver. And the two trumpets were stationed in the midst. The cornet ceased, and the trumpets prolonged their notes, because the obligation of the day was for the trumpets.

5. The jubilee is like the New Year for the sounding and the blessings. R. Judah says, "on the New Year they sounded rams' horns; and on the jubilee wild goats' horns."

6. A cornet, which was rent and cemented, is disallowed. One cemented from fragments of cornets is disallowed. "It had a hole, which was closed?" "If it hinder the sound, it is disallowed; but if not, it is allowed."

7. "If one sound the cornet within a pit, a cistern, or in an earthenware vessel, and one (outside) hears the sound of the cornet?" "He is free." [5] "But if he hear the echo of the sound?" "He is not free." And so, if one be passing behind a synagogue, or his house adjoin the synagogue, and he hear the sound of the cornet, or the reading of the roll of Esther, he is legally free, provided he heard it with due attention; but if not, he is not legally free. Although one hears as well as another, yet one hears with hearty intention, and another without hearty intention.

8. "And it came to pass, when Moses held up his hand that Israel prevailed," [6] etc. And how could the hands of Moses make the battle, or crush the battle? But it is written to tell thee that while Israel looked to Heaven for aid, and subjected their hearts to their heavenly Father, they prevailed; and when they did not do so, they were defeated. Like as He says, "Make thee a fiery serpent, and set it upon a pole, and it shall come to pass that everyone that is bitten, when he looketh upon it, shall live." [7] And how could the serpent kill, or make alive? But when the Israelites looked to Heaven for aid, and subjected their hearts to their heavenly Father, they were healed; and when they did not do so, they perished. One deaf and dumb, or an idiot, or a child, cannot, as proxies, free others from their obligations. This is the

---

[5] From the obligation of hearing or sounding.

[6] Exod. xvii. 11.

[7] Num. xxi. 8.

rule: all who are not responsible for a thing, cannot free others from their obligations.

CHAPTER IV

1. When the feast of New Year happened on the Sabbath, they used to sound the cornet in the Sanctuary; but not in the provinces. After the destruction of the Sanctuary, R. Jochanan, son of Zacai, decreed that they should sound it in every place in which there is a tribunal of justice. R. Eleazar says, " R. Jochanan, son of Zacai, decreed it only for Jamnia." But the Sages said to him, " it was all one for Jamnia, and all one for every place in which there is a tribunal of justice."

2. And again,[1] Jerusalem was privileged above Jamnia, because every city which could be seen, and the sounding heard, and which was near, and to which it was allowed to go, might sound the cornet; but in Jamnia they could only sound it before the tribunal of justice.

3. At first the palm-branch was taken seven days in the Sanctuary, and one day in the provinces. After the destruction of the Temple, R. Jochanan, son of Zacai, decreed, " that the palm-branch should be taken in the provinces for seven days, to commemorate the Sanctuary "; also " that the whole day of the waving[2] it should be forbidden (to eat new corn)."

4. At first they received evidence of the new moon during the whole (thirtieth) day; but once the witnesses delayed coming, and the Levites erred in the chant. They decreed, that they should receive evidence only till the time of the evening sacrifice; and if witnesses came after the evening sacrifice, that and the next day were kept holy. After the destruction of the Sanctuary Rabban Jochanan, son of Zacai, decreed, " that they should receive evidence of the new moon during the whole day." R. Joshua, son of Korcha, says, " and again Rabban Jochanan, son of Zacai, decreed that wherever the chief of the Sanhedrin might be, the witnesses need only go to the place of its meeting."

[1] There is a supposed hiatus in the Mishna text to the following effect: " In Jerusalem they sounded through the whole city during the session of the Sanhedrin (i.e., till noon); but in Jamnia they did not sound in the city, but only before the tribunal of justice. And again," etc.

[2] I.e., of the sheaf of the first-fruits. Lev. xxiii. 10.

5. The order of blessings to be said on the New Year is, " The Fathers," [3] and " The Mighty," and " Sanctification of the Name," and there are comprehended the " Kingdoms " without blowing the trumpet; " The Holiness of the Day," and he blows; " The Remembrances," and he blows; " The Trumpets," and he blows. And he says, " The Service," " The Confession," and " Blessing of the Priests." The words of R. Jochanan, son of Nourri. Said R. Akivah to him, " if the trumpet be not blown after ' The Kingdoms,' why are they mentioned? " But the order is, " The Fathers," and " The Mighty," and " Sanctification of the Name," and there are comprehended " The Kingdoms," with sanctification of the Day," and he blows; " The Remembrances," and he blows; " The Trumpets," and he blows. And he says, " The Service," " The Confession," and " Blessing of the Priests."

6. They cannot read less than ten (texts of Scripture) relating to " The Kingdom," ten relating to " Remembrances," and ten to " Trumpets." [4] R. Jochanan, son of Nourri, says, " if three be read from all of them, the duty is fulfilled, but they mention not the remembrance of the kingdom, and trumpet of vengeance.[5] They must begin with the Law and end with the Prophets." R. José says, " if they end with the Law, the duty is fulfilled."

7. (The minister of the congregation) must go over to the reading-desk on the feast of the New Year. The second minister must blow the trumpet. But at the hour for the hymn the first must read the hymn.

8. For sounding the trumpet of the New Year they may not transgress the Sabbatical limit, they may not remove for it a heap of stones, they may not climb a tree, and they may not ride a beast, or swim over water. Nor may they cut it [6] with anything that violates the Sabbatical rest, or violates a negative command. But if one wish he may pour into it water or wine.[7] They may not prevent children from blowing, but they may practise in teaching them. But he who practises

---

[3] The titles or the headings of the blessings which were used in the services of the Temple and of the synagogues out of Jerusalem.
[4] Three were read from the Law, three from the Psalms, and three from the Prophets—such passages as Exod. xv.

18, Ps. xxiv., Ezek. xx. 33, Zech. xiv. 9, etc.
[5] I.e., they would not read such passages as Ps. lxxviii. 39.
[6] I.e., to improve its tone.
[7] To clear its tone.

blowing is not freed from his obligation, and he who listens to the practice is not freed from his obligation.

9. The order of blowing the trumpet is, three blasts blown thrice. The measure of the blast is as six alarms. The measure of the alarm is as three shrieks. If one blew the first and prolonged the blast for the second to be as two, it reckons but as one. He who has said the blessings, and afterward a trumpet is given to him, must blow a blast, an alarm, and a blast three times. As the minister of the congregation is bound, so is each individual bound. R. Gamaliel says, " the minister of the congregation releases the public from their obligations."

ON FASTING

When Rain is to be Prayed for—Proclamations for Fasting—Ceremonial of Fasting—Prayers—Blowing of Trumpets—R. Gamaliel and R. Meier—Sign of Famine—Partial Rain—Pestilence—Story of Hone Hammeagal—Lifting Up of Hands—Deputies—Bringing Wood—Five Things Happened in Tammuz and Five in Ab—Mortifications—Rejoicings.

CHAPTER I

1. "When do we remember in prayer the heavy rain?" Rabbi Eleazar said, "from the first holiday of the feast (of tabernacles)," Rabbi Joshua said, "from the last holiday of the feast." To him said Rabbi Joshua, "when the rain is no mark of blessing in the feast, why should one remember it?" Said Rabbi Eleazar to him, "even I did not say to ask for it, but to remember the blowing of the wind, and the descent of the rain in its season." He replied to him, "if so, one can remember it always."

2. We ask for rain only near to the season of rains. Rabbi Judah said,[1] "he who passes last before the ark on the last holiday of the feast of tabernacles remembers it; the first does not remember it. On the first holiday of the passover the first remembers it, the last does not remember it." How long do we ask for rain? Rabbi Judah said, "till the passover be ended." Rabbi Meier said, "till Nisan depart,[2] as is said,[3] 'And He will cause to come down for you the rain, the former rain, and the latter rain in the first month.'"

3. On the third day of Marchesvan[4] we ask for the rain. Rabban Gamaliel said, "on the seventh, fifteen days after the feast, that the last Israelite returning home from the feast may reach the river Euphrates."

4. "If the seventeenth day of Marchesvan arrive, and the

[1] I.e., the Chazan that prays Musaph.
[2] Nisan corresponded partly to March and April.
[3] Joel ii. 23.
[4] Marchesvan corresponded partly to October and November.

rain does not come down?" "Men of eminence begin to fast for three days. They may eat and drink by night. And they may work, and wash, and anoint themselves, and put on their sandals, and use their couches."

5. "If the first day of the month Chislev [5] arrive, and the rain does not come down?" "The tribunal proclaims three fast-days [6] for the congregation. Persons may, however, eat and drink by night. And they may work, and wash, and anoint themselves, and put on their sandals, and use their couches."

6. "If these days pass over, and there be no answer?" The tribunal proclaims three other fast-days for the congregation. Persons may, however, eat and drink while it is still day. But they are forbidden work, and washing, and anointing, and putting on sandals, and the use of the couch. And the baths are locked up." "If these days pass over, and there be no answer?" "The tribunal proclaims for them seven more; these are altogether thirteen fast-days for the congregation." "And what are these fast-days more than the first six?" "Because during them men blow with the trumpets and lock up their shops." On Monday they can half open them at dark. But on Thursday they may open them for honor to the approaching Sabbath.

7. "If these days pass over, and there be no answer?" "People diminish business, building, planting, betrothals and marriages, and salutations of peace between man and his friend, as children of men ashamed before OMNIPRES-ENCE." The men of eminence have again recourse to fasting, till Nisan be ended. If Nisan be ended, and the rain comes down, it is a mark of cursing, as is said,[7] "Is it not wheat harvest to-day?" etc.

CHAPTER II

1. "What is the order of the fast-days?" "Men draw out the ark containing the rolls of the Law to the public street of the city, and they put burnt ashes on the top of the ark, and on the head of the prince, and on the head of the president

---

[5] Part of November and part of December.

[6] The fast-days of strict Pharisees were Mondays and Thursdays, because on a Thursday Moses went up to Mount Sinai, and returned on a Monday with the second Tables of the Law.

[7] I Sam. xii. 17.

of the tribunal, and everyone takes and puts ashes on his own head." The most aged of them says before them touching words, " Brethren, it is not said for the men of Nineveh, ' And God saw their sackcloth and their fasting,'[1] but ' God saw their works, that they returned from their evil way.' And in the tradition (of the prophet) he says,[2] ' Rend your hearts and not your garments, and turn unto the Lord your God.' "

2. When they stood in prayer, they placed before the ark an aged man and full of experience, one who had children and an unblemished house, that his heart be not distracted in prayer, and he says before them twenty-four blessings, the usual eighteen for every day, and he adds to them six more.

3. These are they, " remembrances,"[3] and " blowing of the trumpets,"[3] " In my distress I cried unto the Lord, and He heard me,"[4] " I will lift up my eyes unto the hills,"[5] " out of the depths have I cried unto Thee, O Lord,"[6] " A prayer of the afflicted when he is overwhelmed."[7] Rabbi Judah says, " it was not necessary to say the ' remembrances,' and ' the trumpets,' but he said instead of them, ' If there be in the land famine, if there be pestilence,' "[8] etc. " The word of the Lord that came to Jeremiah concerning the dearth."[9] And he said their closing benediction.

4. For the first additional prayer he said, " He who answered Abraham our father on Mount Moriah, He shall answer you, and hear the voice of your cry this day. Blessed be Thou, Lord, the Redeemer of Israel." For the second he said, " He who answered our fathers by the Red Sea, He will answer you, and hear the voice of your cry this day. Blessed be Thou, Lord, who rememberest those forgotten by man." For the third he said, " He who answered Joshua in Gilgal, He will answer you, and hear the voice of your cry this day. Blessed be Thou, Lord, who hearest the blowing of the trumpet." For the fourth he said, " He who answered Samuel in Mizpah, He will answer you, and hear the voice of your cry this day. Blessed be Thou, Lord, who hearest the cry of distress." For the fifth he said, " He who answered Elijah on

[1] Jonah iii. 10.
[2] Joel ii. 13.
[3] Prayers for the New Year.
[4] Ps. cxx
[5] Ps. cxxi. i.
[6] Ps. cxxx.
[7] Ps. cii.
[8] 1 Kings viii. 37.
[9] Jer. xiv. i.

Mount Carmel, He will answer you, and hear the voice of your cry this day. Blessed be Thou, Lord, who hearest prayer." For the sixth he said, "He who answered Jonah from the fish's belly, He will answer you, and hear the voice of your cry this day. Blessed be Thou, Lord, who art ever answering prayer in the time of need." For the seventh he said, "He who answered David and Solomon his son in Jerusalem, He will answer you, and will hear the voice of your cry this day. Blessed be Thou, Lord, who hast pity on the earth."

5. It happened in the days of Rabbi Chelpatha and R. Chauania, son of Teradion, that a minister passed before the ark, and finished the whole blessing, and the congregation did not answer after him, Amen. One cried out, "Let the priests blow the trumpets"; they blew. (The minister prayed,) "May He who answered Abraham our Father on Mount Moriah answer you, and hear the voice of your cry this day." (One cried out,) "Let the sons of Aaron blow an alarm"; they blew an alarm. (The minister prayed,) "May He who answered our fathers by the Red Sea, answer you, and hear the voice of your cry this day." And when the matter came before the Sages they said it was not customary to do so, save in the Eastern gate and on the Mountain of the House.

6. These are the first three fasts. The priests of the weekly Watch of the Temple fasted, but not completely. And the priests of their "Father's House"[10] did not fast at all. In the second three fasts the men of the Watch fasted completely. And the men of their "Father's House" fasted, but not completely. "In the seven last fasts both of them fasted completely." The words of Rabbi Joshua. But the Sages say, "in the three first fasts neither one nor other fasted at all. In the second three fasts the priests of the Watch fasted, but not completely. And the priests of their 'Father's House' did not fast at all. In the seven last fasts the priests of the Watch fasted completely, and the priests of their 'Father's House' fasted, but not completely."

---

[10] Some understand the priests ministering in their course, others explain this expression by Deut. xviii. 8. The priests were divided into twenty-four Watches. Each Watch ministered for a week in the Temple. These Watches were again subdivided into seven "Father's Houses," and each "Father's House" officiated for a day in the Temple. A dispensation from fasting was granted to the priests on duty, that they might not be weak in the service of the Sanctuary.

7. The men of the Watch are allowed to drink wine by night, but not by day, and the men who inherit the patrimony of their fathers [1] may not drink it neither by day nor night. The men of the Watch and the Delegates [2] are not allowed to shave, nor wash, except on Thursdays for the honor of the approaching Sabbath.

8. That which is written in "The Roll of Fasting," [3] "not to mourn" on certain days—the day before them it is not allowed—the day after them it is allowed to mourn. Rabbi José said, "both before and after the day it is not allowed." But when it is written, "not to fast," both the day before and the day after the fast, it is allowed to fast. Rabbi José said, "before the fast it is not allowed—after the fast it is allowed."

9. The rulers must not proclaim fasts for the congregation to begin on Thursday, so as not to raise the market. But the three first fasts are Monday, Thursday, and Monday. And the three second, Thursday, Monday, and Thursday. Rabbi José said, "as the first fasts are not to begin on Thursday, so likewise the second and the last are not to begin on that day."

10. "The rulers must not proclaim fasting for the congregation on the feast of New Moon, and on the feasts of Dedication, and Purim; but if they have already begun, they need not cease." The words of Rabbi Gamaliel. Said R. Meier, "even though Rabbi Gamaliel said they need not cease, he admits that the congregation do not fast the whole day; and so also on the ninth of Ab, the fast for the burning of the Temple, if it happen on the eve of the Sabbath."

CHAPTER III

1. The order of these fasts is said only for the first rains. But if the sprouts wither, men blow an alarm off-hand. And if the rains cease between rain and rain forty days, men blow an alarm off-hand. Because it is a sign of famine.

2. If the rains came down for the sprouts, but did not come down for the trees, for the trees, but not for the sprouts, for

[1] This means the officiating priests.
[2] The delegates were the representatives of the congregation, who attended at the public sacrifices, and prayed on their behalf.
[3] This was a book written in Chaldee, as is proved by the quotations from it.

both these, but not for the wells, pits, and caves, men must blow an alarm for them off-hand.

3. And so also for the city, on which the rain did not come down, as is written,[1] " And I caused it to rain upon one city, and caused it not to rain upon another city; one piece was rained upon, and the piece whereupon it rained not withered."

This city fasts and blows an alarm, and all its neighboring cities fast, but do not blow alarms.   R. Akiba said, " they blow alarms, but do not fast."

4. And so for a city, in which there is pestilence, or falling of buildings, that city fasts and blows an alarm, and all the neighboring cities fast, but do not blow an alarm.   Rabbi Akiba said, " they blow alarms, but do not fast."   " What is pestilence? "   " A city containing 500 men, and there go forth from it three dead in three days, one after the other; this is pestilence, less than this is not pestilence."

5. For these things men blow an alarm in every place—for the blasting and for the blighting, for the locust and for the caterpillar, and for the evil beast, and for the sword, they blow an alarm over them, because it is a spreading wound.

6. It happened that the elders went down from Jerusalem to their cities, and proclaimed fasting, because the blasting appeared, as much as would fill an oven, in Askelon.   And again they proclaimed a fast, because the wolves devoured two children beyond Jordan: Rabbi José said, " not because they devoured them, but because the wolves were seen."

7. For these things men blow an alarm on the Sabbath— for a city, encompassed by Gentiles, or by a flood, and for a ship tossed in the sea.   Rabbi José said, " for help, but not for a cry of distress."   Simon the Temanite said, " also for pestilence," but the Sages did not admit it.

8. For all distress—may it not come on the congregation —men sound an alarm, except for too much rain.   It happened that they said to Honé Hammeagal, " pray that the rain come down ": he said to them, " go and bring in the passover ovens, that they be not dissolved."   He prayed, but the rain did not come down—What did he do?   He dug a hole and stood in it, and said before HIM, " Our Lord of the world, thy sons have turned toward me, because I am a

[1] Amos iv. 7.

son of the House in Thy Presence. I am sworn in Thy great Name, that I move not from hence, till Thou have pity on Thy children." The rain began to drop; he said, " I did not ask it thus, but rains for wells, pits, and caves." The rain began to descend with storm. He said, " I did not ask it thus, but reasonable rain, with blessing and free-will." The showers came down as they ought, until all Israel went up from Jerusalem to the Mount of Olives on account of the rains. They came and said to him, " as thou hast prayed that the rains should come down, so pray that they may depart." He said to them, " go and see if the Stone of Proclamation [2] be covered." Simon the son of Shatach sent to him word, " if thou wert not Honé, I would excommunicate thee; but what shall I do to thee, since thou prayest before OMNIPRES-ENCE, and He does thy will, as a son who plays upon his father, and he does his will? and for thee the Scripture says, 'Thy father and thy mother shall be glad, and she that bare thee shall rejoice.' " [3]

9. " If men were fasting and the rains came down for them before the sun rose? " " They need not complete the day." " If the rains came down after sunrise? " " They must complete it." R. Eliezer said, " before noon they need not complete it, if after noon they must complete it." It happened, that the rulers proclaimed a fast in Lydda, and the rains came down in the forenoon. Said R. Tarphon, " go and eat, and drink, and make holiday." They went and ate and drank, and made holiday, and they came in the evening and read the great Thanksgiving.[4]

CHAPTER IV

1. Three times in the year the priests elevate their hands to bless the people, four times a day—in the morning prayer, in the following prayer, in the evening prayer, and at the locking of the gates. These times are the fast days, on the fasts of the deputies, and on the day of atonement.

2. These are the Delegates, according as is said, " Command the children of Israel, and say unto them, My offering and

---

[2] A stone on which lost property was deposited, and publication of it was made, so that its owner might reclaim it.   [3] Prov. xxiii. 25.   [4] Ps. cxxxvi.

my bread for my sacrifices made by fire." [1] And how is it possible, that the offering of a man should be sacrificed, and he does not stand by it? Therefore, the former prophets decreed four-and-twenty Watches. For every Watch there were Delegates in Jerusalem of priests, Levites, and Israelites. When the time approached (for them) to go up, the priests and Levites went up to Jerusalem, and the Israelites, who belonged to the Watch, gathered in their cities and read in the history of Genesis.

3. And the Delegates used to fast four days in the week, from the second day till the fifth. But they did not fast on the eve of the Sabbath, for honor to the Sabbath. Nor on the first day, that they should not go forth from repose and enjoyment, to toil, and fasting, and death. On the first day they read in Genesis,[2] " and let there be a firmament." On the second, " let there be a firmament and let the waters be gathered together." On the third day, " let the waters be gathered together, and let there be lights." On the fourth, " let there be lights, and let the waters bring forth abundantly." On the fifth, " let the waters bring forth abundantly," and " let the earth bring forth." On the sixth, " let the earth bring forth," and " the heavens were finished." Two men read a large portion, but a small portion was read by one. At morning prayer, at the following prayer, at the evening prayer, they went in and read orally (by heart), as they read the " Hear," [3] etc. On the eve of the Sabbath they did not go in to evening prayer for honor to the Sabbath.

4. Every day when there is praise, the Delegates are not at morning prayer. When there is the additional offering at the following prayer, there is not the closing prayer at the locking up of the gates. " When there is the offering of the wood, there is not the evening prayer." The words of Rabbi Akiba. The son of Azai said to him, R. Joshua thus taught it: " when there was an additional offering, the Delegates did not come to evening prayer; when there was the offering of the wood, they did not come to prayer at the locking up of the gates." R. Akiba changed his opinion, and taught as the son of Azai.

5. The times of bringing wood for the altar by priests and

---

[1] Num. xxviii. 2.   [2] Gen. i. 6, etc.   [3] Deut. vi. 4, etc.

people were nine. On the first of Nisan,[4] the children of
Arach, son of Judah, brought it. On the twentieth of Tammuz,[5] the children of David, the son of Judah, brought it.
On the fifth of Ab,[6] the children of Parhush, the son of Judah,
brought it. On the seventh, the children of Jonadab, the son
of Rechab, brought it. On the tenth, the children of Sinah, the
son of Benjamin, brought it. On the fifteenth, the children of
Zathva, the son of Judah, brought it, and with them the priests
and Levites and all who were ignorant of their tribe. And
the children of Gonebi Eli[7] and the children of Kozhi Kezi-
hoth. On the twentieth, the children of Pachath Moab, the
son of Judah, brought it. On the twentieth of Elul,[8] the children of Adin, the son of Judah, brought it. On the first of
Tebeth, the children of Parush returned the second time. On
the first of Tebeth,[9] there was no meeting of the Delegates,
as there was on it " The Praise," and the additional offering
at the following prayer, and the offering of the wood.

6. Five things happened to our fathers on the seventeenth
of Tammuz, and five on the ninth of Ab. On the seventeenth
of Tammuz the stone tables were broken, and the daily offering ceased, and the city was broken up, and Apostemus[10]
burnt the law, and he set up an image in the Temple. On
the ninth of Ab it was proclaimed to our fathers, that they
should not enter the land, and the House was ruined for the
first and second time, and Bither was taken, and the city was
ploughed up. On entering Ab we must diminish joy.

7. The week in which the ninth of Ab comes, men are not
allowed to clip their hair, or wash their clothes; but on Thursday they are allowed, for honor to the Sabbath. On the eve
of the ninth of Ab one must not eat from two dishes, must not
eat flesh, and must not drink wine. Rabban Simon, the son
of Gamaliel, said, " one must change the style of living." R.
Judah " enjoined to turn over the beds," but the Sages did
not approve him.

8. Said Rabban Simon, the son of Gamaliel, " there were no
holidays in Israel like the fifteenth of Ab, or like the day of

atonement. Because in them the daughters of Jerusalem promenaded in white garments borrowed, that no one might be ashamed of her poverty. All these garments must be baptized. And the daughters of Jerusalem promenaded and danced in the vineyards. And what did they say? 'Look here, young man, and see whom you choose; look not for beauty, look for family;' 'Favor is deceitful, and beauty is vain, but a woman that feareth the Lord, she shall be praised;' and it is said, 'Give her of the fruit of her hands, and let her own works praise her in the gates,'[1] and also it is said, 'Go forth, O ye daughters of Zion, and behold King Solomon with the crown, wherewith his mother crowned him in the day of his espousals, and in the day of the gladness of his heart.'[2] The day of his espousals, this is the gift of the Law; and in the day of the gladness of his heart, this is the building of the Sanctuary, and may it be speedily built in our days. Amen."

[1] Prov. xxxi. 30, 31.   [2] Sol. Song, iii. 11.

THE FEAST-OFFERING [1]

CHAPTER I

1. All are bound to appear in the Temple, except the deaf, an idiot, and a child, and a eunuch, and women, and slaves who are not free, and the lame, and the blind, and the sick, and the aged, and the man who cannot go afoot. " What is a child ? " " Everyone who cannot ride on the shoulder of his father, and go up from Jerusalem to the Mountain of the House." The words of the school of Shammai. But the school of Hillel say, " everyone who cannot grasp his father's hand, and go up from Jerusalem to the Mountain of the House," as is said, " three times." [2]

2. The school of Shammai say, " the appearance in the Temple is with two pieces of silver, and the peace-offering with a meah of silver." [3] But the school of Hillel say, " the appearance is with a meah of silver, and the feast-offering with two pieces of silver."

3. The burnt-offerings of the appointed feasts come from ordinary money; but the peace-offering from tithes. " The offerings on the first holiday of the passover ? " [4] The school of Shammai say, " from ordinary money," but the school of Hillel say, " from tithes."

4. Israelites discharge their duty with vows, with free-will offerings, and with tithes of animals; and priests with sin-offerings, with trespass-offerings, and with the breast and shoulder, and first-born, but not with fowls, nor with meat-offerings.

---

[1] The feast-offering (" chagiga ") was the offering of individual worshippers, and was quite distinct from the sacrifices of the whole congregation. See " Treatise on the Passover," vi. 4, note.
[2] Exod. xxiii. 14.
[3] Worth perhaps 3d.
[4] Jer. Tal. says " Tabernacles."

5. "If one have a large family and small income?" "He must bring more peace-offerings, and less burnt-offerings." "If a small family and large income?" "He must bring more burnt-offerings, and less peace-offerings." "If both be small?" "Of this they say, a silver meah, and two pieces of silver are sufficient." "If both be large?" "Of this it is said, every man shall give as he is able according to the blessing of the Lord thy God which He hath given thee." [5]

6. When one did not bring his peace-offering on the first holiday of the feast, he may bring it during the holidays, and even on the last day of the feast. "If the feast passed over, and he did not bring the peace-offering?" "He is not obliged to bring it." For this it is said, "that which is crooked cannot be made straight, and that which is wanting cannot be numbered." [6]

7. Rabbi Simon, the son of Menasia, said, "if thou shalt say, a thief or a robber, he may return and become straight." R. Simon, the son of Jochai, said, "we do not call one crooked, save one straight at first, and he became afterward crooked; and this is the disciple of the wise, who departs from the Law."

8. The remission of vows is like flying in the air, and it has no foundation. The decisions for the Sabbath, peace-offerings, and trespasses, are as mountains hanging on a hair; because the verse is small, but the decisions are many. Jurisprudence, and the Temple service, cleanness and uncleanness, and illegal connections, have their own foundations; they, they are the body of the law.

CHAPTER II

1. Men may not discourse on illegal connections with three,[1] nor on the work of creation with two,[2] nor on the cherubs with one,[3] save when one is wise, and comprehends it of his own knowledge. Everyone who considers four things, it were suitable for him that he did not come into the world. What is in the height? what is in the depth? what is before? and what is behind? And everyone who is not anxious for the honor of his Creator, it were suitable for him that he did not come into the world.

[5] Deut. xvi. 17.
[6] Eccl. i. 15.
[1] From motives of delicacy.
[2] This must be done only by one (Deut. iv. 32).
[3] Ezek. x.; Isa. vi.

2. José, the son of Joezar, said that " one is not to lay his hand on the offering." José, the son of Jochanan, said, " he is to lay his hand on the offering." Joshua, the son of Perachia, said, that he " is not to lay on his hand." Nittai, the Arbelite, said, " he is to lay on his hand." Judah, the son of Tabai, said, that " he is not to lay on his hand." Simon, the son of Shatach, said, " he is to lay on his hand." Shemaiah, said, " he is to lay on his hand." Abtalion said, " he is not to lay on his hand." Hillel and Menachem did not dispute. Menachem went out and Shammai entered. Shammai said, " he is not to lay on his hand." Hillel said, " he is to lay on his hand." [4] The first were Princes, and the second were Presidents of the Tribunal.

3. The school of Shammai said, " men may bring peace-offerings during the feast, but they are not to lay their hands on them, and they are not to bring burnt-offerings." But the house of Hillel say, " they may bring peace-offerings, and burnt-offerings, and lay their hands on them."

4. " When Pentecost happens to be on the eve of the Sabbath? " The school of Shammai say, " the day of slaughtering the offering is after the Sabbath." But the school of Hillel say, " there is no day of slaughtering after the Sabbath."

But they both acknowledge that if it happened to be on the Sabbath, the day of slaughter is after the Sabbath. And the high priest must not robe in his vestments, though they are allowed in seasons of mourning and fasting, for fear of confirming the words of those who say that " Pentecost is after the Sabbath." [5]

5. Men must wash their hands for ordinary eating, but for tithes and for the heave-offering they must be baptized. And for the sin-offering, if the hands be unclean, the body is unclean.

6. He who baptized himself for ordinary eating, and indicated it to be for ordinary eating, he is prohibited from (eating) the tithe. " If he baptized for the tithe, and indicated it to be for the tithe? " " He is prohibited from eating heave-offerings." " If he baptized for heave-offerings, and indicated

[4] This decision is for private sacrifices, but for public sacrifices there seems (according to the Talmud) to have been no " laying on of hands," except in the case of the scapegoat and the bullock, when the congregation had sinned through ignorance.

[5] I.e., the Sadduccea (Lev. xxiii. 15).

it to be for heave-offerings?" "He is prohibited from eating the holy flesh." "If he baptized for the holy flesh, and indicated it to be for the holy flesh?" "He is prohibited from the sin-offering." "If he baptized for the weighty?" "He is permitted the light." "If he baptized, and did not indicate his intention?" "It is as no baptism."

7. Treading on the garments of an ordinary man defiled the Pharisees. Treading on the garments of the Pharisees defiled those who eat the heave-offering. Treading on the garments of those who eat the heave-offering defiled for the holy flesh. Treading on the garments of those who eat the holy flesh defiles for the sin-offering. Joseph, the son of Joezer, was the most pious of the priesthood, and treading on his cloak defiled for the holy flesh. Jochanan, the son of Gudgada, used to eat with the purification for the holy flesh all his life; and treading on his cloak defiled for the sin-offering.

CHAPTER III

1. There are more weighty rules for holy things, than for the heave-offering. Because vessels may be baptized in vessels for the heave-offering, but not for holy things. The outside and inside and handle (are reckoned separately) for the heave-offering, but not for holy things. He who carries that which defiles by treading upon it, may carry the heave-offering but not the holy flesh. Treading on the garments of those who eat the heave-offering defiles for the holy flesh. The measure of the holy flesh is not as the measure of the heave-offering. Because for the holy flesh one must loose his garments and dry himself, and baptize and afterward bind them up. But in the heave-offering he can bind them up and afterward baptize himself.

2. Vessels completed in purity must be baptized for holy things, but not for the heave-offering. A vessel unites whatever is inside to holy things, but not to the heave-offering. The fourth degree of legal uncleanness [1] is disallowed in holy things, and the third degree in the heave-offering. In the

[1] There are reckoned six degrees of uncleanness: The father of fathers, the fathers, the first, second, third, and fourth children of defilement. There are altogether twenty-nine fathers of uncleanness, of which eleven arise from contact with a dead body.

heave-offering, if one of the hands be unclean, its fellow may be clean, but in holy things one must baptize both hands; because each renders its fellow unclean for holy things, but not for the heave-offering.

3. Men may eat with unwashen hands the dry meat of the heave-offering, but not the holy flesh. The first day mourner, and he who failed in atonement, have need of baptism for the holy flesh, but not for the heave-offering.

4. There are weighty rules for the heave-offering, because in Judah men are credited with the purity of wine and oil during the whole year. And in the time of wine-pressing and oil-pressing (men are credited) even for the heave-offering. When the time for wine and oil pressing has passed over, and a barrel of wine is brought for the heave-offering, it must not be received. But one may let it stand over for the wine-pressing next year. But if one said, " I put into it a quarter log of holy wine," it is credited. " Jugs of wine and jugs of oil which are mixed?" They are credited in the time of wine-pressing and oil-pressing, and seventy days before that time."

5. From Modiyith [2] and inward,[3] men are credited for the purity of earthen vessels. From Modiyith and outward they are not credited. " How?" " The potter, when he is selling pots, comes inward from Modiyith." One says, " this is the potter," and " these the pots," and " these the purchasers," " it is credited." " When he went outward?" " It is not credited."

6. The tax-gatherers when they enter the house, and also the tax-gatherers when they restore the vessels, are credited in saying, " we did not touch them." And in Jerusalem they are credited in holy things (that they did not defile them), and at the time of the feast they are credited even in the heave-offering.

7. " He who opened his barrel of wine,[4] and commenced with his dough for the use of the feast?" R. Judah said, " he may finish it " (after the feast). But the Sages say, " he must not finish it." When the feast was over, the priests looked round for the purity of the Temple court. If the feast ended

---

[2] A city about fifteen miles from Jerusalem.
[3] Toward Jerusalem.
[4] This decision refers to the case of a dealer whose wine or flour might become legally defiled by contact with the common people.

on Friday, they did not look round for honor to the approaching Sabbath.   R. Judah said, " even they did not look round on Thursday, because the priests are not then idle."

8. " How did they look round for the purity of the court? " " The priests baptized the vessels, which were in the Sanctuary, and used to say to the people, ' Watch and do not touch the table and the candlestick, lest you render them unclean.' " All the vessels in the Sanctuary were double and treble, because if the first became unclean, they could bring duplicates instead of them.   " All the vessels which were in the Sanctuary required baptism [5] except the golden altar, and the brazen altar, because they are as earth."   The words of R. Eliezer.   But the Sages say, " because they were overlaid."

[5] The Tosephta relates, that when the Pharisees were baptizing the candle- stick, the Sadducees used to mock them by saying, they were baptizing the sun.

THE SANHEDRIN

CHAPTER I

1. " Judgments for money (require) three (judges). Robbery and beating (require) three. Damages or half damages,
double payments and payments four or five fold (require)
three." Constraint, and enticement, and slander (require)
three " The words of R. Meier. But the Sages say, " slander
(requires) twenty-three judges, because there exist in it judgments of souls."

2. Stripes (require) three judges. In the name of Rabbi
Ishmael, the Sages say, " twenty-three." " The intercalary
month [1] requires three. The intercalary year requires three."
The words of Rabbi Meier. Rabban Simon, the son of Gamaliel, said, " with three judges they begin, and with five they
discuss, and they conclude with seven; and if they concluded
with three it is intercalated."

---

[1] The Jewish year is composed of
twelve lunar months. It is adapted to
the solar year by the use of an intercalary month called Veaddar—the additional Addar. Every nineteen years
there are seven occasions on which this
embolismic month must be introduced
to prevent the various feasts revolving
over the four seasons of the year, like
the Moslem fast of Ramadhan. For-
merly the Sanhedrin arranged this intercalary month to suit the harvest, so
that if it were late, the wave sheaf and
other observances should still be kept
according to their proper dates. When,
however, the Sanhedrin was suppressed
by the Emperor Constantine, Hillel II
of Tiberias ruled that an intercalary
month of twenty-nine days should be
added in the 3d, 6th, 8th, 11th, 13th,
17th, and 19th years of the Metonic Cy-
cle. This decision has since remained
the Jewish standard for reckoning time.

3. " The appointment of elders, and striking off the heifer's neck [2] (require) three." The words of Rabbi Simon. But Rabbi Judah said, " five." The loosing off the shoe,[3] and dissatisfaction in marriage (require) three. The produce [4] of the fourth year,[5] the second tithes, of which the value is unknown (require) three. The valuation of holy things (requires) three. The estimation of movable things requires three. R. Judah said, " one of them must be a priest." Immovable things require nine judges and a priest; and the valuation of a man (slave) is similar.

4. Judgments of souls (require) twenty-three judges. Bestiality (requires) twenty-three, as is said, " and thou shalt slay the woman and the beast," and it is also said, " the beast thou shalt slay." An ox to be stoned (requires) twenty-three judges; as is said, " The ox shall be stoned, and his owner also shall be put to death," [6] as is the death of the owner, so is the death of the ox. The wolf, and the lion, and the bear, and the leopard, and the panther, and the serpent, are to be put to death with twenty-three judges. R. Eliezer said, " everyone who first killed them has gained honor." R. Akiba said, " they are to be put to death after a judgment with twenty-three (judges)."

5. A tribe must not be judged, nor a false prophet, nor a high priest, save before the tribunal of seventy-one. And soldiers must not go forth to lawful warfare, save by a decree of the tribunal of seventy-one. Men must not add to the city or to the temple courts, save by a decision of the tribunal of seventy-one. They must not appoint judges to the tribes, save by a decision of the tribunal of seventy-one. A city must not be excluded, save by the tribunal of seventy-one. And the tribunal must not exclude a city on the border, nor exclude three cities, but only one or two.

6. The Great Sanhedrin consisted of seventy-one members, and the small one of twenty-three. And whence know we that the great one contained seventy-one? as is said, " Gather unto me seventy men of the elders of Israel ": [7] and Moses over them. There are seventy-one. R. Judah said " seventy." And whence know we that the small one consisted of twenty-

---

[2] Deut. xxi. 4.
[3] Deut. xx. 5, 9.
[4] Lev. xix. 24.
[5] Deut. xiv. 22-25.
[6] Exod. xxi. 29.
[7] Num. xi. 17.

three? as is said, " Then the congregation shall judge ";[8] " and the congregation shall deliver." A congregation to judge, and a congregation to deliver, there is twenty. And whence know we that a congregation required ten? as is said, " How long shall I bear with this evil congregation? "[9] Joshua and Caleb were excepted. " And whence know we to produce the other three?" From the meaning, as is said, " Thou shalt not follow a multitude to do evil."[10] I am hearing that " I shall be with them for good." If so, why is it said, " to decline after many to wrest judgment "?[10] " Because thy inclinations to good do not equal thy inclinations to evil. Thy inclinations to good are by the report of one. Thy inclinations to evil are by the report of two. And a tribunal must not be balanced. Another must be added. There are twenty-three." " And how populous must be the city suited for judges?" " One hundred and twenty." R. Nehemiah said " 230 to represent twenty-three overseers of tens."

CHAPTER II

1. The high-priest may judge, and be judged.[1] He may bear witness, and witness may be borne against him. He may have his shoe loosed, and the shoe may be loosed for his wife.[2] His brother may take his wife, but he must not take his brother's wife, because he is prevented from marrying a widow. If there happened a death in his family, he must not go immediately behind the bier. " But when the (mourners) are concealed (in a street), then he is discovered (to the public). They are discovered to the public, and he is concealed in a street. And he may go with them to the entrance gate of the city." The words of R. Meier. R. Judah said, " he must not depart from the sanctuary "; as is said, " neither shall he go out of the sanctuary."[3] And when he comforts others, the fashion of all the people is to pass one after the other, and the deputy priest puts him in the middle between himself and the people.

---

[8] Num. xxxv. 24, 25. A congregation, or " minyan," must not be less than ten men. If there be 10,000 women they cannot form a minyan. The Lord Jesus more mercifully promises His presence to " two or three gathered together." Matt. xviii. 20.

[9] Num. xiv. 27.
[10] Exod. xxiii. 2.
[1] The Great Sanhedrin could whip a high-priest for certain offences, and afterward restore him to his office.
[2] Deut. xxv. 9.
[3] Lev. xxi. 12.

But when he is comforted by others, all the people say to him, "we are thy atonement." And he says to them, "you shall be blessed from heaven." And at the first meal [4] after a funeral, all the people recline on the ground, and he sits on a stool.

2. The king neither judges, nor is he judged. He neither bears witness, nor is witness borne against him. He does not unloose the shoe, and the shoe is not unloosed for his wife. He does not marry his brother's wife, nor is his wife married by his brother. R. Judah said, "if he pleased he may unloose the shoe, or marry his brother's wife. He is remembered in prayer for good." The Sages said to him, "we do not hear him (the king) (for unloosing the shoe) and his widow must not marry." R. Judah said, "the king may marry the widow of a king, as we find with David that he married the widow of Saul"; as is said, "And I gave thee thy master's house, and thy master's wives into thy bosom." [5]

3. If there happened a death in his family, he goes not out from the entrance of his palace. R. Judah said, "if he pleases to go after the bier he may go, as we find in David that he went after the bier of Abner"; as is said, "And King David himself followed the bier." [6] The Sages said to him, "this only happened to pacify the people." And at the first meal after a funeral, all the people recline on the ground, and he sits on a sofa.

4. And he may go forth to lawful warfare by order of the supreme court of seventy-one, and he may break down a road for himself, and none can prevent him. The road of a king is without measure, and all the people plunder and lay it before him. And he takes part first. He must not multiply wives beyond eighteen. R. Judah said, "he may multiply wives for himself so long as they do not turn away his heart." R. Simon said, "even if one turn away his heart, he should not marry her." If so, wherefore is it said, "he must not multiply for himself wives, even though they be as Abigail"? He must not multiply horses, except sufficient for his own riding. And silver and gold he must not multiply much, only sufficient to pay his own expenses. And he must write a book of the law for himself. When he goes out to war, he must bring it with him. When he returns, he must bring it with him. If he sit

[4] 2 Sam. iii. 35.   [5] 2 Sam. xii. 8.   [6] 2 Sam. iii. 31.

in judgment it is with him. When he is seated it is before him, as is said, " And it shall be with him, and he shall read therein all the days of his life." [7]

5. None may ride on his horse, and none may sit on his chair, and none may use his sceptre, and none may see him shaving, either when he is naked, or in the bath, as is said, " Thou shalt in any wise set him king over thee," [8] that his dread be upon thee.

CHAPTER III

1. " Judgments in money matters (require) three judges. This party chooses for himself one, and the other party chooses for himself one. And both parties choose another." The words of R. Meier. But the Sages say, " the two judges choose for themselves the other." " This one may declare the judge of that one illegal. And that one may declare the judge of this one illegal." The words of R. Meier. But the Sages say, " it is only when witness can be brought against them that they are related or unlawful." " But if they be righteous or experienced, they must not be declared illegal." " This one may declare illegal the witness of that one. And that one may declare illegal the witness of this one." The words of R. Meier. But the Sages say, " it is only when witness can be brought against them that they are related or unlawful, but if they be righteous they must not be declared illegal."

2. One said to the other, " I trust my father," " I trust thy father," " I trust three cowherds." R. Meier said, " he may change his mind." But the Sages say, " he must not change." If he must give an oath to his companion, and he said to him, " vow to me by the life of thy head " ? R. Meier said, " he may change his mind." But the Sages say, " he must not change his mind."

3. And these are illegal (as judges or witnesses), one who played at cards, or lent on usury, or bet on the flight of doves, or trades in the Sabbatical year. R. Simon said, " at first they were called gatherers on the Sabbatical year ; when they were forced by Gentiles to cultivate the ground, they changed to

[7] Deut. xvii. 19.　　　　[8] Deut. xvii. 15.

call them traders on the Sabbatical year." R. Judah said, " it is only when they have no other occupation but this one alone: but if they have another occupation, they are allowed."

4. And these are related, his father and his brother, and the brethren of his father, and the brethren of his mother, and the husband of his sister, and the husband of his father's sister, and the husband of his mother's sister. And the husband of his mother and his father-in-law, and his brother in-law, they, their children, and their sons-in-law, and his step son alone. R. José said, " this was the teaching of R. Akiba ; but the first teaching was, his uncle and the son of his uncle, and all suitable for inheritance, and everyone related to him at the present time." " One was related and became estranged?" " He is lawful." R. Judah said, " even if his daughter died, and he has children left by her, they are related."

5. " Who is a friend? and who is an enemy?" " A friend is the bridegroom's best man, an enemy is everyone who has not spoken with him three days in malice." The Sages replied to him, " Israelites are not so suspicious."

6. " How are witnesses examined?" " They are brought in and intimidated; and all other men are driven out. And the chief of the witnesses is left, and they say to him, " tell us how do you know that this man is indebted to that man?" If the witness said, " he told me that I am indebted to him "— " such a man told me that he is indebted to him "—he has said nothing, till he shall say, " he acknowledged in our presence that he owed him 200 zuz." And afterward the second witness is brought in, and examined. If their statements were found agreeing, the judges held a conversation. Two of them said " he is clear," and one said " he is indebted "? " He is cleared." " Two said, he is indebted, and one said, he is clear?" " He is indebted." " One said he is clear, and one said he is indebted? And even if two pronounced him clear or indebted, and one said, ' I don't know'?" " The judges must be increased."

7. The matter is finished. They bring in the plaintiff and defendant. The chief judge says, " thou, such a one, art clear; thou such an one, art indebted." " And whence know we that one of the judges on going out should not say, ' I was

for clearing him, but my colleagues pronounced him indebted, but what shall I do when my colleagues are too many for me'?" " Of this man it is said, 'Thou shalt not go up and down as a tale-bearer among thy people';[1] and it is said, 'A tale-bearer revealeth secrets.'"[2]

8. At any time the one condemned may bring evidence and annul the judgment. The judges said to him, " bring all your evidence within thirty days from this date." If he brought them within thirty days, it is annulled, if after thirty days, it is not annulled. Rabban Simon, the son of Gamaliel, said, " what shall he do if he did not find them within thirty days, but found them after thirty days?" " The judges said to him, ' bring witnesses'; and he said, 'I have no witnesses'; they said, ' bring evidence'; and he said, 'I have no evidence'; but afterward he found evidence, and found witnesses?" "They are nothing." Rabban Simon, the son of Gamaliel, said, " what shall he do if he did not know that he had witnesses, and found witnesses; he did not know that he had evidence, and found evidence?" " They said to him, 'bring witnesses'; he said, 'I have no witnesses.' ' Bring evidence,' and he said, 'I have no evidence.'" " He saw that he will be pronounced indebted in judgment, and he said, 'approach such a one, and such a one, and bear witness for me,' or ' he pulled out evidence from his pocket'?" " It is nothing."

CHAPTER IV

1. Judgments in money and judgments in souls must be equally inquired into and investigated; as is said, " Ye shall have one manner of law."[1] " What is the difference between judgments in money and judgments in souls?" " Judgments in money (require) three judges, judgments in souls twenty-three. Judgments in money open the case either for clearing or proving indebted, but judgments of souls open the case for clearing, and the case is not opened for condemning. Judgments in money are balanced by one judge either for clearing or proving indebted; but judgments in souls are balanced by one for clearing and by two for condemning. Judgments in money may be reversed either for clearing or proving indebted;

---

[1] Lev. xix. 16.   [2] Prov. xi. 13.   [1] Lev. xxiv. 22.

but judgments in souls may be reversed for clearing, but must not be reversed for condemnation. All may express an opinion on judgments in money for clearing or proving indebted. All may express an opinion on judgments in souls for clearing, but all must not express an opinion for condemnation. He who has expressed an opinion on judgments in money for proving indebted, may express an opinion for clearing, and he who has expressed an opinion for clearing, may express an opinion for proving indebted. He who has expressed an opinion on judgments in souls for condemnation may express an opinion for clearing, but he who has expressed an opinion for clearing must not reverse it to express an opinion for condemnation. Judgments in money are conducted by day and settled by night. Judgments in souls are conducted by day and settled by day. Judgments in money are settled on the same day, either for clearing or proving indebted. Judgments in souls are finished on the same day for clearing, and on the day after it for condemnation—wherefore there can be no judgments on Friday or on the eve of a festival." [2]

2. Judgments in legal uncleanness and legal cleansings begin with the Supreme (judge). Judgments in souls begin with a judge at his side. All are eligible to pronounce judgments in money matters, but all are not eligible to pronounce judgments in souls—only priests, Levites, and Israelites who can intermarry into the priesthood.

3. The Sanhedrin was like half a round threshing-floor, in order that the members might observe each other. And two scribes of the judges stood before them—one on the right and one on the left. And they wrote the sentence of acquittal, and the sentence of condemnation. R. Judah said, "three; one scribe wrote the sentence of acquittal, and one wrote the sentence of condemnation; and the third wrote both the sentence of acquittal and the sentence of condemnation."

4. And three rows of the disciples of the wise sat before them. And each one knew his place. When it was necessary to appoint a judge, they appointed one from the first row. One from the second row came instead of him into the first, and one from the third row came instead of him into the second,

---

[2] This rule was violated in the case of our Lord Jesus Christ. Matt. xxvi. xxvii.; Mark xiv.; Luke xxii. xxiii.; John xix.

and they selected another from the congregation, and they seated him in the third row, and he did not sit in the place of his predecessor, but he sat in a place suitable for himself.

5. "How did the judges intimidate witnesses in the testimony for souls?" "They introduced them, and intimidated them." "Perhaps you are speaking from guess? or from hearsay? witness from witness? or from a trustworthy man we heard it?" Or, perhaps, "you don't know that at the last we shall proceed to inquire into your own character and investigate it." "Have a knowledge that the judgments of money are not as the judgments of souls. Judgments for money, when the man pays the money he has atoned. In judgments for souls his blood and the blood of his posterity are suspended till the end of the world." So we find it with Cain when he slew his brother. It is said of him,[3] "the voice of thy brother's bloods crieth." He does not say thy brother's blood, but bloods of thy brother, his blood and the blood of his posterity. Another thing is also meant, that thy brother's bloods are spattered on wood, and on stones. Therefore man is created single, to teach thee that everyone who destroys one soul from Israel, to him is the verse applicable, as if he destroys a full world. And everyone who supports one soul in Israel, to him is the verse applicable, as if he supports the full world. And it is also said, for the peace of creation, that no man may justly say to his companion, my father is greater than thine. And that the Epicureans should not say, that there are more Creators in the heavens, and it is also said, to show forth the greatness of the Holy One, blessed be He! When man stamps many coins with one stamp, all are alike. But the King of Kings, the Holy One, blessed be He! stamped every man with the stamp of the first Adam, and no one of them is like his companion; therefore everyone is bound to say, "for my sake was the world created." But, perhaps, the witnesses will say "what is this trouble to us?" But is it not already said, "And is a witness, whether he hath seen or known of it; if he do not utter it?"[4] But perhaps the witnesses will say, "what is it to us, to be guilty of this man's blood?" But is it not already said, "When the wicked perish, there is shouting"?[5]

[3] Gen. iv. 10.   [4] Lev. v. 1.   [5] Prov. xi. 10.

CHAPTER V

1. The witnesses were examined with seven investigations. "In what Sabbatical year?" "In what year?" "In what month?" "What date in the month?" "What day?" "What hour?" "What place?" R. José said, "What day?" "What hour?" "What place?" "Did you know him?" "Did you warn him?" In a case of idolatry, "whom did he serve?" "And with what did he serve?"

2. Every judge who extends examinations is praiseworthy. It happened that the son of Zacchai examined (even) on the stems of figs. And what difference is there between investigations and examinations? In investigations if one say, "I don't know," their witness is worthless. In examinations, if one say, "I don't know," and even two say, "we don't know," their witness stands. Whether in investigations or examinations, when they contradict each other, their witness is worthless.

3. One witness said, "on the second of the month," and another witness said, "the third of the month." Their witness stands. Because one knows of the intercalary month, and another does not know of the intercalary month. One said, "on the third," and another said, "on the fifth"; their witness is worthless. One said, "at the second hour," and another said, "at the third hour"; their witness stands. One said, "at the third," and another said, "at the fifth"; their witness is worthless. R. Judah said, "it stands." One said, "on the fifth," and another said, "on the seventh"; their witness is worthless, because at the fifth (hour) the sun is in the east, and at the seventh hour the sun is in the west.

4. And afterward they introduce the second (witness) and examine him. If both their statements agree, they open the case with clearing. One of the witnesses says, "I possess information to clear him." Or one of the disciples of the Sanhedrin says, "I possess information for condemning." They order him to keep silence. One of the disciples of the Sanhedrin says, "I possess information to clear him." They bring him up, and seat him between the judges, and he did not go down during the whole day. If there be substantial in-

formation, they give him a hearing. And even when he (the accused) says, "I possess information for clearing myself," the judges give him a hearing; only there must be substantial information in his words.

5. If the judges found him clear, they released him, but if not they deferred his judgment till the morrow. They conversed in pairs, and reduced their eating, and they drank no wine all the day, and discussed the matter the whole night. And on the morrow they came very early to the judgment hall. He who was for clearing said, "I was for clearing, and I am for clearing in my place." And he who was for condemning said, "I was for condemning, and I am for condemning in my place." He who pronounced for condemning, could pronounce for clearing, but he who pronounced for clearing, could not turn round and pronounce for condemning. If the judges erred in a matter, the two scribes of the judges recalled it to their memory. If they found him clear, they released him: but if not, they stood to be counted. "Twelve cleared him, and eleven condemned?" "He is clear." "Twelve condemned him, and eleven cleared him, and even eleven cleared, and eleven condemned," and one said, "I don't know." And even twenty-two cleared or condemned, and one said, "I don't know?" "They must add judges." "How many do they add as judges two by two?" "Up to seventy-one." "Thirty-six cleared him, and thirty-five condemned him?" "He is clear." "Thirty-six condemned him, and thirty-five cleared him?" "They disputed with each other until one of the condemning party acknowledged the statement of the clearing party."

CHAPTER VI

1. When the judgment was finished, they brought him forth to stone him.[1] The place of stoning was outside the judgment-hall; as is said, "Bring him forth that hath cursed."[2] One stood at the door of the judgment-hall with towels in his hand, and another man rode a horse at a distance from him,

---

[1] Before executing a criminal, a quantity of frankincense in a cup of wine was given to him to stupefy him and render him insensible to pain. The compassionate ladies of Jerusalem generally provided this draught at their own cost. This custom was in obedience to Prov. xxxi. 6, "Give strong drink unto him that is ready to perish, and wine unto those that be of heavy hearts."

[2] Lev. xxiv. 14.

but so that he might see him. If one said, " I have something
to tell for clearing," this one waved the towels, and the other
galloped his horse, and stopped the accused. And even though
he himself said, " I have something to tell to clear myself," they
brought him back as many as four or five times, only there
must be substance in his words. If they found him clear, they
freed him; but if not, they took him forth to stone him. And
a herald preceded him (crying), " Such a one, the son of such
a one, is brought out for stoning, because he committed such
a transgression, and so and so are witnesses; let everyone
who knows aught for clearing him come forth and tell it."

2. When he was ten cubits from the place of stoning, they
said to him " confess," as it is the custom of all about to die to
confess, since to everyone who confesses there is a portion in
the world to come. So we find with Achan when Joshua said
to him, " My son, give, I pray thee, glory to the Lord God of
Israel, and make confession unto him." [3] And Achan answered Joshua, and said, " Indeed, I have sinned against the
Lord God of Israel, and thus and thus I have done." " And
from whence know we that his confession made atonement for
him?" " As it is said, ' And Joshua said, Why hast thou
troubled us? the Lord shall trouble thee this day. This day
thou art troubled, but thou shalt not be troubled in the world
to come.' " And if he did not know how to confess, they told
him to say, " let my death be an atonement for all my sins."
Rabbi Judah said, " if he knew that he was falsely condemned,
he said, ' let my death be an atonement for all my sins, except
this one ';" the (Sages) said, " if so, every man will speak thus
to make themselves innocent."

3. When he was four cubits from the place of stoning, they
stripped off his garments. " If a man, they covered him in
front; if a woman, before and behind." The words of Rabbi
Judah. But the Sages say " a man was stoned naked, but the
woman was not stoned naked."

4. The place of stoning was two men high. One of the witnesses thrust him down on his loins. If he turned on his heart,
the witness must turn him on his loins. If he died with that
thrust it was finished; but if not, the second (witness) took the
stone, and cast it upon his heart. If he died with that blow, the

---

[3] Josh. vii. 19, 20, 25.

stoning was finished. But if not, he was stoned by all Israel, as is said, "The hands of the witnesses shall be first upon him to put him to death, and afterward the hands of all the people." [4] "All who were stoned were hung up." The words of Rabbi Eliezer. But the Sages say, "none were hung up, save the blasphemer and the idolater." "The man is to be hung with his face toward the people, but the woman with her face toward the wood." The words of Rabbi Eliezer. But the Sages say, "the man was hung up, but they do not hang up a woman." Rabbi Eleazar said to them, "and did not Simon, the son of Shatach, hang women in Askalon?" They said to him, "he hung up eighty women (witches), and two could not be judged, in one day." "How did they hang him?" "They sunk a beam in the ground, and a traverse beam proceeded from it, and they bound his hands, one over the other, and hung him up" (by them). R. José said, "the beam was inclined against the wall, and he was hung upon it, just as the butchers do." And they loosed him immediately afterward. "But if he was out all night?" "It was a transgression of a negative command, as is said, 'His body shall not remain all night upon the tree, but thou shalt in any wise bury him that day (for he that is hanged is accursed of God),'" [5] etc. As one says, "wherefore is this one hung?" "Because he blasphemed the NAME, and it follows that the heavenly NAME is profaned."

5. Rabbi Meier said, "when man is sorrowful, [6] what language does the Shekinah [7] make him to utter?" If it be lawful so to speak, "my head makes me ashamed, my arm makes me ashamed." If, to speak after the manner of men, OMNIPRESENCE is sorrowful, when the blood of the wicked is poured out, how much more sorrowful is He for the blood of the righteous? And not in the case of the condemned alone, but everyone who leaves his dead overnight, is a transgressor of a negative command. If they left him for the sake of honor, to bring a coffin and a shroud for him, there is no transgression. But they did not bury him (the condemned) in the sepulchres of his fathers. And there were two burial grounds

---

[4] Deut. xvii. 7.
[5] Deut. xxi. 23.
[6] This supposes a man sorrowful, because he is obliged to punish his own son.

[7] I.e., the Divine Presence. The luminous cloud of glory in the Holy of Holies.

prepared for the Judgment Hall—one for the stoned and the burned, and one for those beheaded and strangled.

6. When the flesh of the condemned was consumed, they gathered his bones and buried them in their proper place; and his relatives came and asked after the peace of the judges, and the peace of the witneses, as much as to say, " know there is nothing in our hearts against you, as your judgment was true." And they did not mourn, but were gloomy, since gloominess is only in the heart.

CHAPTER VII

1. Four punishments were permitted to the supreme court —stoning, burning, beheading, and strangling. R. Simon said, "burning, stoning, strangling, and beheading" The preceding chapter is the order of stoning.

2. The order for those burned was to be sunk in dung to their knees. And men put a hard towel in a soft one, and encircled his neck. One pulled on one side, and another pulled on the other side, till the condemned opened his mouth. And one lit a wick, and cast it into his mouth, and it went down to his bowels, and it consumed his intestines. R. Judah said, " if he died in their hands, they did not complete in him the order of burning; only they opened his mouth with tongs against his will, and lit the wick, and cast it into his mouth, and it went down to his bowels and consumed his intestines." Said R. Eleazar the son of Zadok, " it happened with the daughter of a priest, who was immoral, that they surrounded her with dry branches and burned her." The Sages replied, " because the court at that time was unskilled."

3. The order of those beheaded was to have their heads struck off with a sword, as is the custom of governments. R. Judah said, " that was an abuse; they only rested his head on a block, and hewed it off with an axe." The Sages replied to him, " no death is a greater abuse than that." The order for those strangled was, that they were sunk down in dung to their knees, and they put a hard towel inside a soft one, and encircled his neck. One pulled on one side, and another pulled on the other side, till his soul departed.

4. These were stoned; . . . a blasphemer, and an

idolater, and he who gave his seed to Molech, and one with a familiar spirit,[1] and a wizard, and he who profaned the Sabbath, and he who cursed father or mother, and he who came to a betrothed maid, and an enticer to idolatry, and a withdrawer to idolatry, and a sorcerer, and a son stubborn and rebellious.

5. The blasphemer was not guilty till he expressed the NAME. Said R. Joshua, the son of Korcha, every day they examined the witnesses under a substituted (feigned) name, for example, " José shall beat José." When the judgment was finished, they could not execute him under the nickname, but they withdrew all men outside, and interrogated the principal witness, and said to him, " tell us clearly what thou hast heard?" and he said it. And the judges stood up on their feet, and rent their garments,[2] and they were never sewn again. And the second witness said, " even I (heard) as he," and the third said, " even I (heard) as he."

6. One committed idolatry, whether he served the idol, or sacrificed to it, or burned incense to it, or made a libation to it, or bowed down to it, or accepted it for his god. And also, he who said to it, thou art my God." But he who embraced it, and kissed it, and honored it, and dusted it, and washed it, and anointed it, and dressed it, and put shoes on it, transgressed a negative command. He who vowed in its name, and performed the vow in its name, transgressed a negative command. " He exposed himself to Baal peor?" " That is positive service." " He cast a stone to Mercury?" " That is positive service."

7. He who gave his seed to Molech [3] is not guilty till he hand

---

[1] The words in the original, " Baal Aob," are supposed by some to denote a ventriloquist from " Aob," meaning a " bottle " or " stomach." " Aob " seems, however, much more likely to be allied to the Coptic word for " a serpent " or " Python," Acts xvi. 16.

[2] Matt. xxvi. 65.

[3] The image of Molech was made of brass. It was hollow within and heated with fire outside. It stood in the valley of Hinnom without the walls of Jerusalem. Kimchi says the image of Molech contained seven chapels. These chapels are supposed by some to represent the seven planets. In the first chapel flowers were offered; in the second, turtle doves or young pigeons; in the third, lambs; in the fourth, rams; in the fifth, calves; in the sixth, oxen; " but whosoever offered his son, they opened to him the seventh chapel." The face of Molech was like the face of a calf, and the image stretched forth its hands " as a man who opens his hands to receive something of his neigbhor." " They kindled the image with fire, and the priests took the babe and put it into the hands of Molech, and the babe gave up the ghost." They called it Tophet, because they made a noise with drums (" tophim "), that the father might not hear the screams of his child and have pity upon him. And they called it Hinnom, because the child roared (" menahem ") in his anguish. Others say it was called Hinnom, because the priests used to say, " May it profit thee—may it be sweet to thee."

it to Molech, and pass it through the fire. "If he hand it to Molech, and do not pass it through the fire, (or if) he passed it through the fire, and did not hand it to Molech?" "He is not guilty till he hand it to Molech, and pass it through the fire." One has a familiar spirit, when the Python speaks from his arm. But the wizard speaks with his mouth. These are to be stoned, and inquiry from them is forbidden.

8. He who profaned the Sabbath by aught which renders him guilty of presumption is to be cut off;[4] but if he profaned the Sabbath in error, a sin-offering (is required) from him. He who cursed father or mother is not guilty till he curse them by the NAME. "If he curse them with a substituted name of God?" R. Meier pronounces him "guilty"; but the Sages "free him."

9. "If one came to a betrothed maid?" "He is not guilty, except she be a virgin, and betrothed, and in the house of her father." "If two came to her?" "The first is to be stoned and the second strangled."

10. "The enticer to idolatry?" "This ordinary man enticed an ordinary man; he said to him, 'there is an object of fear in such a place, so it eats, so it drinks, so it does good, so it does evil.'" Of all who are guilty of death in the law, we are not to set witnesses in concealment to convict them, except in this case of an enticer to idolatry. When he has spoken of his idolatry to two persons, they as witnesses bring him to the judgment-hall, and stone him. If he spoke thus to one, this one replies, "I have companions who desire to hear so and so." "If he be cunning, and he does not speak before them?" "Witnesses are concealed behind a wall, and he says to the idolater, 'tell me what thou saidst to me alone,' and the idolater told him. And he replied to him, 'how can we leave our God, who is in heaven, and go and serve wood and stone?'" "If the idolater returned from his sin, it is well; but if he said, 'so is our duty, and so it is excellent for us,' they who stood behind the wall bring him to the judgment-hall, and stone him; if he said, 'I shall serve, I shall go and serve, let us go and serve; I will sacrifice, I will go and sacrifice, let us go and sacrifice; I will burn incense, I will go and burn in-

---

[4] Cutting off is generally supposed to have extended to the family as well as the guilty person. It seems to have included the future as well as the present life.

cense, let us go and burn incense; I will pour a libation, I will go and pour a libation, let us go and pour a libation; I will bow down, I will go and bow down, let us go and bow down '—the withdrawer is he who says, ' let us go and serve idols.' "

11. The sorcerer, who has done the act, is guilty of death, but he is not guilty who merely deludes the eyes. R. Akiba said in the name of R. Joshua, " two sorcerers can gather cucumbers—one gathers them and is free, but another gathers them and is guilty. He who has performed the act is guilty. He who has merely deluded the eyes is free."

CHAPTER VIII

1. A son stubborn and rebellious.[1] " From what time is he decidedly a son stubborn and rebellious?" " From the time the two hairs have come, and up to the time the beard has sprouted; but the Sages spoke in modest language. As is usually said, when a man has a son—a son, but not a daughter; a son, but not a man; a child as yet free from coming under the rule of the commandments."

2. " From what time is he guilty?" " From the time he ate three-quarters of a pound of flesh, and drank half a log of Italian wine." R. José said, " a pound of flesh and a log of wine." " He ate it in an appointed feast; he ate it in the intercalary month; he ate it during the second tithes in Jerusalem; he ate of a carcass and of things torn, abominable things and creeping things; he ate of that which had not paid tithes, and the first tithes before the heave-offering was separated from them and the second tithes and holy things which were not redeemed; he ate of a thing which is commanded, and of a thing which is a transgression; he ate every kind of meat; but he did not eat flesh; he drank every kind of fluid, but he did not drink wine?" " He is not a son stubborn and rebellious till he eat flesh and drink wine," as is said, " A glutton and a drunkard ";[2] and even though there is no conclusive evidence, there is a memorial to the matter, as is said, " Be not among winebibbers; among riotous eaters of flesh."[3]

3. " If he steal it from his father, and eat it (with permission) on the property of his father; from others, and eat it

---

[1] Deut. xxi. 18.   [2] Deut. xxi. 20.   [3] Prov. xxiii. 20.

12

on the property of others; from others, and eat it on the property of his father?" "He is not a son stubborn and rebellious till he steal it from his father and eat it on the property of others." R. José, the son of R. Judah, said, "till he steal it from his father and from his mother."

4. "If his father desires (his punishment), and his mother does not desire it; his father does not desire it, and his mother does desire it?" "He is not declared a son stubborn and rebellious until both of them desire it." R. Judah said, "if his mother was not suitable for his father, he is not declared a son stubborn and rebellious." "One of them was broken-handed, or lame, or dumb, or blind, or deaf?" "He is not declared a son stubborn and rebellious," as is said, "'Then shall his father and his mother lay hold on him,[4] which is impossible if they be broken-handed; 'and bring him out,' which is impossible if they be lame; 'and they shall say,' which is impossible if they be dumb; 'this our son,' which is impossible if they be blind; 'he will not obey our voice,' which is impossible if they be deaf. They must warn him before three judges, and then flog him." "He returned to his bad habits?" "He is to be judged before twenty-three judges, but he is not to be stoned till the three first (judges) are present, as is said, 'this our son' who was flogged before you." "He ran away before his judgment was finished, and afterward came to puberty?" "He is free." "But if he ran away after the decision and then came to puberty?" "He is guilty."

5. A son stubborn and rebellious is judged for the sake of his future prospects. The law says, "better die when he is innocent, and not die when he is guilty." The death of the wicked is pleasant for them, and pleasant for the world; but the death of the righteous is evil for them, and evil for the world. Wine and sleep are pleasant to the wicked, and pleasant to the world; but for the righteous, it is evil for them, and evil for the world. Separation for the wicked is pleasant for them, and pleasant for the world; but for the righteous, it is evil for them, and evil for the world. Union for the wicked is evil for them, and evil for the world; but for the righteous, it is pleasant for them, and pleasant for the world. Rest for the wicked

[4] Deut. xxi. 19, 20.

is evil for them, and evil for the world; but for the righteous, it is pleasant for them, and pleasant for the world.

6. If one engaged in burglary, he is judged for the sake of his future prospects. "He engaged in burglary and broke a barrel?" "If the owner might not kill him, he must pay for the barrel; but if the owner might kill him, he is freed from paying for the barrel."

7. These are they who are rescued [5] with their souls—he who pursued after his companion to kill him, and one after a betrothed girl. But one about to profane the Sabbath, and one about to serve idols, such cannot be saved with their souls.[6]

CHAPTER IX

1. And these are to be beheaded. The murderer and the men of a city withdrawn to idolatry. "The murderer who smote his neighbor with a stone or iron, and he pressed him down in the midst of the water, or in the midst of fire, and he could not come out from thence, and he died?" "He is guilty." "He pushed him into the midst of water, or into the midst of fire, and he could come out, but he died?" "He is free." "He encouraged a dog against him, he encouraged a serpent against him?" "He is free." "He caused a serpent to bite him?" Rabbi Judah declared him "guilty," but the Sages "freed him." "He smote his companion either with a stone or his fist, and he was counted for dead, and he became lighter, and afterward became heavier, and died?" "He is guilty." R. Nehemiah said, "he is free, because there are extenuating circumstances in the matter."

2. "His intention was to kill a beast, and he killed a man—a foreigner, and he killed an Israelite—a premature birth, and he killed a timely child?" "He is free." "His intention was to smite his loins, and there was not sufficient force in the blow to cause death in his loins, and it passed to his heart, and there was sufficient force in the blow to cause death in his heart, and he died?" "He is free." "His intention was to smite him

---

[5] I.e., they are saved from crime by immediately depriving them of life. This summary mode of procedure was called "the rebel's beating." It was a kind of lynch law inflicted by the people at once. John viii. 59.

[6] As the former class of intending criminals could at once be killed, so this latter class must be guilty of the act, and they are then judged for it.

on his heart, and there was sufficient force in the blow to cause death on his heart, and it passed on to his loins, and there was not sufficient force in the blow to cause death on his loins, but he died?" "He is free." "His intention was to smite an adult, and there was not sufficient force in the blow to cause death to an adult, and it passed off to a child, and there was sufficient force to kill the child, and he died?" "He is free." "His intention was to smite a child, and there was sufficient force in the blow to cause death to a child, and it passed to an adult, and there was not sufficient force to cause death to the adult, but he died?" "He is free." "But his intention was to smite him on his loins, and there was sufficient force in the blow to cause death on his loins, and it passed to his heart, and he died?" "He is guilty." "His intention was to smite an adult, and there was sufficient force in the blow to cause the death of the adult, and it passed to a child, and he died?" "He is guilty." R. Simon said, "even if his intention be to kill this one, and he killed that one, he is free."

3. "A murderer, who is mingled with others?" "All are to be freed." R. Judah said, "they are to be collected in a prison." "Several condemned to (different) deaths are promiscuously mingled?" They are all to be adjudged the lightest punishment." "Those condemned to stoning with those condemned to burning?" R. Simon said, "they are to be condemned to stoning, because burning is more grievous," but the Sages say, "they are to be condemned to burning, because stoning is more grievous." To them replied R. Simon, "if burning were not more grievous, it would not have been assigned to the daughter of a priest who was immoral." They replied to him, "if stoning were not more grievous, it would not have been assigned to the blasphemer, and the idolater." "Those condemned to beheading, mingled with those condemned to strangling?" R. Simon said, "they are to be put to death with the sword," but the Sages say, " with strangling."

4. "He who is found guilty of two deaths by the judges?" "He is condemned to the more grievous punishment." "He committed a transgression, . which made him deserve two deaths?" "He is condemned to the more grievous." R. José said, "he is condemned for the first deed which he committed."

5. "He who is flogged once and again?" "The judges com-

mit him to prison, and they give him barley to eat till his belly bursts." " He who killed a person without witnesses?" "They commit him to prison, and they give him to eat the bread of adversity, and the water of affliction."[1]

6. "A thief who stole a sacred vessel, and he who cursed in necromancy, and the paramour of an Aramæan?" "The avengers may at once fall upon him" "The priest who served in legal uncleanness?" "His brother priests have no need to bring him to the tribunal, but the young priests drag him outside of the court, and dash out his brains with fagots of wood." "A stranger who served in the sanctuary?" R. Akiba said, he is to be killed "with strangling," but the Sages say, "by the visitation of heaven."

CHAPTER X

1. All Israel have a portion in the world to come, as is said, "Thy people also shall be all righteous,"[1] etc. And these are they who have no portion in the world to come: he who says there is no resurrection of the dead in the law, and that there is no revealed law from heaven, and the Epicurean. R. Akiba said, "even he who reads in forbidden[2] books, and he who mutters over a wound"; and he said, "I will put none of these diseases upon thee, which I have brought upon the Egyptians: for I am the Lord that healeth thee."[3] Aba Shaul said, "even to meditate the NAME[4] in its letters."

2. Three kings and four ordinary persons have no portion in the world to come. Three kings, Jeroboam, Ahab, and Manasseh. R. Judah said, "Manasseh had a portion in the world to come," as is said, "And prayed unto him, and he was entreated of him, and heard his supplication, and brought him again to Jerusalem into his kingdom."[5] The Sages said to him, "He brought him back to his kingdom, but He did not bring him back to life in the world to come." Four ordinary persons, Balaam, and Doeg, and Ahitophel, and Gehazi, have no portion in the world to come.

3. The generation of the deluge has no portion in the world

---

[1] Isa. xxx. 20.
[1] Isa. lx. 21.
[2] Literally, outside.
[3] Exod. xv. 26.

[4] I.e., to meditate with the intention to mutter JEHOVAH over a wound.
[5] 2 Chron. xxxiii. 13.

to come, and they stand not in judgment, as is said, "My
Spirit shall not always strive with man." [6] (They have) neither
judgment nor spirit.   The generation of the dispersion has
no portion in the world to come, as is said, "So the Lord
scattered them abroad from thence upon the face of all the
earth." [7]   And the Lord scattered them in this world, and
from thence the Lord scattered them in the world to come.
The men of Sodom have no portion in the world to come, as
is said, "But the men of Sodom were wicked and sinners before the Lord exceedingly," [8] wicked in this world, and sinners in the world to come.   But they will stand in judgment.
R. Nehemiah said, "neither one nor other will stand in judgment," as is said, "Therefore the ungodly shall not stand in
the judgment, nor sinners in the congregation of the righteous." [9]   "Therefore the wicked shall not stand in judgment;" this is the generation of the deluge: "Nor sinners
in the congregation of the righteous;" these are the men of
Sodom.   The (Sages) said to him, "they do not stand in the
congregation of the righteous, but they stand in the congregation of the wicked."   The spies have no portion in the world
to come, as is said, "Even those men that did bring up the
evil report upon the land, died by the plague before the
Lord." [10]   And they died in this world.   They also died in
the plague in the world to come.   "The generation of the
wilderness has no portion in the world to come, and they will
not stand in judgment, as is said, 'In this wilderness they
shall be consumed, and there they shall die.'" [1]   The words
of R. Akiba.   R. Eliezer said, "of them He said, 'Gather my
saints together unto me, those that have made a covenant
with me by sacrifice.'" [2]   "The congregation of Korah will
not come up, as is said, 'And the earth closed upon them' [3]
in this world.   'And they perished from among the congregation' in the world to come."   The words of R. Akiba.   R.
Eliezer said, "of them he said, 'The Lord killeth and maketh
alive; he bringeth down to the grave and bringeth up.'" [4]
"The ten tribes will not return, as is said, 'And cast them into
another land, as it is this day'; [5] as the day departs and does

[6] Gen. vi. 3.
[7] Gen. xi. 8.
[8] Gen. xiii. 13.
[9] Ps. i. 5.
[10] Num. xiv. 37.

[1] Num. xiv. 35.
[2] Ps. l. 5.
[3] Num. xvi. 33.
[4] 1 Sam. ii. 6.
[5] Deut. xxix. 28.

not return, so they depart and do not return." The words of
R. Akiba. R. Eliezer said, "as the day darkens and brightens,
so will it be with the ten tribes; as it was dark for them, so
will it be bright for them."

4. The men of a city withdrawn to idolatry have no portion in the world to come, as is said, "Certain men, the children of Belial, are gone out from among you and have withdrawn the inhabitants of their city," [6] and they are not to be
killed till the withdrawers be from the city itself and from
the tribe itself, and till it withdraw the majority, and till the
withdrawers be men. If the withdrawers be women, or children, or the minority be withdrawn, or the withdrawers be
outside it, they are to be treated singly, and they need two
witnesses, and a warning to each one of them. It is more
grievous for individuals than for the multitude, because individuals must be stoned, though for that reason their money
is safe for their heirs; but the multitude are cut off with the
sword, and for that reason their money is lost.

5. "Thou shalt surely smite the inhabitants of that city," [7]
etc. A caravan of asses or camels passing from place to place
are delivered, as is said, "Destroying it utterly and all that is
therein," etc. From thence they said, "the property of the
righteous in it is lost, out of the city it is safe. But that of the
wicked, whether inside or outside, is lost."

6. "And thou shalt gather all the spoil of it into the midst
of the street thereof." [8] If it have no street, they must make
a street for it. If there be a street outside of it, they bring
it inside. "And shalt burn with fire the city and all the spoil
thereof," its spoil but not the spoil of heaven. From thence
they say, the holy things therein are to be redeemed, and the
heave-offerings suffered to decay. The second tithes and
holy writings are to be concealed. "Every whit for the Lord
thy God." Said R. Simon, "The Holy One, Blessed be He,
said, If you execute judgment on the withdrawn city, I count
it for you as though you brought a burnt-offering wholly before me." "And it shall be a heap forever; it shall not be
built again." "Thou shalt not make of it even gardens or
parks." The words of R. José, the Galilean. R. Akiba said,
"it shall not be builded again. It must not be built as it was

---

[6] Deut. xiii. 13.   [7] Deut. xiii. 15.   [8] Deut. xiii. 16.

before, but it may be made (into) gardens and parks." "And there shall cleave naught of the cursed thing to thine hand."⁹ Whilst the wicked are in the world, wrath is in the world. When the wicked are destroyed from the world, wrath retires from the world.

CHAPTER XI

1. These are to be strangled—he who beats his father or his mother, and he who steals a soul from Israel, and an "elder" who is rebellious against the judges, and a false prophet, and he who prophesies in the name of idolatry, and false witnesses proved to be perjured against a priest's daughter and her paramour. He who beats father or mother is not guilty till he make a bruise in them. It is more grievous to curse them than to beat them. Because if he cursed them after their death, he is guilty; but if he beat them after their death, he is free. He who stole a soul from Israel is not guilty till he bring him on his property. R. Judah said, "till he bring him on his property and obtain service by him," as is said, "And maketh merchandise of him, or selleth him."¹ "If he steal his own son?" R. Ishmael, the son of R. Jochanan, the son of Beroka, pronounces him "guilty," but the Sages pronounce him "free." "If he stole one, half a servant and half free?" R. Judah pronounces him "guilty," but the Sages pronounce him "free."

2. The elder rebellious against the decision of the judges⁹ as it is said, "If there arise a matter too hard for thee in judgment,"² etc. There were three places of judgment. One place was by the door of the Mountain of the House; and one was by the door of the court; and one was in the chamber of hewn stone. The witnesses against the rebellious elder came to the one by the door of the Mountain of the House, and each one said, "so I expounded, and so my companions expounded; so I taught, and so my companions taught." If the judges listened to them, they told them: but if not, they went to those at the door of the court, and each one said, "so I expounded, and so my companions expounded; so I taught, and so my companions taught." If they listened to them, they told them; but if not, both parties went to the su-

⁹ Deut. xiii. 17.　¹ Deut. xxiv. 7.　² Deut. xvii. 8.

preme court in the chamber of hewn stone, because from it
the Law proceeded forth to all Israel, as is said, " Of that
place which the Lord shall choose." [3] " If the rebellious elder
returned to his city, and taught as before? " " He is free."
" But if he decided to practise false teaching? " " He is
guilty," as is said, " And the man that will do presumptuously " [4] He is not guilty till he decide to practise his false
teaching. A disciple who decided to practise false teaching is
free. It follows that what is a grave offence in the one is a
light offence in the other.

3. The burden in the words of the scribes is greater than
the burden in the words of the law. He who said, " There are
no phylacteries, so as to transgress the words of the law? "
" He is free." He who said, " There are five frontlets, so as
to add to the words of the scribes? " " He is guilty."

4. " The judges do not put such an offender to death in
the tribunal of his city, nor in the tribunal of Jabneh,[5] but
they bring him up to the supreme court in Jerusalem, and
they guard him till a holiday; and they put him to death on
a holiday, as is said, " And all the people shall hear and fear,
and do no more presumptuously." [6] The words of R. Abika.
R. Judah said, " they do not cause him anguish in delaying his
judgment, but they execute him off-hand." And they write
and send messengers to all places, " Such a man, the son of
such a man, is condemned to death by the tribunal."

5. A false prophet, who prophesied what he did not hear,
and what was not told to him, is put to death by the hands of
man. But he who suppressed his prophecy, and he who added
to the words of a prophet, and a prophet who transgressed his
own words, is put to death by the visitation of heaven, as is
said, " I will require it of him." [7]

6. And he who prophesied in the name of idolatry and
said, " so the idol said," even though its decision was exactly
to pronounce unclean the unclean, and to pronounce cleansed
the clean, is to be strangled. And so also the false witnesses
against a priest's daughter. Because all false witnesses are
condemned to the same death which they had intended (for
the accused), except false witnesses against the daughter of a
priest, and they are to be strangled.

ON IDOLATRY[1]

CHAPTER I

1. Three days before the feasts of the idolaters it is forbidden to deal with them, to lend articles to them, or to take
a loan of articles from them ; to make a loan of money to them,
or to borrow money from them ; to repay them, or to take payment from them. Rabbi Judah said, " it is allowed to take
payment from them, since it is unsatisfactory to the idolater."
The (Sages) answered him, " though it is unpleasant to him
now, he rejoices afterward."

2. R. Ishmael said, " three days before and three days after
their feasts it is forbidden." But the Sages say, " before their
feasts it is forbidden, after their feasts it is allowed."

3. " And these are the feasts of the idolaters—the Kalends,
and the Saturnalia, and the Quartesima, and the coronation
day of their kings, and the day of their birth, and the day of
their death." The words of R. Meier. But the Sages say,
" every death anniversary in which there is burning of incense,[2] there is in it the worship of idols. But if there be no
burning of incense there is no worship of idols." " The day
of shaving his beard and cutting his hair, the day of his dis-
embarking from the sea, and the day of his release from prison,
and the day when the heathen makes a feast for his son ? "
" It is not forbidden to deal with them save on this day of his
feast, and with this man who keeps the feast only."

---

[1] Literally, strange worship. It chiefly means the worship of the stars and
other heavenly bodies. [2] Jer. xxxiv. 5.

4. "The city in which there exists idolatry outside the city?" "It is allowed to deal with the idolaters." "If the idolatry be outside?" "Inside it is allowed." "How is it with going there?" "When the road directly leads to the place itself, it is forbidden; but if it be possible to go by it to another place, it is allowed."

5. "If in the city in which there exists idolatry there be shops, some decorated with idolatrous crowns, and some without decoration?" This was the case in Bethshan; and the Sages say, "the decorated ones are forbidden for dealing, and those not decorated are allowed."

6. These things are forbidden to be sold to idolaters—fircones, and the best figs, with their clusters, and incense, and the white cock. R. Judah said, "it is allowable to sell a white cock among many others. But when a man has only one, he must cut its claw before he sell it, since the heathen do not offer that which is blemished in idol worship." And all other things for ordinary uses are allowed—but if they be declared to be for idolatry, they are forbidden. R. Meier said, "even the fine dates, and the date sap,[3] and the Jericho dates, are forbidden for sale to idolaters."

7. Where they are accustomed to sell small cattle to idolaters, they may sell them. Where they are unaccustomed to sell them, they must not sell them. And everywhere they must not sell to them the large cattle, calves, ass foals, unblemished or blemished. R. Judah allowed the broken-boned; and Benbethira allowed even horses.

8. Men must not sell to them bears or lions, or anything in which there is peril to the multitude. They must not build with them royal halls,[4] judgment-seats, and stadiums,[5] and bemas.[6] But men may build with them altars and baths. When they reach to the arching in which they place their idol, it is forbidden to build farther.

9. And Israelites must not make decorations for idols, necklaces, and nose-rings, and rings. R. Eleazar said, "for pay it is allowed." Men must not sell to them what is fastened to the ground. But one may sell it after it is cut down. R. Judah

---

[3] Or sugar-cane.
[4] For executions.
[5] For races.

[6] Where harangues were delivered involving life and death.

said, "one may sell it to a heathen on condition that he cuts
it down."

10. "Men must not let to them buildings [7] in the Land of
Israel, and it is needless to say fields. But in Syria they may
let to them buildings, but not fields. But out of the Land
they may sell to them buildings, and may rent to them fields."
The words of R. Meier. R. José said, "in the Land of Israel
men may let to them buildings, but not fields. But in Syria
they may sell buildings and rent fields to them, and out of the
Land they may sell both." However, where they said to let,
they did not say a dwelling-house; since a heathen can bring
inside of it an idol, as it is said, "Thou shalt not bring in
abomination into thy house." [8] And everywhere a man must
not hire to a heathen his bath, because it is called by his
name.

CHAPTER II

1. Israelites must not put cattle in the stables of idolaters,
because of their evil habits. And a woman must not be alone
with them, because of their evil habits. And no man should
be alone with them, because they are apt to shed blood.

2. A daughter of Israel must not attend an idolatrous
woman, because she helps the birth of a child for idolatry.
But an idolatress may attend a daughter of Israel. A daughter of Israel must not suckle a child of an adolatress; but an
idolatress may suckle a child of a daughter of Israel, under her
observation.

3. "Israelites may take from them medicine to cure property; but not to cure persons. And they are not to be shaved
by them anywhere." The words of R. Meier. But the Sages
say, "under public observation it is allowed, but not entirely
alone."

4. These things of the idolaters are forbidden, and every
use of them is strictly forbidden; wine, and vinegar of the
heathen which was at first wine, and Hadrian's mixture [1] with
its fragments, and hides of animals with their hearts [2] (torn

---

[7] Nor graves.
[8] Deut. vii. 26.
[1] Hadrian's mixture was balls of clay saturated with wine and taken on military expeditions. When the soldiers wished to drink, they soaked them in water so that it had a taste of wine, and the mud settled at the bottom of the vessel.
[2] The heart torn out of the animal when alive to be offered in idolatrous worship.

out). Rabbi Simon, the son of Gamaliel, said, "when the rent is round, it is forbidden, when lengthwise, it is allowed." " The flesh brought in for idolatry is allowed; but that which is brought out is forbidden, because it is the sacrifice for the dead." The words of R. Akiba. It is forbidden to do business with those who go to worship the Penates; but with those who return from them it is allowed. " The skin-bottles of the idolaters and their jugs into which Jewish wine is poured, are forbidden, and every use of them is strictly forbidden." The words of R. Meier. But the Sages say, "every use of them is not forbidden." " Grape-stones and grapeskins of the idolaters are forbidden, and every use of them is strictly forbidden." The words of R. Meier. But the Sages say, "when moist, they are forbidden; but when dry, they are allowed " " Fish-brine and the cheese from Bethuniki,[3] a village of the idolaters, are forbidden, and every use of them strictly forbidden." The words of R. Meier. But the Sages say, "every use of them is not forbidden." R. Judah related, that R. Ishmael asked R. Joshua, as they were journeying along the road—he said to him, " why do they forbid the cheese of idolaters? " He replied to him, " because they cause it to ferment with the stomach of a carcass." R. Ishmael said to him, " and is not the stomach of a burnt-offering of more importance than the stomach of a carcass," and it was said, " the priest who was so minded supped the milk that was in it," but the Sages did not agree with him, and they said, " the priests do not use it, and they are not guilty." He changed the conversation, and said to him, " because they ferment it with the stomach of a calf (devoted) to idolatry." He said to him, " if so, why do they not forbid it for every use? " He turned to another subject, and said to him, " brother Ishmael, how do you read, ' For thy love is better than wine,'[4] or ' For thy love is good '? " He replied to him, " For thy love is good." He said to him, " it is not so, since the next verse explains it, ' Because of the savor of thy good ointments.'"

5. These things of the idolaters are forbidden, but every

---

[3] A village where calves were offered in idolatry. Consequently the rennet was forbidden, and the cheese made from their rennet was also forbidden.
[4] Sol. Song, i. 2. The question is, whether the friendship sprang from the wine or not, and his conclusion is that as the savor is connected with the oil, so is the friendship with the wine, and so is the cheese connected with idolatry.

use of them is not strictly forbidden; milk which a heathen milked, and an Israelite did not see it. "Their bread and oil?" "Rabbi and his colleagues allowed oil." But the cookery, and the gravy into which they are wont to put wine and vinegar, and shred thunny fish, and the sauce in which the fish chalbith is not swimming, and the herring, and the essence of assafœtida, and spiced salt, are forbidden; but every use of them is not strictly forbidden.

6. These things are allowed for eating—milk which an idolater milked, and an Israelite saw, and honey and honeycomb, even if they are dropping, as they do not contain the effect of liquor,[5] and gravy into which they are not wont to put wine and vinegar, and shred thunny fish, and sauce in which there is the fish chalbith, and the leaf of the assafœtida, and olives crushed into round cakes. R. José said, "the kernels detached from the olives are forbidden." The locusts which they bring from their baskets[6] are forbidden; but those brought from their magazines are allowed. And even so is the decision for their heave-offerings.

CHAPTER III

1. "All images are forbidden, because they are worshipped once a year." The words of R. Meier. But the Sages say, "only those are forbidden which have in their hand a staff, or bird, or ball." R. Simon, the son of Gamaliel, said, "all images which have in their hand anything whatever."

2. "If one find the broken pieces of images?" "They are allowed (for useful purposes)." "If one find the figure of a hand, or the figure of a foot?" "They are forbidden, because such as they are worshipped."

3. "(If one find) vessels on which is the form of the sun-disk, the form of the moon, the form of a dragon?" "They are to be carried into the Salt Sea."[1] R. Simon, the son of Gamaliel, said, "when such forms are on precious (vessels) they are forbidden, when they are on insignificant (ones) they are allowed."

---

[5] I.e., for legal defilement.
[6] The locusts might be mixed in the basket with wine or liquor, which would cause legal defilement.

[1] The Salt Sea generally means in the Talmud the Dead Sea. It is now called by the Arabs "Bahr-Lût," i.e., the Sea of Lot.

4. R. José said, "one must grind the image to powder and scatter it to the wind, or cast it into the sea." The Sages said to him, "then it will make dung," and it is said, "And there shall not cleave to thy hand aught of the accursed thing." [2]

5. Proclus, the son of a philosopher, asked R. Gamaliel, in Acho,[3] as he was bathing in the bath of Venus, an'd said to him, "it is written in thy law, 'and there shall not cleave to thy hand aught of the accursed thing'; why dost thou bathe in the bath of Venus?" He said to him, "men do not give replies in the bath"; and when he came out he said to him, "I came not within its district; it came into my district." They did not say, "let us make a bath to the honor of Venus, but they said, let us make Venus an honor to the bath." Another thing: "if they gave thee money wouldst thou enter naked before thy idol, or wouldst thou do aught disgraceful in its presence? yet if it stands on a canal everyone dishonors it." It is not said, save for their heathen gods, "that which is customary from its being a god, is forbidden, that which is not customary from its being a god, is allowed."

6. Though idolaters worship the mountains and the hills, the mountains and the hills are allowed, but what is upon them is forbidden; as is said, "Thou shalt not covet the silver and the gold upon them to take them."[4] R. José, the Galilean, said, "their gods of the mountains, but not the mountains their gods; their gods of the hills, but not the hills their gods." "But why are the groves forbidden?" "Because they are prepared by man's hands, and every object of idolatry which is prepared by man's hands is forbidden." Said R. Akiba, "I will consider and decide before thee; every place in which you find a high mountain, and an elevated hill, and a flourishing tree, know that there is idolatry."

7. "He who had a house joined to an idol, and it fell down?" "It is forbidden to rebuild it." "What shall he do?" "He must first reduce the size of the house by four cubits, and then rebuild it." "If the house be in common between him and the idol?" "It is decided to leave the four cubits unoccupied, as its stones, wood, and dust cause defilement like a worm, 'Thou shalt utterly detest it.'"[5]

[2] Deut. xiii. 17.
[3] The modern Akka (Acre).
[4] Deut. vii. 25.
[5] Deut. vii. 26.

8. There are three sorts of buildings. The house originally built for idolatry is forbidden. " If the idolater whitewashed, and painted, and repaired it for the idol? " " He must take down his repairs." " If he brought in and afterward took out the idol? " " It is allowed."

9. There are three sorts of stones. The stone originally hewn for a pedestal to the idol is forbidden. " If the idolater whitewashed, and painted, and repaired it to honor an idol? " " He must take down his repairs." " If he placed his idol upon it, and afterward took it away? " " It is allowed."

10. There are three sorts of groves. The tree originally planted to honor an idol is forbidden. " If the idolater cut it, and hewed it, and made changes to honor an idol? " " He must take down his changes " " If he placed an idol beneath it and abused it? " " It is allowed."

11. " What is a grove? " " That in which there is an idol." R. Simon said, " everything that is worshipped, as it happened in Zidon at the tree where they worshipped, and they found beneath it a heap. Said R. Simon to them, ' examine this heap.' And they examined it and found in it an image. He said to them, ' as the object of service is the image, we shall allow the tree to you.' "

12. One must not sit in the shadow of an idolatrous grove, and though he sit, he is legally clean. And one must not pass underneath it ; even if one pass he is defiled. " If it occupy the public thoroughfare and one pass beneath it? " " He is clean."

13. One may sow underneath it vegetables in winter, but not in summer. But lettuce⁶ must not be sown either in summer or winter. R. José said, " not even vegetables in winter, since the leaves would fall upon them and serve them for dung."

14. " Has one taken wood from it? " " Its wood is forbidden for every use." " Has one heated an oven with it ? " " If the oven be new it must be broken down, and if old it must be cooled down." " Has one baked bread in it? " " The use of the bread is forbidden." " Are the loaves mixed with other loaves, and these again with others? " " The use of all the loaves is forbidden." R. Eliezer said, " its value is to be

---

⁶ Lest the lettuce might derive profit from the shade of the idolatrous grove.

cast into the Salt Sea." The Sages replied to him, "there is
no redemption for idolatry." "Has one made out of such a
tree a weaver's shuttle?" "Its use is forbidden." "Has one
woven a garment with it?" "The use of the garment is forbidden." "Is the garment mixed with other garments, and
these again with others?" "The use of all the garments is
forbidden." Rabbi Eleazar said, "its value is to be cast into
the Salt Sea." The Sages replied to him, "there is no redemption for idolatry."

15. "How is the tree to be desecrated?" "Has the idolater
broken off dry bark, or green boughs; has he taken from it a
staff, or a twig, or even a leaf—it is desecrated." "Has he
trimmed it for the sake of the tree?" "It is forbidden." "Has
he trimmed it, but not for the sake of the tree?" "It is al
lowed."

CHAPTER IV

1. Rabbi Ishmael said, "three stones [1] beside each other at
the side of the image of Mercury are forbidden, but two are
allowed." But the Sages say, "when they are within his view
they are forbidden, but when they are not within his view they
are allowed."

2. "Has one found money on his head, a garment, or implements which are not offerings?" "They are allowed."
Festoons of grapes, wreaths of ears of corn, and wines, and
oils, and fine flour, and everything similar offered on his altar
are forbidden.

3. A garden or a bath for idolatry is permitted for use
when it is gratuitous. But neither is to be used if a present
for the worship of the idol be expected. If it be in partner-
ship with others that are not so employed, either can be
used, whether it be with the expectation of a present or
gratuitous. The idol of idolaters is at once forbidden, but the
idol of Israel is not forbidden until it be served.

4. An idolater may desecrate his own idol, or the idol of
his companion. But Israël must not desecrate the idol of an
idolater. In desecrating the idol he desecrates what apper-

---

[1] These stones must be arranged as
two on the ground, and one over them,
and not more than four ells distant
from the image, to fulfil the conditions
of being an idolatrous offering. If the
stones did not fulfil these conditions,
an Israelite might use them for building
purposes.

tains to it. "Has he desecrated what appertains to it?"
"What appertains to it is allowed, but the idol itself is forbidden."

5. "How is it to be desecrated?" "He cuts off the lobe of
its ear, the tip of its nose, the end of its finger—he deforms
even though he does not diminish it—it is desecrated." "He
spits before it, he drags it, and throws dirt upon it?" "It is
not desecrated." "Has he sold it or pledged it?" Rabbi says,
"it is desecrated." But the Sages say, "it is not desecrated."

6. The idol, the service of which is abandoned in the time
of peace, is allowed. "But if its service be abandoned in time
of war?" "It is forbidden."[2] The royal pedestals[3] are forbidden, because they are erected at the time when kings are
travelling.

7. The elders were asked in Rome, "If God has no pleas-
ure in idolatry, why does He not destroy it?" They replied
to the Romans, "If the idolaters were serving a thing which
was not necessary to the world, He would destroy it, but they
serve the sun-disk, and the moon, and the stars, and the signs
of the zodiac. Shall he destroy his world on account of the
fools?" They replied to them, "If so He can destroy the
object which is not wanted for the world, and leave that which
the world wants." They replied to them, "even we should be
strengthening the hands of the worshippers of such objects;
they would say, there is a proof that they are gods, because
they are not destroyed."

8. One may buy a wine-press pressed by an idolater, even
though he take *grapes* with his hand and lay them on the
heap of grapes, as it is not made the wine of idolatrous libation till it runs into the vat. "Has it run into the vat?"
"That which is in the vat is forbidden, but the remainder is
allowed." One may tread with an idolater in the wine-press,
but one must not gather grapes with him. One must not tread
or gather grapes with an Israelite who works in a state of defilement. But one may carry with him empty barrels to the
press and bring them away with him from the press. One

---

[2] If the idol be disregarded in time
of peace, the heathen have ceased to
esteem it as a god, and Israelites might
use it for some purpose. But if the
heathen neglected it during the confusion of war, there was no proof that
they would not worship it at another
time.

[3] I.e., triumphal arches with statues
upon them.

must not knead nor prepare with the baker who works in (a state of) legal defilement, but one may carry the bread with him to the dealer in bread.

9. "If an idolater be found standing by the side of a wine vat, and if he have any loan upon it?" "It is forbidden." "If he have no loan on it?" "It is allowed" "Has he fallen into the vat and come out again, or measured it with a cane; has he driven away a hornet with a cane; or has he given a slap to the fermentation on the top of the barrel?" All these things once happened, and the (Sages) decided, "Let it be sold." But R. Simon "allowed it." He took the barrel and flung it in a rage into the vat. This once happened, and the Sages allowed it.

10. "Has one made the wine of an idolater without legal defilement, and left it in his possession in a house open to public concourse—in a city in which there are idolaters and Israelites?" "It is allowed." "In a city in which all are idolaters?" "It is forbidden till he leave a watchman, and it is not needful that the watchman sit and watch. Even though he goes in and out it is allowed." R. Simon, the son of Eleazar, said, "all possession of wine by idolaters is alike." "Has one made the wine of a heathen without legal defilement, and left it in his possession, and the idolater afterward wrote to him, I have received from you the money for the wine?" "It is allowed." "But if the Israelite wish to withdraw it, and the idolater do not permit him, till he shall give him his money for it?" This once happened in Bethshan, and the Sages "forbade it."

CHAPTER V

1. "Has an idolater hired an Israelite to make with him wine of idolatrous libation?" "His wages are forbidden." "But if he hired him to do with him another work, even though he say to him, 'carry for me a barrel of wine of libation from place to place?'" "His wages are allowed." "Has one hired an ass to bring on him wine of idolatrous libation?" "The hire is not allowed." "Has one hired out the ass for riding, even though the idolater put his wine flask upon him?" "The hire is allowed."

2. Wine of idolatrous libation which fell on grapes must be cleansed away, and they are allowed. But if the grapes be crushed, they are forbidden. " Has the idolatrous wine fallen on figs or on dates?" "If it convey to them a taste, they are forbidden." It happened once with Baithus, son of Zonan, that he brought dried figs in a boat, and a barrel of wine of idolatrous libation was broken, and it fell upon them, and he consulted the Sages and they allowed them. This is the rule: In every use where the taste is conveyed, it is forbidden. But where in its use no taste is conveyed, it is allowed. It is like vinegar which has fallen on peas.

3. " An idolater who was carrying with an Israelite pitchers of wine from place to place?" "If it be certain that the idolater is watched, it is allowed." "If the Israelite let him know that he is departing—if there be time to bore, to close, and to seal the pitcher?" R. Simon, son of Gamaliel, said, " it is not allowed if there be time to open, to cork, and to seal it again." " And an Israelite put his wine into a carriage, or into a boat, and he has gone a near cut—he entered the city and washed?" " It is allowed." " But if he let the idolater know that he is departing, if there be time to bore, and cork, and seal it again?" R. Simon, son of Gamaliel, said, " it is not allowed if there be time to open the barrel and cork and seal it again." "If he leave the idolater in the wine-shop, even though he go in and out?" " It is allowed." " But if he let the idolater know that he departs, if there be time to bore, and cork, and seal it again?" R. Simon ben Gamaliel said, " it is not allowed if there be time to open, and to cork, and to seal it again." " Did he dine with the idolater at table, and he left a flask on the table, and a flask on the sideboard, and he left them and went out?" " That one which is on the table is forbidden, but that one on the sideboard is allowed." " But if he said to him, ' you may mix and drink wine, even that one on the sideboard is forbidden?'"[1] Open barrels are forbidden, also sealed ones, when there is time to open, and cork, and seal them up again."

4. If foreign banditti have entered into a city in time of peace, open barrels are forbidden—closed ones are allowed.

---

[1] Because the idolater might have made an idolatrous libation from both flasks.

If the banditti have entered in time of war, both are equally allowed, because there is no time for idolatrous libation.

5. When an idolater has sent to workmen of Israel a barrel of wine of idolatrous libation for wages, it is allowed to say, "give us its value." "But if it has come into their possession?" "It is forbidden."

6. "Has one sold wine to an idolater?" "If he agreed for the price before it is measured, its payment is allowed." "Has he measured it before he agreed for the price?" "Its payment is forbidden."

7. "Has one taken a funnel and measured wine into the bottle of an idolater, and he then turned round and measured wine into the bottle of an Israelite?" "If the funnel retain a drop of the wine of the idolater, the wine is forbidden." "Has one poured the wine from vessel to vessel?" "That vessel from which he poured it is allowed, and that one into which he poured it is forbidden."

8. Wine of idolatrous libation is forbidden, and even a little of it renders forbidden—wine in wine, and water in water —how much soever they be, and wine in water, and water in wine, in giving a taste. This is the rule: If both be of one sort, however little; if they be of different sorts, in giving a taste.

9. These things are forbidden, and even a little of them renders other things forbidden. Wine of idolatrous libation, and idols, and skins of beasts with the hearts torn out, and an ox that was stoned,[2] and a heifer that is beheaded,[3] and the birds from the leprosy, and the hair of the Nazarite,[4] and the first-born of the ass, and flesh in milk, and the scapegoat, and the profane animals [5] which were slaughtered in the Temple court. These are forbidden to be mixed with other things; and if so mixed, even a little of them renders other things forbidden.

10. "Wine of idolatrous libation which has fallen into a vat?" "All its use is forbidden." R. Simon ben Gamaliel said, "it may all be sold to heathens, excepting the value of the wine of idolatrous libation which is in it."

---

[2] Exod. xxi. 29.
[3] Deut. xxi. 4.
[4] Num. vi. 18.
[5] This refers to the killing or slaugh-

tering of cattle and fowls for profane or domestic purposes. They were called profane to distinguish them from the holy sacrifices.

11. "A stone-press which an idolater has prepared with pitch?" "It must be cleansed, and it is clean." "And if of wood?" Rabbi said, "it should be cleansed"; and the Sages said, "one must peel off the pitch; but if it be made of earthenware, even though one peel off the pitch, it is forbidden."

12. "If one buy culinary utensils from an idolater?" "That which it is usual to dip (in water), one must dip; to scour, one must scour; to whiten in the fire, one must whiten in fire. The spit and the fork, one must whiten in the fire;[8] and the knife must be rubbed down, and it is clean."

<hr />

[8] Num. xxxi. 23.

THE FATHERS

The Oral Law—Its Transmission—Names of the " Receivers "—Maxims
—Apothegms—Wisdom of the Wise.

CHAPTER I

1. Moses received the Oral Law from Sinai and delivered
it to Joshua, and Joshua delivered it to the elders, and the
elders to the prophets, and the prophets to the men of the
great synagogue.[1] They said three things, " be deliberate in
judgment, raise up many disciples, and make a fence for the
law."

2. Simon the Just was one of the last of the men of the
great synagogue. He used to say that the world stood on
three things—" on the law, the service, and the acts of the
pious."

3. Antigonus of Soco received (the law) from Simon the
Just. He used to say, " be not as servants, who serve their
master for the sake of receiving a reward, but be like servants
who serve their master without the view of receiving a reward; and let the fear of heaven be upon you."

4. José, son of Joezer of Zeredah, and José, son of Jochanan
of Jerusalem, received (the oral law) from him. José, son of
Joezer of Zeredah, said, " let thy house be a house of assembly
for the wise, and dust thyself with the dust of their feet, and
drink their words in thirstiness."

5. José, son of Jochanan of Jerusalem, said, " let thy house
be wide open, and let the poor be thy children. Discourse
not much with women, not even with thy wife, much less with

---

[1] The men of the great synagogue
were the " Scribes " who flourished from
the return out of Babylon till the Græco-
Syrian persecution, 220 B.C. Their object was to preserve the sacred text
with scrupulous minuteness, and make
a " fence " for the law. They added
numberless directions for the better observance of the old precepts. The
Scribes were succeeded by the " learn-
ers," the " repeaters," and the " master builders," who continued from 220
B.C. till 220 A.D. In their time fall the
Maccabæan revolution, the birth of
Christ, the overthrow of the Temple by
Titus, the rebellion of Barchochba, the
complete destruction of Jerusalem, and
the dispersion of the Jews.

thy neighbor's wife." Hence the wise men say, "whoever converses much with women brings evil on himself, neglects the study of the law, and at last will inherit hell."

6. Joshua, son of Perechiah, and Natai the Arbelite received the oral law from them. Joshua, son of Perechiah, said, "get thyself a master, and obtain a companion, and judge all mankind with favor."

7. Natai the Arbelite said, "withdraw from an evil neighbor, and associate not with the wicked, neither flatter thyself to escape punishment."

8. Judah, son of Tabai, and Simon, son of Shetach, received it of them. Judah, son of Tabai, said, "consider not thyself as the arranger of the law, and when the parties are before thee in judgment, consider them as guilty; but when they are departed from thee, consider them as innocent, when they have acquiesced in the sentence."

9. Simon, son of Shetach, said, "be extremely careful in the examination of witnesses, and be cautious in thy words, lest they from thence should learn to utter a falsehood."

10. Shemaiah and Abtalyon [2] received it from them. Shemaiah said, "love thy business and hate dominion, and be unknown to government."

11. Abtalyon said, "ye Sages, be cautious of your words, lest ye be doomed to captivity, and carried captive to a place of bad waters, and the disciples who follow you should drink of them, by which means the name of God may be profaned."

12. Hillel and Shammai received it of them. Hillel said, "be thou of the disciples of Aaron, who loved peace, and pursued peace, so that thou love mankind, and allure them to the study of the law."

13. He used to say, "whoever aggrandizes his name, destroys his name, and he who does not increase his knowledge in the law, shall be cut off, and he who does not study the law, is deserving of death, and he who serves himself with the crown of the law, will perish."

14. He also said, "if I perform not good works myself, who can do them for me?" and "when I consider myself, what am I?" and "if not now, when shall I?"

---

[2] Supposed by some to be the Sameas and Pollio of Josephus. Though others try to identify Sameas with Simon, son of Shetach.—"Antiq." xiv. ix. 4, etc.

15. Shammai said, " let thy study of the law be fixed, say little and do much, and receive all men with an open, pleasant face."

16. Rabban Gamaliel said, "procure thyself an instructor, that thou mayest not be in doubt, and accustom not thyself to give tithes by conjecture."

17. Simon, his son, said, " I have all my life been brought up among wise men, and never found anything so good for the body as silence, neither is the study of the law the principal thing, but its practice," and " whoever multiplies words causes sin."

18. Rabban Simon, son of Gamaliel, said the duration of the world depends on three things, justice, truth, and peace, as is said, " judge truth, and justice, and peace in your gates."

CHAPTER II

1. Rabbi Judah said, "which are the most eligible paths for man to choose? All such as are an ornament to those who tread therein; and get them honor from man. Be also as careful of the observance of a light precept, as of a weighty one; because thou knowest not the due reward of the precepts, and balance the loss sustained by the omission of a precept against its recompense, and the reward of sin against its loss of happiness. Consider also three things, and thou wilt not transgress. Understand what is above thee: an All-seeing Eye and a Hearing Ear; and that all thy actions are written in a Book."

2. Rabban Gamaliel, the son of Rabban Judah the Prince, said, " that the study of the law and intercourse with the world are commendable together, as the joining of these two annihilates sin; and all the study of the law, that is not supported by business, will become of none effect, and will be the cause of sin; and whoever is engaged in the service of the congregation, ought to act for God's sake, then will the merit of their ancestors support them, and their charitable deeds exist to eternity; and I (God) shall account you deserving of a great recompense, as if ye had actually done it."

3. " Be ye warned of following princes, as they only bestow favors on men for their own interest. They show themselves

as friends while men are useful to them; but they will not support a man in time of need."

4. He used to say, "do His will as if it were thine own will, that He may accomplish thy will as if it were His will; abolish thy will for the sake of His will, that He may abolish the will of others for the sake of thy will." Hillel said, "separate not thyself from the congregation, nor have confidence in thyself, until the day of thy death. Judge not thy neighbor till thou art in his situation, neither utter a sentence as if it were incomprehensible, that afterward may be comprehended, nor say, when I shall have leisure I shall study; mayhap thou wilt not have leisure."

5. He also said, "a boor cannot be fearful of sin, nor can a rustic be a saint; the bashful will not become learned, nor the passionate man a teacher; neither will he, who is much engaged in traffic, become wise; and where there are no men, strive thou to be a man."

6. He having also seen a skull floating on the water, said, "because thou didst make others float, have they floated thee! and the end of those who made thee float will be that they will float."

7. He also said, "he who increases flesh, increases worms; he who increases riches, increases care; he who increases wives, increases witchcraft; he who increases female servants, increase lewdness; he who increases men servants, increases robbery; but he who increases his knowledge of the law, increases life; he who increases his study in college, increases wisdom; he who increases counsel, increases prudence; he who increases justice, increases peace; if a man have gained a good name, he has gained it for himself; if he have gained the words of the law, he has gained for himself everlasting life in the world to come."

8. Rabbi Jochanan, son of Zaccai, received the oral law from Hillel and Shammai. He used to say, "if thou hast spent much time in the study of the law, yet pride not thyself thereon, because for that wast thou created." Rabbi Jochanan, son of Zaccai, had five disciples, and these are they: Rabbi Eleazar, son of Hyrcanus, Rabbi Joshua, son of Chananya, Rabbi José the priest, Rabbi Simon, son of Nathanael, Rabbi Eleazar, son of Arach. He used thus to estimate their merits:

"R. Eleazar, son of Hyrcanus, is as a well-plastered cistern which loses not a drop; Joshua, son of Chananya, happy are his parents; José the priest is a saint; Simon, son of Nathanael, fears sin; Eleazar, son of Arach, is a mighty spring." He used to say, "if all the Sages of Israel were in one scale of the balance, and R. Eleazar, son of Hyrcanus, in the other, he would outweigh them all." Abba Saul said in his name, "if all the Sages of Israel were in one scale, and even R. Eleazar, son of Hyrcanus, with them, and R. Eleazar, son of Arach, in the other, he would outweigh them all."

9. He also said to them, "go forth and consider which is the good path for man to cleave to?" To this R. Eleazar answered, "a good eye." R. Joshua said, "a good companion." R. José said, "a good neighbor." R. Simon said, "he who foresees the future." R. Eleazar said, "a good heart." He then said to them, "I prefer the words of R. Eleazar, son of Arach, above yours, as his words include yours." He also said to them, "go forth and consider which is the bad way that man should shun"; to which R. Eleazar said, "a bad eye." R. Joshua said, "a bad companion." R. José said, "a bad neighbor." R. Simon said, "he who borrows and pays not; for when one borrows from man, it is as if he borrows from God, as is said, 'The wicked borroweth and payeth not again; but the righteous showeth mercy and giveth.'"[1] R. Eleazar said, "a bad heart." He then said to them, "I prefer the words of R. Eleazar, son of Arach, above yours, as his words include yours."

10. They also said three things. R. Eleazar said, "let the honor of thy companion be as dear to thee as thine own; and be not easily moved to anger; and repent one day before thy death; and warm thyself by the fire of the Sages, and be careful that their coal does not burn thee, for their bite is as a bite of a fox, and their sting is as the sting of a scorpion, and their burn is the burn of a fiery serpent, and all their words are as fiery coals."

11. R. Joshua said, "the bad eye, the bad thought, and envy of companions, cause the death of man."

12. R. José said, "let thy companion's property be as dear to thee as thine own; and prepare thyself to study the law, as it

[1] Ps. xxxvii. 21.

cometh not to thee by inheritance; and let all thine actions be in the name of God."

13. R. Simon said, " be careful of reading the ' Hear,'[2] etc., and the other prayers; and when thou art praying consider not thy prayer as fixed, but as supplicating mercy in the presence of the Supreme, as is said, ' For He is gracious and merciful, slow to anger and of great kindness, and repenteth Him of the evil ';[3] and be not impious in thine own sight."

14. R. Eleazar said, " be diligent to study the law, that thou mayest know how to confute the Epicurean; consider also in whose presence thou art laboring, for the Master of thy work is faithful to pay thee the reward of thy labor."

15. R. Tarphon said, " the day is short, the labor vast, but the laborers are slothful, though the reward is great, and the Master of the house presseth for despatch."

16. He used to say, " it is not incumbent upon thee to complete the work, neither art thou free to cease from it. If thou hast studied the law, great shall be thy reward; for the Master of thy work is faithful to pay the reward of thy labor; but know that the reward of the righteous is in the world to come."

CHAPTER III

1. Akabia, son of Mahallalel, said, " ponder on three things, and thou wilt not be led to the commission of sin; consider from whence thou comest, and whither thou goest; and in whose presence thou must in futurity stand to account in judgment. From whence comest thou? from a foul drop. And whither goest thou? to a place of dust—worms—and reptiles; and in whose presence art thou in future to account in judgment? even before the King Who is King of kings, and the HOLY ONE, blessed be He."

2. Rabbi Chanina, suffragan of the priests, said, " pray for the peace of the kingdom, for, were it not for its fear, men would swallow each other alive." Rabbi Chanina, son of Theradion, said, " two who are sitting together and speak not of the law are an assembly of scorners; as is said, " Nor sitteth in the seat of the scornful."[1] But two who sit together,

Deut. vi. 4, etc.   **Joel ii. 13.**   **Ps. i. 1.**

and speak of the law, the DIVINE PRESENCE (Shechinah) rests between them; as is said, "Then they that feared the Lord spake often one to another; and the LORD hearkened and heard; and a book of remembrance was written before him for them that feared the Lord; and for them that thought upon His name."[2] This refers to two; but whence may we infer, that if but one sits engaged in the study of the law the Holy One, blessed be He, will appoint him a reward? Because it is said, "He sitteth alone and keepeth silence, because he hath borne it upon him."[3]

3. Rabbi Simon said, "three who have eaten at one table and have not spoken of the law, are to be considered as if they had eaten of the sacrifices of the dead, for it is said, 'For all tables are full of vomit and filthiness, so that there is no place clean.'[4] But three who have eaten at one table and have spoken of the law, are considered as if they had eaten at GOD'S table, as is said, 'And he said unto me, This is the table that is before the LORD.'"[5]

4. R. Chanina, son of Chanina, said, "he who wakes in the night and travels in the road alone, and turns his heart to vanity, is guilty of the death of his own soul."

5. R. Nechunya, son of Hakana, said, "whoever lays on himself the yoke of the law is relieved from the yoke of the kingdom and the yoke of the custom of the world, and whoever breaks off the yoke of the law, imposes on himself the yoke of the kingdom and the yoke of the custom of the world."

6. R. Chalaphta of the village of Chananya said, "ten men who assemble together and study the law, the Shechinah rests among them, as is said, 'God standeth in the congregation of the mighty.'"[6] And hence it is inferred that it is also so with five, because it is said, "and hath founded his troop in the earth."[7] And hence it is inferred that it is likewise so with three, because it is said, "He judgeth among the gods."[8] And hence it is inferred that it is also thus with two, because it is said, "Then they that feared the Lord spake often one to another, and the Lord hearkened and heard, etc."[9] And

[2] Mal. iii. 16.
[3] Lam. iii. 28.
[4] Isa. xxviii. 8.
[5] Ezek. xli. 22.
[6] Ps. lxxxii. 1.
[7] Amos ix. 6.
[8] Ps. lxxxii. 1.
[9] Mal. iii. 16.

hence it is inferred that it is likewise so with one, because it is said, "In all places where I record my name I will come unto thee, and I will bless thee."[10]

7. R. Eleazar of Barthota said, "give unto Him of His own, for thou and all that thou hast are His." And thus said David, "For all things come of Thee, and of thine own have we given Thee."[1] R. Simon said, "he who journeys on the road, meditating on the law, and ceases therefrom to admire this beautiful tree or that beautiful fallow ground, is considered in Scripture as endangering his life."

8. R. Dosthai, the son of Jonai, in the name of R. Meier, said, "whoever forgetteth anything of what he had obtained by study, is considered in Scripture as having endangered his life"; as is said, "Only take heed to thyself and guard thy soul diligently, lest thou forget the things which thine eyes have seen."[2] "Perhaps his study has been too powerful for him?" "But it is said, 'And lest they depart from thy heart all the days of thy life.'"[3] Hence he endangers not his life, till he deliberately removes them from his heart."

9. Rabbi Chanina, son of Dose, said, "whosoever's fear of sin precedes his wisdom, his wisdom will remain; but whosoever's wisdom precedes his fear of sin, his wisdom will not remain." He used to say, "whosoever's good deeds exceed his wisdom, his wisdom will remain; but whosoever's wisdom exceeds his good deeds, his wisdom will not remain."

10. He also used to say, "with whomsoever the spirit of his companions is gratified, the Spirit of God is gratified; but with whomsoever the spirit of his companions is not gratified, the Spirit of God is not gratified." R. José, son of Harchinas, said, "that morning sleep, noontide wine, childish conversation, and the assembly of the ignorant, take man out of the world."

11. R. Eleazar Hamodai said, "he who profanes the holy offerings, despises the solemn feasts, puts his neighbor to shame in public, makes void the covenant of our father Abraham, and expounds the law contrary to its true sense, although he be well learned in the law and possessed of good deeds, yet has he no share in the world to come."

[10] Exod. xx. 24.　　　　　[2] Deut. iv. 9.
[1] 1 Chron. xxix. 14.　　　　[3] Deut. iv. 9.

12. R. Ishmael said, " be humble to thy superior, and affable to thy inferior, and receive all mankind with joy."

13. R. Akiba said, " laughter and levity accustom mankind to lewdness, tradition is a fence to the law, tithes are a fence to riches, vows are a fence to abstinence, the fence to wisdom is silence."

14. He used to say, " man is beloved as he was created in the image of God, but an addditional love was shown to him that he was created in the image of God, as is said, ' In the image of God he made man.' [4] Beloved are Israel in that they are called the children of God, but an additional love was shown to them in that they are called the children of God, as is said, ' Ye are the children of the Lord your God.' [5] Beloved are Israel, to whom was given the desirable vessel wherewith the world was created, but an additional love was shown unto them, that the desirable vessel wherewith the world was created was given unto them, as is said, ' For I give you good doctrine, forsake ye not my law.' " [6]

15. " Everything is seen by God, though freedom of choice is given unto man ; the world is judged in goodness, though all is according to the greatness of the work."

16. He used to say, " everything is given to man on pledge, and a net is spread over all living ; the shop is open, and the merchant credits ; the ledger is open, and the hand records, and whosoever chooses to borrow may come and borrow, as the collectors are daily coming round and getting payment of man, whether with his consent or without it, for they have good authority to support them, and the judgment is true justice, and all things are ready for the feast."

17. R. Eleazar, son of Azariah, said, " if there be no law, there is no morality, and if there be no morality, there is no law ; if there be no wisdom, there is no reverence, and if there be no reverence, there is no wisdom ; if there be no understanding, there is no knowledge, and if there be no knowledge, there is no understanding ; if there be no meal, there can be no study of the law, and if there be no law, there will be no meal." He used to say, " to what may he be likened whose wisdom exceeds his goods deeds ? To a tree whose branches are many and his roots few, so that the wind comes and plucks

[4] Gen. ix. 6.　　　　[5] Deut. xiv. 1.　　　　[6] Prov. iv. 2.

it up and overturns it, as is said, 'For he shall be like the heath in the desert, and he shall not see when good cometh, but shall inhabit the parched places in the wilderness in a salt land and not inhabited.' [7] But to what is he like whose good deeds exceed his wisdom? To a tree whose branches are few and its roots many, so that if all the winds in the world come and assail it, they cannot move it from its place, as is said, 'For he shall be like a tree planted by the waters, and that spreadeth out her roots by the river, and shall not see when heat cometh, but her leaf shall be green and shall not be careful in the year of drought, neither shall cease from yielding fruit.' " [8]

18. R. Eleazar, son of Chisma, said, "sacrifices of doves and observance of times are important constitutions. As tronomy and geometry are the ornaments of wisdom."

CHAPTER IV

1. The son of Zoma said, "Who is wise? He who is willing to receive instruction from all men, as is said, 'Than all my teachers' [1] Who is mighty? He who subdues his evil imagination, as is said, 'He that is slow to anger is better than the mighty, and he that ruleth his spirit than he that taketh a city.' [2] Who is rich? He who rejoices in his lot, as is said, 'For thou shalt eat the labor of thine hands, happy shalt thou be and it shall be well with thee '; [3] happy shalt thou be in this world, and it shall be well with thee in the world to come. Who is honorable? He who honors mankind, as is said, 'For them that honor me I will honor, and they that despise me shall be lightly esteemed.' " [4]

2. Ben Asai said, " run to the performance of a slight precept as though it were a grave one, and flee from transgression, for the performance of a precept causes another precept, and transgression causes transgression, as the reward of a commandment is a commandment, and the reward of transgression is transgression."

3. He used to say, "despise not all men, nor oppose all

[7] Jer. xvii. 6.
[8] Jer. xvii. 8.
[1] Ps. cxix. 99.

[2] Prov. xvi. 32.
[3] Ps. cxxviii. 2.
[4] 1 Sam. ii. 30.

things, for there is no man who has not his hour, neither is there anything that has not its place."

4. Rabbi Levitas of Jabneh said, "be very humble of spirit, as all the hope of man is to be food for worms." Rabbi Johanan, son of Beroka, said, "whosoever profanes God's name in secret will be punished publicly, whether it be done ignorantly or presumptuously, it is all one in the profanation of God's name."

5. Rabbi Ishmael, his son, said, "he who learns that he may be able to teach others, will be enabled to study and to teach others; but he who studies in order to perform the precepts, will be enabled to study, teach, observe, and do the commandments." Rabbi Zadok said, "make not the study of the law subservient to thy aggrandizement, neither make a hatchet thereof to hew therewith." And thus said Hillel, "whosoever receiveth any emolument from the words of the law deprives himself of life."

6. Rabbi José said, "he who honors the law, his person shall be honored by mankind; and he who profanes the law, his person shall be dishonored by mankind."

7. Rabbi Ishmael, his son, said, "he who avoids being a judge, delivers himself from enmity, robbery, and false swearing; but he who is arrogant in judging, is a proud wicked fool."

8. He used to say, "judge not alone, for none ought to judge alone save ONE; neither say, receive ye my opinion, for they are at liberty to accept it, but thou canst not compel them."

9. Rabbi Jonathan said, "whosoever performs the law in poverty, shall in the end perform it in riches; but he who neglects the law for riches, will in the end neglect it for poverty."

10. Rabbi Meier said, "diminish your worldly affairs and engage in the study of the law, and be humble in spirit before all men; and if thou neglect the law, there are many hinderances to oppose thee, but if thou hast labored in the study of the law, there is much reward to be given thee."

11. Rabbi Eliezer, the son of Jacob, said, "he who performs but one precept gains for himself an advocate; and he who commits a single sin, gains for himself an accuser; re-

14

pentance and good deeds are a shield before the divine punishment." Rabbi Johannan Hasandelar said, "every congregation formed for God will be permanent, but that which is not for God will not be permanent."

12. Rabbi Eliezer, son of Shamna, said, "let the honor of thy disciple be as dear to thee as thine own, and the honor of thy companion as the fear of thy master, and the fear of thy master as the fear of God."

13. Rabbi Judah said, "be careful in doctrine, for an error in doctrine is presumptuous sin." Rabbi Simon said, "there are three crowns—the crown of the law, the crown of the priesthood, and the crown of monarchy, but the crown of a good name is better than all of them."

14. Rabbi Nehorai said, "flee to a place where the law is studied, and do not say that it will follow thee, for thy companions will establish it for thee, and lean not to thine own understanding."

15. Rabbi Janai said, "the prosperity of the wicked and the chastisements of the righteous are not in our hands." Rabbi Mathia, son of Charash, said, "be forward to greet all men, and be rather as the tail of the lion, than as the head of the foxes."

16. Rabbi Jacob said, "this world may be likened to a courtyard before the world to come, therefore prepare thyself in the hall, to enter into the dining-room."

17. He used to say, "one hour employed in repentance and good deeds in this world is better than the whole life in the world to come; and one hour's refreshment of spirit in the world to come is better than the whole life in this world."

18. Rabbi Simon, son of Eleazar, said, "try not to pacify your neighbor in the moment of his anger, and do not console him while his dead lies before him; inquire not of him in the moment of his vowing, nor desire to see him in the time of his calamity."

19. The younger Samuel used to say, "rejoice not when thine enemy falls, and let not thy heart be glad when he stumbles, lest the Lord see it and it be evil in His sight, and He turn His wrath from him."

20. Elisha, son of Abuya, said, "he who teaches a child, is like to one who writes on clean paper; but he who teaches

old people, is like to one who writes on blotted paper." Rabbi José, the son of Judah, of a village near Babylon, said, " to what may he who learns the law from little children be likened? To one who eats unripe grapes and drinks new wine." And to what may he who learns the law from old men be likened? To one who eats ripe grapes and drinks old wine." Rabbi Meier said, " look not at the flask, but that which is therein, for there are new flasks full of old wine, and old flasks which have not even new wine in them."

21. Rabbi Eleazer Hakapher said, " envy, lust, and ambition take men out of the world."

22. He used to say, " those who are born are doomed to die, the dead to live, and the quick to be judged, to make us know, understand, and be informed that He is God. He is the Former, Creator, Omniscient, Judge, Witness, and Claimant, and He will judge thee hereafter, blessed be He ; for in His presence there is no unrighteousness, forgetfulness, respect of persons, or acceptance of a bribe, for everything is His. Know also that everything is done according to the account, and let not thine evil imagination persuade thee that the grave is a place of refuge for thee, for against thy will wast thou formed, and against thy will wast thou born, and against thy will dost thou live, and against thy will shalt thou die, and against thy will must thou hereafter render an account and receive judgment in the presence of the King of kings, the Holy God, blessed be He."

CHAPTER V

1. With ten expressions [1] the world was created. " But wherefore is this taught, since God could have created it with one expression?" " This is to punish the wicked, who destroy the world that was created with ten expressions, and to reward the righteous who establish the world created with ten expressions."

2. There were ten generations from Adam to Noah, to let us know that God is long-suffering, as all those generations provoked him before he brought the deluge upon them. There

[1] The Rabbis reckon that the expression " God said " is used nine times in the first chapter of Genesis, and that the tenth expression is to be found in the first verse, " In the beginning God created the heaven and the earth."

were ten generations from Noah to Abraham, to let us know
that God is long-suffering, as all those generations provoked
him, until Abraham our father came and took the reward of
them all.

3. Our father Abraham was proved with ten trials, and in
all of them he stood firm; to let us know how great was the
love of our father Abraham to God.

4. Ten miracles were wrought for our fathers in Egypt, and
ten at the Red Sea. Ten plagues did the blessed God send
on the Egyptians in Egypt, and ten at the Red Sea. Ten
times did our fathers tempt the blessed God in the wilderness,
as is said, "And have tempted me now these ten times, and
have not hearkened to my voice." [2]

5. Ten miracles were wrought for our fathers in the holy
temple—no woman miscarried from the scent of the flesh of
the sacrifices; nor did the flesh of the sacrifices ever stink;
nor was a fly seen in the slaughter house; nor did legal uncleanness happen to the high priest on the day of atonement;
nor did the rain extinguish the fire of the wood arranged on
the altar; nor did the wind prevent the straight ascension of
the pillar of smoke; nor was any defect found in the omer,
the two loaves, and the showbread; and though the people
stood close together, yet when they worshipped there was
room enough for all; nor did a serpent or scorpion injure a
person in Jerusalem; nor did a man say to his neighbor, I have
not room to lodge in Jerusalem.

6. Ten things were created on the eve of the Sabbath in the
twilight, and these are they—the mouth of the earth; the
mouth of the well; the mouth of the ass; the rainbow; the
manna; the rod of Moses; the shameer; [3] the letters; writing;
and the tables of stone. And some say also the demons; and
the grave of our lawgiver Moses; and the ram of our father
Abraham; and some say the tongs, the model of the tongs.

7. Seven things are to be met with in a rude person, and
seven in a wise man. The wise man will not speak before
one who excels him in wisdom and years; nor will he interrupt
his companion in his discourse; nor is he in haste to answer;
he inquires according to the subject, and answers according

---

[2] Num. xiv. 22.
[3] The shameer is the worm which knows how to hew stones, and helped Solomon to build the Temple.

to the decision, and he will answer the first proposition first, and the last proposition last; and what he has not heard he will acknowledge he has not heard it; and he confesses the truth. But the opposites of these are to be met with in a rude person.

8. Seven kinds of punishment are brought on the world for seven important sins; for when a part of the people give tithes and the others do not, a scarcity and a dearth ensue, so that some are filled and others suffer hunger; but when the whole agree not to give tithes, a famine of dearth and confusion ensues. If they offer not up the "cake," [4] confusion and fire ensue. Pestilence comes into the world for the commission of sins said to be punished with death in the law, but which are not recognized by our judges; and for not observing the law concerning the fruits of the Sabbatical year. The sword enters the world on account of the delay of justice and its perversion; and on account of those who explain the law contrary to its true sense.

9. Evil beasts come into the world on account of false swearing, and the profanation of God's name. Captivity enters the world on account of idolatry, immorality, bloodshed, and not suffering the land to rest on the Sabbatical year. At four seasons the pestilence is prevalent—in the fourth year, the seventh, and the end of the seventh, and the end of the feast of tabernacles in every year. In the fourth year, for not giving the poor's tithe of the third year; in the seventh, for withholding the poor's tithe of the sixth year; and at the end of the seventh, on account of the fruits of the Sabbatical year; and at the end of the feast of tabernacles yearly, on account of robbing the poor of the gifts due to them.

10. There are four sorts of men: He who says, that which is mine is mine, and that which is thine is thine, is a passable custom, and some say this was the custom of Sodom. He who says, what is thine is mine, and what is mine is thine, is the custom of the ignorant. He who says, what is mine is thine, and what is thine is also thine, is the custom of the pious. He who says, what is mine is mine, and what is thine is mine, is the custom of the wicked.

11. There are four sorts of passionate men: He who is

<hr />

4 Num. xv. 20.

easily provoked and easily pacified loses more than he gains; he whom it is difficult to provoke and difficult to pacify gains more than he loses; he whom it is difficult to provoke and easy to pacify is pious; but he who is easily provoked and with difficulty pacified is wicked.

12. There are four sorts of disciples: He who is quick to hear and quick to forget loses more than he gains; he who is slow to hear and slow to forget gains more than he loses; he who is quick to hear and slow to forget is wise; he who is slow to hear and quick to forget has an evil portion.

13. There are four sorts in those who bestow charity: He who is willing to give but does not wish that others should give, has an envious eye toward others; he who likes to see others give but will not give, has an evil eye toward himself; he who is willing to give and that others should also give, acts piously; he who will not give and likes not that others should give, acts wickedly.

14. There are four sorts in those who go to college: He who goes but does not study, has only the reward of going; he who studies and does not go, has the reward of action; he who goes and studies, is pious; he who neither goes nor studies, is wicked.

15. There are four sorts in those who sit before the Sages: Those who act as a sponge, a funnel, a strainer, and a sieve; as a sponge which sucks up all, as a funnel which receives at one end and lets out at the other, as a strainer which lets the wine pass through, but retains the lees, and as a sieve which lets the bran pass through but retains the fine flour.

16. Every affection that depends on some carnal cause, if that cause ceases the affection ceases, but that which does not depend on such a cause will never cease. Where do we meet with an affection dependent on a carnal cause? Such was the love of Ammon to Tamar; but that which does not depend on such a cause was the love of David and Jonathan.

17. Every dispute that is carried on for God's sake, will in the end be established; but that which is not for God's sake, will not be established. "What may be considered a dispute for God's sake?" "Such as the disputes of Hillel and Shammai; but that which was not for God's sake was the contention of Korah and all his company."

18. He who by his conduct justifies the public, no sin will be caused through his means, and whosoever causes the public to sin is not suffered to repent. Moses acted justly and caused the public to obtain merit: the merit of the public was attributed to him, as is said, " He executed the justice of the Lord and his judgments with Israel." [5] Jeroboam, the son of Nebat, sinned, and caused Israel to sin: the sin of the public was attributed to him, as is said, " Because of the sins of Jeroboam, who did sin, and who made Israel to sin." [6]

19. He who possesses these three virtues is of the disciples of our father Abraham, and he who is possessed of the three opposites is of the disciples of the wicked Balaam. The disciples of our father Abraham possess a benevolent eye, a humble spirit, and a contented mind. The disciples of Balaam have an evil eye, a haughty spirit, and a narrow mind. " What is the difference between the disciples of our father Abraham and the disciples of the wicked Balaam?" " The disciples of our father Abraham eat of the fruit of their good works in this world, and inherit the future one, for it is said, ' That I may cause those that love me to inherit substance, and I will fill their treasures.' [7] But the disciples of the wicked Balaam inherit hell and descend to the pit of destruction, as is said, ' But Thou, O God, shalt bring them down into the pit of destruction; bloody and deceitful men shall not live out half their days, but I will trust in Thee.' " [8]

20. Judah, son of Tamai, said, " be bold as a leopard, light as an eagle, swift as a roe, and strong as a lion, to do the will of Thy Father, who is in heaven." He used to say, " the impudent are for hell and the modest for paradise. May it be acceptable in Thy presence, O Lord our God! that Thy city may speedily be rebuilt in our days, and let our portion be in Thy law."

21. He also said, " at five years of age a child should study the Bible; at ten he should study the Mishna; at thirteen he should observe the precepts; at fifteen he should study the Gemara; at eighteen he should get married; at twenty he should study the law; at thirty he is arrived at full strength; at forty he is arrived at understanding; at fifty he is able to give counsel; at sixty he is accounted aged; at seventy he is hoary; at

[5] Deut. xxxiii. 21.   [6] 1 Kings xiv. 16.   [7] Prov. viii. 21.   [8] Ps. lv. 23.

eighty he may still be accounted strong; at ninety he is only fit for the pit;[9] at 100 he is as if already dead and forgotten from the world."

22. The son of Bagbag said, "ponder the law again and again, for all things are in it; contemplate it always, and depart not from it, for there is nothing to be preferred to it."

23. The son of Haha said, "the reward is proportioned to the labor."

CHAPTER VI

1. The Sages studied in the language of the Mishna; blessed be He who made choice of them and their learning. R. Meier said, "he who is engaged in the study of the law for its own sake merits many things, and not only so, but the whole world is under the greatest obligation to him; he is called a dear friend, dear to God and dear to mankind; he rejoices God and rejoices His creatures. It clothes him with meekness and the fear of God, and directs him to become just, pious, righteous, and faithful; it removes him from sin, and brings him near to merit, and the world is benefited by his counsel, sound wisdom, understanding, and strength; as is said, " Counsel is mine, and sound wisdom; I am understanding, I have strength "[1] It also bestows on him empire, dominion, and perception in judgment. It reveals the secrets of the law to him, and he shall be an increasing fountain, and a never-failing river; and it will cause him to be modest, slow to anger, and ready to pardon an injury done to him; and it will magnify and exalt him above all things."

2. R. Joshua, son of Levi, said, " every day a Divine voice (*bath kol*) proceeds from Mount Horeb, which proclaims and says, ' Woe be to those who contemn the law; for whoever is not engaged in the study of the law may be considered as excommunicate '; for it is said, ' as a jewel of gold in a swine's snout, so is a fair woman which is without discretion ';[2] and it is said, ' And the tables were the work of God, and the writing was the writing of God, graven upon the tables.'[3] Read not graven but freedom; for who are counted free but those engaged in the study of the law, and whoever is engaged

---

[9] Or, perhaps, "for meditation."
[1] Prov. viii. 14.
[2] Prov. xi. 22.
[3] Ex. xxxii. 16.

in the study of the law is exalted; as it is said, 'And from Mattanah to Nahaliel, and from Nahaliel to Bamoth.'"[4]

3. He who learns from his companion one chapter, sentence, verse, or expression, ought to behave toward him with respect; for thus we find by David, King of Israel, who having learned only two things from Ahitophel, called him his teacher, guide, and acquaintance, as is said, "But it was thou, a man mine equal, my guide, and mine acquaintance."[5] Hence it may be deduced that if David, King of Israel, who having learned only two things from Ahitophel, called him his "teacher, guide, and acquaintance," how much more ought he who learns from his companion a single chapter, sentence, verse, or expression, to show him the utmost respect? And there is no glory but the knowledge of the law; as is said, "The wise shall inherit glory";[6] and the perfect shall inherit the good; but nothing is really good but the law, as is said, "For I give you good doctrine, forsake ye not my law."[7]

4. Thus is the law to be observed: Thou shalt eat bread and salt, and water by measure shalt thou drink; on the earth shalt thou sleep, and a life of trouble shalt thou live; and thou shalt labor in the study of the law. If thou doest thus, thou shalt be happy, and it shall be well with thee; thou shalt be happy in this world, and it shall be well with thee in the world to come.

5. Seek not grandeur for thyself, neither covet more honor than thy learning merits. Crave not after the tables of kings; for thy table is greater than their table, and thy crown is greater than their crown; and the Master who employs thee is faithful to pay thee the reward of thy labor.

6. The law is more excellent than the priesthood and royalty; for royalty is acquired by thirty properties, and the priesthood by twenty-four; but the law is acquired by forty-eight things, and these are they—with study, attention, eloquence; an understanding heart, an intelligent heart; with dread and meekness, fear and joy; with attendance on the Sages, the acuteness of companions, and disputations of the disciples; with sedateness, the study of the Bible, and the Mishna; in purity, in taking little sleep, in using little discourse, in being little engaged in traffic, in taking little sport, in enjoying little

[4] Num. xxi. 19.　　[5] Ps. lv. 13.　　[6] Prov. iii. 35.　　[7] Prov. iv. 2.

delight and little worldly manners; in being slow to anger, in having a good heart, in having faith in the Sages, and in bearing chastisements; in being sensible of his situation, and rejoicing in his portion; in being circumspect in his language, in not pretending to pre-eminence, in sincerely loving God, and loving His creatures; in loving admonition, and that which is right; in avoiding honor, and in not priding himself on his acquired knowledge; not rejoicing in pronouncing sentence, in bearing the burden equally with his companion, and inclining him to merit, and confirming him in the truth and in peace; is sedate in his study, inquires according to the subject, and answers according to the constitution; is attentive to study, and extends it; learns it with a view to the teaching of others, and also with a view to perform the precepts; increases his teacher's knowledge, and is attentive to his instruction, and reports everything in the name of the person who said it; hence it is inferred that whoever reports anything in the name of the person who said it, procures redemption for the world, as is said, "And Esther certified the king thereof in Mordecai's name." [8]

7. Great is the law, which bestows life on the doers of it, both in this world and in the world to come; as is said, "For they are life unto those that find them, and health to all their flesh." [9]   And it is said, "It shall be health to thy navel, and marrow to thy bones." [10]   And it is said, "She is a tree of life to them that lay hold upon her; and happy is everyone that retaineth her." [1]   And it is said, "For they shall be an ornament of grace unto thy head, and chains about thy neck." [2] And it is said, "She shall give to thine head an ornament of grace; a crown of glory shall she deliver to thee." [3]   And it is said, "Length of days is in her right hand, and in her left hand riches and honor." [4]   And it is said, "For length of days and long life, and peace shall they add to thee." [5]

8. Rabbi Simeon, son of Judah, in the name of Rabbi Simeon, son of Jochai, said, "beauty, strength, riches, honor, wisdom, age, hoariness, and many children, are suitable for the righteous, and suitable for the world; as is said, "The

---

[8] Esther ii. 22.
[9] Prov. iv. 22.
[10] Prov. iii. 8.
[1] Prov. iii. 18.

[2] Prov. i. 9.
[3] Prov. iv. 9.
[4] Prov. iii. 16.
[5] Prov. iii. 2.

hoary head is a crown of glory, if it be found in the way of righteousness."[6] And it is said, "Children's children are the crown of old men, and the glory of children are their fathers."[7] And it is said, "Then the moon shall be confounded, and the sun ashamed, when the Lord of Hosts shall reign on Mount Zion, and in Jerusalem; and before his ancients gloriously."[8]

9. Rabbi Simeon, son of Manasya, said, "those seven qualities which the Sages counted as proper for the righteous, were all established in the Rabbi (Judah) and his children." Rabbi José, son of Kishma, said, "I was once travelling along the road and met a certain person, who saluted me with peace, and I returned his salutation. He then said to me, 'Rabbi, whence art thou?' I answered him, 'from a great city abounding in sages and scribes:' said he to me, 'if thou be willing to dwell with us in our city, then will I give thee a thousand thousand golden dinars, and precious stones and pearls.' To this I answered, 'if thou wouldst give me all the silver and gold, and precious stones and pearls in the world, I would only dwell in a place where the law is studied; because at the time of man's departure from this world he is not accompanied either with silver and gold, and precious stones and pearls, but with the law and good deeds alone, as is said, 'When thou goest it shall lead thee: when thou sleepest it shall keep thee: and when thou awakest it shall talk with thee.'"[9] "When thou goest it shall lead thee," that is in this world. "When thou sleepest it shall keep thee," in the grave; "and when thou awakest it shall talk with thee," in the world to come. And thus it is written in the book of Psalms by the hand of David, King of Israel, "The law of thy mouth is better to me than thousands of gold and silver."[10] And it is said, "The silver is mine, and the gold is mine, saith the Lord of Hosts."[1]

10. Five possessions hath the Holy One, blessed be He, obtained in this world, and these are they—the law is one possession; heaven and earth another; Abraham another; Israel another; and the holy Temple another. Now whence is it to be proved that the law is one possession? Because it is written, "The LORD possessed me in the beginning of

[6] Prov. xvi. 31.
[7] Prov. xvii. 6.
[8] Isa. xxiv. 23.
[9] Prov. vi. 22.
[10] Ps. cxix. 72.
[1] Hag. ii. 8.

His way before His works of old." [2]   And whence is it proved
that heaven and earth is another possession?   Because it is
said, " Thus saith the Lord, The heaven is my throne and the
earth is my footstool; where is the house that ye build unto
me? and where is the place of my rest?" [3]   And it is said,
" O Lord, how manifold are thy works! in wisdom hast thou
made them all; the earth is full of thy riches." [4]   Whence is
it proved that Abraham is one possession?   Because it is
written, " And he blessed him, and said blessed be Abraham
of the most high God, possessor of heaven and earth." [5]
Whence is it proved that Israel is one possession?   Because
it is written, " Till thy people pass over, O Lord, till the people
pass over, which thou hast purchased." [6]   And it is said, " But
to the saints that are in the earth, and to the excellent, in whom
is all my delight." [7]   Whence can it be proved that the holy
temple is one possession?   Because it is said, " The sanctuary,
O Lord, which thy hands have established." [8]   And it is said,
" And he brought them to the border of his sanctuary, even
to this mountain which his right hand hath purchased." [9]
Everything which God created, he created but for his glory;
as is said, " Everyone that is called by my name; for I have
created him for my glory, I have formed him; yea, I have
made him." [10]   And the Lord will reign forever and ever.
R. Chanina, son of Akasea, said, " the Holy One, Blessed be
He, wished to purify Israel, wherefore He magnified for them
the Law and the Commandments, as is said, ' The Lord is
well pleased for his righteousness' sake; he will magnify the
law and make it honorable." [1]

[2] Prov. viii. 22.
[3] Isa. lxvi. 1.
[4] Ps. civ. 24.
[5] Gen. xiv. 19.
[6] Exod. xv. 16.
[7] Ps. xvi. 3.
[8] Exod. xv. 17.
[9] Ps. lxxviii. 54.
[10] Isa. xliii. 7.
[1] Isa. xlii. 21.

THE DAILY SACRIFICE

Guarding the Temple at Night—Taking the Ashes Off the Altar—Casting
Lots—Opening the Temple in the Morning—Arranging the Fire on
the Altar—The Wood-Kindling—Allotting Services—Examination
of the Daily Sacrifice—Slaughter-house—Sounds Heard at Jericho—
Snuffing the Candlestick—Position of the Lamb when Slain—Pour-
ing Out its Blood—Preparations for Burning—Order of Carrying the
Members to the Altar—Blessings—Cleansing the Vessels of the Holy
Place—The High Priest on the Altar—Music and Psalm-Singing.

CHAPTER I

1. The Priests guarded the sanctuary in three places [1]—in
the House Abtinas, in the House Nitzus, and in the House
Moked. The House Abtinas and the House Nitzus had
upper chambers, and the young priests guarded there. The
House Moked was arched, and its large chamber was surrounded with stone divans, and the elders of the House of
the Fathers slept there, with the keys of the court in their
hands; and the younger priests also slept there, each with
his cushion on the ground. They did not sleep in the holy
garments, but they undressed, and folded them, and put
them under their heads, and they covered themselves with
their own dresses. If legal defilement happened to one of
them, he went out, and proceeded in the circuit that went
under the Temple, and candles flamed on either side, until he
arrived in the house of baptism. And the fire pile was there,
and the place of the seat of honor; and this was its honor,
when he found it closed, he knew that someone was there;
when he found it open he knew that no one was there. He
descended and washed; he came up and wiped himself, and
warmed himself before the fire pile. He came and sat beside
his brethren the priests, till the doors were opened; then he
went out on his own way.

[1] See the treatise on " Measurements," chap. i.

2. He who wished to take the ashes from the altar, rose
up early and bathed before the Captain of the Temple came.
And in what hour did the Captain come? All times were
not equal; sometimes he came at cockcrow, or near to it, before or after it. The Captain came, and knocked for them,
and they opened to him. He said to them, " let whoever is
washed, come, and cast lots." They cast lots, and he gained
who gained.

3. He took the key and opened the wicket door, and entered from the House Moked to the court, and the priests
went after him with two lighted torches in their hands. And
they divided themselves into two parties. These went in the
gallery eastward, and those went in the gallery westward.
They observed everything as they walked till they approached
the place of the pancake-makers. They arrived. Both parties said, peace! all peace! The pancake-makers began to
make pancakes.

4. He who gained the lot to take the ashes from the altar,
took them; and they said to him, " be careful that thou touch
not the vessels, till thou dost sanctify thy hands and thy feet
from the laver." And the ash dish was placed in the corner
between the ascent to the altar and the west of the ascent.
No man entered with the priest, and there was no candle in
his hand, but he walked toward the light of the fire on the
altar. They did not see him, and they did not hear his voice,
till they heard the creaking of the wheel, which the son of
Kattin made for the laver, and they said, " the time has come
to sanctify his hands and feet from the laver." He took the
silver ash dish, and he went up to the top of the altar, and he
turned the live coals on one side, and he piled up those that
were well burned inward, and he descended, and came on the
pavement of the altar. He turned his face northward, and
went eastward of the ascent about ten cubits. He packed the
coals on the pavement three hand-breadths distant from the
ascent, at the place where they put the crops of the fowls, and
the ashes of the inner altar, and of the candlestick.

CHAPTER II

1. His brethren saw him come down, and they came running to him. They hastened and sanctified their hands and their feet from the laver. They took the brushes and the forks, and went up to the top of the altar. The members and the cauls [1] (of the sacrifices) which were not consumed over night, they moved to the side of the altar. If the sides could not contain them, they laid them out in a closet at the ascent.

2. They commenced to bring up the ashes to the top of the heap,[2] and the heap was on the middle of the altar. Sometimes there was on it about 300 cors;[3] but in the holidays they did not clear away the ashes, since they were an honor for the altar. Never was the priest lazy in removing the ashes.

3. The priests began bringing up the fagots to arrange the fire of preparation on the altar. " Was, then, all wood allowed for preparation? " " Yes, all wood was allowed for the fire of preparation, except that of the olive and that of the vine. But these they preferred—branches of the fig-tree, of the nut, and of the pine."

4. The priests arranged the great fire of preparation eastward, and then made an opening eastward, so that the heads of the inward fagots touched the heap on the altar. And there was a division between the fagots, that the priests might kindle the chips there.

5. The priest chose from the fagots the best figwood to arrange the second fire of preparation for the incense opposite the western horn southward. He prolonged it from the horn toward the north four cubits, reckoning for five seahs [4] of live coals, and on the Sabbath he reckoned for eight seahs of live coals. As they placed there the two cups of frankincense of the showbread. The members and cauls (of the sacrifices) which were not consumed by the fire overnight, were returned again by the priests to the great fire of preparation. And they kindled both the preparations with fire; and they came down, and entered into the chamber of hewn stone.[5]

[1] Membranes over the fat.
[2] In the form of an apple.
[3] A cor was equal, according to the Rabbis, to 44.286 gallons, but Josephus reckons it to have been 86.696 gallons.
[4] A seah, according to the Rabbis, was 1.4762 gallon.
[5] Or, of " the treasurers."

CHAPTER III

1. The Captain of the Temple said to the priests, "come and cast lots." "Who is to slaughter?" "Who is to sprinkle?" "Who is to take the ashes from the inner altar?" "Who is to take the ashes from the candlestick?" "Who is to bring up the members to the ascent, the head and the right foot, and the two hind feet, the chine, and the left foot, the breast, and the throat, and the two sides, the inwards, and the fine flour, and the pancakes and the wine?" They cast lots, and he gained who gained.

2. The Captain said to them, "go and see if the time for slaughter approaches?" If it approached, the watchman said, "it brightens." Matthia, son of Samuel, said, "is it light in the whole east, even to Hebron?" and he said, "yes."

3. He said to them, "go and bring the lamb from the lamb-chamber." The lamb-chamber was in the northwest corner of the court, and there were four chambers there, one the lamb-chamber, one the seal-chamber,[1] and one chamber for the burning materials, and one chamber where they made showbread.

4. The priests entered the chamber for the vessels, and they brought out ninety-three vessels of silver and gold. They made the daily sacrifice drink in a golden cup. Even though he was examined the night before, they examined him again by torch-light.

5. He who gained the lot for the daily sacrifice, led the lamb to the slaughter-house, and those who gained the lots for the members, went after him. The slaughter-house was to the north of the altar, and in it were eight dwarf pillars, and beams of cedar-wood were fastened upon them, and iron hooks were fastened in them. And there were three rows of hooks to each of them. Upon them the priests hung the sacrifices, and skinned them, near the marble tables between the pillars.

6. Those who gained the lot for the removal of the ashes

---

[1] In this chamber were kept the "seals" or "tokens" given to those persons who bought their offerings from the Levites. These "seals" were of four sorts, and were respectively inscribed with "calf" or "kid," according to the offerings to be presented; and with the word "male" when the offering was to be a ram; and "sinner" when it was to be a sin-offering.

from the inner altar, and the ashes from the candlestick, advanced with four vessels in their hands, a flagon [2] and a cup [3] and two keys. The flagon resembled a great golden measure containing two cabs and a half. And the cup resembled a great golden jug. And the two keys to the sanctuary. One key entered the lock up to the shoulder of the priest, and one opened quickly.

7. The priest came to the wicket on the north, and there were two wickets in the great gate, one in the north and one in the south. Through that in the south man never entered, and Ezekiel explains it. " Then said the Lord unto me : This gate shall be shut, it shall not be opened, and no man shall enter in by it; because the Lord, the God of Israel, hath entered in by it, therefore it shall be shut." [4]   He took the key and opened the wicket; he entered the chamber, and he went from the chamber into the sanctuary, until he came to the great gate. When he came to the great gate, he took down the bar and the bolts and opened it. The slaughterer did not slaughter till he heard the noise of the opening of the great gate.

8. From Jericho [5] people heard the opening of the great gate. From Jericho they heard the noise of the shovel.[6] From Jericho they heard the noise of the wooden wheel which the son of Kattin made for the laver. From Jericho they heard the voice of Gabini the herald. From Jericho they heard the sound of the cornet. From Jericho they heard the sound of the cymbal. From Jericho they heard the voice of the song. From Jericho they heard the clang of the horn, and some say even the voice of the High Priest at the time when he mentioned the Name on the Day of Atonement. From Jericho they smelled the odor of the preparation of incense. Said R. Eleazar, the son of Daglai, " the family of Aba had goats on the mountains of Mikvor,[7] and they used to sneeze from the odor of the preparation of the incense."

9. The priest who gained the lot for removing the ashes from the inner altar entered, and took the flagon and laid it

---

[2] Others read " a basket."
[3] Or jug.
[4] Ezek. xliv. 2.
[5] Jericho is about eighteen miles distant from Jerusalem.
[6] Perhaps " a gong " or " a bell."

Some think it to have been a " musical instrument," and others consider it to have been " an organ."
[7] Some think " Machærus " on the east of the Dead Sea, about fifty miles distant from Jerusalem.

before him, and he took handfuls of ashes and filled them into the flagon, and at last he brushed the remainder into it. And he left it and went out (of the holy place). He who gained the lot for removing the snuff from the candlestick, entered and found the two eastern lights burning. He snuffed the rest, and left these burning in their place. If he found them extinguished, he snuffed them, and lighted them again from those still burning, and afterward he snuffed the rest. And there was a stone before the candlestick, and in it were three steps, on which the priest stood and trimmed the lights. And he placed the cup with the snuff on the second step, and went out.

CHAPTER IV

1. The priests did not tie the four feet of the lamb together, but they bound its fore and hind feet. He who gained the lot for carrying the members, held it; and thus was it bound, its head southward, and its face westward. The slaughterer stood in the east with his face westward. The morning sacrifice was slaughtered at the northwestern corner on the second ring. The evening sacrifice was slaughtered at the northeastern corner on the second ring. The slaughterer slaughtered, and the receiver caught (the blood). The priest came to the northeastern corner of the altar, and he sprinkled the blood northeast. He came to the southwest, and sprinkled the blood southwest:[1] the remainder of the blood he poured out on the southern altar-base.

2. The priest did not break its leg, but he made a hole in the midst of its side, and by that it was hung up. He skinned it downward till he came to the breast. When he came to the breast, he cut off the head, and gave it to him who had gained (its lot). He cut off the two hind feet, and gave them to him who had gained them for his lot. He finished the skinning; he tore out the heart, that the blood should come out. He cut off the two fore feet, and gave them to him who had gained them for his lot. He came to the right leg; he cut it off, and gave it to him who had gained it for his lot. He cleft the

---

[1] In each act of sprinkling, the priest, standing before a corner, sprinkled the blood on two sides of the altar. And thus, in two acts of sprinkling, he put the blood on its four sides.

body, and it became all open before him. He took out the caul, and put it on the place of slaughter, with the head on the top of it. He took out the intestines and gave them to him who had gained them for his lot to cleanse them. And the belly they cleansed in the house of the washers, as much as was needful. And the intestines were cleansed three times at least, upon the marble tables between the pillars.

3. The priest took the knife and separated the lungs from the liver, and the finger of the liver from the liver, but he did not remove it from its place. He made a hole in the breast, and gave it to him who gained it for his lot. He came to the right side, and he cut it downward to the backbone, but he did not touch the backbone, till he came to the two tender ribs. He cut it off and gave it to him who gained it for his lot, with the liver hanging upon it. He came to the neck, and left the two side bones on both sides. He cut it off and gave it to him who had gained it for his lot, with the windpipe and the heart and the lungs hanging upon it. He came to the left side, and left on it the two tender ribs, above and below, and so he left it on the corresponding side. It follows that he left on the two sides, two and two ribs above, and two and two ribs below. He cut it off, and gave it to him who gained it for his lot, the backbone with it, and the spleen hanging upon it. And it was large, but the right side is called large, as the liver hangs upon it. He came to the tail; he cut it off and gave it to him who gained it for his lot, and the fat, and the finger of the liver, and the two kidneys with it. He took the left hind leg, and gave it to him who gained it for his lot. It follows that all the priests stood in one row with the members in their hands. The first priest with the head and hind foot, the head in his right hand with the nose toward his arm, and the horns between his fingers, and the place of slaughter upward, and the caul placed on it; and the right hind foot in his left hand with the skin outside. The second priest stood with the two fore legs, the right in his right hand, and the left in his left hand, and the skin outside. The third priest stood with the tail and the hind foot; the tail in his right hand, and the fat wrapped between his fingers, and the finger of the liver and the two kidneys with it; the left foot was in his left hand with the skin outward. The fourth priest stood with the

breast and the throat. The breast was in his right hand, and
the throat in his left, and its side bones between his fingers.
The fifth priest stood with the two sides, the right side in his
right hand, and the left side in his left hand, and the skinny
side outward. The sixth priest stood with the intestines placed
in a pan, and the legs over them. The seventh priest stood
with the fine flour. The eighth priest stood with the pancakes. The ninth priest stood with the wine. They then proceeded and deposited the members on the lower half of the
ascent westward, and they salted them, and descended, and
came to the chamber of the hewn stone to read the " Hear," [2]
etc.

CHAPTER V

1. The Captain of the Watch said, " give one blessing,"
and the priests blessed and read the ten commandments,
" Hear," [1] etc. " And it shall come to pass if ye shall
hearken," [2] etc. And " He spake," [3] etc. They then gave the
three blessings to the people, " Truth and Sureness," and " the
Service," and " the Blessing of the Priests." And on the Sabbath they added one blessing for the outgoing Temple-guard.

2. He said to them, " novices [4] to the incense, come and
cast lots." They cast lots. He gained who gained. He said
to them, " novices with old men come and cast lots, who shall
bring up the members of the lamb from the ascent to the
altar." R. Eliezer, the son of Jacob, said, " those priests who
brought the members to the ascent must also bring them to
the top of the altar."

3. He handed the priests over to the sextons. They di-
vested them of their dresses, leaving them their breeches only,
and there were windows there, and over them was written,
" used for vestments." [5]

4. He who gained the lot for the incense, took the spoon;
and the spoon resembled a great measure of gold containing

---

[2] Called the Shema. It consisted of
the following three passages of Scripture:
  [1] Deut. vi. 4-9.
  [2] Deut. xi. 13-21.
  [3] Num. xv. 37-41.
[4] The lot for the incense was always
arranged for a new man who had never

burned it before. It might come to a
priest once in his lifetime, and never
again afterward. Luke i. 9.
  [5] The chambers for vestments had
separate rooms for each of the twenty-
four courses, and separate wardrobes for
each of the four kinds of vestments.

three cabs. And the pan was heaped full of incense; and it had a covering like a kind of weight upon it.

5. He who gained the lot for the censer, took the silver censer, and went up to the top of the altar, and he turned the live coals here and there, and he put them into the censer. He descended, and poured them into a censer of gold. There was dispersed from them about a cab of live coals, and he brushed them into the channel for refuse. On the Sabbath he put over them a cover. And the cover was a great vessel containing a letech.[6] And there were two chains to it, one by which the priest drew it down, and one by which he held it from above, that it should not be rolled about; and it was useful for three purposes, as a covering over the live coals, and as a covering over the reptile on the Sabbath, and it was also used to carry down the ashes from the altar.

6. The priests arrived between the porch and the altar. One of them took the shovel,[7] and flung it between the porch and the altar. No one could hear the voice of his neighbor in Jerusalem from the rattling of the shovel. And it was useful for three purposes: when the priest heard its rattle, he knew that his brother priests were entering to worship, and he came running; and the Levite, when he heard its rattle, knew that his brother Levites were entering to chant, and he came running; and the chief of the Delegates [8] compelled the defiled men to stand in the eastern gate of the Temple.

CHAPTER VI

1. The priests began ascending the steps of the porch. They who gained the lot for the removal of ashes from the inner altar and from the candlestick, proceeded in front. He who gained the lot for the removal of ashes from the inner altar, entered the Holy Place, and took the flagon, and he bowed down and went out. He who gained the lot for the removal of snuff from the candlestick, entered the Holy Place, and found the two eastern lamps burning; he removed the snuff from the eastern one and left the western one burning, and from it he lighted the candlestick in the evening. If he found

[6] About 37½ gallons.
[7] See note 5, chap. iii. 8.
[8] The Delegates were appointed to represent the whole congregation of Israel in the temple services.

it extinguished, he removed the snuff, and lit it from the altar of burnt offerings. He took the cup from the second step, and he bowed down, and went out.

2. He who gained the lot for the censer, gathered the live coals on the top of the altar of incense ; and he smoothed them with the bottom of the censer, and he bowed down, and went out.

3. He who gained the lot for the incense, took the pan from the cup, and gave it to his friend or to his neighbor. When the incense was dispersed in it, he supplied it to him in handfuls. And he instructed him, " be careful and do not begin too near yourself, lest you be burned." He smoothed it and went out. The offerer could not offer the incense, till the Captain said to him, " offer incense." If the offerer were the high priest, the captain said, " My Lord, High Priest, offer the incense." The people dispersed, and he offered the incense, and he bowed down and went out from the Holy Place.

CHAPTER VII

1. When the High Priest entered to worship, three priests had hold of him, one on his right hand, one on his left hand, and one by the jewels on his breast-plate. And so soon as the Captain of the Temple heard the sound of the footsteps of the High Priest as he proceeded on his way, he lifted the veil for him. He entered the holy place, bowed himself, and went out. And his brethren the priests entered, and bowed down, and went out.

2. The priests came and stood on the steps of the porch. The first came and stood to the south of his brother priests. And they had five vessels in their hands—the flagon in the hand of one, and the cup in the hand of one, and the censer in the hand of one, and the pan in the hand of one, and the spoon with its cover in the hand of one. They blessed the people once. In the city they said the service in three blessings, but in the sanctuary they said it in one blessing. In the sanctuary they pronounced the Name [1] as it is written, but in the city they pronounced it by its substitute.[2] In the

[1] Jchovab.
[2] That is by substituting for the Name (Jehovah) the word " Adonai," except where " Adonai " and " Jehovah " come together. In such cases ,, Elohim " is substituted for " Jehovah.',

city the priests raised their hands (in blessing) opposite their shoulders, but in the sanctuary they raised them above their heads, excepting the High Priest, who could not lift his hands above the golden plate. R. Judah said, " even the High Priest could lift his hands above the golden plate, as is said, ' Aaron lifted up his hand toward the people and blessed them.' " [3]

3. When the High Priest desired to offer incense he went up on the ascent to the altar, and the Sagan (Suffragan) was on his right. When he reached the half of the ascent, the Sagan took him by his right hand and helped him up. The first (priest) reached to him the head and hind foot of the lamb, and he laid his hand on them, and then pushed them away. The second priest reached out to the first one the two forelegs, and he handed them to the High Priest, and he laid his hands upon them, and then pushed them away; the second priest was dismissed, and he departed, and so they reached out to him all the members of the lamb, and he laid his hands upon them and pushed them away; but when he desired, he merely laid his hands on them, and others pushed them away. He next came to make a circuit of the altar. " From what place did he begin? " " From the southeastern corner, northeastern, northwestern, southwestern." They gave to him the wine for libation. The Sagan stood by the corner of the altar with the banners in his hand, and two priests stood by the table of the fat with two silver trumpets in their hands: They sounded a blast, they blew an alarm, and again they sounded the trumpets. They came and took their position beside the son of Arza.[4] One stood on his right hand and one stood on his left. The High Priest bowed down to make the libation, and the Sagan waved the banners, and the son of Arza clanged the cymbals, and the Levites intoned the chant. When they came to a full stop, the trumpets sounded, and the people bowed themselves. At every full stop there was a blast, and at every blast there was bowing down. This is the order of the daily offering for the service of the House of our God. May it be His will to build it speedily in our days. Amen.

4. The chant which the Levites intoned in the sanctuary on the first day of the week was, " The earth is the Lord's and the fulness thereof; the world, and they that dwell therein." [5]

[3] Lev. ix. 22. [4] Who had charge of the channels from the altar. [5] Ps. xxiv. 1.

On the second day they said, " Great is the Lord, and greatly to be praised, in the city of our God, in the mountain of his holiness " [6]   On the third day they said, " God standeth in the congregation of the mighty: He judgeth among the gods." [7]   On the fourth day they said, " O Lord God, to whom vengeance belongeth ; O God, to whom vengeance belongeth, show thyself " [8]   On the fifth day they said, " Sing aloud unto God our strength, make a joyful noise unto the God of Jacob." [9] On the sixth day they said, " The Lord reigneth, he is clothed with majesty," [10] etc.   On the Sabbath they said the chant composed for the Sabbath day, the chant composed for the future, for the day to come, when all will be rest and repose for life everlasting.

[6] Ps. xlviii. 1.   [7] Ps. lxxxii. 1.   [8] Ps. xciv.
[9] Ps. lxxxi.   [10] Ps. xciii.

ON MEASUREMENTS

Priests and Levites Guarding the Temple—Officer of the Watch—Gates —Chambers—Keys—Manner of Entering the House—Nicanor— Steps—Altar—Place of Slaughter—The Laver—The Porch—The Sanctuary—Repairing the Holy of Holies—Measurements—Judging the Priesthood.

CHAPTER I

1. The priests guarded the sanctuary in three places, in the House Abtinas,[1] in the House Nitzus,[2] and in the House Moked;[3] and the Levites in twenty-one places, five at the five gates of the Mountain of the House, four at its four corners inside, five at the five gates of the Court, four at its four corners outside, and one in the chamber of the Offering, and one in the chamber of the Vail, and one behind the House of Atonement.

2. The Captain of the Mountain of the House went round to every Watch in succession with torches flaming before him, and to every guard who did not stand forth, the Captain said, " Peace be to thee." If it appeared that he slept, he beat him with his staff; and he had permission to set fire to his cushion.[4] And they said, " what is the voice in the Court? " " It is the voice of the Levite being beaten, and his garments burned, because he slept on his guard."[5] Rabbi Eliezer, the son of Jacob, said, " once they found the brother of my mother asleep, and they burned his cushion."

3. There were five gates to the Mountain of the House, two Huldah gates in the south which served for going in and out, Kipunus in the west served for going in and out; Tadi[6] in the north served for no (ordinary) purpose. Upon

---

[1] A famous maker of incense.
[2] Sparkling.
[3] Burning. The watch at certain gates seems to have been hereditary in certain families. Just as at the present time the custody of Rachel's tomb is the privilege of a certain family in Jerusalem. Each guard consisted of ten men, so that there were 210 Levites in the twenty-one stations. The three more important places contained guards of both Levites and Priests, thirty of each. There were therefore 240 Levites on guard each night.
[4] He rolled up his overcoat and laid it down for a cushion.
[5] Rev. xvi. 15.
[6] Obscurity.

the east gate was portrayed the city Shushan. Through it one could see the High Priest who burned the heifer, and all his assistants going out to the Mount of Olives.

4. In the court were seven gates—three in the north, and three in the south, and one in the east. That in the south was called the gate of Flaming, the second after it, the gate of Offering; the third after it the Water-gate. That in the east was called the gate Nicanor. And this gate had two chambers, one on the right, and one on the left; one the chamber of Phineas, the vestment keeper, and the other the chamber of the pancake maker.

5. And at the gate Nitzus on the north was a kind of cloister with a room built over it, where the priests kept ward above, and the Levites below; and it had a door into the Chel.[7] Second to it was the gate of the offering. Third the House Moked.

6. In the House Moked were four chambers opening as small apartments into a saloon—two in the Holy place, and two in the Unconsecrated place; and pointed rails separated between the Holy and the Unconsecrated. And what was their use? The southwest chamber was the chamber for offering. The southeast was the chamber for the showbread. In the northeast chamber the children of the Asmoneans deposited the stones of the altar which the Greek Kings had defiled.[8] In the northwest chamber they descended to the house of baptism.

7. To the House Moked were two doors; one open to the Chel, and one open to the court. Said Rabbi Judah, " the one open to the court had a wicket, through which they went in to sweep the court."

8. The House Moked was arched, and spacious, and surrounded with stone divans, and the elders of the Courses slept there with the keys of the court in their hands; and also the young priests each with his pillow on the ground.

9. And there was a place a cubit square with a tablet of marble, and to it was fastened a ring, and a chain upon which the keys were suspended. When the time approached for locking the gates, the priest lifted up the tablet by the ring, and took the keys from the chain and locked inside, and the

---

[7] Platform or rampart.   [8] 1 Mac. ii. 25.

Levites slept outside. When he had finished locking, he returned the keys to the chain, and the tablet to its place, laid his pillow over it, and fell asleep. If sudden defilement happened, he rose and went out in the gallery that ran under the arch, and candles flamed on either side, until he came to the house of baptism. Rabbi Eleazar, the son of Jacob, says, " in the gallery that went under the Chel, he passed out through Tadi."

OUR BEAUTY BE UPON THEE IN THREE PLACES.

CHAPTER II

1. The Mountain of the House was 500 cubits square. The largest space was on the south, the second on the east, the third on the north, and the least westward. In the place largest in measurement was held most service.

2. All who entered the Mountain of the House entered on the right-hand side, and went round, and passed out on the left: except to whomsoever an accident occurred, he turned to the left. "Why do you go to the left?" "I am in mourning." "He that dwelleth in this House comfort thee." "I am excommunicate." "He that dwelleth in this House put in thy heart (repentance), and they shall receive thee." The words of Rabbi Meier. To him said Rabbi José, "thou hast acted as though they had transgressed against him in judgment; but, 'may He that dwelleth in this House put it in thy heart that thou hearken to the words of thy neighbors, and they shall receive thee.'"

3. Inside of the (Mountain of the House) was a reticulated wall, ten hand-breadths high; and in it were thirteen breaches, broken down by the Greek kings. The (Jews) restored, and fenced them, and decreed before them thirteen acts of obeisance. Inside of it was the Chel, ten cubits broad, and twelve steps were there. The height of each step was half a cubit, and the breadth half a cubit. All the steps there were in height half a cubit, and in breadth half a cubit, except those of the porch. All the doors there were in height twenty cubits, and in breadth ten cubits, except that of the porch. All the gateways there had doors, except that of the porch. All the gates

there had lintels, except Tadi; there two stones inclined one
upon the other. All the gates there were transformed into
gold, except the gate Nicanor,[1] because to it happened a wonder, though some said " because its brass glittered like gold."

4. And all the walls there were high, except the eastern
wall, that the priest who burned the heifer, might stand on
the top of the Mount of Olives, and look straight into the
door of the Sanctuary when he sprinkled the blood.

5. The Court of the women was 135 cubits in length, by
135 in breadth. And in its four corners were four chambers,
each forty cubits square, and they had no roofs; and so they
will be in future, as is said, " Then he brought me forth into
the utter court, and caused me to pass by the four corners of
the court; and, behold, in every corner of the court there was
a court." [2]   In the four corners of the court there were courts
smoking, yet not smoking, since they were roofless. And
what was their use? The southeast one was the chamber of
the Nazarites, for there the Nazarites cooked their peace-
offerings, and polled their hair, and cast it under the pot. The
northeast was the chamber for the wood, and there the priests
with blemishes gathered out the worm-eaten wood. And
every stick in which a worm was found, was unlawful for the
altar. The northwest was the chamber for the lepers. The
southwest? Rabbi Eleazar, the son of Jacob, said, " I forget
for what it served." Abashaul said, " there they put wine,
and oil." It was called the chamber of the house of oil. And
it was open at first and surrounded with lattice-work, that the
women might see from above and the men from beneath, lest
they should be mixed. And fifteen steps corresponding to
the fifteen steps in the Psalms, ascended from it to the court
of Israel; upon them the Levites chanted. They were not
angular, but deflected like the half of a round threshing-floor.

6. And under the court of Israel were chambers open to
the court of the women. There the Levites deposited their
harps, and psalteries, and cymbals, and all instruments of
music. The court of Israel was 135 cubits long, and eleven
broad; and likewise the court of the priests was 135 cubits

[1] So called either because Nicanor, a
Pharisee, had the gate made in Alexandria, and though it was thrown over-
board from a ship in a storm, it yet
came safe to land; or because Nicanor,
a Greek prince, was slain there in the
time of the Asmoneans.
[2] Ezek. xlvi. 21.

long, and eleven broad. And pointed rails separated the
court of Israel from the court of the priests. Rabbi Eleazar,
the son of Jacob, said, "there was a step a cubit high, and a
dais placed over it. And in it were three steps each half a
cubit in height." We find that the priests' court was two
and a half cubits higher than the court of Israel. The whole
court was 187 cubits in length, and 135 cubits in breadth, and
the thirteen places for bowing were there. Abajose, the son
of Chanan, said, "in front of the thirteen gates." In the south
near to the west were the upper gate, the gate of flaming, the
gate of the first-born, the water gate. And why is it called
the water gate? Because through it they bring bottles of
water for pouring out during the feast of Tabernacles. Rabbi
Eleazar, the son of Jacob, said, "through it the water returned
out, and in future it will issue from under the threshold of the
house." And there were opposite to them in the north, near
to the west, the gate of Jochania, the gate of the offering, the
gate of the women, the gate of music. And "why was it
called the gate of Jochania?" "Because through it Jochania
went out in his captivity." In the east was the gate Nicanor,
and in it were two wickets, one on the right, and one on the
left, and two in the west which were nameless.

OUR BEAUTY BE UPON THEE, O MOUNTAIN OF THE HOUSE.

CHAPTER III

1. The altar was thirty-two cubits square. It ascended a
cubit and receded a cubit. This was the foundation. It remains thirty cubits square. It ascended five cubits, and
receded one cubit. This is the circumference. It remains
twenty-eight cubits square. The place for the horns was a
cubit on each side. It remains twenty-six cubits square.
The place of the path for the feet of the priests was a cubit
on each side. The hearth remains twenty-four cubits square.
Rabbi José said, "at first it was only twenty-eight cubits
square." It receded and ascended until the hearth remained
twenty cubits square; but when the children of the captivity
came up, they added to it four cubits on the north, and four
cubits on the west, like a gamma it is said; and the altar was

twelve cubits long by twelve broad, being a square. One
might say it was only "a square of twelve," [1] as is said. Upon
its four sides we learn that it measured from the middle twelve
cubits to every side. And a line of red paint girdled it in
the midst to separate the blood sprinkled above from the blood
sprinkled below. And the foundation was a perfect walk
along on the north side; and all along on the west, but it
wanted in the south one cubit, and in the east one cubit. [2]

2. And in the southwestern corner were two holes as two
thin nostrils, that the blood poured upon the western and
southern foundation should run into them; and it commingled
in a canal and flowed out into the Kidron.

3. Below in the plaster in the same corner there was a place
a cubit square, with a marble tablet, and a ring fastened in it.
Through it they descended to the sewer and cleansed it. And
there was a sloping ascent [3] to the south of the altar, thirty-two
cubits long by sixteen broad. In its western side was a closet,
where they put the birds unmeet for the sin-offering.

4. Either the stones of the sloping ascent, or the stones
of the altar were from the valley of Bethcerem. [4] And they
digged deeper than virgin soil, and brought from thence perfect stones over which iron [5] was not waved. For the iron
defiles by touching. And a scratch defiles everything. In
any of them a scratch defiled, but the others were lawful.
And they whitewashed them twice in the year; once at the
passover, and once at the feast of Tabernacles. And the
Sanctuary (was whitewashed) once at the passover. The
Rabbi said, "every Friday evening they whitewashed them
with a mop on account of the blood." They did not plaster
it with an iron trowel, "mayhap it will touch and defile."
Since iron is made to shorten the days of man, and the altar
is made to lengthen the days of man, it is not lawful, that
what shortens should be waved over what lengthens.

5. And there were rings to the northern side of the altar,

---

[1] Ezek. xliii. 16.
[2] As this corner would have been in
the tribe of Judah, it was not added,
that the whole altar might remain in
the tribe of Benjamin. Gen. xlix. 27.
   This sloping ascent to the altar was
strewn with salt. This salt was brought
from the mountain of Sodom at the
south of the Dead Sea. The salt was

intended to keep the priests from slipping and falling, which might easily
happen, as they were obliged to minister barefooted. The coldness of the
pavement in winter, and eating so much
flesh of the sacrifices, brought various
diseases on the priests.
[4] House of the vineyard.
[5] Deut. xxvii. 5.

six rows of four each: though some say four rows of six each. Upon them the priests slaughtered the holy beasts. The slaughter-house was at the north side of the altar. And in it were eight dwarf pillars with a beam of cedar-wood over them. And in them were fastened iron hooks—three rows to each pillar. Upon them they hung up (the bodies), and skinned them upon marble tables between the pillars.

6. The laver was between the porch and the altar, but inclined more to the south. Between the porch and the altar were twenty-two cubits, and there were twelve steps. The height of each step was half a cubit, and its breadth a cubit—a cubit—a cubit—a landing three cubits—a cubit—a cubit and a landing three cubits. And the upper one a cubit—a cubit, and the landing four cubits. Rabbi Jehudah said, " the upper one a cubit—a cubit, and the landing five cubits."

7. The doorway of the porch was forty cubits high, and twenty broad. Over it were five carved oak beams. The lower one extended beyond the doorway a cubit on either side. The one over it extended a cubit on either side. It follows that the uppermost was thirty cubits; and between each one there was a row of stones.

8. And stone buttresses were joined from the wall of the sanctuary to the wall of the porch, lest it should bulge. And in the roof of the porch were fastened golden chains, upon which the young priests climbed up, and saw the crowns. As it is said, " And the crowns shall be to Helem, and to Tobijah, and to Jedaiah, and to Hen, the son of Zephaniah, for a memorial in the temple of the Lord." [6] And over the doorway of the sanctuary was a golden vine supported upon the buttresses. Everyone who vowed a leaf, or a berry, or a cluster, he brought it and hung it upon it. Said Rabbi Eleazar, the son of Zadok, " it is a fact, and there were numbered 300 priests to keep it bright."

OUR BEAUTY BE UPON THEE, O ALTAR.

[6] Zech. vi. 14.

CHAPTER IV

1. The doorway of the Sanctuary [1] was twenty cubits in height, and ten in breadth. And it had four doors, two within and two without, as is said, "Two doors to the temple and the holy place." [2] The outside (doors) opened into the doorway to cover the thickness of the wall, and the inside doors opened into the Sanctuary to cover (the space) behind the doors, because the whole house was overlaid with gold excepting behind the doors. Rabbi Judah said, "they stood in the middle of the doorway, and like a pivot these folded behind them two cubits and a half; and those two cubits and a half, half a cubit and a jamb on this side, and half a cubit and a jamb on the other side." It is said, "two doors to two doors folding back, two leaves to one door and two leaves to the other." [3]

2. And the great gate had two wickets, one in the north, and one in the south. Through the one in the south no man ever entered. And with regard to it Ezekiel declared, as is said, "The Lord said unto me; this gate shall be shut, it shall not be opened, and no man shall enter in by it; because the Lord, the God of Israel, hath entered in by it, therefore it shall be shut." [4] The priest took the key, and opened the wicket, and went into the little chamber, and from the chamber to the Sanctuary. Rabbi Judah said, "he went in the thickness of the wall, until he found himself standing between the two gates, and he opened the outside gates from inside, and the inside from outside."

3. And there were thirty-eight little chambers, fifteen in the north, fifteen in the south, and eight in the west. The northern and southern ones were (placed) five over five, and five over them; and in the west three over three, and two over them. To each were three doors: one to the little chamber on the right, one to the little chamber on the left, and one to the little chamber over it. And in the northeastern corner were five gates: one to the little chamber on

[1] The Rabbis say that "the world is like an eye. The ocean is the white of the eye. The pupil is Jerusalem. And the image in the pupil is the Sanctuary." [3] Ezek. xli. 23.
[5] Ezek. xli. 24.   [4] Ezek. xliv. 2.

the right, and one to the little chamber over, and one to the gallery, and one to the wicket, and one to the Sanctuary.

4. The lowest row was five cubits, and the roofing six cubits, and the middle row six, and the roofing seven, and the upper was seven, as is said, " the nethermost chamber was five cubits broad, and the middle six cubits broad, and the third seven cubits broad." [5]

5. And a gallery ascended from the northeastern corner to the southwestern corner. Through it they went up to the roofs of the little chambers. One went up in the gallery with his face to the west. So he proceeded all along the northern side, till he reached the west. On reaching the west, he turned his face southward, going along the west side, till he reached the south. On reaching the south, with his face to the east, he went along the south side till he arrived at the door of the upper story, because the door of the upper story opened in the south side. And at the door of the upper story were two cedar beams. By them they went up to the roof of the upper story, and on its summit rails separated between the Holy and the Holy of Holies. And in the attic, trap-doors opened to the Holy of Holies. Through them they let down the workmen in boxes, lest they should feast their eyes in the Holy of Holies.

6. The Sanctuary was a square of 100 cubits, and its height 100. The foundation six cubits, and the height (of the wall) forty cubits, and the string course [6] one cubit, and the rain channel two cubits, and the beams one cubit, and the covering plaster one cubit; and the height of the upper story was forty cubits, and the string course one cubit, and the rain channel two cubits, and the beams one cubit, and the covering plaster one cubit, and the battlement three cubits, and the scarecrow one cubit. Rabbi Judah said, " the scarecrow was not counted in the measurement; but the battlement was four cubits."

7. From east to west there were 100 cubits, the wall of the porch five, and the porch eleven, and the wall of the Sanctuary six, and the interior forty, and the partition space (between the Vails) one, and the Holy of Holies twenty cubits. The wall of the Sanctuary was six, and the little chamber six, and

---

[5] 1 Kings vi. 6.   [6] Curiously graven and gilt.

16

the wall of the little chamber five. From north to south there
were seventy (cubits). The wall of the gallery five, the gallery
three, the wall of the little chamber five, the little chamber six,
the wall of the Sanctuary six, its interior twenty, the wall of
the Sanctuary six, the little chamber six, the wall of the little
chamber five, the place of the descent of the water three, and
the wall five cubits. The porch was extended beyond it fifteen
cubits in the north, and fifteen in the south; and this space
was called, "the house of the instruments of slaughter," because the knives were there deposited. And the Sanctuary
was narrow behind and broad in the front, and it was like a
lion, as is said, "Ho! Ariel, the city where David dwelt,[7] as
a lion is narrow behind and broad in front, so the Sanctuary
is narrow behind and broad in front."

OUR BEAUTY BE UPON THEE, DOOR OF THE SANCTUARY.

CHAPTER V

1. The length of the whole court[1] was 187 cubits. The
breadth 135. From east to west 187. The place for the tread
of the feet of Israel was eleven cubits. The place for the
tread of the priests eleven cubits. The altar thirty-two. Between the porch and the altar twenty-two cubits. The temple
100 cubits; and eleven cubits behind the House of Atonement.

2. From north to south there were 135 cubits. From the
sloping ascent to the altar sixty-two. From the altar to the
rings eight cubits. The space for the rings twenty-four.
From the rings to the tables four. From the tables to the
pillars four. From the pillars to the wall of the court eight
cubits. And the remainder lay between the sloping ascent
and the wall and the place of the pillars.

3. In the court were six chambers, three in the north, and
three in the south. In the north, the chamber of salt, the
chamber of parva, the chamber of washers. In the chamber
of salt they added salt to the offerings. In the chamber of

[7] Is. xxix. 1.
[1] "The king only, and no man else
(remarks Maimonides) might sit in the
court of the Temple in any place; and
even this privilege was confined to a
king of the family of David." Cunœus
further observes, that the king was esteemed nearer to God than the priests
themselves, and a greater president of
religion."

parva they salted the skins of the offerings; and upon its roof
was the house of baptism for the High Priest on the day of
atonement. In the chamber of washers they cleansed the inwards of the offerings; and from thence a gallery extended up
to the top of the house of parva.

4. In the south were the chamber of wood, the chamber of
the captivity, and the chamber of hewn stone. The chamber
of wood, said Rabbi Eleazar, the son of Jacob, " I forget for
what it served." Abashaul said, " the chamber of the High
Priest was behind them both, and the roof of the three chambers was even. In the chamber of the captivity was sunk the
well with the wheel attached to it, and from thence water was
supplied to the whole court. In the chamber of Hewn Stone
the great Sanhedrin of Israel sat, and judged the priesthood,
and the priest in whom defilement was discovered, clothed
in black, and vailed in black, went out and departed; and when
no defilement was found in him, clothed in white, and vailed
in white, he went in and served with his brethren the priests.
And they made a feast-day, because no defilement was found
in the seed of Aaron the Priest, and thus they said, " Blessed
be the Place. Blessed be He, since no defilement is found
in the seed of Aaron. And blessed be He who has chosen
Aaron and his sons to stand and minister [2] before the Lord
in the House of the Holy of Holies.

OUR BEAUTY BE UPON THEE, WHOLE COURT;

AND COMPLETION TO THEE, TRACT

MEASUREMENTS.

[2] The Temple services were arranged
by the council of fourteen. This council was composed of the High Priest,
the Sagan (the deputy or Suffragan of
the High Priest), two Katholikin, who
had charge of the treasuries, three Giz-
barim, who were assistants of the Katholikin, and seven Ammarcalin, who had
charge of the gates.

THE TABERNACLE

CHAPTER I

Rabbi Judah the Holy, said, there were ten heave-offerings, the heave-offering of the Lord, and the heave-offering
of the tithes, of the dough, and of the first-fruits; and the
heave-offering of the Nazarite, and the heave-offering of
thanksgiving, and the heave-offering of the land, and the
heave-offering of Israelites dwelling in Midian, and the
heave-offering of the shekels, and the heave-offering of the
tabernacle. The heave-offering of the Lord, and the heave-
offering of the tithes, and of the dough, and of the first-fruits,
and the heave-offering of the Nazarite, and the heave-offering
of thanksgiving, were for the priests. The heave-offering of
the land was for the priests, the Levites, and the Nethinim,[1]
and the Sanctuary and Jerusalem. The heave-offering of
Midian was for Eleazar the priest, the heave-offering of shekels
was for the sockets of the tabernacle, the heave-offering of
the tabernacle furnished the material of the tabernacle, and
the oil for lighting, and the sweet incense, and the garments
of the priests, and the garments of the High Priest. The
length of the tabernacle was thirty cubits, and its breadth was

[1] The Nethinim, or the " given ones,"
were added, it is supposed, from among
the Gibeonites to fill up the deficiencies
in the number of Levites who returned
from the captivity in Babylon. They
were held in low estimation, and were
forbidden to intermarry with Israelites.

ten cubits, and its height was ten cubits. Rabbi José said,
" its length was thirty-one cubits." " How was the tabernacle
set up?" " Forty sockets of silver were placed on the north,
and forty sockets of silver on the south, and sixteen on the
west, and four on the east. These are 100 sockets. As is
said,[2] 'An hundred sockets of the hundred talents, a talent
for a socket.'" " How were the boards set up?" " Twenty
boards were placed on the north, and twenty boards on the
south, and eight on the west. On the east there was no board,
but there were four pillars of shittim-wood. Upon them the
vail was hung. As is said,[3] 'thou shalt make a vail,' etc., 'and
thou shalt hang it upon four pillars of shittim-wood, overlaid
with gold,' etc., and 'thou shalt hang up the vail under the
taches.'" And the sockets were made with holes, and these
were cut out in the boards below, a quarter from one side and
a quarter from the other side, and there was cut out half of it
in the middle, and it made two pins like two supports, and
they entered into two sockets, as is said, " two sockets under
one board for its two tenons."[4] The pins extended from the
boards two and two, to every one which was inserted, the
positive into the negative, as it is said,[5] " Set in order one
against the other." The words of Rabbi Nehemiah, when
Rabbi Nehemiah said, "there is no meaning in saying, 'set
in order.'" "And what is meant by set in order?" "It is
meant that there should be made for them rungs like an
Egyptian ladder." There was cut out from the board above
a finger-breadth from one side, and a finger-breadth from the
other side, and they were put into the golden ring, that they
should not separate one from the other, as is said, " And they
shall be coupled together beneath, and they shall be coupled
together above the head of it unto one ring."[6] There is no
meaning in saying, " unto one ring," and what is meant by
saying, " unto one ring?" " The place where the bar was
put in, and every board had in it two rings of gold, one above,
and one below; in them were put in the bars." And there
were two upper bars, and two lower (bars) on the south side;
the length of each of them was fifteen cubits. It follows that
two were in length thirty cubits against twenty boards, and

[2] Exod. xxxviii. 27.   [3] Exod. xxvi. 31-33.   [4] Exod. xxvi. 19.
          [5] Exod. xxvi. 17.   [6] Exod. xvi. 24.

the middle (bar) was in length thirty cubits against twenty boards, which was inserted in the middle of the boards from east to west, as is said, "And the middle bar in the midst of the boards shall reach from end to end."[7] As the boards were made in the south, so the boards were made in the north, but in the west they were not so; but the length of the upper bar and the lower one was six cubits against four boards, and the middle (bar), twelve cubits against eight boards. And the boards, and the bars, and the pillars, and the sockets, the place of the thickness of the boards were overlaid with gold, as is said, "And the boards thou shalt overlay with gold."[8] "The places for the bars," there is no meaning in saying, "places for the bars"; and what is the meaning of saying, "places for the bars"? "The place where the bar entered the boards." "And the bars themselves shall be overlaid with gold."[9] "How was it done?" "Two pipes of gold were introduced—the length of each of them was a cubit and a half; and they were put into the hole of the board, the place where the bars were put in."

CHAPTER II

"How was the tabernacle covered?" "There were provided ten curtains of blue, of purple, and scarlet, and fine-twined linen." As is said, "Moreover, thou shalt make the tabernacle (with) ten curtains of fine-twined linen, and blue, and purple, and scarlet."[1] "Their threads were doubled thirty-two times," the words of Rabbi Nehemiah, when R. Nehemiah said, "thread," *i.e.*, one doubled in two, "twined," *i.e.*, to four, "fine-twined," *i.e.*, to eight. It follows that their threads were doubled thirty-two times. But the Sages say, "thread," *i.e.*, one doubled in two, "twined," *i.e.*, to three, "fine-twined," *i.e.*, to six. It follows that their threads were doubled twenty-four times. They were coupled in two vails, one of five, and one of five.[2] As is said, "the five curtains shall be coupled together one to another: and (other) five curtains (shall be) coupled one to another," and they were coupled with loops of blue, as is said,[3] "And thou shalt make loops

[7] Exod. xxvi. 28. [9] Exod. xxvi. 29. [3] Exod. xxvi. 3.
[8] Exod. xxvi. 29. [1] Exod. xxvi. 1. [2] Exod. xxvi. 4.

of blue upon the edge of the one curtain from the selvedge in the coupling; and likewise shalt thou make in the uttermost edge of (another) curtain, in the coupling of the second." And they were coupled to fifty taches of gold, as is said,[4] " And thou shalt make fifty taches of gold, and couple the curtains together with the taches; and it shall be one tabernacle." And the taches appeared in the tabernacle as stars in the firmament. The length of the curtains was twenty-eight cubits, as is said,[5] " the length of one curtain (shall be) eight and twenty cubits." Take from them ten cubits for the breadth of the tabernacle, there will remain nine cubits from the one side, and nine cubits from the other side. They hung down and covered the boards till they reached the sockets. This teaches that the sockets were one cubit high. And the breadth of the curtains was forty cubits. As is said,[6] " and the breadth of one curtain four cubits." Take from them thirty cubits from the east to the west, which were on the roof of the tabernacle, and ten cubits to the west behind the tabernacle, there are forty.

CHAPTER III

There were provided eleven curtains of goats' hair, and the length of every one of them was thirty cubits, as is said, " And thou shalt make curtains of goats' (hair) to be a covering upon the tabernacle: eleven curtains shalt thou make. The length of one curtain (shall be) thirty cubits." [1] And they were coupled in two vails, one of five, and one of six, as is said, " And thou shalt couple five curtains by themselves, and six curtains by themselves," [2] and they were coupled with fifty loops, as is said, " And he made fifty loops upon the outmost edge of the curtain in the coupling, and fifty loops made he upon the edge of the curtain which coupleth the second." [3] And the loops were coupled to fifty taches of brass, as is said, " And thou shalt make fifty taches of brass, and put the taches into the loops, and couple the tent together that it may be one." [4] The length of the curtains was thirty cubits. Take from them ten cubits for their breadth, there will remain ten

---

[4] Exod. xxvi. 6.
[5] Exod. xxvi. 2.
[6] Exod. xxvi. 2.
[1] Exod. xxvi. 7, 8.
[2] Exod. xxvi. 9.
[3] Exod. xxxvi. 17.
[4] Exod. xxvi. 11.

cubits from one side, and ten cubits from the other side, as they hung down and covered the boards and the sockets. The breadth of the curtains was forty-four cubits, as is said, " And the breadth of one curtain four cubits; and the eleven curtains shall be all of one measure." [5] Take from them thirty cubits for the length of the tabernacle, and ten cubits behind the tabernacle—these are forty. There was left there one curtain which was doubled in front of the tent, as is said, " And thou shalt double the sixth curtain in the fore-front of the tabernacle." [6] Rabbi Judah said, " half of it was doubled in the fore-front of the tabernacle, and half of it was hanging behind the tabernacle," as is said, " And the remnant that remaineth of the curtains of the tent, the half curtain that remaineth shall hang over the back-side of the tabernacle." [7] There was also provided one great cover of rams' skins dyed red, its length thirty cubits, and its breadth ten cubits; with it they clothed the tent upon the tabernacle from east to west, as is said, " And thou shalt make a covering for the tent of rams' skins dyed red, and a covering above of badgers' skins," [8] and it was made " like patchwork," the words of Rabbi Nehemiah. Rabbi Judah said, " there were two covers—the lower one of rams' skins dyed red, and the upper one of badgers' skins," as is said, " his covering and the covering of the badgers' skins that is above upon it." [9]

CHAPTER IV

The vail was woven ten cubits square, and there were made in it four loops, and it was hung on hooks on the tops of the pillars, and it was spread in the third portion of the tabernacle, that there should be from it inward ten cubits, and from it outward twenty cubits, as is said, " And thou shalt hang up the vail under the taches." [1] It follows that the place of the Holy of Holies was ten cubits square, and there were put the ark, and the pot of manna, and the pan of anointing oil, and Aaron's rod with its almonds and flowers; and there Aaron entered four times on the day of atonement. Outside the vail

[5] Exod. xxvi. 8.
[6] Exod. xxvi. 9.
[7] Exod. xxvi. 12.
[8] Some commentators explain these to be " skins of seals " or " dolphins," and

others understand the meaning to be a " blue color." Exod. xxvi. 14.
[9] Num. iv. 25.
[1] Exod. xxvi. 33.

were placed the table and candlestick. But the table was on the north, and opposite to it was the candlestick on the south; as is said, "And thou shalt set the table without the vail, and the candlestick over against the table."[2] And as they were placed in the tent of the congregation, so were they placed in the everlasting House.[3] Now the tent of the congregation was in length thirty cubits, and in breadth ten cubits. But the everlasting House was in length sixty cubits, and in breadth twenty cubits. This teaches that the tent of the congregation was one-fourth part of the everlasting House. And as the vail was woven, so was woven the ephod and the breastplate, only in these there was an additional thread of gold; as is said, "And they did beat the gold into thin plates and cut *it into* wires."[4] As was the weaving of the covering vail, so was the weaving of the covering for the entrance. But the vail was cunning work, as is said, "Thou shalt make the vail of blue and purple," etc.; "cunning work"[5] But the covering of the entrance was needle-work, as is said, "And thou shalt make an hanging for the door of the tent," etc., "of needle-work."[6] The words of R. Nehemiah. R. Nehemiah usually said, "every place where it is said cunning work (there were) two figures—in the needlework (there was) but one figure only." And the branches of the candlestick were right opposite to the breadth of the table. And the golden altar was placed in the middle of the house, and divided the house, and its half inward was right opposite to the ark; as is said, "And thou shalt put it before the vail that is by the ark of the testimony before the mercy-seat"[7] From the boards on the south to the branches of the candlestick (there were) two cubits and a half. And from the branches of the candlestick to the table (there were) five cubits. And from the table to the boards on the north (were) two cubits and a half. This teaches that the breadth of the Holy Place (was) ten cubits. From the boards on the west to the vail (were) ten cubits. From the vail to the table were five cubits. From the table to the golden altar (were) five cubits. From the golden altar to the boards on the east (were) ten cubits. This teaches that the length of the tabernacle was thirty cubits.

[2] Exod. xxvi. 35.
[3] Or, in the "House of dispensations."
[4] Exod. xxxix. 3.
[5] Exod. xxvi. 31.
[6] Exod. xxvi. 36.   [7] Exod. xxx. 6.

CHAPTER V

The court of the tabernacle was in length 100 cubits, and in breadth fifty cubits, as is said, " And thou shalt make the court of the tabernacle for the south side, etc., 100 cubits,[1] and likewise for the north side an hundred cubits," as is said, " and likewise for the north side in length there shall be hangings of 100 cubits long." [2] And on the west fifty cubits, as is said, " On the west side shall be hangings of fifty cubits." [3] And on the east fifty cubits, as is said, " On the east side eastward *shall be* fifty cubits." [4] Take from them fifty cubits for hangings, as is said, " The hangings of one side of the gate shall be fifteen cubits," [5] etc. " And for the other side," etc. From both sides the hangings on the south to the tent were twenty cubits, and the tent was ten cubits broad, and from the tent to the hangings on the north were twenty cubits. This teaches that the breadth (of the court) was fifty cubits. From the hangings on the west to the tent were twenty cubits, and the tent was thirty cubits long; and from the tent to the hangings on the east, there were fifty cubits. This teaches that its length was 100 cubits, as is said, " The length of the court shall be 100 cubits, and the breadth fifty everywhere." [6] Rabbi José said there is no meaning in saying " fifty everywhere," and what is meant by saying " fifty everywhere "? " That is in front of the tent." This teaches that its length was 100 cubits, and its breadth fifty cubits. But you could not know the breadth of the hangings till you know the height of the court, as he (Moses) said, " And the height five cubits "; [6] as the height was five cubits, so was the breadth five cubits. " How was the court set up? " Twenty sockets of brass were put on the north side, and twenty on the south side, and there was a pillar in every one of them. And there were beams, and a ring was fastened in their middle, and the beams were fastened with ropes and pillars; and the length of every beam was six hand-breadths, and its breadth was three (hand-breadths). And the ring was hung on the hook in the pillar; and the hanging was rolled on it like the sail of a ship. It follows that the hanging extended from the pillar two cubits and a

---

[1] Exod. xxvii. 9. [3] Exod. xxvii. 12. [5] Exod. xxxviii. 14, 15.
[2] Exod. xxvii. 11. [4] Exod. xxvii. 13. [6] Exod. xxvii. 18.

half on one side, and two cubits and a half on the other side; and so with the second pillar. This teaches that between each pillar there were five cubits. The beams were coupled with ropes and pillars, and they were coupled in the pins of brass; and as there were pins to the tabernacle, so were there pins to the court, as is said, " All the vessels of the tabernacle in all the service thereof, and all the pins thereof, and all the pins of the court, shall be of brass." [7] But you could not know how much space there was from the hangings to the entrance of the court, till he said, " And the hangings of the court, and the hanging for the door of the gate of the court, which is by the tabernacle, and by the altar." [8] As between the tabernacle and the altar there were ten cubits, so from the hangings to the entrance of the court there were ten cubits. But you could not know how high was the entrance of the court, till he said, " And for the gate of the court shall be a hanging of twenty cubits," in length and height. In breadth it was five cubits. " There was no meaning in saying five cubits, and what is the meaning of saying five cubits? " " To instruct thee that its length was ten cubits, and its breadth five cubits." As was the entrance of the tent, so was the entrance of the court. As was the entrance of the court, so was the entrance of the sanctuary. As was the height of the entrance of the sanctuary, so was the breadth of the entrance of the porch. " The length of the court shall be 100 cubits, and the breadth of it fifty everywhere." [9] The oral law says, " Take fifty and surround them with fifty." [10] Hence said Rabbi José, the son of Rabbi Judah,[1] " an enclosed space which can contain two seahs (of sown grain) as the court of the tabernacle, is lawful for carrying burdens on the Sabbath day."

CHAPTER VI

THE ARK which Moses made in the desert was in length two cubits and a half, and in breadth one cubit and a half, and in height one cubit and a half, as is said, " And they shall make an ark of shittim-wood, two cubits and a half shall be

[7] Exod. xxvii. 19.
[8] Num. iv. 26.
[9] Exod. xxvii. 18.
[10] Some explain this to mean " multiply fifty with 100 " (Aruch); others

think that the measurement is to be made with a rope of fifty cubits (Eruvin).
[1] Some read " in the name of," etc.

the length thereof, and a cubit and a half the breadth thereof,
and a cubit and a half the height thereof." [1]   R. Meier said,
" with a cubit containing six hand-breadths—thus they make
fifteen hand-breadths.   Take from them twelve hand-breadths
for the breadth of the tables, and two hand-breadths for the
place where the roll of the Law lay, and half a hand-breadth
from either side for the thickness of the ark.   And the breadth
of the ark was nine hand-breadths.   Take from them six hand-
breadths for the length of the tables, and for the place where
the roll of the Law lay, two hand-breadths, that it should not
be pressed going in and out, and half a hand-breadth on either
side for the thickness of the ark."   R. Judah said, " with a
cubit containing five hand-breadths, thus there were twelve
hand-breadths and a half, and four tables lay in it—two perfect,
and two broken.   And the length of each table was six hand-
breadths, and their breadth six, and their thickness three.
Take from them twelve hand-breadths for the breadth of the
tables, and a finger-breadth on either side for the thickness
of the ark.   And the breadth of the ark was seven hand-
breadths and a half.   Take from them six hand-breadths for
the length of the tables, and one hand-breadth for the place
where the handles (pillars) lay; and on it the explanation of
the prophets is, " King Solomon made himself a chariot of the
wood of Lebanon.   He made the pillars thereof of silver." [2]
And (there was) a finger-breadth on either side for the thickness of the ark, but the roll of the Law was put on the side,
as is said, " And put it in the side of the ark of the covenant
of the LORD." [3]   And so with the Philistines, he said, " And
put the jewels of gold, which ye return for a trespass-offering,
in a coffer by the side thereof." [4]   R. Judah, the son of Lachish,
said, " there were two arks, one which abode in the encampment, and one which went forth with them to war, and in
it were the broken tables," as is said, " And the ark of the
covenant of the Lord went." [5]   But the one with them in the
encampment contained the roll of the Law.   That is what is
written, " Nevertheless the ark of the covenant of the Lord;
and Moses departed not out of the camp." [6]   And so he said
with regard to Saul, " And Saul said unto Ahiah, bring hither

[1] Exod. xxv. 10.   [3] Deut. xxxi. 26.   [5] Num. x. 33.
[2] Sol. Song, iii. 9, 10.   [4] 1 Sam. vi. 8.   [6] Num. xiv. 44.

the ark of God." [7]   And so of Uriah it is said, " The ark, and
Israel, and Judah abide in tents." [8]   But the ark of the covenant went not forth to war, save once only, as is said, " So
the people sent to Shiloh, that they might bring from thence
the ark of the covenant of the Lord of hosts." [9] R. Judah said,
" there was nothing in the ark save the tables of the covenant
only," as is said, " There was nothing in the ark save the
two tables of stone." [10]

CHAPTER VII

" How did Bezaleel make the ark ? " " He made three
boxes, two of gold and one of wood. He put the wooden
one inside the golden one, and the golden one inside the
wooden one, and covered the upper edge with gold; as is
said, " And thou shalt overlay it with pure gold: within and
without shalt thou overlay it." [1]   " And what is the meaning
of saying, ' thou shalt overlay it '? "   " It means that he covered the upper edges (with) gold." The golden mercy-seat
was placed above upon it; as is said, " And thou shalt put the
mercy-seat above upon the ark." [2] And four rings of gold
were fastened in it, two on the north and two on the south,
and in them the staves were put, and they were never moved
from thence; as is said, " The staves shall be in the rings of
the ark; they shall not be taken from it." [3] Even though
Solomon made the pattern of all the vessels, the pattern of
the ark he did not make; as is said, " And all the elders of
Israel came, and the priests took up the ark." [4] The ark was
placed in the midst of the House, and divided the House ten
cubits by ten cubits. And two cherubs of gold stood on their
feet on the ground. From the wall to the cherub there were
five cubits, and from the cherub to the wall five cubits.
" Where is it mentioned, that as soon as the priests brought
in the ark the staves were drawn out, and they reached to the
vail, and they touched the entrance? " As is said, " And they
drew out the staves, that the ends of the staves were seen out in
the holy place before the oracle." [5] For that reason the doors
of the Holy of Holies were never closed. " And they were

[7] 1 Sam. xiv. 18.
[8] 2 Sam. xi. 11.
[9] 1 Sam. iv. 4.
[10] 1 Kings viii. 9.
[1] Exod. xxv. 11.
[3] Exod. xxv. 21.
[2] Exod. xxv. 15.
[4] 1 Kings viii. 3.
[5] 1 Kings viii. 8.

not seen without "⁶   It is not possible to say that they were
not seen, since it was already said " they were seen."   Neither
is it possible to say that they were seen, since it is already said
" they were not seen."   " How is it?"   " They were push-
ing out in the vail, and were seen in the sanctuary like the two
paps of a woman."   " And from whence (do we know) that
they were drawn out from the inside?"   As is said, " And
they were not seen without."   There we learned that they were
drawn out from the inside.   And from thence (we learned)
that they were drawn out to the outside, as is said, " And the
ends of the staves were seen."   And where thou sayest that as
the staves were drawn out, so were drawn out the wings of
the cherubim, and they covered the ark, and overshadowed
the house from above, as is said, " And the cherubims covered
the ark and the staves thereof, above."⁷   " And where was
the ark concealed?"   Rabbi Judah, the son of Lachish, said,
" in its place in the house of the Holy of Holies, as is said, ' And
there they are unto this day.' "⁸   But the Sages say, " in the
chamber of the wood."   " And who concealed it?"   Rabbi
Judah the Holy said, Josiah concealed it, as it is said, ' And
said unto the Levites that taught all Israel, which were holy
unto the Lord, Put the holy ark in the house which Solomon,
the son of David, King of Israel, did build; it shall not be a
burden upon your shoulders."⁹   He said to them, " it shall
not be carried captive with you to Babylon, that you should
bear it upon your shoulders."   Rabbi Eleazar said, " it went
to Babylon, as is said, ' Nothing shall be left saith the Lord,'¹⁰
nothing, not even the words in it."   The house of the Holy
of Holies, which Solomon made for it, had a wall, entrance,
and doors, as is said, " And the temple and the sanctuary had
two doors."¹   But in the latter house there was no wall, only
two boards were there, and the length of each one was a cubit
and a half.   And two vails of gold were there, spread over
them from above, and it was called the place of Partition.²

⁶ 1 Kings viii. 8
⁷ 1 Kings viii. 7, 8.
⁸ 1 Kings viii. 8.
⁹ 2 Chron. xxxv. 3.
¹⁰ 2 Kings xx. 17.
¹ Ezek. xli. 23.

² Some   commentators   interpret
" Traksin " to mean " place of doubting," as zealots continually disputed the
exact division between the Holy Place
and the Holy of Holies.

CHAPTER VIII

THE TABLE which Moses made in the wilderness was in length two cubits, and its breadth one cubit, and its height was one cubit and a half, as is said, " Thou shalt also make a table of shittim-wood, two cubits shall be the length thereof, and a cubit the breadth thereof, and a cubit and a half the height thereof." [1] Rabbi Judah said, " the cubit (contained) five hand-breadths, thus there are ten hand-breadths." From thence the Sages said, " the table was in length ten hand-breadths, and in breadth five hand-breadths. And the show-bread was in length ten hand-breadths, and in breadth five. The length of the showbread was placed against the breadth of the table. It extended over two hand-breadths and a half on either side. It follows that its length quite filled the breadth of the table." Rabbi Meier said, " the table was in length twelve hand-breadths, and in breadth six hand-breadths. And the showbread was in length ten (hand-breadths), and in breadth five. And its length was placed against the breadth of the table. It extended over two hand-breadths on either side; and there was an opening of two hand-breadths in the middle, that the air might blow through them (the loaves)." Aba Shaul said, " they put there two cups of incense of the showbread." The Sages said to him, " and is it not already said, ' And thou shalt put pure frankincense upon each row.' " [2] He replied to them, " and is it not already said, ' And by him shall be the tribe of Manasseh '? " [3] Although Solomon made ten tables, and all of them were lawful for service, as is said, " He made also ten tables, and placed them in the temple, five on the right side, and five on the left." [4] " If thou sayest five on the south, and five on the north, is not a table on the south worthless? " But what is the meaning of saying, " five on the right and five on the left "? " Five to the right of the table of Moses, and five to the left of the table of Moses, even though he did not arrange the showbread, save for the table of Moses only, as is said, ' And the table whereupon the show-bread was.' " [5] Rabbi José, the son of Rabbi Judah, said,

---

[1] Exod. xxv. 23.   [2] Lev. xxiv. 7.
[3] Num. ii. 20. עַל therefore means " by " or " next," as well as " upon."
[4] 2 Chron. iv. 8.   [5] 1 Kings vii. 48.

" all the tables were arranged for showbread as is said, 'And the tables whereon the showbread was set.' " [6]

CHAPTER IX

THE CANDLESTICK which Moses made in the wilderness was wrought from gold, and required hammering, and required knops and flowers, as is said, " And thou shalt make a candlestick of pure gold; of beaten work shall the candlestick be made: his shaft and his branches, his bowls, his knops, and his flowers, shall be of the same." [1]   " Do I hear that he shall make separate members and join them to it?"   " The teaching says, that 'they shall be of the same.' "   " Whence know we that it extends to the light?"   " The teaching says, 'Thou shalt make.' "   " I am of opinion that it should be extended to the bowls, knops, and flowers. The teaching says ' it,' and what dost thou see to extend it to the light, and withhold it from the bowls, the knops, and the flowers?"   " Because the verse extends and withholds, (therefore) I extend (it to) the lights that they should be made with it, and I withhold the bowls, the knops, and the flowers, that they should not be made with it."   " Whence know we to extend (it to) the tongs and snuff-dishes?"   " The teaching says, 'thou shalt make.' "   " I am of opinion to extend (it to) the snuffers, and the tweezers."   " The teaching says, ' it,' and what dost thou see to extend (it to) the tongs and snuff-dishes, and to withhold (it from) the snuffers?"   " Because the verse extends and withholds. I extend (it to) the tongs and snuff-dishes, since they are used with it. And I withhold (it from) the snuffers and tweezers, since they are not used with it." As it was made of gold, it required hammering; when it was not of gold it did not require hammering. When it was made of gold it required bowls, knops, and flowers; when it was not of gold it did not require bowls, knops, and flowers. When it was made of gold it required a talent; when it was not of gold it did not require a talent. Rabbi Joshua, the son of Korcha, said, " it (the candlestick) was made of a talent, but the lights, and the tongs, and the snuff-dishes, were not from the talent;" as is said, " Of a talent of pure gold shall he make it." [2] " And what do I establish?" " That all these vessels were vessels of pure gold. But the trumpets which Moses made in the wilderness were made of silver only, as is said, ' Make thee two trumpets of silver.' " [3]

CHAPTER X

" How did Bezaleel make the candlestick?" " He made it from an ingot of gold, and it was like a beam. And above and below he made bowls, knops, and flowers, and drew out from it two branches, one on either side, and from it he drew out two other branches, one on either side, and again drew out two branches, one on either side, as is said, ' And six branches shall come out of the sides of it.' " [1] But we could not understand the hammering of the bowls, until it be said, " And in the candlesticks shall be four bowls made like unto almonds with their knops and their flowers." [2] Aisi, the son of Judah, said, " there are five expressions in the Law, and they have no fixed meaning. These are they, ' accepted,' [3] ' cursed,' [4] ' to-morrow,' [5] ' made like unto almonds,' [6] ' and will rise up.' " [7] " If thou doest well, shalt thou not be accepted?" or, " thou shalt be accepted even if thou doest not well." " Cursed be their anger for it was fierce," or, " for in their anger they slew a man, and in their self-will they houghed cursed oxen." " To-morrow I will stand " or " go out, fight with Amalek to-morrow." " Made like unto almonds with their knops, and their flowers," or " four bowls made like unto almonds." " And this people will rise up," or, " thou shalt sleep with thy fathers, and thou shalt rise up." These are the five expressions in the Law which have no fixed meaning. Aisa, the son of Akiba, said, " it happened once to be more (than a talent by) a dinar of gold, and it was brought into the crucible eighty times." The body of the candlestick was eighteen hand-breadths, the feet and the flowers were three hand-breadths, and two hand-breadths were smooth, and one hand-breadth was for the bowl, a knop and a flower, and two hand-breadths were smooth, and one hand-breadth a knop, and two branches proceeded from it, one on either side. And

[2] Exod. xxv. 39.　　[3] Exod. xxv. 34.　　[5] Exod. xvii. 9.
[3] Num. x. 2.　　[6] Gen. iv. 7.　　[6] Exod. xxv. 34.
[1] Exod. xxv. 32.　　[4] Gen. xlix. 7.　　[7] Deut. xxxi. 16.

two hand-breadths were smooth, and one hand-breadth a knop, and two branches proceeded from it, one on either side, and two hand-breadths were smooth, and one hand-breadth a knop, and two branches proceeded from it on either side. There remained three hand-breadths, in which were the bowls, the knops, and the flowers, as is said, " Three bowls made like unto almonds with a knop and a flower in one branch." [8]   It follows that the bowls were twenty-two, and the knops eleven, and the flowers nine.   " The bowls, to what were they like ? " " To cups of Alexandria."   " The knops, to what were they like ? "   " To the apples of pine-trees." [9]   " The flowers, to what were they like ? "   " To the flowers on the pillars of the temple."   It is found that you learn that there exist in the candlestick difficulty and forgetfulness more than in all the other vessels.   " And whence know we that OMNIPRES-ENCE showed to Moses, the vessels ready, and the candle-stick ready ? "   As it is said, " see and make them according to their patterns." [10]   Although Solomon made ten candle-sticks and all of them were lawful for service, as is said, " And he made ten candlesticks of gold according to their form, and set them in the temple, five on the right hand and five on the left." [1]   If you say, five on the south and five on the north, is not the candlestick on the north worthless ?   " And what is meant by saying, five on the right hand and five on the left ? " " Five on the right side of the candlestick of Moses, and five on the left side of the candlestick of Moses, even though they lighted the candlestick of Moses only, as is said, ' And the candlestick of gold, with the lamps thereof, to burn every evening,' " [2] Rabbi José, the son of Rabbi Judah, said, " they were all lighted," as is said, " Moreover the candlesticks with their lamps, that they should burn after the manner, before the oracle of pure gold; and the flowers, and the lamps, and the tongs made he of gold, and that perfect gold." [3]   All these completed the golden one of Moses.   Those on the west and east flamed in front of the middle light, as is said, " The seven lamps shall give light over against the candlestick." [4]   From thence Rabbi Nathan said, " the middle one is the most honor-

[8] Exod. xxv. 33.
[9] Or, " egg-shaped, oval."
[10] Exod. xxv. 40.
[1] 2 Chron. iv. 7.

[2] 2 Chron. xiii. 11.
[3] 2 Chron. iv. 20, 21.
[4] Num. viii. 2.

able." The seven lamps flamed alike, and their lamps were equal, and they resembled each other. "How did they snuff it?" "They removed the snuff from the candlestick and deposited it in the tent, and rubbed it with a sponge." "It follows that many priests were busied on one lamp." The words of Rabbi José. But the Sages say, "they did not remove the lamps from their places; they only removed the snuff from the candlestick, as is said, ' He shall order the lamps upon the pure candlestick.' "[5]

CHAPTER XI

THE ALTAR OF INCENSE was in length a cubit, and in breadth a cubit, and in height two cubits, as is said, "And thou shalt make an altar to burn incense upon; of shittim-wood shalt thou make it. A cubit shall be the length thereof, and a cubit the breadth thereof: four square shall it be: and two cubits shall be the height thereof: the horns thereof shall be of the same."[1] And it was all overlaid with gold.[2] This altar had three names, the altar of incense, the altar of gold, the inner altar. THE ALTAR OF BURNT-OFFERINGS was in length five cubits, and in breadth five cubits, and in height three cubits, as is said, "And he made the altar of burnt-offering of shittim-wood: five cubits was the length thereof, and five cubits the breadth thereof; it was four-square; and three cubits the height thereof."[3] The words of Rabbi Meier. To him said Rabbi José, "from hearing what is said five by five do we not know that it is four-square? What is the meaning of saying four-square?" "It is superfluous, save for identification in pronouncing with regard to it an equal decision. It is said here four-square, and there four-square." "What four-square is meant there?" "That its height is double its breadth, even the four-square mentioned here means that its height is double its breadth." Rabbi Meier said to him, "if it be according to thy words, it follows that the altar is higher than the curtains." Rabbi José answered him, "and is it not already said, ' And the hangings of the court, and the hanging for the door of the gate of the court, which is by the tabernacle, and by the altar round about.' "[4] As the tabernacle

[5] Lev. xxiv. 4.   [1] Exod. xxx. 1.   [2] Exod. xxx. 3.
[3] Exod. xxxviii. 1.   [4] Num. iv. 26.

was ten cubits broad, so the altar of burnt-offerings was ten
cubits broad. A painted line girdled it in the middle to divide
between the blood (sprinkled) above, and the blood (sprinkled)
below. The painted line and downward was five cubits. The
foundation was a cubit. And three cubits was the compass,
and the circuit was a cubit, and there they put the blood
sprinkled below. The painted line and upward was five cubits
—a cubit the horns, and three cubits the compass, and one
cubit the circuit. And there they put the blood which was
sprinkled above. And the blood intended to be sprinkled on
the painted line and downward, if it were put on the painted
line and upward, was worthless. And the blood that was intended to be sprinkled above the painted line, if it were put
on the painted line and downward, was worthless. The altar
which Moses made in the wilderness was in height ten cubits,
and the one which Solomon made was in height ten cubits,
and the one which the children of the captivity made was in
height ten cubits, and the one prepared for the Future, its
height is ten cubits. The altar of burnt-offerings was placed
in the midst of the court (with) its ascent on the south, with
the laver on the west, with the slaughter-house on the north,
and all the Israelites to the east, as is said, " And all the congregation drew near and stood before the Lord." [5] This altar
had three names, the altar of burnt-offering, the altar of brass,
the outer altar.

CHAPTER XII

Moses made one LAVER, as is said, " Thou shalt also make
a laver of brass " [1] Solomon made ten lavers, as is said, " He
made also ten lavers, and put five on the right hand, and five
on the left, to wash." [2] " There is no meaning in saying ' five
on the right hand, and five on the left,' and what is the meaning of saying ' five on the right hand, and five on the left ' ? "
" Five on the right of the laver of Moses, and five on the left
of the laver of Moses." Solomon added to it when he made
the sea, as is said, " And he made a molten sea, ten cubits
from the one brim to the other ; it was round all about, and
his height was five cubits ; and a line of thirty cubits did com-

---

[5] Lev. ix. 5.   [1] Exod. xxx. 18.   [2] 2 Chron. iv. 6.

pass it round about. And it was an hand-breadth thick, and
the brim thereof was wrought like the brim of a cup, with
flowers of lilies, it contained two thousand baths." [3] It is not
possible to say "two thousand," since before it is said "three
thousand," [4] and it is not possible to say "three thousand,"
since before it is said "two thousand" "How can it be?"
"Two thousand liquid make three thousand dry measure." But
you don't know how much is the bath until it be said, "The
ephah and the bath contain one measure," [5] "for ten baths
are a homer." Allow ten baths for every cur—there are 200
curs. Subtract from them fifty curs, and allow fifty square,
there are 150 cleansing-pools; since every pool contains forty
seahs." "And from whence do we know that every pool contains forty seahs?" "As is said, 'And bathe his flesh in
water,' [6] water to cover all his flesh." "And how much is it?"
"A square cubit, in height three cubits." From thence the
Sages judged the measure of a pool to be forty seahs. "And
how can it contain 150 cleansing-pools, if thou shalt say it
was all round?" "It could not contain them." "If thou
shalt say it was all square?" "It therefore contained more."
But the three lowest cubits were square; allow for ten cubits
square, there are 100 cubits. Allow for a hundred square;
there are 100 cleansing-pools. The two highest cubits were
round. Allow for ten cubits square; there are seventy-five
cubits. Allow for seventy-five square; there are 150. Allow
for fifty square; there are fifty cleansing-pools; since the square
exceeds the round by a fourth. "And whence do we know
that the square exceeds the round by a fourth?" "As is said,
'Ten cubits from brim to brim, round in compass, and a line
of thirty cubits did compass it round about.'" [7] This teaches
that the square exceeds the round by a fourth. "And whence
do we know that it was round above?" "As is said, 'And
it was an hand-breadth thick, and the brim thereof was
wrought like the brim of a cup.'" "And whence know we
that it was square below?" "As is said, 'It stood upon twelve
oxen, three looking toward the north, and three looking toward
the west, and three looking toward the south, and three looking toward the east.'" [8] And what is meant by saying "look

---

[3] 1 Kings vii. 23, 26.   [6] Ezek. xlv. 11, 14.   [7] 2 Chron. iv. 2.
[4] 2 Chron. iv. 5.   [5] Lev. xv. 13.   [8] 2 Chron. iv. 4.

ing toward " four times; but that when one entered the temple he looked toward the right; when he entered into the court, he looked toward the right; when he entered the Mountain of the House, he looked toward the right; when the priest went up to the top of the altar, he looked toward the right. " And under it was the similitude of oxen, which did compass it round about, ten in a cubit, compassing the sea round about. Two rows of oxen." [9] It follows that (there were) four rows of the heads of oxen, which served for the four sides, as is said, " And the similitude of oxen, two rows of oxen were cast when it was cast." [10] And it was all cast even from the feet of the ox.

CHAPTER XIII

" How did the Levites guard the tabernacle?" " The family of Kohath watched on the south, as is said, 'The families of the sons of Kohath shall pitch on the side of the tabernacle southward.' [1] And they were overseers of the vessels of the ark, as is said, 'And their charge shall be the ark, and the table, and the candlestick, and the altars, and the vessels of the sanctuary wherewith they minister, and the hanging and all the service thereof.' [2] Outside of them were the three tribes of Reuben, Simeon, Levi. The family of Gershon watched in the west, as is said, 'The families of the Gershonites shall pitch behind the tabernacle westward.' [3] And they were intrusted with all the vessels of the tabernacle, as is said, 'And they shall bear the curtains of the tabernacle, and the tabernacle of the congregation.' [4] Outside of them were the three tribes of Ephraim, and Manasseh, and Benjamin. The family of Merari watched on the north, as is said, 'And the chief of the house of the father of the families of Merari was Zuriel the son of Abihail: these shall pitch on the side of the tabernacle northward.' [5] And they were intrusted with the taches, and boards, and bars, and pillars, and the sockets of the tabernacle, as is said, 'And under the custody and charge of the sons of Merari shall be the boards of the tabernacle, and the bars thereof, and the pillars

---

[9] 2 Chron. iv. 3.
[10] The Jerusalem Talmud states that the water poured through the feet of the oxen, and that this was the well of Etham.

[1] Num. iii. 29.
[2] Num. iii. 31.
[3] Num. iii. 23.
[4] Num. iv. 25.
[5] Num. iii. 35.

thereof, and the sockets thereof.'[6] And outside of them were the three tribes of Dan, Asher, and Naphtali. On the east were Moses, Aaron, and their families, as is said, ' But those that encamp before the tabernacle toward the east, even before the tabernacle of the congregation eastward, shall be Moses and Aaron and his sons.'[7] And outside of them were the three tribes of Judah, Issachar, and Zebulon. The whole encampment of Israel was twelve miles. The standard of Judah was four miles, and the encampment of the Levites, and the encampment of the SHECHINAH, four miles. The standard of Reuben was four miles. The standard of Ephraim was four miles. The encampment of the Levites and the encampment of the SHECHINAH was four miles. And the encampment of Dan was four miles. It follows *that* the four corners of the tabernacle were four encampments for service on every side, as is said, ' Then the tabernacle of the congregation shall set forward with the camp of the Levites in the midst of the camp; as they encamp so shall they set forward, every man in his place by their standards.'[8] So soon as Israel set forward, the pillar of cloud which was standing still rolled up and spread out over the children of Judah like a kind of beam. The (trumpet) sounded, and blew an alarm, and sounded, and the standard of Judah moved forward first, as is said, ' In the first place went the standard of the camp of the children of Judah according to their armies.'[9] At once Aaron and his sons entered (the Tabernacle) and took down the vail, and with it they covered the ark, as is said, ' And when the camp setteth forward, Aaron shall come and his sons, and they shall take down the covering vail, and cover the ark of testimony with it.'[10] The (trumpet) sounded, and blew an alarm, and sounded, and the standard of the encampment of Reuben set forward. At once the sons of Gershon, and the sons of Merari entered, and took down the tabernacle, and loaded it on the wagon. And they set up the tabernacle before the sons of Kohath came, as is said, ' And the Kohathites set forward, bearing the sanctuary; and the other did set up the tabernacle against they came.'[1] And the trumpet sounded, and blew an alarm, and sounded, and the standard of Ephraim moved for-

---

[6] Num. iii. 36.
[7] Num. iii. 38.
[8] Num. ii. 17.
[9] Num. x. 14.
[10] Num. iv. 5.
[1] Num. x. 21.

ward; the children of Kohath entered and took down the holy
vessels, and loaded them on their shoulders, as is said, 'And
when Aaron and his sons have made an end of covering the
sanctuary and all the vessels of the sanctuary, as the camp is
to set forward; after that the sons of Kohath shall come to
bear it.'[2] The (trumpet) sounded, and blew an alarm, and
sounded. And the standard of Dan moved forward, as is said,
'And the standard of the camp of the children of Dan set
forward.'[3] It follows that two standards were in front, and
two standards were in the rear, and the encampment of the
Levites, and the encampment of the SHECHINAH was in the
middle, as is said, 'Then the tabernacle of the congregation
shall set forward with the camp of the Levites in the midst of
the camp.'[4] And as they encamped, so they set forward, as
is said, 'As they encamp, so shall they set forward.' Israel
set forward by three commands, by command of the HOLY
BLESSED ONE, by command of Moses, and by command of
the trumpets." "Whence know we the command of the HOLY
BLESSED ONE?" "As is said, 'At the commandment of the
Lord, the children of Israel journeyed, and at the commandment of the Lord they pitched,'"[5] etc. "By the commandment of the Lord by the hand of Moses."[6] "By commandment of Moses—how?" "Moses said in the evening, 'early
in the morning you must go forward.'" At once the Israelites
began to gather their cattle, and prepared their furniture for the
march. "By commandment of the trumpets whence know we
it?" "As is said, 'Make thee two trumpets of silver, etc., that
thou mayest use them for the calling of the assembly, and for
the journeying of the camps.'"[7] "How?" "The trumpets
sounded, blew an alarm, and sounded three blasts for every
standard." Rabbi Judah said, "there were three blasts for every
tribe."

CHAPTER XIV

When Israel was to encamp, the pillar of cloud rose up and
spread out over the children of Judah like a kind of booth, and
it covered the tent outward, and filled the tabernacle inward;
as is said, "Then a cloud covered the tent of the congregation,

---

[2] Num. iv. 15.   [4] Num. ii. 17.   [6] Num. ix. 23.
[3] Num. x. 22.   [5] Num. ix. 18.   [7] Num. x. 2.

and the glory of the Lord filled the tabernacle." [8] And this was one of the clouds of glory, which served the Israelites in the wilderness forty years. One on the right hand, and one on the left, and one before them, and one behind them. And one over them, and a cloud dwelling in their midst (and the cloud, the SHECHINAH which was in the Tent), and the pillar of cloud which moved before them, making low before them the high (places), and making high before them the low (places), and killing serpents and scorpions, and burning thorns and briers, and guiding them in a straight way. Rabbi Simon, the son of José, said, " during the forty years, when the Israelites were in the wilderness, none of them had need of the light of the sun by day, nor the light of the moon by night. When it became reddish they knew that the sun had set, and when it became whitish they knew that the sun rose. And when one looked into a barrel, he knew what was in it; and into a pitcher, and he knew what was in it, by reason of the cloud, the SHECHINAH in their midst," as is said, " For the cloud of the Lord was upon the tabernacle by day, and fire was on it by night, in the sight of all the house of Israel throughout all their journey." [9] And so it is prepared to come in the future: as is said, " Arise, shine; for thy light is come, and the glory of the Lord is risen upon thee." " The sun shall be no more thy light by day; neither for brightness shall the moon give light unto thee: but the Lord shall be unto thee an everlasting light." " Thy sun shall no more go down; neither shall thy moon withdraw itself; for the Lord shall be thine everlasting light, and the days of thy mourning shall be ended." [10] " From whence did the SHECHINAH speak with Moses?" Rabbi Nathan said, " from the altar of incense," as is said, " And thou shalt put it before the vail that is by the ark of the testimony, etc.,

WHERE I WILL MEET WITH THEE." [1]

Rabbi Simon, the son of Yochai, said, " beside the altar of incense," as is said, " And thou shalt beat some of it very small, and put of it before the testimony in the tabernacle of the congregation,

WHERE I WILL MEET WITH THEE." [2]

[8] Exod. xl. 34.   [9] Exod. xl. 38.   [10] Isa. lx. 1, 19, 20.
[1] Exod. xxx. 6.   [2] Exod. xxx. 36.

The disciples of Rabbi Ishmael said, " beside the altar of burnt-offering," as is said, " This shall be a continual burnt-offering throughout your generations at the door of the tabernacle of the congregation, before the Lord,

WHERE I WILL MEET YOU." [8]

[8] Exod. xxix. 42.

THE HEIFER [1]

CHAPTER I

1. Rabbi Eliezer said, "the red heifer must be a calf of a
year old or a heifer of two years." But the Sages say, "a
calf of two years and a heifer of three years or of four years."
Rabbi Meier said, "even of five years she is allowed, or older.
But they are not to wait (longer) for her, lest she turn black
and be disallowed." Rabbi Joshua said, "I only heard,
third." They said to him, "what is the meaning of 'third'?"
He said to them, "thus I heard it, without explanation." The
son of Azai said, "I will explain it, if you say 'third,' that is
to others in counting; but if you say 'one of three,' that is, of
three years." As when they say, "a fourth vineyard." They
said to him, "what means 'fourth'?" He said to them, "thus
I heard it, without explanation." Said the son of Azai, "I
will explain. If you say 'fourth,' that is, to others in counting. But as you say 'one of four,' that is, of four years. As
when they say, he who eats in a leprous house a half-loaf,[2]
of three loaves to the cab of flour." They say to him, "say

---

[1] The Jews say that Solomon, who
understood all the commands of God,
could not comprehend the full meaning
of the Red Heifer.
[2] The meaning is that he who spends

as much time in a leprous house as is
sufficient for eating a loaf of such a size,
becomes defiled in his garments. See
"Leprosy," xiii. 10.

eighteen loaves to the seah of flour." He said to them, " Thus I heard it, without explanation." Said the son of Azai, " I will explain. If you say, ' three to the cab,' there is no dough-offering. But if you say, ' eighteen to the seah,' the dough-offering diminishes it."

2. R. José the Galilean said, " the cleansing of the Levites required bullocks of two years old," as is said, " And another young bullock shalt thou take for a sin-offering." [3] But the Sages say, " even of three years." R. Meier said, " bullocks even of four and five years are allowed, but old ones are not brought, for honor's sake."

3. Sacrifices required lambs of a year old and rams of two years old, and all (are reckoned) from day to day.[4] If they be thirteen months old, neither ram nor lamb is allowed. R. Tarphon called it, " half and between." The son of Azai called it, " pointed out." R. Ishmael called it, " recalled coin." If the ram be brought for offering, and the libation of the ram be brought with him, it does not pass for his offering, except he be thirteen months and one day old. That is the law for the ram.

4. The sin-offering of the congregation and their burnt-offerings, the sin-offering of an individual and the trespass-offering of the Nazarite and the trespass-offering of the leper are allowed for thirty days and upward, and even on the thirtieth day. And if they are brought on the eighth day, they are allowed; vows, freewill-offerings, the first-born, and the tithe and the passover are allowed from the eighth day and upward, and even on the eighth day

CHAPTER II

1. Rabbi Eliezer said, " a heifer for a sin-offering is allowed even in pregnancy." But the Sages disallow her. R. Eliezer said, " she is not to be taken from foreigners." But the Sages allow her. And not only she, but all the offerings of the congregation, and of the individual, may come from the Land (of Israel), or from outside the land, from the fresh harvest and

---

[3] Num. viii. 8.
[4] The age of the lamb was reckoned from its birthday in Elul of last year till the first day of Elul in the current year.

from the old harvest, except the omer,[1] and the two loaves,[2] which may only come from the fresh harvest, and from the Land.

2. A heifer whose horns and hoofs are black should have them cut away. The pupil of the eye and the teeth and the tongue cause no blemish in the heifer. If she be diminutive, she is allowed. " Had she a wen which was cut away? " R. Judah " disallowed her." Rabbi Simon said, " every place which was cut down, and no red hair sprang up in its place, renders her blemished."

3. A heifer produced from the side or from the hire of immorality or exchanged for a dog is disallowed. R. Eliezer allowed it, " as is said, ' Thou shalt not bring the hire of a whore or the price of a dog into the house of the Lord thy God.' [3] But she did not come into the house." All blemishes which are disallowed in holy things are disallowed in the heifer. If one rode on her or leaned on her or hung something on her tail or crossed a river on her or doubled the rope over her or put his garment on her, she is disallowed. But if one bound her with a rope or made a shoe to prevent her slipping or spread his garment over her because of the flies, she is allowed. This is the rule: Everything which was necessary for her is allowed; if there be any use of her for another's benefit, she is disallowed.

4. If a bird rested on her, she is allowed. If the male came to her, she is disallowed. R. Judah said, " if he were brought, she is disallowed, but if he came of himself, she is allowed."

5. If she had two black or white hairs in one cavity, she is disallowed. R. Judah said, " even in one pore." " If they be in two pores and they prove united? " " She is disallowed." Rabbi Akiba said, " even four or five, if they be scattered, may be plucked out." Rabbi Eleazar said, " even fifty." R. Joshua, son of Bathira, said, " if there be even one in her head

---

[1] Lev. xxiii. 10, 17. The omer or wave-sheaf of barley was always cut on the evening of the 15th Nisan, even though it were a Sabbath. It must always have been gathered from a fresh harvest cultivated even in the Sabbatical year. The reapers asked these questions three times of those who were witnesses, " Has the sun gone down? " " With this sickle? " " Into this basket? " " On this Sabbath [first day of the Passover]? " " Shall I reap? " After the witnesses answered these questions the sheaf was reaped. It was finally ground into flour, and a handful of it mixed with frankincense was burned on the altar. The remainder belonged to the priests.

[2] Num. xxviii. The two wave-loaves of wheaten flour were always offered on the Jewish Pentecost.

[3] Deut. xxiii. 18.

and one in her tail, she is disallowed." " If there be two hairs,
their roots black and their tops red, their roots red and their
tops black?" "All follows after the appearance," the words
of Rabbi Meier. But the Sages say, "after the root."

CHAPTER III

1. Seven days before the burning of the heifer, the priest
who burned the heifer was removed from his house to the
chamber in front of the Temple Palace toward the northeast;[1]
and it was called the Stone House. And he was sprinkled
during all the seven days from all the ashes of red heifers
which were there. R. José said, "they did not sprinkle him
save on the third and seventh days only." R. Hananiah, the
deputy high-priest, said, " on the priest who burned the heifer
they sprinkled during all the seven days, but on him who took
service on the Day of Atonement they did not sprinkle save
on the third and seventh days only."

2. There were courts in Jerusalem built of stone, and beneath they were hollow,[2] through fear of an unseen grave.
And pregnant women were brought, and they were delivered
there. And there they reared their sons, and oxen were
brought with doors on their backs, and the lads were seated
on them with stone cups in their hands. They came to
Siloam, they dismounted, and filled them. They remounted,
and returned on the backs of the oxen." R. José said, " from
their seats on the backs of the oxen they let down (the cups)
and filled them (with water)."

3. The lads came back to the Mountain of the House and
dismounted. The Mountain of the House and its courts were
hollow below, through fear of an unseen grave. And at the
door of the court there were prepared the ashes of the red
heifers; and they brought a ram from the sheep, and they
twisted a rope between his horns, and they twisted a stick and

---

[1] Nehem. ii. 8. 1 Chron. xxix. 1.
[2] According to Jewish tradition a dead
body covered in with earth conveyed
legal uncleanness to everyone who
walked over it; but if a vault was over
the body, or if air intervened between
the corpse and the surface of the
ground, it was regarded as a non-con-
ductor. There are reckoned six degrees
of uncleanness—the father of fathers,
the fathers, the first, second, third, and
fourth children of defilement. There
are altogether twenty-nine fathers of
uncleanness, of which eleven arise from
contact with a dead body.

stuck it into the end of the rope, and it was dipped into the ashes, and the ram got a blow, and he skipped backward, and took them, and caused them to appear on the surface of the water. R. José said, " you should not give an opportunity to the Sadducees for scoffing: but (the lad) took and prepared the ashes."

4. They did not make use of (what pertained) to one red heifer for a second one, nor did they use another lad for [3] his (prepared) companion. "And the lads themselves were in need of sprinkling," the words of Rabbi José the Galilean. R. Akiba said, " they had no need of sprinkling."

5. If they did not find (ashes) of seven red heifers, six were sufficient, five, four, three, two, one. " And who made them? " " Moses made the first, and Ezra the second, and (there were) five from Ezra and afterward," the words of Rabbi Meier. But the Sages say, " seven from Ezra and afterward." " And who made them? " " Simon the Just, and John the High-priest made each two. Elihueni, son of Hakuf, and Hanamel the Egyptian, and Ishmael, son of Piani, made one each."

6. And a causeway was made from the Mountain of the House to the Mount of Olives, with arches over arches. And there was an arch in front of the last pillar for fear of an un-seen grave. Over it the priest who burned the heifer, and the heifer with all her attendants, proceeded to the Mount of Olives.

7. If the heifer were unwilling to go, they did not bring with her a black one, lest it be said, " they slaughtered a black one " nor a red one, lest it be said, " they slaughtered two." R. José said, this was not the reason, but because it is only said, "That he may bring her forth "[4] And the elders of Israel preceded her on foot to the Mount of Olives. And a house for washing was there. And the priest who burned the heifer was rendered unclean because of the Sadducees,[5] lest they should say, " it is needful for sunset to pass over him."[6]

8. The elders put their hands on the priest and said, " my Lord High-priest, wash once." He descended and washed,

---

[3] Some commentators explain that " each heifer requires a fresh lad."
[4] Num. xix. 3.
[5] The Pharisees asserted that a priest might be defiled, and that after washing he was legally clean for burning the red heifer. But the Sadducees maintained that he was not legally clean before sun-set. Num. xix. 9, 10.
[6] Lev. xxii. 7.

and he came up and wiped himself. And wood was set in order there, cedar and ash and cypress and fig-wood smoothed. And it was made like a tower, and windows were opened in it, and their direction was westward.

9. The red heifer was bound with a rope of bulrushes and she was put on the place of preparation, with her head southward and with her face westward. The priest stood in the east with his face westward. He slaughtered the heifer with his right hand, and received (the blood) in his left hand. R. Judah said, " he received it in his right hand and put it into his left, and sprinkled it with his right hand." He dipped his hand, and sprinkled the blood seven times in front of the House of the Holy of Holies. For every sprinkling of blood he dipped his hand. When he finished sprinkling the blood he wiped his hand on the body of the heifer. He went down and kindled the fire with chips. Rabbi Akiba said, " with palm-branches."

10. She burst and moved from her place. He took cedar-wood and hyssop and scarlet (wool). He said to them, " is this cedar-wood, is this cedar-wood? " " is this hyssop, is this hyssop? " " is this scarlet, is this scarlet? " three times for each thing. And they said to him, " yes," " yes," three times for each thing."

11. He wrapped them in the remainder [7] of the tongue of scarlet wool, and cast them into the midst of the burning. When the fire was burned down, the ashes were beaten with sticks and sifted with sieves. R. Ishmael said, " with stone hammers, and the work was finished with stone sieves." A black piece in which there are ashes must be pulverized, and that which has no ashes is left. Bones with or without ashes were pulverized. And they were divided into three parts. One part was put in the Chel, and one was put on the Mount of Olives, and one was divided for all the guards [8] (i.e., the representatives of all Israel).

[7] The cedar, hyssop, and scarlet wool were laid parallel to each other, and whatever portion of the scarlet wool remained too long was wrapped round the bundle.

[8] Num. xix. 9.

CHAPTER IV

1. " The heifer which was slaughtered without the proper intention, (the priest) caught the blood and sprinkled it with out the proper intention, or with the proper intention and afterward without the proper intention, or without the proper intention and (afterward) with the proper intention? " " She is disallowed." R. Eliezer " allowed her." " And if the priest did not wash his hands and his feet? " " She is disallowed." R. Eliezer " allowed her." " If she was not slaughtered by the High-priest? " " She is disallowed." R. Judah " allowed her " " If any of his garments were wanting? " " She is disallowed." And the rites were performed in white vestments.

2. If the priest burned her out of her prepared place, or in two places, or burned two in one place? " " She is disallowed." " If he sprinkled her blood but not straight in front of the DOOR? " " She is disallowed." " If he sprinkled her blood the sixth time for the seventh—he then turned and sprinkled the seventh? " " She is disallowed." " If the priest sprinkled the seventh time for the eighth—he then turned and sprinkled the eighth? " " She is allowed."

3. If the priest burned the red heifer without wood, or with every sort of wood, even with stubble and dung? "[1] " She is allowed." " If he skinned and cut her? " " She is allowed." " If he slaughtered her on condition of eating from her flesh and drinking from her blood? " " She is allowed." Rabbi Eliezer said, " intention does not disallow the heifer."

4. All who are busied about the heifer from the beginning to the end render their garments legally unclean. And any work gained from her renders her disallowed. If any illegality happened during her slaughter, she does not render their gar ments unclean. If it happened during the sprinkling of her blood, everyone busied before her disallowance renders his garments unclean. After her disallowance he does not render his garments unclean. It follows that her difficulty is his convenience. They who are busied about her are always liable for a trespass-offering. They may add wood to her during her burning. And her business is done in the day and by a priest.

[1] Or thick parts of straw.

Every work for gain with her causes her disallowance until she be reduced to ashes. And work for gain causes disallowance in the water also, until the ashes be strewn upon it.

CHAPTER V

1. He who brings earthen vessels for the ashes of the heifer must wash them, and place them in the furnace over night. Rabbi Judah said, " even if he bring them from his house they are allowed. Since everyone is trusted about the heifer. But in the heave-offering he opens the furnace and takes out the vessels." R. Simon said, "from the second [1] row." R. José said, "from the third row."

2. He who washes vessels for the ashes of the red heifer, in water unsuitable for purification, must dry them. If he wash them in water suitable for purification, it is not necessary to dry them. If he add therein water for purification, whether of one sort or the other sort of water, he must dry them.

3. A pumpkin bottle which is washed in water unsuitable for purification, may be used for purification, till it becomes legally unclean. When it is unclean, they may no longer purify in it. R. Joshua said, "if one purify in it at first, one may purify in it to the last; if it cannot purify at last, it cannot purify at first." Whether it be clean or unclean, one must not add therein water for purification."

4. "A hollow reed cut for the ashes of the red heifer?" R. Eliezer said, "it must be washed at once." R. Joshua said, "it must be rendered legally unclean, and afterward washed." Everyone is suitable for purifying excepting a deaf person, an idiot, and a child. R. Judah "allows a child, but disallows a woman and a neuter."

5. Water may be prepared for purification in every vessel, even in vessels of dung, in vessels of stone and vessels of clay and in a boat. Water must not be prepared for purification in the sides of vessels nor in the bottom of a vase nor in the cork of a barrel nor in one's fists, since they are not used for filling water, and they must not purify with them. And the

---

[1] If the vessels had been in the first row, someone might have touched them, or some vessel might have come in contact with them, so as to render them unclean.

water of the ashes of the heifer is not sprinkled without a vessel. There is no safety from defilement in the covering [2] bound except in proper vessels—there is no safety from the defilement of earthen vessels except in proper vessels.

6. An egg-shaped vessel of the potters is allowed for the purifying water. R. José " disallows it." " The egg (shell) of a hen? " R. Meier and R. Judah " allow it," but the Sages " disallow it."

7. " A trough in a rock? " " They do not fill water with it, they do not purify in it, and they do not sprinkle from it, and it does not need the covering bound, and it does not disallow [3] the purifying-pool." " If there were a vessel united (to it) with lime? " " They may fill water with it, they may purify in it, and sprinkle from it, and it needs a covering bound, and (if it becomes legally unclean) it disallows the purifying pool." " It had a hole in the bottom, and it was stuffed with a rag? " " The water in it is disallowed, because it is not (entirely) surrounded with the vessel." " If the hole were in the side, and it was stuffed with a rag? " " The water within it is allowed, because it is surrounded with the vessel." " If a rim of mud was made for it, and the water rose up to it? " " It is disallowed " " If it were so strong that the vessel could be lifted by it? " " It is allowed."

8. " There are two troughs in one stone. One of them is legally purified. The water in the second is not purified. There arc holes from one trough to the other like the pipe of a bottle, or water overflowed from above only as much as the peeling of a garlic, and the owner had purified one of them? " " The water in the second can also purify."

9. " Two stones which are placed near to each other, and one made of them a (drinking-) trough, and also two kneading-troughs, and also a drinking-trough, which was divided? " " The water, which is between them, does not purify." " If one connected them with lime or gypsum, and they can be lifted at once? " " The water, which is between them, can purify."

---

[2] Num. xix. 15.
[3] It does not disallow the purifying pool if water flowed through a crevice in the rock into the pool.

CHAPTER VI

1. "When one wishes to purify, and the ashes of purification have fallen on his hand or upon the side (of the vessel), and they afterward fell on a drinking-trough?" "They are disallowed." "If water of purification fell from a pipe on the trough?" "It is disallowed." "He took the water of purification out of the pipe, and covered the pipe or shut the door with it?" "The ashes of purification are allowed, but the water is disallowed." "He laid it on the ground?" "It is disallowed " "He laid it in his hand?" "It is allowed, because it is not otherwise possible."

2. "If the ashes swam on the surface of the water?" R. Meier and Rabbi Simon said, "one may take them and purify"; but the Sages say, "all ashes which have once touched water, cannot purify." "If one have sprinkled the water, and the ashes be found at the bottom?" R. Meier and R. Simon said, "He may dry them and purify"; but the Sages say, "all ashes which have (once) touched water, cannot purify."

3. "If one prepare water for purification in a trough, and there be a jug in it?" "Though its mouth be ever so narrow, the water therein can purify." "If there be a sponge?" "The water in it is disallowed." "How is one to act?" "He is to sprinkle till he come to the sponge. When he has touched the sponge, even if the water swim over it ever so little, it is dis allowed."

4. "One has put in his hand or his foot, or leaves of vegetables, so that the water of purification has run over to another vessel?" "It is disallowed." If they were leaves of reeds or leaves of nuts, they are allowed. This is the rule: The thing which contracts uncleanness is disallowed; and the thing which does not contract uncleanness is allowed.

5. "If one divert a well into a vat-shaped pool or into a marsh?" "The water in them is disallowed for issues and leprosies, or to purify with it as with the water of the ashes of the heifer, since it is not filled in a vessel."

CHAPTER VII

1. " When five persons filled five barrels with water of purification, to purify five persons requiring purification, and they
changed their mind for one purification, or they prepared for
one purification, and they changed their mind for five?"
" They are all allowed." " One person who filled five barrels
to purify five persons requiring purification, and changed his
mind for one purification?" " None is allowed but the last."
" Or he made ready for one purification, and changed his
mind for five purifications?" " None is allowed but the first
purification." " If he said to one, ' purify all those for thee?'"
" None is allowed but the first." " Purify all those for me?"
" They are all allowed."

2. " He who fills (water of purification) with one hand, and
does work with the other hand, if he fill for himself or for
another person, or if he fill for both at once?" " Both are
disallowed, since work disallows in filling (water of purification) whether for himself or for another."

3. " He who puts in ashes with one hand, and does work
with the other hand?" " If it be for himself, it is disallowed;
but if it be for another person, it is allowed." " He who while
doing work puts in ashes for himself and for another?" " His
own is disallowed, and the other's is allowed." " He who puts
in ashes for two persons at once?" " Both are allowed."

4. " Put in ashes for me; and I will put in ashes for thee?"
" The first case is allowed." " Fill water for me; and I will fill
water for thee?" " The latter case is allowed." " Put in
ashes for me, and I will fill water for thee?" " Both cases
are allowed." " Fill water for me; and I will put in ashes for
thee?" " Both cases are disallowed."

5. " A person filled water for his own use, and (also) for
purification?" " He fills first for himself and binds it on the
shoulder-pole; and afterward he fills that for purification."
" And if he fill that for purification first, and afterward fill for
himself?" " It is disallowed." He must put his own water
behind him, and the water for purification before him. " And
if he put that for purification behind him?" " It is disallowed." " Both are water for purification, he put one in

front and one behind him?" "It is allowed, because it is not otherwise possible."

6. "If one carry a rope in his hand?"[1] "If he go in the (straight) way, it is allowed." "If he go out of his way?" "It is disallowed." One went to Jabneth[2] during three feasts, about this matter, and in the third feast it was allowed to him as a decision for the time.

7. "If one rolled the rope round his hand?" "It is allowed; but if he rolled it after (drawing the water), it is disallowed." Said R. José, "this act they allowed as a decision for the time."

8. "If one put aside the barrel lest it be broken, or turned it on its mouth for the purpose of drying it, intending to fill it with water?" "It is allowed." "But if he did so to carry in it ashes?" "It is disallowed." If one turned out potsherds from the trough, that it might contain more water, it is allowed; but if they would be no hinderance to him in the time of sprinkling, it is disallowed.

9. "One who had water on his shoulder, and he taught a decision in the law or he showed the way to others or he killed a serpent or a scorpion or he took food to put it aside?" "It is disallowed." "The food was for eating?" "It is allowed." "The serpent or scorpion hindered him?" "It is allowed." Said Rabbi Judah, "this is the rule: An act for work, whether a man stood or did not stand, is disallowed; and an act which is not for work, if he stood, is disallowed; but if he did not stand, it is allowed."

10. "He who handed over his water of purification to an unclean (person)?" "It is disallowed." "But if he handed it to a legally clean person?" "It is allowed." R. Eleazar said, "even to a (person legally) unclean it is allowed, if its owner did no work."

11. "Two persons drew water for purification, and each helped the other, or each took a thorn from the other?" "For one purification it is allowed, for two purifications, it is disallowed." R. José said, "even for two purifications it is allowed, if it were made a condition between them."

---

[1] The principle laid down in this mishna is that if one merely carried the rope for drawing the water, it was allowed to him to do so. But if he used the rope for any work advantageous to himself it was disallowed.
[2] The modern Yebna (Jamnia).

12. "He who has broken (something) during drawing water for purification with the view of preparing it afterward?" "The water is allowed" "But if he prepared it?" "The water is disallowed."[3] "He ate with the view of drying the remainder of his food?" "The water is allowed." "But if he dried it?" "The water is disallowed." "He ate and left some, and he threw away what was left in his hand under a fig-tree, or into the place of drying, that it might not be lost?" "The water is disallowed."

CHAPTER VIII

1. "Two persons watched a trough containing water for purification; one of them becomes legally unclean?" "It is allowed, because it was in the safe-keeping of the second." "He became clean and the second unclean?" "It is allowed, because it was in the safe-keeping of the first." "Both became unclean at once?" "It is disallowed." "One of them did work?" "It is allowed, because it was in the safe-keeping of the second." "He stood still, and the second did work?" "It is allowed, because it was in the safe-keeping of the first." "Both worked at once." "It is disallowed."

2. If one put ashes in the water for purification, he must not put on his sandal, for if the water fall on the sandal, it becomes legally unclean, and renders him legally unclean. This is the proverb, "What makes thee unclean, cannot make me unclean, but thou canst make me unclean." "If water fall on his flesh?" "He is clean." "If it fall on his garment?" "It becomes unclean, and renders him unclean." This is the proverb, "What makes thee unclean, cannot make me unclean, but thou canst make me unclean."

3. He who burned the red heifer and the bullocks,[1] and he who sent forth the scapegoat, render garments unclean. The heifer and the bullocks, and the scapegoat which was sent forth, cannot of themselves render garments unclean. This is the proverb: "What makes thee unclean, cannot make me unclean, but thou canst make me unclean."

---

[3] The water is disallowed, because the man gained something for himself during the act of drawing it. His intention was not single-minded and pure.

[1] Lev. iv. 12, 21.

4. If one eat from the carcass of a clean bird, as it is in his throat, it renders garments unclean. The carcass itself does not render garments unclean. This is the proverb: "What makes thee unclean, cannot make me unclean, but thou canst make me unclean."

5. Every [2] secondary uncleanness does not render vessels unclean, but fluid does so. If fluid become unclean, it renders Vessels unclean. This is the proverb, "What makes thee unclean, cannot make me unclean, but thou canst make me unclean."

6. Earthen vessels cannot render each other unclean, but fluid does so. If fluid becomes unclean, it renders vessels unclean. This is the proverb, "What makes thee unclean, cannot make me unclean, but thou canst make me unclean."

7. Everything [3] which disallows the heave-offering renders the fluid unclean so as to be a primary uncleanness, for rendering a person unclean, and disallowing him, except he was one who washed by day.[4] This is the proverb, "What makes thee unclean, cannot make me unclean, but thou canst make me unclean."

8. All seas are reckoned for a pool of purification, as is said, "And the gathering together of the waters called He seas," [5] the words of R. Meier. R. Judah said, "the great sea is as a purifying-pool; it is not said seas, but there is in it many kinds of seas." R. José said, "all seas may purify in flowing, but they are disallowed for issues, and leprosies, and for purifying with them the water of the ashes of the red heifer."

9. Waters with a nickname are disallowed. These are the nicknames—"salt" and "lukewarm." Deceitful [6] waters are disallowed. These are deceitful waters—they failed once in seven years, they failed during war and during famine—yet they are allowed. R. Judah "disallows them."

10. The waters of Kirmion (Kishon?), and the waters of Pygah (Belus?) are disallowed, because they are the waters of marshes. The waters of the Jordan and the waters of Jar-

---

[2] Primary uncleanness arises from touching a dead body, leprosy, etc. Secondary uncleanness arises from touching one who had primary uncleanness.

[3] A tertiary uncleanness follows from contact with secondary uncleanness.

[4] That is one over whom evening had not yet come, nor was his offering yet made. Lev. xxii. 6, 7.

[5] Gen. i. 10.

[6] Isa. lviii. 11.

muk [7] are disallowed, because they are mixed. And these are
mixed waters, one allowed and one disallowed are mixed.
Two which are allowed and mixed, are allowed. R. Judah
" disallows them."

11. " The well of Ahab [8] and the cave of Panias [9] are
allowed. Water which changed, but changed   itself, is allowed. A well of water which came from a distance is allowed,
only it must be watched, that no man check it. R. Judah said,
" it is taken for granted and allowed." " A well into which
earth or clay fell? " " One must wait till it clear," the words
of R. Ishmael. R. Akiba said, " there is no need of waiting."

CHAPTER IX

1. " A pan full of the water of purification into which ordinary water, however little, has fallen? " R. Eliezer said,
" one must sprinkle twice with it." But the Sages " disallow
it." " If dew fell into it? " R. Eliezer said, " let him leave it
in the sun, and the dew evaporates." But the Sages " disallow it." " If fluid has fallen into it, or fruit juice? " " Let
him pour it out, and it is necessary to dry it." Ink, gum, and
vitriol, and everything which can be remarked, must be poured
out, and there is no necessity to dry it.

2. " If insects and worms have fallen in and burst or
changed their appearance? " " The water is disallowed." A
black beetle, though not burst nor changed, disallows it, since
it is like a pipe. Rabbi Simon and R. Eliezer, the son of
Jacob, said, " the wheat-worm and the grain-worm are allowed, because there is no matter in them."

3. " If a beast or animal drink of it? " " They disallow it."
All fowls disallow it, excepting the dove, because it sucks.
All creeping animals do not disallow it, excepting the weasel,
because it laps. Rabban Gamaliel said, " also the serpent, because it spews." R. Eliezer said, " also the mouse."

4. " If one think to drink the water of purification? " R.

[7] The river Jarmuk is the Hieromax
of the Greeks. It falls into the Jordan
about four miles below the Lake of
Tiberias. The Arabs now call it the
Sheriat el Mandhur.
[8] The well of Ahab is supposed by
some to be the source of a river near
Beirût. This supposition is, however,
very doubtful.
[9] The modern Banias, one of the
sources of the Jordan. It is situated
under Mount Hermon, close to the remains of the ancient Cæsarea Philippi.

Eliezer said, "it is disallowed." R. Joshua said, "when he drew it (toward him)." R. José said, "of what are they talking, of water in which there are no ashes." "But of water in which there are ashes?" R. Eliezer said, "when he drew it (toward him)." R. Joshua said, "when he drinks." But if it be poured into his throat, it is allowed.

5. Water of purification which is disallowed, must not be kneaded in mortar, lest it bring misfortune to others. R. Judah said, "it is worthless." "A cow which drank water of purification?" "Her flesh is unclean for twenty-four hours."[1] R. Judah said, "it becomes worthless in her intestines."

6. The water of purification and the ashes of purification must not be passed over a river even in a boat, nor may they be floated on the surface of water. Nor may one stand on one side and throw them to the other side. But one may pass with them through water, which is up to his neck. He who is cleansed for purification, may pass over water with empty vessels in his hand cleansed for purification, and with water in which there are no ashes.

7. "Ashes which are allowed for purification, when they are mixed in ordinary ashes?" "We must follow the majority[2] (in reference to uncleanness) and they do not purify with them." Rabbi Eleazar said, "they may purify with them all."

8. Water intended for purification which was disallowed, renders unclean (him who was) cleansed for the heave-offering in his hands and body, but it does not render unclean him who was cleansed for purification, either in his hands or in his body. "If it were rendered unclean?" "It renders unclean (him who was) cleansed for the heave-offering in his hands and in his body, but (him who was) cleansed for purification it renders unclean, in his hands, but not in his body."

9. Ashes which are allowed when put on the surface of water, which is unsuitable for purification, render unclean him who was cleansed for the heave-offering in his hands and body, but it does not render unclean him who was cleansed for purification, either in his hands or in his body.

---

[1] Literally, "from time to time."
[2] The meaning is, that if the greater part of the ashes be legal, purification would follow; but if the greater part be ordinary ashes, there would be no purification.

CHAPTER X

1. Everything suited for causing legal uncleanness in that which is trodden must be expelled from the ceremony of purification, whether it be unclean or clean, and man likewise. "Everything suited for producing defilement of the dead, whether it be unclean or clean?" R. Eliezer said, "it is not expelled." R. Joshua said, "it is expelled." But the Sages say, "if unclean it is expelled, but the clean thing is not expelled."

2. He who is cleansed for purification, when he touches that which is expelled, is unclean. A jug for purification, when it touches that which is expelled, is unclean. He who is cleansed for purification, when he touches eatable or drinkable things with his hand, is unclean. "But with his foot?" "He is clean." "The thing was moved with his hand?" R. Joshua pronounces him "unclean"; but the Sages pronounce him "clean."

3. "An earthen vessel for purification, which touched a creeping thing?" "It is clean." "It was placed upon it?" R. Eleazar pronounces it "clean"; but the Sages pronounce it "unclean." "It touched eatable or drinkable things or holy writings?" "It is clean" "It was placed upon them?" R. José pronounced it "clean"; but the Sages pronounced it "unclean."

4. "When he who was cleansed for purification touched a fireplace [1] with his hand?" "He is unclean." "But with his foot?" "He is clean." "He stood on the fireplace, and stretched his hand with the jug, and the water and ashes in it beyond the fireplace, and also the shoulder-pole, which he placed over the fireplace, and on it were two earthen vessels, one on either side?" R. Akiba pronounces him "clean"; [2] but the Sages pronounce him "unclean."

5. "He stood outside the fireplace, and stretched his hand to the window, and took the jug (with water and ashes) and passed it over the fireplace?" R. Akiba pronounces him "unclean," but the Sages pronounce him "clean." But he who was cleansed for purification, may stand over the fire-

[1] The dispute is now about what constitutes "a clean place." [2] Heb. ix. 13, 14.

place, and in his hand an empty vessel cleansed for purification or (one) with water without ashes.

6. "When a jug for purification touched (one) in which there were holy things, or one in which there was a heave-offering?" "The one for purification is unclean; but those of the holy things and the heave-offering are clean." "If both be in his two hands?" "Both are unclean." "If both be in two papers?" "Both are clean." "If the one for purification be in paper, and the one for the heave-offering be in his hand?" "Both are unclean." "If the one for the heave-offering be in paper, and the one for purification be in his hand?" "Both are clean." R. Joshua said, "the one for the purification is unclean." "They were placed on the ground and one touched them?" "The one for purification is unclean, the one containing the holy things, and the one with the heave-offering are clean." "He moved them?" R. Joshua pronounces them "unclean," but the Sages pronounce them "clean."

CHAPTER XI

1. "A pan for purification which one left open, and he found it covered?" "It is disallowed." "He left it open and found a covering on it?" "If a weasel could drink of it, or a serpent, according to the words of Rabban Gamaliel, or there fell in it dew by night, it is disallowed." Water with ashes cannot be saved (from legal impurity) by the covering [1] bound upon it. And water in which there are no ashes, is saved by the covering bound upon it.

2. Every doubt implies cleanness in the heave-offering and cleanness in purification. Every reason for suspense in the heave-offering causes pouring away of the water in purification. If acts requiring legal cleanness be afterward performed, they are in suspense. Shallow water [2] is clean for holy things, and the heave-offering and purification. R. Eleazar said, "trickling water [3] is unclean for purification."

3. "A dried fig of the heave-offering which has fallen into water for purification, and one has taken it out and eaten it?" "If it be the size of an egg, whether it be unclean or clean,

---

[1] Num. xix. 15.   [2] Maimonides translates "lattice-work."   [3] Or trelliswork.

the water is unclean, and he who ate it is guilty of death." R. José said, "if it be clean the water is clean." He who was cleansed for the sin-offering, and afterward put his head and the greater part of his body into water of purification, is unclean.

4. Everyone charged by the words of the Law to enter water, renders unclean holy things, and the heave-offering and ordinary things and the tithe, and is prevented from entering the temple. "After entering (the water) he renders unclean holy things, and disallows the heave-offering," the words of R. Meier, but the Sages say, "he disallows holy things and the heave-offering, but he is permitted in ordinary things and tithes, and if he came to the temple, whether before or after entering (water), he is a debtor (to the Law)."

5. "Everyone charged by the words of the Scribes to enter water, renders unclean holy things, and disallows the heave-offering, but allows ordinary things and the tithes," the words of R. Meier; but the Sages "disallow him in tithes." After his entering (water) he is permitted in all these. And if he come to the temple whether before or after entering water, he is free.

6. Everyone charged to enter water, whether by the words of the Law or the words of the Scribes, renders unclean the water for purification and the ashes for purification, and the sprinkler of the water of purification, by touching or lifting. "The hyssop, and the water without ashes, and empty vessels cleansed for purification (render unclean), by touching or lifting," the words of R. Meier; but the Sages say, "by touching, but not by lifting."

7. All hyssop which has a distinctive name is forbidden, simple hyssop is allowed; Grecian hyssop, colored hyssop, Roman hyssop, desert hyssop, are forbidden, and that of the unclean heave-offering is forbidden, but if it were of the clean (heave-offering) one should not sprinkle with it, but if one sprinkled with it, it is allowed. Men must not sprinkle with the sprouts or the berries of hyssop. When sprinkled with the sprouts, they are not prevented from entering the temple. R. Eliezer said, "not even with the berries." These are sprouts—stalks which have not ripened.

8. Hyssop used for sprinkling is allowed to cleanse the

leper. "If one gathered it for wood, and fluid fell on it?"
" He may dry it, and it is allowed." "If one gathered it for
food, and fluid fell on it?" "Even though he dried it, it is
disallowed" "If one gathered it for purification?" "It is
reckoned as food," the words of R. Meier. R. Judah and R.
José and R. Simon say, "it is reckoned as wood."

9. The order of the hyssop (requires) three roots, and in
them three stalks. R. Judah said, "to every root three
stalks." Hyssop which has three roots is to be separated and
bound; if separated and not bound, if bound and not separated, if neither separated nor bound, it is allowed. R. José
said, "the order of the hyssop is three roots and in them three
stalks, and if there remain over from sprinkling two, and their
fibres however small, they are allowed."

CHAPTER XII

1. Short hyssop is made sufficient for sprinkling with a
thread and spindle, and it is dipped and lifted, and one holds
the hyssop and sprinkles. R. Judah and R. Simon say, "as is
the rule for sprinkling with the hyssop, so is the dipping with
the hyssop " (i.e., in holding it).

2. "If one sprinkled and there is a doubt if the water with
ashes came from the thread, or a doubt if it came from the
spindle, or a doubt if it came from the stalk?" "His sprinkling is disallowed." "If he sprinkled on two vessels, there
is a doubt; if he sprinkled on both, there is a doubt that the
sprinkling splashed from one to the other?" "His sprinkling
is disallowed." "A needle is placed on a potsherd, and he
sprinkled it, there is a doubt if he sprinkled on the needle,
there is a doubt if the sprinkling splashed from the potsherd
upon it?" "His sprinkling is disallowed." "A pan for
purification with a narrow mouth?" "He is to dip the hyssop
in and lift it out as usual." R. Judah says, "the first sprinkling (is allowed)." "The water of purification which became
diminished?" "One may dip in even the tops of the stalks
and sprinkle, except that he should not dry up the vessel."
"His intention [1] was to sprinkle before him, and he sprinkled

<hr>

[1] This doctrine of intention has also
been adopted into the system of Roman-
ism. The Council of Trent (Session vii.
Canon xi.) teaches that " Whoever

behind him; to sprinkle behind him, and he sprinkled before him?" "His sprinkling is disallowed." "Before him, and he sprinkled sidewise in front?" "His sprinkling is allowed." He may sprinkle a man whether he be aware of it or not. He may sprinkle a man, or vessels, even should they be 100.

3. "His intention was to sprinkle on anything which can receive defilement, and he sprinkled on a thing which cannot receive defilement?" "If there remain (water) in the hyssop he must not repeat it." "His intention was to sprinkle on something which does not receive defilement, and he sprinkled on something which does receive defilement?" "If there remain (water) in the hyssop, he may repeat it." "If upon man, and he sprinkled on a beast?" "If there remain (water) in the hyssop, he must not repeat it." "Upon beast and he sprinkled on man?" "If there be (water) in the hyssop he may repeat it." Water which has dropped from the hyssop is allowed, because it renders everything unclean like the water of purification.[2]

4. He who sprinkled from a public window and entered the sanctuary, and the water was afterward found (to be) disallowed, is free. He who sprinkled from a private window and entered the sanctuary, and the water was afterward found (to be) disallowed, is a debtor. But the high-priest, whether he sprinkled from a private, or from a public window, is free, since no high-priest is indebted (for an offering) on his entering the sanctuary. Persons were slipping in water of purification before a public window, and treading in it and were not hindered, because the (Sages) say, "the water of purification, which has done its duty, causes no uncleanness."

5. A clean man who took the axe of one legally unclean by the handle,[3] and sprinkled it, even though there be so much water upon it as is sufficient for sprinkling, is clean. "How much water is sufficient for sprinkling?" "Sufficient that the tops of the stalks of hyssop be dipped and sprinkled." R. Judah said, "we regard them as though the hyssop were copper."

shall affirm that when ministers perform and confer a sacrament, it is not necessary that they should have at least the intention to do what the Church does; let him be accursed." It follows, that if, for example, in the sacrament of or-ders, any bishop in any age failed in due intention, all the orders which flowed from him are invalid.

[2] Chap. ix. 9; viii. 5.

[3] Another rendering is, "in his garment."

6. "He who sprinkled with unclean hyssop?" "If it be the size of an egg, the water is disallowed, and the sprinkling is disallowed." "If it be not the size of an egg?" "The water is allowed, but the sprinkling is disallowed, and he who is sprinkled renders his companion unclean, and he again his companion, even though there be 100.

7. He who was cleansed for purification, if his hands became unclean, his body is unclean, and he renders his companion unclean, and he again his companion, even though there be 100.

8. A jug for purification, which became unclean on the outside, becomes unclean inside, and renders unclean the one next to it, and it again the next one, even though they be 100. The bell and its clapper are reckoned as one. The spindle for bulrushes is not to be sprinkled either on the spindle or on the ring. But if it be sprinkled, it is sprinkled. If it be a spindle for flax, its parts are all reckoned as one. The skin which covers a couch which is joined to rings, is reckoned as one with it. The canopy is neither reckoned for uncleanness or cleanness. All handles of vessels which enter them are reckoned as one with them. Rabbi Jochanan, the son of Nuri, said, "even if they be only attached."

9. The panniers of an ass, and the staff of the threshing-wagon, and the pole of a bier, and the horn vessels of travellers, and a chain for keys, and the stitch-hooks of washers, and a garment sewed with a mixture of wool and linen, are reckoned as one for uncleanness, but not reckoned as one for sprinkling.

10. "The cover of a kettle which is bound by a chain?" The school of Shammai say, "it is reckoned as one for uncleanness, but not reckoned as one for sprinkling." The school of Hillel say, "he sprinkled the kettle, he sprinkled the cover; he sprinkled the cover, he did not sprinkle the kettle." All are permitted to sprinkle, except a neuter and a woman, and a child without understanding. A woman may help a man when he sprinkles, and she may hold for him the water. And he dips the hyssop and sprinkles. If she take hold of his hand even in the moment of sprinkling, it is disallowed.

11. "One dipped the hyssop by day and sprinkled by day?"

" It is allowed." " He dipped the hyssop by day and sprinkled by night, by night and sprinkled by day? " " It is disallowed." " By day, and sprinkled on the day following? " " It is disallowed." But he himself washed by night, and sprinkled by day, since we do not sprinkle till the sun rise; and everything done in sprinkling when the pillar of the morn ascends, is allowed.

19

HANDS

CHAPTER I

1. A quarter-log [1] of water is poured on the hands of one
person; also on the hands of two persons. Half a log on
three or four. From a log for five, ten, or even 100 (persons).
R. José says, " provided there be not less for the last than a
quarter-log." Men may add (water) for the second washing,[2]
but they must not add it for the first.

2. They may put water for hands in all vessels, even in vessels of dung or vessels of stone or vessels of earth. But
they must not pour it on hands out of the (broken) sides of
vessels or the bottom of a tub or the bung of a cask. Nor
may one give it to his neighbor out of the hollow of his hand:
because they must not draw or consecrate, or sprinkle the
water of purification, or put it on hands, except it be in a vessel.
They can only preserve vessels by the covering bound [3] upon
them. Nor can they preserve from uncleanness water in open
earthen vessels,[4] only in (covered) vessels.

3. Water which is unfit for animals to drink, is unfit (for
washing) in vessels; but on the ground it is fit. If ink, gum,

---

[1] A log is about half a pint.
[2] Before eating ordinary food the
hands must be washed once. Before
eating consecrated food they must be
washed twice.

[3] Num. xix. 15.
[4] I.e., from the uncleanness of a dead
reptile.

or vitriol black drop into it, and its color be changed, it is unfit. If one made use of it, or soaked his bread in it, it is unfit. Simeon the Temanite said, "even if he intended to soak it in one vessel and it dropped into another, it is fit."

4. If one rinsed vessels in it, or rinsed out measures, it is unfit. If one rinsed in it vessels already washed, or new ones, it is fit. R. José "disallows it for new vessels."

5. Water in which the baker had dipped rolls, is unfit; but if he only dipped in his hands, it is fit. All are allowed to pour water on hands, even one deaf, an idiot, or a minor. A man may rest a cask between his knees and pour it. He may incline the barrel on its side and pour it. An ape may pour water on hands. R. José "disallows these two cases."

CHAPTER II

1. "If one poured on his hand one gush?" "His hand is clean." "If on both hands one gush?" R. Meier pronounces them "unclean, until one poured out of a quarter-log (vessel) upon them." "If a heave-loaf fall (on the water)?" "It is clean." R. José "pronounces it unclean."

2. "If one poured out his first (ablution) in one place, and his second in another place, and a heave-loaf fall on the first?" "It is unclean." "If on the second?" "It is clean." "If one poured out both the first and second (ablutions) into one place, and a heave-loaf fall on them?" "It is unclean" "If one poured out his first ablution, and find on his hand a splinter or small stone?" "His hands are unclean, as the second water only purifies the first washing on the hand."[1] R. Simon, the son of Gamaliel, says, "whatsoever is a creation of the water is clean."

3. The hands become legally unclean, or legally clean up to the wrist. "How?" "If one poured the first (ablution) up to the wrist, and the second above the wrist, and the water ran back into the hand?" "It is clean." "If one poured the first and second (ablutions) above the wrist, and the water ran back into the hand?" "It is unclean." "If one poured the first (ablution) over one hand, and afterward the second

---

[1] And consequently does not purify the place covered by the splinter or stone, which remained unwashed by the first water.

over both hands?" "They are unclean." "If one poured the first (ablution) over both hands, and afterward the second over one hand?" "His hand is clean." "If one poured water on one hand and then rubbed it against its fellow?" "It is unclean." "If he rubbed it against his head, or against the wall?" "It is clean." Men may pour water over four or five persons alongside of each other, or above each other, provided they be separated, so that the water can come on them.

4. "There is a doubt if the water has been used, there is a doubt if it has not been used; there is a doubt if it be the prescribed quantity, there is a doubt if it be not the prescribed quantity: there is a doubt if it be (legally) unclean, there is a doubt if it be (legally) clean?" "In doubting he is clean," because the Sages said, "if there be a doubt of his hands being unclean, or imparting uncleanness, or being clean, he is clean." R. José said, "if there be a doubt of cleanness it is uncleanness." "How?" "His hands are clean, and before him are two unclean loaves, it is doubtful if he touched them, it is doubtful if he did not touch them: his hands are unclean, and before him are two clean loaves, it is doubtful if he touched them, it is doubtful if he did not touch them?" "His hands are one unclean and one clean." "And before him are two clean loaves: he touched one of them, it is doubtful if he touched the unclean, it is doubtful if he touched the clean?" "His hands are clean." "And before him are two loaves, one unclean and one clean, he touched one of them, it is doubtful if he touched the unclean, it is doubtful if he touched the clean?" "His hands are one unclean and one clean." "And before him are two loaves, one unclean and one clean, he touched both of them, it is doubtful if it were the unclean (loaf) with the unclean (hand), or the clean (loaf) with the clean (hand), or the clean loaf with the unclean (hand), or the unclean loaf with the clean hand?" "The hands remain as they were, and the loaves as they were." [2]

[2] Those that were legally clean continue clean, and those legally unclean continue unclean.

CHAPTER III

1. "Whosoever puts his hands into a house smitten with leprosy?" "His hands are unclean in a primary degree."[1] The words of R. Akiba. But the Sages say, "his hands are unclean in a secondary degree."[2] "Whatever renders garments unclean at the time of contact, renders hands unclean in a primary degree." The words of R. Akiba. But the Sages say, "in a secondary degree." They said to R. Akiba, "where do we find the hands (unclean) in a primary degree?" "Everywhere," he said to them; "and how is it possible for them to be unclean in a primary degree, unless his body is unclean, excepting this."[3] "Victuals, and vessels which are unclean through liquids render hands unclean in a secondary degree." The words of R. Joshua. But the Sages say, "that which is unclean through a source of uncleanness,[4] renders the hands unclean; but derived uncleanness [5] does not render the hands unclean." Rabban Simeon, the son of Gamaliel, said, "it happened that a woman came before my father. She said to him, 'my hands entered into the hollow of an earthen vessel.' He said to her, 'my daughter, from what was its uncleanness?' But I did not hear what she said to him." The Sages said, "the thing is clear, that which is unclean through a source of uncleanness renders the hands unclean; but derived uncleanness does not render the hands unclean."

2. "Whatever disallows the heave-offering, renders the hands unclean in a secondary degree. One hand can render the other hand unclean." The words of R. Joshua. But the Sages say, "a secondary cannot make a secondary."[6] He said to them, "and are not Holy Scriptures secondaries, and they render the hands unclean?" They said to him, "we cannot judge the words of the Law from the words of the scribes, nor the words of the scribes from the words of the Law, nor the words of the scribes from other words of the scribes."

---

[1] His hands render unclean what they touch.
[2] His hands render sacred things unclean.
[3] I.e., the putting his hands into a house infected with leprosy.
[4] Literally "father of uncleanness," such as a corpse or dead reptile, etc.
[5] I.e., uncleanness not containing the principle of uncleanness.
[6] An object unclean in the secondary degree cannot make another unclean in the same degree.

3. Straps of phylacteries with the phylacteries, render the hands unclean. R. Simeon says, " the straps of phylacteries do not render the hands unclean."

4. The margin in a book of the Law, at the top and bottom, at the beginning and end, renders the hands unclean. R. José says, " in the end it does not render the hands unclean, until the roller be attached."

5. A book of the Law which is erased, but in which there remain eighty-five letters like the portion, " And it came to pass when the Ark set forward," [7] renders the hands unclean. Any roll in which there are written eighty-five letters like the portion, " And it came to pass when the Ark set forward," renders the hands unclean. All sacred Scriptures render the hands unclean. The Canticles and Ecclesiastes render the hands unclean. R. Judah says, " Canticles render the hands unclean, but Ecclesiastes is in dispute." R. José says, " Ecclesiastes does not render the hands unclean, but the Canticles are in dispute." R. Simeon says, " Ecclesiastes is one in which the school of Shammai is less strict, and the school of Hillel more rigid." R. Simeon, the son of Azai, said, " I received by tradition from the mouths of the seventy-two elders, on the day they inducted R. Eleazar, the son of Azariah, into the president's seat, that Canticles and Ecclesiastes render the hands unclean." R. Akiba said, " God forbid! no man in Israel ever questioned that the Canticles render the hands unclean, as the whole world is not equal to the day on which the Canticles were given to Israel; for all the Scriptures are holy, but the Canticles are Holy of Holies. They only disputed in reference to Ecclesiastes." R. Jochanan, the son of Joshua, the son of R. Akiba's father-in-law, said, " according to the words of the son of Azai, thus they disputed, and thus they decided."

[7] Num. x. 35, 36. The rabbis count these verses a distinct book of the law.

CHAPTER IV.

1. On that day [1] they voted and decided, "that a foot-bath containing from two logs to nine cabs,[2] which was split,[3] may become unclean from pressure," [4] although R. Akiba says, "that a foot-bath is as its name." [5]

2. On that day they said, "that all sacrifices offered without due intention are allowed, but they do not absolve the owners from their obligation, except the passover-offering, and the sin-offering—the passover-offering in its time, and the sin-offering at all times." R. Eleazar says, "also the trespass-offering, the passover-offering in its time, and the sin or trespass-offering at all times." R. Simeon, the son of Azai, said, " I received it by tradition from the mouth of the seventy-two elders, on the day they inducted R. Eleazar, the son of Azariah, into the president's seat, that all sacrifices offered without due intention, are allowed, but they do not absolve the owners from their obligation, except the passover-offering, and the sin-offering." The son of Azai only added the burnt-offering, but the Sages did not agree with him.

3. On that day they said, "how is it with Ammon and Moab [6] in the Sabbatical year?" R. Tarphon decided "they must pay tithes for the poor ";[7] but R. Eleazar, son of Azariah, decided " second tithes."[8] R. Ishmael then said, " Eleazar, son of Azariah, it behoves thee to prove it, for thou addest to the burden (of the Law); and whoever adds to the burden (of the Law) it behoves him to prove it." R. Eleazar, son of Azariah, said to him, " Ishmael, my brother, I have not changed from the order of the years,[9] but my brother Tarphon has changed, therefore it behoves him to prove it." R. Tarphon replied, " Egypt is out of the land, and Ammon and Moab are out of the land: as Egypt pays tithes for the poor in the Sabbatical year, so Ammon and Moab pay tithes for

---

[1] When R. Eleazar, the son of Azariah, was made president of the school in Jamnia.

[2] A cab is about three pints.

[3] And could not contain water enough to wash one foot.

[4] Of an unclean person.

[5] It continues as long as its name, and as such cannot become unclean from pressure.

[6] I.e., with Israelites dwelling there.

[7] Tithe for the poor could be eaten anywhere.

[8] Second tithes could only be eaten in Jerusalem. Deut. xiv. 22, 23.

[9] The sixth year was fixed for the tithe to the poor, consequently in countries outside the land of Israel, and not subject to the Sabbatical rest, Israelites should pay the second tithe.

the poor in the Sabbatical year." R. Eleazar, son of Azariah, replied: " Babylon is out of the land, and Ammon and Moab are out of the land; even as Babylon pays second tithes in the Sabbatical year, so Ammon and Moab pay second tithes in the Sabbatical year." R. Tarphon replied, " Egypt being near, is subject to tithes for the poor, in order that the poor in Israel may be supported in the Sabbatical year; so Ammon and Moab, which are near, must also be subject to tithes for the poor, in order that the poor in Israel may be supported in the Sabbatical year." R. Eleazar, the son of Azariah, replied, "thou seekest to increase money, but thou only losest souls; wouldest thou be the cause that heaven should neither send down dew nor rain, as is said, 'Will a man rob God?' Yet ye have robbed me. But ye say, Wherein have we robbed thee? In tithes and offerings." [10] R. Joshua said, " Behold I will answer for my brother Tarphon, but not according to the sense of his words—Egypt is a new arrangement, Babylon is an old arrangement; the judgment before us is a new arrangement. Let the new arrangement be judged from the new arrangement, but let not a new arrangement be judged from an old arrangement. Egypt is an arrangement by the elders (of the Sanhedrin), but Babylon is an arrangement by the prophets—the judgment before us is an arrangement by the elders. Let therefore the arrangement by the elders be judged from an arrangment by the elders; but let not an arrangement by the elders be judged from an arrangement by prophets." They voted and decided " that Ammon and Moab must pay tithes for the poor in the Sabbatical year." When R. José, son of Dormiskith, came to R. Eleazar at Lydda, he said to him, " what had you new in the college to-day?" He answered, "they voted and decided that Ammon and Moab must pay tithes in the Sabbatical year." R. Eleazar wept and said, "'The secret of the LORD is with them that fear him; and He will show them His covenant.' [1] Go and tell them, be not anxious about your vote, for I received it by tradition from Rabban Jochanan, the son of Zachai, who heard it from his teacher, up to the decision

---

[10] Mal. iii. 8. It is assumed that the prophet means the consecrated second tithe, and not the unconsecrated tithe for the poor.
[1] Ps. xxv. 10.

of Moses from Sinai, that Ammon and Moab must pay tithes to the poor, in the Sabbatical year."

3. On that day came Judah, an Ammonitish proselyte, and stood before them in the college. He said to them, "How am I to come into the congregation?" Rabban Gamaliel said to him, "thou art forbidden." R. Joshua said to him, "thou art allowed." Rabban Gamaliel said, "the Scripture says, 'An Ammonite or Moabite shall not enter into the congregation of the LORD; even to their tenth generation, etc.'"[2] To him said R. Joshua, "Are then the Ammonites or Moabites still in their own land? Sennacherib, King of Assyria, aforetime came up, and commingled the nations, as is said, 'And I have removed the bounds of the people, and have robbed their treasures, and I have put down the inhabitants like a valiant (man).'"[3] Rabban Gamaliel said to him, "the Scripture says, 'And afterward I will bring again the captivity of the children of Ammon';[4] and they are already returned." To him said R. Joshua, "the Scripture says, 'And I will bring again the captivity of my people of Israel,[5] and Judah.' But they are not yet returned." And they allowed him to come into the congregation.

4. The Chaldee passages in Ezra and Daniel render the hands unclean. Chaldee written in Hebrew, and Hebrew written in Chaldee, or in Hebrew,[6] do not render the hands unclean. In no case do they cause uncleanness, unless the writing be Assyrian, on parchment with ink.

5. The Sadducees said, "we blame you Pharisees, because you say sacred Scriptures render the hands unclean, but the books Hameram[7] do not render the hands unclean." Rabban Jochanan, the son of Zachai, said, "and have we nothing else against the Pharisees but this? Behold they say, 'that the bones of an ass are clean, but the bones of Jochanan the high-priest are unclean.'" They said to him, "according to their value is their uncleanness, so that no one may make the bones of his father and mother into spoons." He said to them, "so

---

[2] Deut. xxiii. 3.
[3] Isa. x. 13.
[4] Jer. xlix. 6.
[5] Amos ix. 14.
[6] The ancient Hebrew letters are now called Samaritan. They are still used for writing by the small community of Samaritans who dwell in Nablùs, in the Holy Land. The Jews now use the Chaldee characters; and the Talmud therefore errs in calling the old national letters Assyrian.

[7] Some suppose the writings of Homer are meant; others think that these were books against revealed religion.

(are) the sacred Scriptures: according to their value is their uncleanness. The books Hameram, which are not valued, do not render the hands unclean."

6. The Sadducees said, "we blame you Pharisees, that you declare the stream flowing (from a clean into an unclean vessel) to be clean." The Pharisees said, "we blame you Sadducees, that you declare a stream of water flowing from a graveyard to be clean." The Sadducees said, "we blame you Pharisees, because you say, if my ox or my ass cause damage, we are responsible; but if my slave or my bondwoman cause damage, we are free. What! if I be responsible for my ox and my ass, for which I have no obligation, I am bound for my slave or bondwoman for whom I have obligation. It is just that I should be bound for their damages." They said to them "no! if you speak of my ox and my ass which have no knowledge, as you speak of my slave and bondwoman who have knowledge: then, if I offend them, they may go and set fire to the stacks of corn of another, and I should be bound to pay."

7. A Galilean Sadducee said, "I blame you Pharisees, because you write the name of the reigning sovereign in the letter of divorce with Moses." The Pharisees said, "we blame you Galilean Sadducee, that you write the sovereign on the same page with the NAME, and not only so, but you write the sovereign above, and the name below, as is said, "And Pharaoh said, 'Who is the Lord, that I should obey his voice to let Israel go?'"[8] But when he was punished, what did he say? "The LORD is righteous."[9]

[8] Exod. v. 2. The name of Pharoah cannot be considered an insult to Moses, since it precedes the name of God.

[9] Exod. ix. 27. This is merely added to avoid ending with Pharoah's blasphemy.

est doneie la lumiere al doleur·
Pen la mime esterniere signefier a la sou
tiuere la propriete· z la mau ladustuur de cest mil
de· Do ne li pscalmistes dist· Si est ses tenebres end
z sa lumiere· Car ti charur home aissi destoschent
et desprenent la proprieu del munde· co il en soffra
 et porter sa adulter· z p̃ ore hatrece de euer ser
uiilent· z les biens z les mals del munde desor les
pier· z si dient si com ses tenebres cust z sa lumi
ere· Aissi com se il deldient ouuenie· y ieur p̃ le
sie grauance naissilent la fente de vie etuencion
nele oute ronpent atu agonist· Mais grant si est
mas amour dit ke il desturbent les penses des tos·
ia sber ce ke il nes elliencur· fi suuenr li sanct p̃
me la charnf sor conoissenf en la dolor de cest ecl
estue cleir en la proprieu de cest munde· z de car
alt aluus dur· Por cor est la lumiere doneie al
dolent· Doue est la lumiere doneie al dolent· car
est en eschanteur les touuaines choses· z churr sor
conoissenc eucest ertst· resiouent la clareu de
la resplaiceur· p̃prteur· Que cant il muuir plo
rent de ce ke il tardient repatent al pus il
lur deseur loin soffre les sait donor· Li amour
des pmanables choses les courrebles· z la glore
des tempurel les tolenier· Que quant il penseur ques
cee choses ff eug il muuisir es badtues· z quil oeles
eug il emor ne noient es haltrecees· Quz oeles sour
ki et les tamoeunent en uie· z quiz oeles cuidonc
peines et cuita· fi les reuort la dolus de lur p̃o
prietur   ia sber ce ke il ne noient mie· ke ele

Por coi est donee la lumiere al dolent?

En la sainte escriture signefier a la foiz la lumiere la prosperitet · z la nuit la dui siteit de cest mũ-
de. Donc li psalmistes dist · Si cũ ses tenebres · ensi
z sa lumiere. Car li saint home alsi destoidrent
z desprirent la prosperitet del munde · cõ il en soffrã-
ce poroient sa aduisiteit · z p gint haitece de cuer sier-
missent · z les biens z les malz del munde desor lor
piez · z si dient si com ses tenebres · ensi z sa lumiere. Alsi com se il disoient ouitemt · Hient plus ke
ses greuances naissent la force de nre entencion
nele corrumpent a saiagemt · Mais prant si cõ
nos auons dit · ke il desturbent les penses des bõs
la foiz ce ke il nes el'lieuent si fuient li saint home ke chaitif soi conoissent en la dolor de cest exil
estre cleir en la prosperitet de cest munde. J de ce
est adroit dit · Por coi est la lumiere donee al
dolent? Donc est la lumiere doueie al dolent · car
cil ki esgardent les soutaines choses · z chaitif soi
conoissent en cest exil · rezoiuent la clartet de
la tresplaisant prosperitet. Ob cant il mult plo-
rent de ce ke il tardient repairent al pais · si
lur destient loim soffrir les fait donor · Li amors
des pmanables choses les courroblet · z la glore
des temporen les losenger. Ob cant il pensent giles
cez choses ff cui il cuient et baisseces · z gilz celes
cui il encor ne voient et haitteces · gilz celes sont
ki et les stancemment en tet · z gilz celes cui il ont
pdues et enel · si les remort la dolors de lur prosperitet · car ia foir ce ke il ne voient mie · ke ele

THE KABBALAH UNVEILED

THE LESSER HOLY ASSEMBLY

—

[*Translated by S. L. Macgregor Mathers*]

THE LESSER HOLY ASSEMBLY

CHAPTER I

WHICH CONTAINETH THE INTRODUCTION

Tradition.—On that day on which the Companions were as-sembled together in the house of Rabbi Schimeon, and on which he had arranged his affairs because he was about to depart from the world, before him were Rabbi Eleazar his son, and Rabbi Abba, and the rest of the Companions; and the house was full.

Therefore lifting up his eyes, Rabbi Schimeon saw that the house was full. And Rabbi Schimeon wept, saying: " The second time when I was sick, and Rabbi Benchas Ben Yair was in my presence, and until I had chosen my place, life hath been prolonged unto me even until now.

" When I was restored, fire surrounded (my habitation) which hitherto hath never ceased, neither did any man enter in unto me without permission.

" But now I see that it is taken away, and that the house is filled."

While they were sitting down, Rabbi Schimeon, opening his eyes, beheld a certain vision, and lo! fire surrounded the house!

Therefore all (the others) went forth, and Rabbi Eleazar his son, and Rabbi Abba remained; but the other Companions sat without.

Rabbi Schimeon said unto Rabbi Eleazar his son: " Go forth, and see whether Rabbi Yitzchaq be present for whom I have made myself surety.

" And say thou unto him that he dispose his affairs, and that he may sit down with me. Blessed is his portion."

Rabbi Schimeon arose and again sat down; and he laughed aloud, and rejoicing said, " Where are the companions?"

Rabbi Eleazar arose and introduced them, and they sat down in his presence.

Rabbi Schimeon lifted up his hands and prayed a prayer, and was joyful.

And he said, " Let those Companions who were in the former Conclave [1] assembled here."

Therefore, all the others having gone forth, there remained Rabbi Eleazar his son, and Rabbi Abba, and Rabbi Yehudah, and Rabbi Yosi Bar Yoqeb, and Rabbi Chiya.

In the meantime Rabbi Yitzchaq entered, to whom Rabbi Schimeon said: " How excellent is thy lot! How much joy is this day stored up for thee!"

Rabbi Abba sat down behind his (*i.e.*, Rabbi Schimeon's) back, and Rabbi Eleazar before him (*i.e.*, Rabbi Schimeon).

Rabbi Schimeon spake and said: " Surely now is the time of benevolence, and I desire to enter without confusion into the world to come.

" And verily these sacred things, which hereunto have never been revealed, I desire to reveal before the Schekhinah;

" Lest they should say that I have kept back anything, and that I have been taken away from the world; for even until now these things have been concealed in my heart, so that having entered into these very matters I may be with them in the world to come.

" But this is my arrangement of you; let Rabbi Abba write, and let Rabbi Eleazar my son speak openly; but let the rest of the Companions in silence meditate in their heart."

Rabbi Abba arose from his seat behind him, and Rabbi Eleazar his son sat down.

He said unto him, " Arise, O my son, for another shall sit in that seat "; and Rabbi Eleazar arose.

Rabbi Schimeon covered himself and sat down; and he commenced, and said, Ps. cxv. 17: "' The dead shall not praise IH, *Yah*, nor all they who go down into silence!

"' The dead shall not praise Yah;' so it is certain that it is assuredly those who are called dead; for He, God, the most Holy One—may He be blessed!—is called the Living One, and is Himself commemorated among those who are called living, and not with those who are called dead.

[1] That is, who had formed part of the Greater Holy Assembly.

"And the end of this text runneth thus: 'Nor all they who go down into silence;' for all they who go down into silence remain in Gehenna.

"There is another reason appertaining to those who are called living, for God the most Holy One—may He be blessed!—desireth their glory."

Rabbi Schimeon said: "How different is this occasion from that of the former conclave! For into a certain conclave [2] came He, the most Holy and Blessed God, and His Chariot.

"Now verily He, the Holy One, is here—may He be blessed—and He hath approached with those Just who are in the Garden of Eden,[3] which did not occur in the former conclave.

"And God, the Most Holy One—may He be blessed—more promoteth the glory of the Just than His own glory.

"As it is written concerning Jeroboam, who sacrificed unto and served other gods, and yet God, the Most Holy One—may He be blessed!—waited for him.

"But because he stretched forth his hand against Iddo the prophet, his hand became withered.

"For it is written, 1 Kings xiii. 4, 'And his hand became withered, etc.' Here it is not written that it was because he served other gods, but because he extended his hand against Iddo the prophet, etc.

"Now, therefore, God the Most Holy One—may He be blessed!—promoteth their glory (i.e., that of the Just), and they all come with Him."

He said, "Verily, Rav Hamenuna the elder is here, and around him are seventy Just represented in his circle, of whom certain shine with the splendor of the Ancient and Most Holy One, the Concealed with all Concealments.

"He, I say, cometh, in order that with joy he may hear those words which I shall speak."[4]

And when he had sat down he said: "Assuredly here a seat hath been set aside for Rabbi Benchas Ben Yair."

The companions who were there trembled greatly, and they arose, and sat down in the lowest part of the house; but Rabbi Eleazar and Rabbi Abba (still sat) before Rabbi Schimeon.

---

[2] Meaning that the Greater Holy Assembly had been as it were the reflection of the conclave of the Sephiroth above. The word used for "chariot" is not "Mercavah," but "Rethikh."

[3] I.e., the Paradise above.

[4] In the original both this and the foregoing section, apparently by an oversight, have the number thirty-three attached to them.

Rabbi Schimeon said: " In the former Assembly we acted thus; namely, that all the companions spoke, and I also with them, by turns.

" Now I shall speak alone, and let all hear my words, superiors and inferiors; blessed be my portion this day ! "

Rabbi Schimeon commenced, and said, Cant. vii. 10: " ' I am my beloved's, and his desire is toward me.'

" As long as I have been bound unto this world in one link with God, the Most Holy One—may He be blessed !—have I been bound, and therefore now is His desire toward me.

" For He Himself and His whole holy company come, so that with joy they may hear the concealed words, and the praise of Him, the Most Holy Ancient One, the Concealed with all Concealments.

" And He separateth Himself ever more and more; He is separated from all things, neither yet doth He altogether separate Himself, seeing that unto Himself all things adhere, and that He Himself adhereth unto all; HVA, *Hoa*, He Himself is all; He the Most Holy Ancient of all Ancients, the Concealed with all Concealments.

" He hath been formed, and yet as it were He hath not been formed. He hath been conformed, so that He may sustain all things; yet is He not formed, seeing that He is not discovered.

" When He is conformed He produceth nine Lights, which shine forth from Him, from His conformation.

" And from Himself those Lights shine forth, and they emit flames, and they rush forth and are extended on every side, like as from an elevated lantern the rays of light stream down on every side.

" And those rays of light,[5] which are extended, when anyone draweth near unto them, so that they may be examined, are not found, and there is only the lantern alone.

" So also is He the Most Holy and Ancient One: He is that highest Light concealed with all concealments, and He is not found; those rays [6] (proceeding from Him) being excepted, which are extended, which are revealed, and which are hidden.

" And they are called the Holy Name, and therefore are all things One.

" Which truly our companions have said in former books,

[5] Carrying on the simile of the lantern and its rays.   [6] The Sephiroth.

,that certain paths have been created by the Most Holy Ancient One, who is revealed through them collectively and severally; since they are the conformations of the Most Holy Ancient One, concerning them now there is not time for examination.

" I have spoken concerning them in the Holy Assembly, and I have beheld that which before I did not understand in such a manner, and I have hidden the matter in my heart.

" But now I alone will describe these things before the Holy King, and all those assuredly just men who have assembled to hear these words."

CHAPTER II

Concerning the Skull of the Ancient One, and Concerning His Brain; and Concerning the Three Heads, and the Hair, and the Discriminatory Paths

The skull of the White Head hath not beginning, but its end is the convexity of its joining together, which is extended, and shineth.

And from it the just shall inherit 400 [1] desirable worlds in the world to come.

And from this convexity of the joining together of this White Skull daily distilleth a dew into Microprosopus, into that place which is called Heaven; and in that very place shall the dead be raised to life in the time to come.

Like as it is written, Gen. xxvii. 27: " And Elohim shall give thee from the dew of heaven."

And His head is filled with that dew, and all the place of the apple-trees distilleth therewith.

He, the Most Holy Ancient One, is hidden and concealed, and in that Skull is the Supernal Wisdom concealed, who is found and who is not found.

For assuredly in Him, the Ancient One, nothing is revealed save the Head alone, seeing that that Head is itself the Head of all heads.

The beginning of that Supernal Wisdom which also is itself the Head, is hidden therein, and is called the Supernal Brain,

---

[1] Which is the number of Th, the last letter of the Hebrew alphabet, which includes the symbology of the cross.

the Hidden Brain, the Tranquil and Calm Brain; neither doth any man know it, save He Himself.

Three Heads have been formed forth, one within the other, and the other above the other.

One Head is the Concealed Wisdom, which is covered and is not disclosed.

And this Hidden Wisdom is the Head of all things, and the Head of the remaining Wisdoms.

The Supernal Head is the Most Holy Ancient One, the Concealed with all Concealments.

The Head of all Heads, the Head which is not a Head [2]— namely, that which is *in* that Head—neither knows nor is known, because it cannot be comprehended either by Wisdom or Understanding.

And therefore is it read, Num. xxiv. 11· "Fly thee in thy place;" and Ezek. i. 14. The *Chaioth,* living creatures, are said to run forth and return.

And therefore is the Most Holy Ancient One called AIN, *Ain*, the Negatively Existent; seeing that back from Him dependeth the AIN, the Negative Existence.[3]

But all those hairs and all those locks depend from the Hidden Brain.

And all are calm (otherwise, are disposed) in the Equilibrium; neither in any manner is the neck seen (*i.e.,* because of the locks which overshadow it).

Because He the Most Holy Ancient One is in an unvarying condition of joy, neither changeth He from mercy forever.

But in the thirteen measurements [4] of mercies is He found, because that Wisdom hidden in Him is divided into three [5] paths in a quaternary, and He Himself the Ancient One com-

---

[2] That is to say, which will hardly admit even of so vague a definition, seeing it is the Indefinite Absolute in Kether.

[3] We must be most careful not to misapprehend the meaning intended to be conveyed in this passage. Kether, the Ancient One, Macroprosopus, is not in the more restricted sense of the first Sephira, the AIN, but that that idea links back from Him must be manifest on consideration. Yet even He, the Vast Countenance, is hidden and concealed; how much more, then, the AIN! From Negative to Positive, through Potential Existence, eternally

vibrates the Divine Absolute of the Hidden Unity of processional form masked in the Eternal Abyss of the Unknowable, the synthetical hieroglyph of an illimitable pastless futureless Present. To the uttermost bounds of space rushes the Voice of Ages, unheard save in the concentrated unity of the thought-formulated Abstract, and eternally that Voice formulates a Word which is glyphed in the vast ocean of limitless life.

[4] The thirteen conformations of the beard of Macroprosopus.

[5] The Trinity completed by the Quaternary.

prehendeth them, and through them doth He reign over all things.

One (path) which shineth in the midst of the hairs going forth from the Skull, is that path by whose light the just are led into the world to come.

Like as it is written, Prov. iv. 18, " And the path of the just shineth as the Light."

And concerning this it is written, Isa. lviii. 14, " Then shalt thou delight thyself in Tetragrammaton."

And from that path [6] are all the other paths illuminated which depend from Microprosopus.

He the Eternal Ancient of the Ancient Ones is the highest Crown among the Supernals, wherewith all Diadems and Crowns are crowned.

And from Him are all the Lights illuminated, and they flash forth flames, and shine.

But He verily is the Supreme Light, which is hidden, which is not known.

And all the other Lights are kindled by Him, and derive (their) splendor (from him).

He the Most Holy Ancient One is found to have three heads, which are contained in the One Head.[7]

And He Himself is that only highest supreme Head.

And since He the Most Holy Ancient One is thus symbolized in the Triad, hence all the other Lights which shine are included in Triads.[8]

Moreover, the Most Holy Ancient One is also symbolized by the Duad.

And the division of the Ancient One in the Duad is so that the (one form is) the Highest Crown of all the Supernals, the Head of all Heads.

And (the other is) that superior Head, and It is not known.

---

[6] Kether, the first Sephira, from which all the other Sephiroth proceed, namely, those which are summed up in the Tetragrammaton.

[7] I.e., his manifestation is triune.

[8] This refers to the Triads in the Sephiroth, when the Autz Chaiim is formed. (See Introduction.) It will be found that in this arrangement of the ten Sephiroth there are ten Triads, viz.:
(1) Kether, Chokmah, Binah.
(2) Chesed, Geburah, Tiphereth.
(3) Netzach, Hod, Yesod.

(4) Chokmah, Chesed, Netzach.
(5) Tiphereth, Yesod, Malkuth.
(6) Binah, Geburah, Hod.
(7) Chokmah, Tiphereth, Hod.
(8) Binah, Tiphereth, Netzach.
(9) Chesed, Tiphereth, Hod
(10) Geburah, Tiphereth, Netzach.
Wherein Kether and Malkuth are each repeated once; Chokmah, Binah, Chesed, and Geburah, thrice; Tiphereth, six times; Netzach and Hod each four times; and Yesod twice.

So also all the remaining Lights are mystically divided into Duads.

Furthermore, the Most Holy Ancient One is symbolized and concealed under the conception of the Unity, for He himself is One, and all things are One.

And thus all the other Lights are sanctified, are restricted, and are bound together in the Unity or Monad, and are One; and all things are HVA, *Hoa,* Himself.

CHAPTER III

CONCERNING THE FOREHEAD OF THE MOST HOLY ANCIENT ONE

The Forehead, which is uncovered in the Most Holy Ancient One, is called Grace.

For that Supernal Head concealed in the Higher, which no man hath known, expandeth a certain external manifestation, beautiful and gracious, which is comprehended in the Forehead.

And since He Himself is the grace of all graciousness; hence He assumeth the conformation of the Forehead, which is disclosed in the most intense light (otherwise, hath a formation in the figure of a leaf).

And when It is disclosed, the grace of all graciousness is found in all worlds.

And all the prayers of the Inferiors are accepted; and the countenance of Microprosopus is illuminated, and all things are found to exist in mercy.

And since (through this) all judgments are hidden and subjected, hence in the Sabbath, in the time of the afternoon prayers, in which all judgments are excited, that Forehead is disclosed.

And all the judgments are turned aside, and mercies are found.

And therefore is the Sabbath found without judgment, as well that which is above as that which is below; also the fire of Gehenna is restrained in its place, and the transgressors are at rest.

And therefore is the Spirit NSHMTH, of joy added on the Sabbath.

And it behoveth man to rejoice with three feasts on the Sabbath; for all truth, and the whole system of true faith, is found therein (*i.e.*, in the Sabbath).

And it behoveth man to prepare the table, that he may eat in the three feasts of true faith, and rejoice in them.[1]

Rabbi Schimeon said: " I attest concerning myself, before all these who are here present, that through all my days I have not omitted these three feasts, and that because of them I have not been compelled to fast on the Sabbath.

" Furthermore, also on other days I have not been compelled (to fast), much less on the Sabbath, for he who rightly acteth concerning these (feasts) is the adept of perfect truth.

" The first feast is that of the Great Mother; the second that of the Holy King; and the third that of the Most Holy Ancient One, the Concealed with all Concealments.[2]

" And in this world, who can thoroughly follow out, through them, those paths?

" If this RTzVN, *Ratzon,* Grace, be revealed, all those judgments are enlightened, and are diverted from their concentrated rigor.

" The conformation of Him, the Most Holy Ancient One, is instituted through one form, which is the ideal Syntagma of all forms.

" The same is the Concealed Supernal Wisdom, the synthesis of all the rest.

And this is called ODN, *Eden,* or the supernal Paradise, concealed with all occultations.

" And it is the Brain of the Most Holy Ancient One, and that Brain is expanded on every side.

" Therefore is it extended into Eden, or another Paradise,[3] and from this is Eden or Paradise formed forth.

" And when this Head, which is concealed in the Head of the Ancient One, which is not known, extendeth a certain frontal formation, which is formed for brilliance, then flasheth forth the Lightning of His Brain.

[1] In many of the ancient mysteries a " feast " was part of the ceremony, analogous to our Eucharist. Verbum sapientibus.
[2] That is, the greatest triad of the Sephiroth, the Crown, King, and Queen; which finds a parallel in the Osiris, Isis, and Horus; the Axieros, Axiochersos, and Axiochersa of Lemnos and Samothrace, etc.
[3] Described in other places as the Supernal Eden and the Inferior Eden.

" And it is formed forth and illuminated with many Lights.

" And it produceth and designeth (a certain effect) in this Light (otherwise, in this opening), in this Forehead, whereon is inscribed a certain Light, which is called RTzVN, *Ratzon*, Grace.

" And that Grace is extended backward into the beard, even unto that place where it can remain in the beard, and it is called the Supernal, CHSD, *Chesed*, Mercy.

" And when this Grace is uncovered, all the Lords of Judgment behold It, and are turned aside."

CHAPTER IV

CONCERNING THE EYES OF THE MOST HOLY ANCIENT ONE

The eyes of the Head of the Most Holy Ancient One are two in one,[1] equal, which ever watch, and sleep not.

Like as it is written, Ps. cxxi. 4, " The Keeper of Israel neither slumbereth nor sleepeth," etc.; namely, of Israel the holy.

And therefore are there no eyebrows nor eyelashes unto His eyes.

This Brain is conformed and illuminated with three supernal white brilliances.

With this white brilliance are the eyes of Microprosopus bathed.

As it is written, Cant. v. 12, " Washed with milk," flowing down from the fullness of that primal white brilliance.

And with the remaining white brilliances are the other lights cleansed and purified.

The Brain is called the Fountain of Benevolence, the fountain wherein all blessings are found.

And since this Brain radiateth into the three white brilliances of the eye (of Microprosopus), hence is that called the " good eye," concerning which it is said, Prov. xxii. 9, " It shall be blessed," or rather that from it dependeth blessing.

For through the Brain are manifested the white brilliances of the eye.

[1] The Duad equated in the Monad. Compare what I have previously re- marked concerning the profile symbolism of Macroprosopus.

And when this eye looketh upon Microprosopus, all the worlds are (in a state of) happiness.

This is the right eye. The inferior eyes are right and left, two in duplicate color.

In the " Book of Concealed Mystery " have we taught that there is a Superior Yod, an Inferior Yod; a Superior He, an Inferior He; a Superior Vau, an Inferior Vau.

Unto the Ancient One pertain all the Superiors, and unto Microprosopus the Inferiors.

They depend not in another manner, but only thus; for from the Most Holy Ancient One do they depend.

For the Name of the Ancient One is concealed in all things, neither is it found.

But those letters which depend from the Ancient One, so that they may be established, are all inferiors. For were it not so, they could not be established.

And therefore is the Holy Name [2] *alike* concealed and manifest.

For that which is concealed pertaineth unto the Most Holy Ancient One, the Concealed in all things.

But that, indeed, which is manifested, because it dependeth, belongeth unto Microprosopus. (Otherwise, that which is manifested, is so for this reason—that it is manifested because it dependeth, etc.)

And therefore do all the blessings require both concealment and manifestation.

Those concealed letters which hang behind depend from the Most Holy Ancient One.

Wherefore do they hang behind? For the purpose of establishing the Inferior Yod. (Otherwise, assuredly from the Skull, from the Forehead, from the Eyes, do they depend. And the Yod Maternal [3] dependeth toward the Inferior Yod.)

[2] The student will observe throughout the Qabalah that great stress is laid on the power of names, which arises from the fact that each qabalistical name is the synthesis of a power. Hence to " pronounce that name " is to use that power.

[3] The word I have translated " Maternal " is AMH, Amah, with a double Kametz point. Rosenroth renders it, " Yod Membri."

CHAPTER V

CONCERNING THE NOSE OF THE MOST HOLY ANCIENT ONE

The Nose. From this nose, from the openings of the nostrils, the Spirit of Life rusheth forth upon Microprosopus.

And from that opening of the nose, from those openings of the nostrils, dependeth the letter He, in order to establish the other and inferior He.

And that Spirit proceedeth from the hidden brain, and She is called the Spirit of Life, and through that Spirit [1] will all men understand CHKMTHA, *Chokmatha,* Wisdom, in the time of King Messiah.

As it is written, Isa. xi. 2: " And the Spirit of Wisdom and Understanding, *RVCH CHKMH VBINH, Ruach Chokmah Va-Binah,* shall rest upon Him," etc.

This nose is life in every part; perfect joy, rest of spirit, and health.

The nose of Microprosopus is as we have (before) conformed it.

Since concerning Him it is said, Ps. xviii. 9, " There ascendeth a smoke in his nose," etc.

But concerning this it is written, Isa. xlviii. 9, " And for my name's sake will I defer mine anger (literally, lengthen my nose) for thee."

(But in the book which is called " The Treatise of the School of Rav Yeyeva the Elder," the letter He is located in the mouth, and he doth not argue in the same manner as in the text, neither doth he bring about the same combination, although the matter eventuateth in the same manner.)

But yet from the letter the judgment dependeth, and judgment pertaineth unto the nose (of Microprosopus). Like as it is written, Ps. xviii. 9, " Smoke ascendeth out of His nose."

And if thou sayest that behold also it is written, " And fire out of His mouth consumeth," surely the foundation of wrath dependeth from His nose.

All the conformations of the Most Holy Ancient One are formed forth from the calm and concealed brain.

---

[1] Speaking of the unity, the " Sepher Yetzirah " says: " One is She, the Spirit of the Elohim of life (blessed and more than blessed be His name who is the life of ages), Voice, and Spirit, and Word—this is She, the Spirit of holiness.

And all the conformations of Microprosopus are formed through the Inferior *Chokmah*, Wisdom. Like as it is written, Ps. civ. 24, " All these hast thou made in Chokmah." And certainly it (Wisdom) is the epitome of all things.

Now what is the difference between H, *He,* and H, *He?* By the Inferior *He* is judgment stirred up; but in this instance, through the other *He,* mercy unto mercy is denoted.

CHAPTER VI

Concerning the Beard of the Most Holy Ancient One

From the Beard of the Most Holy Ancient One hangeth the whole ornament of all, and the Influence; for all things are called from that beard, Influence.

This is the Ornament of all Ornaments, and this influence do all the superiors and inferiors alike behold.

From this Influence dependeth the life of all things.

From this Influence heavens and earth depend, the rains of grace, and the nourishment of all things.

From this Influence cometh the providence of all things. From this Influence depend all the superior and inferior hosts.

Thirteen fountains of excellent and precious oil depend from this beard of most glorious Influence, and they all flow down into Microprosopus.

Say not thou, however, that all do so, but nine of them are found (in Microprosopus) for the purpose of diverting the judgments.

And whensoever this Influence hangeth down in equilibrium even unto the heart, all the Holinesses of the Holinesses of Holiness depend from it.

In that Influence is extended an expansion of the Supernal Emanation,[1] which is the Head of all Heads, which is not known nor perfected, and which neither superiors nor inferiors have known, because from that Influence all things depend.

In this beard the Three Heads concerning which we have spoken are expanded, and all things are associated together in this Influence, and are found therein.

[1] The word is QVTRA. Rosenroth translates it by "Aporrhea." It may also be translated "vapor," or "nebula."

And therefore every ornament of ornaments dependeth from that Influence.

Those letters which depend from this Ancient One all hang in that beard, and are associated together in that Influence.

And they hang therein for the purpose of establishing the other letters.

For unless those letters could ascend into the Ancient One, those other letters could not be established.

And therefore Moses saith when necessary IHVH, IHVH, twice; and so that an accent distinguishes the one from the other.

For assuredly from the Influence all things depend.

By that Influence are both superiors and inferiors brought unto reverence, and are prostrate before it.

Blessed is he who attaineth hereunto.

CHAPTER VII

CONCERNING THE BRAIN AND THE WISDOM IN GENERAL

Of this Most Holy Ancient One, Concealed with all Concealments, there is no mention made, neither is He found.

For since this Head is the supreme of all the supernals, hence He is only symbolized as a head alone without body, for the purpose of establishing all things.

And He Himself is concealed, and hidden, and kept recondite by all things.

His conformation is that He is formed forth in that brain, the most hidden of all things, which is expanded and formed forth, and hence proceedeth the superior and inferior ChSD, *Chesed*, Mercy.

And the superior Chesed is formed forth and expanded, and all things are comprehended in this concealed brain.

For when that White Brilliance is formed forth in that Light, it acteth upon that which acteth upon this brain, and it is enlightened.

And the second brain dependeth from that very glorious Influence, it is expanded into the thirty-two [1] paths, when it is

---

[1] The ten numbers and twenty-two letters.

illuminated, then it shineth from that very glorious Influence.[2]

Therefore are the Three Supernal Heads illuminated; Two Heads, and One which comprehendeth them; and they hang in that Influence, and by It are they comprehended.

Hence becometh the ornament of the beard to be manifested, which is the occult Influence.

And those inferiors are conformed, like as the Most Holy Ancient One.

The Three Heads surround Him; thus all things can appear in the Three Heads; and when they are illuminated all things depend together from Him in the Three Heads, whereof two are on the two sides, and one which includeth them.

And if thou sayest, " Who is the Most Holy Ancient One? " come and see. The Supreme Head is that which is not known, nor comprehended, nor designated, and that (Head) comprehendeth all things.

And the Two Heads are contained in Itself. (Otherwise hang, etc.)

And then are all these things thus ordained; truly Himself existeth not in numeration, nor in system, nor in computation, but in the judgment of the heart.

Concerning this it is written, Ps. xxxix. 2, " I said I will take heed unto my ways, that I offend not with my tongue."

The place of commencement is found from the Most Holy Ancient One, and it is illuminated by the Influence. That is the Light of Wisdom.

And it is extended in thirty-two directions, and departeth from that hidden brain, from that Light which existeth in Itself.

And because the Most Holy Ancient One shineth in the beginning (otherwise, in the wisdom), this itself is this. And the same is that beginning from which manifestation is made.

And is conformed in the Three Heads, which One Head includeth.

And those three are extended into Microprosopus, and from them all things shine forth.

Thenceforth this Wisdom instituteth a formation, and pro-

---

[2] MZL = $40 \times 7 \times 30 = 77$, which is OZ, Strength or Vigor. This Gematria is worthy of note as giving the idea of foundational power.

duceth a certain river which floweth down and goeth forth to water the garden.

And it entereth into the head of Microprosopus, and formeth a certain other brain.

And thence it is extended and floweth forth into the whole body, and watereth all those plants (of the garden of Eden).

This is that which standeth written, Gen. ii. 9: "And a river went out of Eden to water the garden," etc.

But also this Wisdom instituteth another formation, and is extended and goeth into the head of Microprosopus, and formeth another brain.

That is the Light from which are produced those two rivulets' which are associated together, carved out hollows in the One Head, which is called the depth of the fountain.[3]

Concerning which it is written, Prov. iii. 20, "In DOTH, *Daath*,[4] Knowledge, the depths are broken up."

And it entereth into the head of Microprosopus, and formeth another brain.

And thenceforth is it extended and goeth into the interior parts of His body, and filleth all those conclaves and assemblies of His body.

This is that same which is written, Prov. xxiv. 4, "In Daath shall the secret places be filled."

And those shine from the Light of that supernal concealed brain which shineth in the Influence, MZL, of the Most Holy Ancient One.

And all things depend mutually from Himself, and mutually are bound together unto Himself, until He is known, because all things are one, and HVA, *Hoa*, He, the Ancient One, is all things, neither from Him can anything whatsoever be separated.

Into three other Lights, which are called the Fathers, do these three Lights shine, and these fathers shine into the children, and all things shine forth from the one place.[5]

When He, that Ancient One, who is the Grace of all Grace, is manifested, all things are found in light and in perfect happiness.

---

[3] I.e., the containing power.

[4] Daath is the conjunction of Chokmah and Binah. (See "Book of Concealed Mystery," chap. i. § 40.)

[5] This is analogous to the teaching of the "Sepher Yetzirah," that the Three Mothers, A, M, Sh, radiate into three paternal forms of the same. A, M, and Sh symbolize the potencies of Air, Water, and Fire.

This Eden is derived from the superior Eden, the Concealed with all Concealments.

And therefore is that Eden called the beginning in the Ancient One; neither yet, however, is there beginning or end.[6]

And since in Him beginning and end exist not, hence He is not called AThH, *Atah*, Thou; seeing that He is concealed and not revealed. But HVA, *Hoa*, He, is He called.

But in that aspect wherein the beginning is found, the name AThH, *Atah*, Thou, hath place, and the name AB, *Ab*, Father. For it is written, Isa. lxiii. 16: "Since *Atah*, Thou, art *Ab*, our Father."

In the teaching of the school of Rav Yeyeva the Elder, the universal rule is that Microprosopus be called AThH, *Atah*, Thou; but that the Most Holy Ancient One, who is concealed, be called HVA, *Hoa*, He; and also with reason.

Now truly in that place wherein beginning is found, is He thus called, although He is concealed.

And therefrom is the beginning, and it is called AThH, *Atah*, Thou; and He is the Father of the Fathers.

And that Father proceedeth from the Most Holy Ancient One, like as it is written, Job xxviii. 12: "And ChKMH, *Chokmah*,[7] Wisdom, is found from AIN, *Ain*, the Negatively Existent One;" and therefore is He not known.

Come and see! It is written *ibid.* 22, "The Elohim have known the path"; His path, properly speaking.

But again, further on: "VHVA, *Va-Hoa*, and He Himself knoweth His place;" His place properly speaking; much more His path; and much more this WISDOM which is concealed in the Most Holy Ancient One.

This Wisdom is the beginning of all things. Thencefrom are expanded the thirty-two paths. ShBILIN, *Shebilin*, Paths, I say; and not ARChIN, Archin, By-ways.

And in them is the Law comprehended, in the twenty-two letters and in the ten utterances.[8]

This Chokmah is the Father of Fathers, and in this Chokmah is beginning and end discovered; and therefore is there one Chokmah supernal, and another Chokmah inferior.

---

[6] For "commencement" denotes end, and end denotes "commencement"; how, then, in the Absolute can there be either? Nevertheless, in the Absolute must we seek for the hypothetical starting-point of life.

[7] Let the student carefully note that this is the second Sephira, the I of IHVH, the Father proceeding from Macroprosopus, Kether, as He proceedeth from Ain Soph.

[8] The Sephiroth, or numbers.

When Chokmah is extended, then is He called the Father of Fathers, for in none else are all things comprehended save in Him. (Otherwise, when they are expanded all things are called Chokmoth,[9] and the Father of Fathers; all things are comprehended in no place, save herein.)

As it is written, Ps. civ. 25, " All things in Chokmah hast Thou formed."

Rabbi Schimeon lifted up his hands, and rejoiced, and said, " Assuredly it is Eden or Paradise, and all things have their operation in this hour."

CHAPTER VIII

Concerning the Father and the Mother in Special

Come and behold. When the Most Holy Ancient One, the Concealed with all Concealments, desired to be formed forth, He conformed all things under the form of Male and Female; and in such place wherein Male and Female are comprehended.

For they could not permanently exist save in another aspect of the Male and the Female (their countenances being joined together).

And this Wisdom embracing all things, when it goeth forth and shineth forth from the Most Holy Ancient One, shineth not save under the form of Male and Female.

Therefore is this Wisdom extended, and it is found that it equally becometh Male and Female.

CHKMH AB BINH AM, *Chokmah Ab Binah Am:* Chokmah[1] is the Father, and Binah is the Mother, and therein are Chokmah, Wisdom, and Binah, Understanding, counterbalanced together in most perfect equality of Male and Female.

And therefore are all things established in the equality of Male and Female; for were it not so, how could they subsist!

This beginning is the Father of all things; the Father of all Fathers; and both are mutually bound together, and the one

---

[9] " Chokmoth " is plural of " Chokmah," Wisdom.

[1] Chokmah is the second and Binah is the third of the Sephiroth. This section is a sufficient condemnation of all those who wish to make out that woman is inferior to man.

path shineth into the other—Chokmah, Wisdom, as the Father; Binah, Understanding, as the Mother.

And therefore is it called BINH, as if (it were a transposition of) BN IH, *Ben Yah*, Son of IH (or *I, Yod, H, He*, and *BN*, the Son).

But They both are found to be the perfection of all things when They are associated together, and when the Son is in Them the Syntagma of all things findeth place.

For in Their conformations are They found to be the perfection of all things—Father and Mother, Son and Daughter.

These things have not been revealed save unto the Holy Superiors who have entered therein and departed therefrom, and have known the paths of the Most Holy God (may He be blessed!), so that they have not erred in them either on the right hand or on the left.

For thus it is written, Hos. xiv. 9, " The paths of Tetragrammaton are true, and the just shall walk in them," etc.

For these things are concealed, and the Holy Highest Ones shine in them, like as light proceedeth from the shining of a lantern.

These things are not revealed save unto those who have entered therein and departed therefrom; for as for him who hath not entered therein and departed therefrom. better were it for him that he had never been born.

For it hath been manifested before the Most Holy Ancient One, the Concealed with all Concealments, because these things have shone into mine heart in the perfection of the love and fear of the Most Holy God, may He be blessed!

And these, my sons, who are here present, know these things; for into these matters have they entered and therefrom have they departed; but neither yet into all (the secrets of them).[2]

But now are these things illustrated in (their) perfection, even as it was necessary. Blessed be my portion with them in this world!

Rabbi Schimeon said: All which I have said concerning the Most Holy Ancient One, and all which I have said concerning

---

[2] This clause refers to the " Unwritten Qabalah."

Microprosopus, all are one, all are HVA, *Hoa*, Himself, all are Unity, neither herein hath separation place.

Blessed be HVA, *Hoa*, He, and blessed be His Name unto the Ages of the Ages.

Come, behold! This beginning which is called Father,[3] is comprehended in I, *Yod*,[4] which dependeth from the Holy Influence.

And therefore is I, *Yod*, the Most Concealed of all the other letters.[5]

For I, *Yod*, is the beginning and the end of all things.

And that river which floweth on and goeth forth is called the World, which is ever to come and ceaseth never.

And this is the delight of the just, that they may be made worthy of that world which is to come, which ever watereth the garden of Eden, nor faileth.

Concerning this it is written, Isa. lviii. 11, " And like a fountain of water, whose waters fail not."

And that world to come is created through I, *Yod*.

As it is written, Gen. ii. 9, " And a river went forth out of Eden to water the garden."

For I, *Yod*, includeth two letters.

In the teaching of the school of Rav Yeyeva the Elder thus is the tradition. Wherefore are VD, *Vau Daleth*,[6] comprehended in IVD, *Yod?* Assuredly the planting of the garden is properly called V, *Vau;* and there is another garden which is D, *Daleth*, and by that Vau is Daleth watered, which is the symbol of the quaternary.[7]

And an Arcanum is extended from this passage, where it is written, " And a river went forth out of Eden."

What is Eden? It is the supernal CHKMH, *Chokmah*, Wisdom, and that is I, *Yod* (in *I, V, D*).

" To water the garden." That is V, *Vau*.

---

[3] Chokmah, the second Sephira, which, however, is as it were the repetition of Kether.

[4] That is, the letter I, Yod, in IHVH, which is said in the " Book of Concealed Mystery " to symbolize Macroprosopus only in its highest point.

[5] See " Book of Concealed Mystery," chap. ii. § 37; chap. iv. § 11.

[6] See " Book of Concealed Mystery," chap. ii. § 37.

[7] The amount of occult symbolism in this section is enormous, and the key of it is the name of the letter I, which

is IVD, Yod. This is a trinity of letters, and their numerical value is I = 10, V = 6, D = 4, total 20, equivalent to double I; but for reasons given in the " Book of Concealed Mystery " the second I is reproduced by a Hexad and a Tetrad—namely, V and D. I = 10, the decimal scale of Sephirotic notation, the key of processional creation; V = 6 = Tiphereth, and Microprosopus the Son united to D = 4, the Cross. Here is the mystery of the crucifixion of the Son on the tree of life; and again the Qabalah agrees with Christian symbolism.

" And thence it is divided, and goeth forth into four heads."
That is D, *Daleth*.

And all things are included in IVD, *Yod*, and therefore is
the Father called All, the Father of Fathers.

The beginning of all is called the Home of All. Whence
IVD, *Yod*, is the beginning and the end of all; like as it is
written, Ps. civ. 24, " All things in Chokmah hast Thou
made."

In His place He is not manifested, neither is He known;
when He is associated with the Mother, BAMA, *Be-Ama*,
then is He made known (otherwise, symbolized) in the
Mother, BAIMA, *Be-Aima*.[8]

And therefore is Aima known to be the consummation of
all things, and She is signified to be the beginning and the
end.

For all things are called Chokmah, and therein are all things
concealed; and the Syntagma of all things is the Holy Name.

Thus far have we mystically described that which we have
not said on all the other days. But now are the aspects shown
forth.

(As to the Sacred Name *IHVH*) I, *Yod*, is included in this
Chokmah, Wisdom; H, *He*, is Aima, and is called Binah, Understanding; VH, *Vau He*, are those two Children who are
produced from Aima, the Mother.

Also we have learned that the name BINH, Binah, comprehendeth all things. For in Her is I, *Yod*, which is associated with Aima, or the letter H, *He*, and together they
produce BN, *Ben*, the Son, and this is the word Binah. Father
and Mother, who are I, *Yod*, and H, *He*, with whom are interwoven the letters B, *Beth*, and N, *Nun*, which are BN, *Ben;*
and thus far regarding Binah.

Also is She called TнBVNH, *Thebunah*, the Special Intel-
ligence. Wherefore is She sometimes called Thebunah, and
not Binah?

Assuredly Thebunah is She called at that time in which Her
two Children appear, the Son and the Daughter, BN VBTн,

---

[8] " Be Ama," " with the Mother; "
here Ama, AMA, Mother = 42. Be
Aima, in the Mother; here Aima,
AIMA = 52 = BN, Ben, Son. This
Gematria is most important, because,
be it noted, Aima, AIMA, is the letter
I, Yod, which we have just been told
represents Chokmah, joined to AMA,
Mother, which is Binah, BINH, which
again is BN IH by Metathesis, Ben
Yod He—i.e., son of IH, eternally con-
joined in Briah.

Ben Va-Bath, who are VH, *Vau He;* and at that time is She called ThBVNH, *Thebunah.*

For all things are comprehended in those letters, VH, *Vau He,* which are BN VBTh, *Ben Va-Bath,* Son and Daughter; and all things are one system, and these are the letters ThBVNH.

In the Book of Rav Hamenuna the Elder it is said that Solomon revealeth the primal conformation (that is, the Mother) when he saith, Cant. i. 15, " Behold, thou art fair, my love "; wherefore he followeth it out himself.

And he calleth the second conformation the Bride, which is called the Inferior Woman.

And there are some who apply both these names (those, namely, of Love and Bride) to this Inferior Woman, but these are not so.

For the first H, *He* (of *IHVH*), is not called the Bride; but the last H, *He,* is called the Bride at certain times on account of many symbolic reasons.

Together They (*Chokmah* and *Binah, IH*) go forth, together They are at rest; the one ceaseth not from the other, and the one is never taken away from the other.

And therefore is it written, Gen. ii. 10, " And a river went forth out of Eden "—*i.e.,* properly speaking, it continually goeth forth and never faileth.

As it is written, Isa. lviii. 11, " And like a fountain of waters, whose waters fail not."

And therefore is She called " My love," since from the grace of kindred association They rest in perfect unity.

But the other is called the Bride, for when the Male cometh that He may consort with Her, then is She the Bride, for She, properly speaking, cometh forth as the Bride.

And therefore doth Solomon expound those two forms of the Woman; and concerning the first form indeed he worketh hiddenly, seeing it is hidden.

But the second form is more fully explained, seeing that it is not so hidden as the other.

But at the end all his praise pertaineth unto Her who is supernal, as it is written, Cant. vi. 9, " She is the only one of Her Mother, She is the choice one of Her that bare Her."

And since this Mother, Aima, is crowned with the crown

of the Bride, and the grace of the letter I, *Yod*, ceaseth not from Her forever, hence unto Her arbitration is committed all the liberty of those inferior, and all the liberty of all things, and all the liberty of sinners, so that all things may be purified.

As it is written, Lev. xvi. 30, " Since in that day he shall atone for you."

Also is it written, Lev. xxv. 10, " And ye shall hallow the fiftieth year." [9] This year is IVBL, *Yobel*, Jubilee.

What is Yobel? As it is written, Jer. xvii. 8, " VOL IVBL, *Va-El Yobel*, And spreadeth out her roots by the river "; therefore that river whichever goeth forth and floweth, and goeth forth and faileth not.

It is written, Prov. ii. 3, " If thou wilt call Binah the Mother, and wilt give thy voice unto Thebunah."

Seeing it is here said, " If thou wilt call Binah the Mother," wherefore is Thebunah added?

Assuredly, according as I have said, all things are supernal truth: Binah is higher than Thebunah. For in the word BINH, *Binah*, are shown Father, Mother, and Son; since by the letters IH, Father and Mother are denoted, and the letters BN, denoting the Son, are amalgamated with them.

ThBVNH, *Thebunah*, is the whole completion of the children, since it containeth the letters BN, *Ben*, BTh, *Bath*, and VH, *Vau He*, by which are denoted the Son and Daughter.

Yet AB VAM, *Ab Ve-Am*, the Father and the Mother, are not found, save BAIMA, *Be-Aima*, in the Mother, for the venerable Aima broodeth over Them, neither is She uncovered.

Whence it cometh that that which embraceth the two Children is called ThBVNH, *Thebunah*, and that which embraceth the Father, the Mother, and the Son is called BINH, *Binah*.

And when all things are comprehended, they are comprehended therein, and are called by that name of Father, Mother, and Son.

And these are ChKMH, *Wisdom*, Father; BINH, *Understanding*, Mother; and DOTh, *Däath*, Knowledge.

Since that Son [10] assumeth the symbols of His Father and

---

[9] The number answering to the " fifty gates of Binah." See " Book of Concealed Mystery," chap. i. § 46.

[10] Compare this with the Egyptian Horus, the son of Isis and Osiris. Also notice the interchange of symbols between Amen, Kneph, and Khom. The name of the great Egyptian God Amen is noticeable when we compare it with the qabalistic name AMN.

of His Mother, and is called DOTH, *Däath*, Knowledge, since He is the testimony of Them both.

And that Son is called the first-born, as it is written, Exod. iv. 22, " Israel is my first-born son."

And since He is called first-born, therefore it implieth dual offspring.

And when He increaseth, in His Crown appear three divisions.[1]

But whether it be taken in this way or in that, there are as well two as three divisions herein, for all things are one; and so is it in this (light) or in that.[2]

Nevertheless, He (the Son) receiveth the inheritance of His Father and of His Mother.

What is that inheritance? These two crowns, which are hidden within Them, which They pass on in succession to this Son.[3]

From the side of the Father (*Chokmah*) there is one Crown concealed therein, which is called Chesed.

And from the side of the Mother (*Binah*) there is one Crown, which is called Geburah.

And all those crown His head (*i.e.*, the Head of Microprosopus), and He taketh them.

And when that Father and Mother shine above Him, all (these crowns) are called the phylacteries of the Head, and that Son taketh all things, and becometh the heir of all.

And He passeth on His inheritance unto the Daughter, and the Daughter is nourished by Him. But, properly speaking, henceforth (from the parents) doth the Son become the heir, and not the Daughter.

The Son becometh the heir of His Father and of His Mother, and not the Daughter, but by Him is the Daughter cherished.

As it is written, Dan. iv. 12, " And in that tree food for all."

And if thou sayest all, assuredly He as well as She are

---

[1] Compare with this the alchemical symbolism of Duenech, the King of Earth, after being overwhelmed by the waters, rising again, glorified and crowned with the triple crown of silver, iron, and gold—Chesed, Geburah, and Tiphereth, in the alchemic Sephiroth of the metals.

[2] The meaning is, that Father and Mother are contained in the Son; for these are the second, third, and sixth Sephiroth—i.e., 2, 3, and 6; and both 2 and 3 are contained in 6, for $2 \times 3 = 6$.

[3] The reflexive essence of Kether, the Crown, which operates in Chokmah and Binah.

called TzDIQ, *Tzediq*, Just, and TzDQ, *Tzedeq*, Justice, which are in one and are one.

All things are thus. Father and Mother are mutually contained in and associated with Themselves.

And the Father is the more concealed (of the two), and the whole adhereth unto the Most Holy Ancient One.

And dependeth from the Holy Influence, which is the Ornament of all Ornaments.

And they, the Father and the Mother, constitute the abode, as I have said.

As it is written, Prov. xxiv. 3, 4, " Through Chokmah is the abode constructed, and by Thebunah is it established, and in Däath shall the chambers be filled with all precious and pleasant riches."

Also it is written, Prov. xxii. 18, " For it is a pleasant thing if thou keep (*Däath*) within thee."

This is the system of all things, even as I have said, and (all things) depend from the Glorious Holy Influence.

Rabbi Schimeon said : In the (former) Assembly I revealed not all things, and all those things have been concealed even until now.

And I have wished to conceal them, even unto the world to come, because there also a certain question will be propounded unto me.

As it is written, Isa. xxxiii. 6, " And Chokmah and Däath shall be the stability of thy times, and strength of salvation ; the fear of Tetragrammaton is His treasure," etc., and they shall seek out Wisdom, Chokmah.

Now truly thus is the will of the Most Holy and Blessed God, and without shame will I enter in before His palace.

It is written, 1 Sam. ii. 3, " Since AL DOVTh, *El Daoth*,[4] is Tetragrammaton." Daoth, or of Knowledges (plural), properly speaking, for He acquireth Daoth by inheritance.

Through Daoth are all His palaces filled, as it is written, Prov. xxix, " And in Däath shall the chambers be filled."

And therefore Däath is not furthermore revealed, for It occultly pervadeth Him inwardly.

And is comprehended in that brain and in the whole body, since " El Daoth is Tetragrammaton."

[4] Plural of " Däath."

In the "Book of the Treatise" it is said concerning these words, "Since El Daoth is Tetragrammaton," read not DOVTh, *Daoth*, of knowledges, but ODVTh,[5] *Edoth*, of *testimony*.

For HVA, *Hoa*, He Himself, is the testimony of all things, the testimony of the two portions.

And it is said, Ps. lxxviii. 5, "And He established a testimony, ODVTh, in Jacob."

Moreover, also, although we have placed that matter in the "Book of Concealed Mystery," still also there what is mentioned of it is correct, and so all things are beautiful and all things are true.

When the matter is hidden, that Father and Mother contain all things, and all things are concealed in them.

And they themselves are hidden beneath the Holy Influence of the Most Ancient of all Antiquity; in Him are they concealed, in Him are all things included.

HVA, *Hoa*, He Himself, is all things; blessed be Hoa, and blessed be His Name in eternity, and unto the ages of the ages.

All the words of the conclave of the Assembly are beautiful, and all are holy words—words which decline not either unto the right hand or unto the left.

All are words of hidden meaning for those who have entered in and departed thence, and so are they all.

And those words have hereunto been concealed; therefore have I feared to reveal the same, but now they are revealed.

And I reveal them in the presence of the Most Holy Ancient King, for not for mine own glory, nor for the glory of my Father's house, do I this; but I do this that I may not enter in ashamed before His palaces.

Henceforth I only see that He, God the Most Holy—may He be blessed!—and all these truly just men who are here found, can all consent (hereunto) with me.

For I see that all can rejoice in these my nuptials, and that they all can be admitted unto my nuptials in that world. Blessed be my portion!

Rabbi Abba saith that when (Rabbi Schimeon) had finished

---

[5] By Metathesis.

this discourse, the Holy Light (*i.e.*, Rabbi **Schimeon**) lifted up his hands and wept, and shortly after smiled.

For he wished to reveal another matter, and said: I have been anxious concerning this matter all my days, and now they give me not leave.

But having recovered himself he sat down, and murmured with his lips and bowed himself thrice; neither could any other man behold the place where he was, much less him.

CHAPTER IX

CONCERNING MICROPROSOPUS AND HIS BRIDE IN GENERAL

He said: Mouth, mouth, which hath followed out all these things, they shall not dry up thy fountain.

Thy fountain goeth forth and faileth not: surely concerning thee may this be applied, "And a river went forth out of Eden"; also that which is written, "Like a fountain of waters whose waters fail not."

Now I testify concerning myself, that all the days which I have lived I have desired to behold this day, yet was it not the will (of God).

For with this crown is this day crowned, and now as yet I intend to reveal certain things before God the Most Holy—may He be blessed!—and all these things crown mine head.

And this day [1] suffereth not increase, neither can it pass on into the place of another day, for this whole day hath been yielded unto my power.

And now I begin to reveal these things, that I may not enter ashamed into the world to come. Therefore I begin and say:

"It is written, Ps. lxxxix. 14: ' TzDQ VMShPT, *Tzedeq Va-Meshephat*, Justice and Judgment are the abode of Thy throne; CHSD VAMTH, *Chesed Va-Emeth*, Mercy and Truth shall go before Thy countenance.'"

What wise man will examine this, so that he may behold His paths, (those, namely) of the Most Holy Supernal One, the judgments of truth, the judgments which are crowned with His supernal crowns.

---

[1] Meaning the period of revealing these matters, not exactly a day of twenty-four hours: day in the scriptural and qabalistical sense.

For I say that all the lights which shine from the Supreme Light, the Most Concealed of All, are all paths (leading) toward that Light.

And in that Light which existeth in those single paths, whatsoever is revealed is revealed.

And all those lights adhere mutually together, this light in that light, and that light in this light.

And they shine mutually into each other, neither are they divided separately from each other.

That Light, I say, of those lights, severally and conjointly, which are called the conformations of the King, or of the Crown of the King, that which shineth and adhereth to that Light, which is the innermost of all things, nor ever shineth without them.

And therefore do all things ascend in one path, and all things are crowned by one and the same thing, and one thing is not separated from another, since HVA, *Hoa*, Himself, and His Name, are one.

That Light which is manifested is called the Vestment; for He Himself, the King, is the Light of all the innermost.

In that Light is Hoa, Who is not separated nor manifested.

And all those lights and all those luminaries shine forth from the Most Holy Ancient One, the Concealed with all Concealments, who is the Highest Light.

And whensoever the matter is accurately examined, all those lights which are expanded are no longer found, save only that Highest Light.

Who is hidden and not manifested, through those vestments of ornament which are the vestments of truth, QShVT, *Qeshot,* the forms of truth, the lights of truth.

Two light-bearers are found, which are the conformation of the throne of the King; and they are called TzDQ, *Tzedeq,* Justice, and MShPT, *Meshephat,* Judgment.

And they are the beginning and the consummation. And through them are all the Judgments crowned, as well superior as inferior.

And they all are concealed in Meshephat. And from that Meshephat is Tzedeq nourished.

And sometimes they call the same, MLKI TzDQ MLK

SHLM, *Meleki Tzedeq Melek Shalem*, Melchizedek, King of Salem.

When the judgments are crowned by Meshephat, all things are mercy; and all things are in perfect peace, because the one temperateth the other.

Tzedeq and the Rigors are reduced into order, and all these descend into the world in peace and in mercy.

And then is the hour sanctified, so that the Male and the Female are united, and the worlds all and several exist in love and in joy.

But whensoever sins are multiplied in the world, and the sanctuary is polluted, and the Male and the Female are separated.[2]

And when that strong Serpent beginneth to arise, Woe, then, unto thee, O World! who in that time art nourished by this Tzedeq. For then arise many slayers of men and executioners (of judgment) in thee, O World. Many just men are withdrawn from thee.

But wherefore is it thus? Because the Male is separated from the Female, and Judgment, Meshephat, is not united unto Justice, Tzedeq.

And concerning this time it is written, Prov. xiii. 23, " There is that is destroyed, because therein is not Meshephat." Since Meshephat is departed from this Tzedeq which is not therefore restrained; and Tzedeq hath operation after another manner.

And concerning this (matter) thus speaketh Solomon the king, Eccles. vii. 16: " All these things have I seen in the days of my HBL, *Hebel;* there is a just man who perisheth in his Tzedeq," etc.

Where by the word HBL, *Hebel* (which is usually translated " vanity "), is understood the breath from those supernal breathers forth which are called the nostrils of the King.

But when he saith HBLI, *Hebeli,* of my breath, Tzedeq, Justice, is to be understood, which is MLKVThA QDIShA, *Malkutha Qadisha,* the holy Malkuth (*Sanctum Regnum,* the Holy Kingdom).

For when She is stirred up in Her judgments and severities,

---

[2] In other words, where there is unbalanced force, there is the origin of evil.

then hath this saying place, " There is a just man who perished in his Tzedeq."

For what reason? Because Judgment, Meshephat, is far from Justice, Tzedeq. And therefore is it said, Prov. xiii. 23, " And there is that is destroyed because therein is not Meshephat."

Come and see! When some sublimely just man is found in the world, who is dear unto God the Most Holy One—may He be blessed!—then even if Tzedeq, Justice, alone be stirred up, still on account of him the world can bear it.

And God the Most Holy—may He be blessed!—increaseth His glory so that He may not be destroyed by the severity (of the judgments).

But if that just man remaineth not in his place, then from the midst is he taken away for example by that Meshephat, Judgment, so that before it he cannot maintain his place, how much less before Tzedeq, Justice.

David the king said at first, Ps. xxvi. 2, " Try me, O Tetragrammaton, and prove me!" For I shall not be destroyed by all the severities, not even by Tzedeq, Justice Herself, seeing that I am joined thereunto.

For what is written, Ps. xvii. 15, " In Tzedeq, Justice, I will behold Thy countenance." Therefore, properly speaking, I cannot be destroyed through Tzedeq, seeing that I can maintain myself in its severities.[3]

But after that he had sinned, he was even ready to be consumed by that Meshephat, Judgment. Whence it is written, Ps. cxliii. 2, " And enter not into Meshephat, Judgment, with Thy servant!"

Come and see! When that Tzedeq, Justice, is mitigated by that Meshephat, Judgment, then it is called TzDQH, Tzedeqah, Liberality.

And the world is tempered by Chesed, Mercy, and is filled therewith.

As it is written, Ps. xxxii. 5: " Delighting in TzDQH, Liberality, and MShPT, Judgment; the earth is full of the ChSD, Mercy, of Tetragrammaton.

I testify concerning myself, that during my whole life I have

---

[3] Because in those severities, and behind them, he can see the Countenance of God.

been solicitous in the world, that I should not fall under the severities of Justice, nor that the world should be burned up with the flames thereof.

As it is written, Prov. xxx. 20, " She eateth and wipeth her mouth."

Thenceforward and afterward all and singular are near unto the Abyss.

And verily in this generation certain just men are given (upon earth); but they are few who arise that they may defend the flock from the four angels (otherwise, but judgments arise against the world, and desire to rush upon us).

CHAPTER X

Concerning Microprosopus in Especial, with Certain Digressions; and Concerning the Edomite Kings

Hereunto have I propounded how one thing agreeth with another; and I have expounded those things which have been concealed in the most Holy Ancient One, the Concealed with all Concealments; and how these are connected with those.

But now for a time I will discourse concerning the requisite parts of Microprosopus; especially concerning those which were not manifested in the Conclave of the Assembly, and which have been concealed in mine heart, and have not been given forth in order therefrom.

Hereunto have I mystically and in a subtle manner propounded all those matters. Blessed is his portion who entereth therein and departeth therefrom, and (blessed the portion) of those who shall be the heirs of that inheritance.

As it is written, Ps. cxliv. 15, " Blessed are the people with whom it is so," etc.

Now these be the matters which we have propounded. The Father [1] and the Mother [2] adhere unto the Ancient One, and also unto His conformation; since they depend from the Hidden Brain, Concealed with all Concealments, and are connected therewith.

And although the Most Holy Ancient One hath been con-

---

[1] Chokmah.   [2] Binah.

formed (as it were) alone (*i.e.*, apparently apart from all things
at first sight); yet when all things are accurately inspected, all
things are HVA, *Hoa*, Himself, the Ancient One, alone.

Hoa is and Hoa shall be; and all those forms cohere with
Himself, are concealed in Himself, and are not separated from
Himself.

The Hidden Brain is not manifested, and (Microprosopus)
doth not depend immediately from it.

The Father and the Mother proceed from this Brain, and depend from It, and are connected with It.

(Through Them) Microprosopus dependeth from the Most
Holy Ancient One, and is connected (with Him). And these
things have we already revealed in the Conclave of the Assembly.

Blessed is his portion who entereth therein and departeth
therefrom, and hath known the paths; so that he declineth not
unto the right hand, or unto the left.

But if any man entereth not therein and departeth there-
from, better were it for that (man) that he had never been born.
For thus it is written, Hos. xiv. 10, " True are Thy ways, O
Tetragrammaton! "

Rabbi Schimeon spake and said: Through the whole day
have I meditated on that saying where it is said, Ps. xxxiv. 2,
" My Nephesch [3] shall rejoice in Tetragrammaton, the humble shall hear thereof and rejoice "; and now that whole text
is confirmed (in my mind).

" My Nephesch shall rejoice in Tetragrammaton." This is
true, for my Neschamah is connected therewith, radiateth
therein, adhereth thereto, and is occupied thereabout, and in
this same occupation is exalted in its place.

" The humble shall hear thereof and rejoice." All those
just and blessed men who have come into communion with
God, the Most Holy—blessed be He!—all hear and rejoice.

Ah! now is the Holy One confessed; and therefore " magnify Tetragrammaton with me, and let us exalt His Name
together! "

Thus is it written, Gen. xxxvi. 31, " And those are the kings
who reigned in the land of Edom." And also it is written

[3] See Introduction concerning the parts of the soul, Chiah, Neschamah,
Ruach, and Nephesch.

thus, Ps. xlviii. 4, "Since, lo! the kings assembled, they passed away together."

"In the land of Edom." That is, in the place wherewith the judgments are connected.

"They passed away together." As it is written, "And he died, and there reigned in his stead."

"They themselves beheld, so were they astonished; they feared, and hasted away." Because they remained not in their place, since the conformations of the King had not as yet been formed, and the Holy City and its walls were not as yet prepared.

This is that which followeth in the text, "As we have heard, so have we seen, in the city," etc. For all did not endure.

But She (the Bride) now subsisteth beside the Male, with Whom She abideth.

This is that which is written, Gen. xxxvi. 39, "And Hadar reigned in his stead, and the name of his city was Pau, and the name of his wife was Mehetabel, the daughter of Matred, the daughter of Mizaheb."

Assuredly this have we before explained in the Assembly.[4]

Now, also, in the book of the teaching of Rav Hamenuna the Elder it is said, "And Hadar reigned in his stead." The word HDR, *Hadar*, is properly to be expounded according unto that which is said, Lev. xxiii. 40, "The fruit of trees which are HDR, *Hadar*, goodly."

"And in the name of his wife Mehetabel," as it is written (in the text just cited), "branches of palm-trees." ⸱

Also it is written, Ps. xcii. 3, "The just man shall flourish as the palm-tree." For this is of the male and female sex.

She is called "the daughter of Matred"; that is, the Daughter from that place wherein all things are bound together, which is called AB, Father.

Also it is written, Job xxviii. 13, "Man knoweth not the price thereof, neither is it found in the land of the living."

She is the Daughter of Aima, the Mother; from Whose side the judgments are applied which strive against all things.

"The Daughter of Mizaheb;" because She hath nourishment from the two Countenances (Chokmah and Binah, which are within Kether); and shineth with two colors—

---

[4] See "Greater Holy Assembly," ch. xlii. §§ 984-996; ch. xxvi. §§ 513-532.

namely from CHSD, *Chesed*, Mercy; and from DIN, *Din*, Judgment.

For before the world was established Countenance beheld not Countenance.[5]

And therefore were the Prior Worlds destroyed, for the Prior Worlds were formed without (equilibrated) conformation.

But these which existed not in conformation are called vibrating flames and sparks, like as when the worker in stone striketh sparks from the flint with his hammer, or as when the smith smiteth the iron and dasheth forth sparks on every side.

And these sparks which fly forth flame and scintillate, but shortly they are extinguished. And these are called the Prior Worlds.

And therefore have they been destroyed, and persist not, until the Most Holy Ancient One can be conformed, and the workman can proceed unto His work.

And therefore have we related in our discourse that that ray sendeth forth sparks upon sparks in 320 directions.

And those sparks are called the Prior Worlds, and suddenly they perished.

Then proceeded the workman unto His work, and was conformed, namely as Male and Female.

And those sparks became extinct and died, but now all things subsist.

From a Light-Bearer of insupportable brightness proceeded a Radiating [6] Flame, dashing off like a vast and mighty hammer those sparks which were the Prior Worlds.

And with most subtle ether were these intermingled and bound mutually together, but only when they were conjoined together, even the Great Father and Great Mother.

From *Hoa*, Himself, is AB, the Father; and from *Hoa*, Himself, is Ruach, the Spirit; Who are hidden in the Ancient of Days, and therein is that ether concealed.

And It was connected with a light-bearer, which went forth from that Light-Bearer of insupportable brightness, which is hidden in the Bosom of Aima, the Great Mother.

[5] See " Book of Concealed Mystery," chap. i. §§ 2, 3, 4 et seq.
[6] Compare this with Miölner, the hammer of Thor, of Scandinavian mythology.

CHAPTER XI

Concerning the Brain of Microprosopus and its Connections

And when both can be conjoined and bound together mutually (*i.e.*, the Father and the Mother), there proceedeth thenceforth a certain hard Skull.

And it is extended on its sides, so that there may be one part on one side, and another one on another side.

For as the Most Holy Ancient One is found to include equally in Himself the Three Heads,[1] so all things are symbolized under the form of the Three Heads, as we have stated.

Into this skull (of Microprosopus) distilleth the dew from the White Head (of Macroprosopus), and covereth it.

And that dew appeareth to be of two colors, and by it is nourished the field of the holy apple trees.

And from this dew of this Skull is the manna prepared for the just in the world to come.[2]

And by it shall the dead be raised to life.

But that manna hath not at any other time been prepared so that it might descend from this dew, save at that time when the Israelites were wandering in the wilderness, and the Ancient One supplied them with food from this place; because that afterward it did not fall out so more fully.

This is the same which is said, Exod. xvi. 4, " Behold I rain upon you bread from heaven." And also that passage where it is thus written, Gen. xxvii. 28, " And the Elohim shall give unto thee of the dew of heaven."

These things occur in that time. Concerning another time it is written, " The food of man is from God the Most Holy One—blessed be He! "—and that dependeth from MZLA, *Mezla*, the Influence; assuredly from the Influence rightly so called.

And therefore is it customary to say, " Concerning children, life, and nourishment, the matter dependeth not from merit,

---

[1] Chokmah and Binah, included in Kether.
[2] It is to be noted that this word is MNA, Manna, and is a Metathesis of the letters of AMN, Amen, which has been shown in the " Book of Concealed Mystery " to be equal by Gematria to IHVH ADNI.

but from the Influence." For all these things depend from this
Influence, as we have already shown.

Nine thousand myriads of worlds receive influence from and
are upheld by that GVLGLThA, *Golgeltha*, Skull.

And in all things is that subtle AVIRA, *Auira*, Ether,[3] contained, as It Itself containeth all things, and as in It all things
are comprehended.

His countenance is extended in two sides,[4] in two lights,
which in themselves contain all things.

And when His countenance (*i.e.*, that of Microprosopus)
looketh back upon the countenance of the Most Holy Ancient
One, all things are called ARK AFIM, *Arikh Aphim*, Vastness of Countenance.

What is ARK APIM, or Vastness of Countenance? Also
it should rather be called ARVK AFIM, *Arokh Aphim*, Vast
in Countenance.

Assuredly thus is the tradition, since also He prolongeth
His wrath against the wicked. But the phrase ARK APIM,
Arikh Aphim, also implies the same as "healing power of
countenance."

Seeing that health is never found in the world save when
the countenances (of Macroprosopus and Microprosopus)
mutually behold each other.

In the hollow of the Skull (of Microprosopus) shine three
lights. And although thou canst call them three, yet not-
withstanding are there four,[5] as we have before said.

He (Microprosopus) is the heir of His Father and of His
Mother, and there are two inheritances from Them; all which
things are bound together under the symbol of the Crown of
His Head. And they are the phylacteries of His Head.

After that these are united together after a certain manner they shine, and go forth into the Three Cavities of the
Skull.

(And then) singly they are developed each after its own manner, and they are extended through the whole body.

[3] ? Astral Light.
[4] Right and left; while in Macroprosopus "all is right."
[5] At first sight this seems a contradiction, but on careful examination the
difficulty disappears. A triangle is a fit
expression of the number 3. It has
three angles, it has three sides; but

there is the whole figure itself also,
which is the synthesis of the sides and
the angles. So there are the three angles
and the whole figure itself which contains them, and thus completes the
Trinity by the Quaternary: in the
Tetragrammaton, IHV, and H final,
which forms the synthesis.

But they are associated together in two Brains, and the third Brain containeth the others in itself.[6]

And it adhereth as well to the one side as to the other, and is expanded throughout the whole body.

And therefrom are formed two colors mixed together in one, and His countenance shineth.

And the colors of His countenance are symbols of Ab (the Father) and Aima (the Mother), and are called Däath (Knowledge) in Däath.

As it is written, 1 Sam. ii. 3, "Since El Däoth (plural) is Tetragrammaton," because in Him there are two colors.

Unto Him (Microprosopus) are works ascribed diversely; but to the Most Holy Ancient One (operations) are not ascribed diversely.

For what reason doth He (Microprosopus) admit of variable disposition? Because He is the heir of two inheritances (i.e., from Chokmah and Binah).

Also it is written, Ps. xviii. 26, "With the merciful man thou shalt show thyself merciful."

But also truly and rightly have the Companions decided concerning that saying where it is written, Gen. xxix. 12, "And Jacob declared unto Rachel that he was her father's brother, and that he was Rebekah's son."

It is written "Rebekah's son," and not "the son of Isaac." And all the mysteries are in Chokmah.[7]

And therefore is (Chokmah) called the Perfection of all; and to it is ascribed the name of Truth.

And therefore is it written, "And Jacob declared," and not written, "and Jacob said."

Those (two) colors are extended throughout the whole Body (of Microprosopus), and His Body cohereth with them.

In the Most Holy Ancient One, the Concealed with all Concealments, (things) are not ascribed diversely, and unto Him do they not tend (diversely), since the whole is the same (with itself) and (thus is) life unto all (things); and from Him judgment dependeth not (directly).

---

[6] Thus rigidly following out the rule of the symbolism before given, that Chokmah and Binah are contained in Kether. In this is the key of all religions.

[7] BChKMThA, Be-Chokmatha; ChK-MThA is the emphatic Chaldee form of ChKMA, which is Chaldee for Hebrew ChKMH.

But concerning Him (Microprosopus) it is written, that unto Him are ascribed (diverse) works, properly speaking.

CHAPTER XII

CONCERNING THE HAIR OF MICROPROSOPUS

From the skull of the Head (of Microprosopus) depend all those chiefs and leaders (otherwise, all those thousands and tens of thousands), and also from the locks of the hair.

Which are black, and mutually bound together, and which mutually cohere.

But they adhere unto the Supernal Light from the Father, AB, *Ab*, which surroundeth His Head (*i.e.*, that of Microprosopus); and unto the Brain, which is illuminated from the Father.

Thencefrom, even from the light which surroundeth His Head (*i.e.*, that of Microprosopus) from the Mother, Aima, and from the second Brain, proceed long locks upon locks (of hair).

And all adhere unto and are bound together with those locks [1] which have their connection with the Father.

And because (these locks are) mutually intermingled with each other, and mutually intertwined with each other, hence all the Brains are connected with the Supernal Brain (of Macroprosopus).

And hence all the regions which proceed from the Three Cavities of the Skull are mingled mutually together, as well pure as impure, and all those accents and mysteries are as well hidden as manifest.

And since all the Brains have a secret connection with the ears of Tetragrammaton, in the same way as they shine in the crown of the Head, and enter into the hollow places of the Skull.

Hence all these locks hang over and cover the sides of the ears, as we have elsewhere said.

And therefore is it written, 2 Kings xix. 16, " Incline, O Tetragrammaton, Thine ear, and hear ! "

---

[1] That is, the locks which have their origin in the influence of the Great Mother are interwoven mutually with those which originate from Chokmah.

Hence is the meaning of this passage, which is elsewhere given, " If any man wisheth the King to incline His ear unto him, let him raise [2] the head of the King and remove the hair from above the ears; then shall the King hear him in all things whatsoever he desireth."

In the parting of the hair a certain path is connected with the (same) path of the Ancient of Days, and therefrom are distributed all the paths of the precepts of the Law.

And over these (locks of hair) are set all the Lords of Lamentation and Wailing; and they depend from the single locks.

And these spread a net for sinners, so that they may not comprehend those paths.

This is that which is said, Prov. iv. 18, " The path of the wicked is as darkness."

And these all depend from the rigid locks; hence also these are entirely rigid, as we have before said.

In the softer (locks) adhere the Lords of Equilibrium, as it is written, Ps. xxv. 10, " All the paths of Tetragrammaton are ChSD, *Chesed*, and AMTh, *Emeth*, Mercy and Truth."

And thus when these developments of the Brain emanate from the Concealed Brain, hencefrom each singly deriveth its own nature.

From the one Brain the Lords of Equilibrium proceed through those softer locks, as it is written, Ps. xxv. 10, " All the paths of Tetragrammaton are Chesed and Emeth."

From the second Brain the Lords of Lamentation and Wailing proceed through those rigid locks and depend (from them). Concerning whom it is written, Prov. iv. 19, " The path of the wicked is as darkness; they know not wherein they stumble."

What is this passage intended to imply? Assuredly the sense of these words: " they know not," is this: " They do not know, and they do not wish to know."

" Wherein they stumble." Do not read " BMH, *Bameh*, wherein," but " BAIMA, *Be-Aima*, in Aima, the Mother," they stumble; that is, through those who are attributed unto the side of the Mother.

---

[2] Meaning, let him supplicate Macroprosopus, developed in the forms of Chokmah and Binah, which are summed up in Aima the Great Mother, to incline Microprosopus to be favorable. This is identical with the Catholic custom of invoking the intercession of the Virgin with her Son; for Mary = Mare = Sea; and the great Sea is Binah.

What is the side of the Mother? Severe Rigor, whereunto are attributed the Lords of Lamentation and Wailing.

From the third Brain the Lords of Lords proceed through those locks arranged in the middle condition (*i.e.*, partly hard and partly soft), and depend (therefrom); and they are called the Luminous and the Non-Luminous Countenances.

And concerning these it is written, Prov. iv. 26, " Ponder the path of thy feet."

And all these are found in those locks of the hair of the Head.

CHAPTER XIII

Concerning the Forehead of Microprosopus

The forehead of the Skull (of Microprosopus) is the forehead for visiting sinners (otherwise, for rooting out sinners).

And when that forehead is uncovered there are excited the Lords of Judgments against those who are shameless in their deeds.

This forehead hath a rosy redness. But at that time when the forehead of the Ancient One is uncovered over against this forehead, the latter appeareth white as snow.

And that time is called the Time of Grace for all.

In the " Book of the Teaching of the School of Rav Yeyeva the Elder " it is said: The forehead is according as the forehead[1] of the Ancient One. Otherwise, the letter *Cheth*, CH, is placed between the other two letters, according to this passage, Num. xxiv. 17, " VMCHTz, *Ve-Machetz*, and shall smite the corners of Moab? "

And we have elsewhere said that it is also called NTzCH, *Netzach*, the neighboring letters (M and N, neighboring letters in the alphabet, that is, and allied in sense, for *Men* = Water, and *Nun* = Fish, that which lives in the water) being counterchanged. (*Netzach* = Victory, and is the seventh Sephira.)

But many are the NTzCHIM, *Netzachim*, Victories;[2] so

[1] The word translated " forehead " is MTzCh, Metzach; now if a metathesis be formed of this word by placing the last letter between the first and second letters, we get MChTz, " he shall smite." Hence the first form symbolizes Mercy, and the second Severity.

[2] And therefore is the divine name of Tzabaoth, or hosts, attributed both to Netzach and to Hod, the seventh and eighth Sephiroth.

that another (development of) Netzach may be elevated into another path, and other Netzachim may be given which are extended throughout the whole body (of Microprosopus).

But on the day of the Sabbath, at the time of the afternoon prayers, the forehead of the Most Holy Ancient One is uncovered, so that the judgments may not be aroused.

And all the judgments are subjected; and although they be there, yet are they not called forth. (Otherwise, and they are appeased.)

From this forehead depend twenty-four tribunals, for all those who are shameless in their deeds.

And it is written, Ps. lxxiii. 11: "And they have said, 'How can El know? and is there knowledge in the Most High?'"

But truly (the tribunals) are only twenty; wherefore are four added? Assuredly, in respect of the punishments of the inferior tribunals which depend from the Supernals.

Therefore there remain twenty.[3] And therefore unto none do they adjudge capital punishment until he shall have fulfilled and reached the age of twenty years, in respect of these twenty tribunals.

But in our doctrine regarding our Arcana have we taught that the books which are contained in the Law refer back unto these twenty-four.

CHAPTER XIV

Concerning the Eyes of Microprosopus

The Eyes of the Head (of Microprosopus) are those eyes from which sinners cannot guard themselves; the eyes which sleep, and yet which sleep not.

And therefore are they called "Eyes like unto doves, KIVNIM, Ke-Ionim." What is IVNIM, Ionim? Surely it is said, Lev. xxv. 17, "Ye shall not deceive any man his neighbor.'

And therefore is it written, Ps. xciv. 7, "IH, Yah, shall not behold." And shortly after verse 9, "He that planteth the ear, shall He not hear? He that formeth the eye, shall He not see?"

---

[3] And 20 is H, He, in the four worlds, for H = 5. which multiplied by 4 = 20.

The part which is above the eyes (the eyebrows) consisteth of the hairs, which are distributed in certain proportions.

From those hairs depend 1,700 Lords of Inspection for striving in battles. And then all their emissaries arise and unclose the eyes.

In the skin which is above the eyes (the eyelids) are the eyelashes, and thereunto adhere thousand thousands Lords of Shields.

And these be called the covering of the eyes. And all those which are called (under the classification of) the eyes of IHVH, Tetragrammaton, are not unclosed, nor awake, save in that time when these coverings of the eyelashes be separated from each other; namely, the lower from the upper (eyelashes).

And when the lower eyelashes are separated from the upper, and disclose the abode of vision, then are the eyes opened in the same manner as when one awaketh from his sleep.

Then are the eyes rolled around, and (Microprosopus) looketh back upon the open eye (of Macroprosopus), and they are bathed in its white brilliance.

And when they are thus whitened, the Lords of the Judgments are turned aside from the Israelites. And therefore it is written, Ps. xliv. 24: "Awake: wherefore sleepest thou, O Tetragrammaton? Make haste," etc.

Four colors appear in those eyes; from which shine the four coverings of the phylacteries, which shine through the emanations of the Brain.

Seven, which are called the eyes of Tetragrammaton, and the inspection, proceed from the black color of the eyes; as we have said.

As it is written, Zech. iii. 9, "Upon one stone seven eyes." And these colors flame forth on this side.

From the red go forth others, the Lords of Examination for Judgment.

And these are called: "The eyes of Tetragrammaton going forth throughout the whole earth."

Where it is said (in the feminine gender) "MShVTTVTh, Meshotetoth, going forth," and not "MShVTTIM, Meshotetim," in the masculine, because all are judgment.

From the yellow proceed others who are destined to make manifest deeds as well good as evil.

As it is written, Job xxxiv. 21, " Since His eyes are upon the ways of man." And these, Zach. iv. 10, are called " The eyes of Tetragrammaton, MShVTTIM, *Meshotetim,* going forth around, but in the masculine gender, because these extend in two directions—toward the good and toward the evil.

From the white brilliance proceed all those mercies and all those benefits which are found in the world, so that through them it may be well for the Israelites.

And then all those three colors are made white, so that He may have pity upon them.

And those colors are mingled together mutually, and mutually do they adhere unto each other. Each one affecteth with its color that which is next unto it.

Excepting the white brilliance wherein all are comprehended when there is need, for this enshroudeth them all.

So therefore no man can convert all the inferior colors—the black, red, and yellow—into the white brilliance.

For only with this glance (of Macroprosopus) are they all united and transformed into the white brilliance.

His eyelashes (*i.e.,* those of Microprosopus, for to the eye of Macroprosopus neither eyebrows nor eyelashes are attributed) are not found, when (his eyes) desire to behold the colors; seeing that his eyelashes disclose the place (of sight) for beholding all the colors.

And if they disclose not the place (of vision) the (eyes) cannot see nor consider.[1]

But the eyelashes do not remain nor sleep, save in that only perfect hour, but they are opened and closed, and again closed and opened, according to that Open Eye (of Macroprosopus) which is above them.

And therefore is it written, Ezek. i. 14, " And the living creatures rush forth and return."

Now we have already spoken of the passage, Isa. xxxiii. 20, " Thine eye shall see Jerusalem quiet, even Thy habitation."

Also it is written, Deut. ii. 12, " The eyes of Tetragrammaton thy God are ever thereon in the beginning of the year," etc.

For so Jerusalem requireth it, since it is written, Isa. i. 21, " TzDQ, *Tzedeq,* Justice abideth in Her."

---

[1] The simple meaning of this and the preceding section is, that the eyes can only see when the upper eyelashes are separated from the lower ones by the lids being raised.

And therefore (is it called) Jerusalem, and not Zion. For it is written, Isa. i. 26: " Zion is redeemed in MShPT, *Meshephat,* Judgment, etc.," which are unmixed mercies.

Thine eye: (therefore) is it written OINK, *Ayinakh* (in the singular number). Assuredly it is the eye of the Most Holy Ancient One, the Most Concealed of All (which is here referred to).

Now it is said, " The eyes of Tetragrammaton thy God are thereon " ; in good, that is to say, and in evil; according as either the red color or the yellow is required.

But only with the glance (of Macroprosopus) are all things converted and cleansed into the white brilliance.

The eyelids (of Microprosopus) are not found when (His eyes) desire to behold the colors. But here (it is said), " Thine eyes shall behold Jerusalem." Entirely for good, entirely in mercy.

As it is written, Isa. liv. 7, " And with great mercies will I gather thee."

The eyes of Tetragrammaton thy God are ever thereon from the beginning of the year. Here the word " MRShITh, *Merashith,* from the beginning," is written defectively without A, for it is not written RAShITh with the A.

Hence it remaineth not always in the same condition. What doth not? The inferior H, *He* (of IHVH).

And concerning that which is supernal it is written, Lam. ii. 1: " He hath cast down MShMIM, *Me-Shamaim,* from the heavens; ARTz, *Aretz,* the earth, the Tiphereth, Israel."

Wherefore hath he cast down Aretz from Shamaim? Because it is written, Isa. l. 3, " I will cover the heavens, Shamaim, with darkness," and with the blackness of the eye (of Microprosopus), namely, with the black color, are they covered.

" From the beginning of the year." What, then, is that place whence those eyes of Tetragrammaton behold Jerusalem?

Therefore he [2] hasteneth to expound this (saying immediately), " From the beginning, MRShITh, of the year," which (word " *MRShITH* " being written thus), without the Aleph, A,[3] symbolizeth judgment; for judgment is referred unto that side, although virtually (the word " Merashith ") is not judgment.

[2] Moses, in this passage of Deuteronomy.

[3] That is, MRShITh, instead of MRAShITh.

"Even unto the end of the year." Herein, properly speaking, is judgment found. For it is written, Isa. i. 21, "Justice dwelt in her." For this is "the end of the year." Come and see! A, *Aleph,* only is called the first (letter). In A, *Aleph,* is the masculine power hidden and concealed; that namely, which is not known.

When this Aleph is conjoined in another place, then is it called RAShITh, *Rashith,* beginning.

But if thou sayest that (*A*) is conjoined herewith,[4] truly it is not so, but (*A*) is only manifested therein and illuminateth it; and in that case only is it called RAShITh, *Rashith,* beginning.

Now therefore in this (passage) RAShITh (spelt with the A) is not found as regards Jerusalem; for were (the letter A) herein, it would (denote that it would) remain forever.

Hence it is written defectively MRShITh, *Me-Rashith.* Also concerning the world to come it is written, Isa. xli. 27,[5] "The first shall say to Zion, Behold, behold them," etc.

CHAPTER XV

CONCERNING THE NOSE OF MICROPROSOPUS

The nose of Microprosopus is the form of His countenance, for therethrough is His whole countenance known.

This nose is not as the nose of the Most Holy Ancient One, the Concealed with all Concealments.

For the nose of Him, the Ancient One, is the life of lives for all things, and from His two nostrils rush forth the *Ruachin De-Chiin,* RVChIN DChIIN, spirits of lives for all.

But concerning this (nose of) Microprosopus it is written, Ps. xviii. 9, "A smoke ascendeth in His nose."

In this smoke all the colors are contained. In each color are contained multitudes of lords of most rigorous judgment, who are all comprehended in that smoke.

Whence all those are not mitigated save by the smoke of the inferior altar.

---

[4] That is, irrevocably, so that the word would cease to bear the same meaning were A not there. In other words, were A a radical letter of it.

[5] The first, RAShVN, Rashon, where this word, derived from the same root as RAShITh, is spelt with A.

Hence it is written, Gen. viii. 21, " And IHVH smelled a sweet savor." It is not written (He smelled) the odor of the sacrifice. What is " sweet " save " rest " ? Assuredly the spirit at rest is the mitigation of the Lords of Judgment.

(When therefore it is said) " And IHVH smelled the odor of rest," most certainly the odor of the sacrificed victim is not meant, but the odor of the mitigation of all those severities which are referred unto the nose.

And all things which adhere unto them, all things, I say, are mitigated. But most of these severities mutually cohere.

As it is written, Ps. cvi. 2, " Who shall recount GBVRVTH IHVH, the Geburoth of Tetragrammaton? "

And this nose (of Microprosopus) emitteth fire from the two nostrils, which swalloweth up all other fires.

From the one nostril (goeth forth) the smoke, and from the other nostril the fire, and they both are found on the altar, as well the fire as the smoke.

But when He the most Holy Ancient One is unveiled, all things are at peace. This is that which is said, Isa. xlviii. 9, " And for My praise will I refrain from thee " (literally, " block up thy nostrils " [1]).

The nose of the Most Holy Ancient One is long and extended, and He is called Arikh Aphim, Long of Nose.

But this nose (of Microprosopus) is short, and when the smoke commenceth, it issueth rapidly forth, and judgment is consummated.

But who can oppose the nose of Him the Ancient One? Concerning this, all things.are as we have said in the Greater Assembly, where concerning this matter the Companions were exercised.

In the book of the treatise of Rav Hamenuna the Elder he thus describeth these two nostrils (of Microprosopus), saying that from the one proceed the smoke and the fire, and from the other, peace and the beneficent spirits.

That is, when (Microprosopus) is considered as having (in Himself the symbolism of) right side and left side. As it is written, Hosea xiv. 7, " And his smell like Lebanon."

And concerning His Bride it is written, Cant. vii. 9, " And

---

[1] The Hebrew idiom for having mercy always refers to the nose, as " to defer anger " is in Hebrew " to lengthen the nose," etc.

the smell of thy nostril like apples." Which if it be true concerning the Bride, how much more concerning Himself? And
this is a notable saying.

When therefore it is said, " And Tetragrammaton smelled the
odor of peace," the word " HNICHCH," *Ha-Nichach*, of peace,
can be understood in a double sense.

One sense is primary, when the Most Holy Ancient One, the
Concealed with all Concealments, is manifested; for HVA, *Hoa*,
He, is the peace and mitigation of all things.

And the other respecteth the inferior mitigation, which is
done through the smoke and fire of the altar.

And because of this duplicate meaning is the word NICHCH,
Nichach, written with a double CH. And all these things are
said concerning Microprosopus.

CHAPTER XVI

CONCERNING THE EARS OF MICROPROSOPUS

There **are** two ears for hearing the good and the evil, and
these two can be reduced into one.

As it is written, 2 Kings xix. 18, " Incline, O Tetragrammaton, Thine ear, and hear."

The ear from within dependeth upon certain curves which
are therein formed, so that the speech may be made clearer before its entrance into the brain.

And the brain examineth it, but not with haste. For every
matter which is accomplished in haste cometh not from perfect
wisdom.

From those ears depend all the Lords of Wings who receive
the Voice of the Universe; and all those are called thus, the
Ears of Tetragrammaton.

Concerning whom it is written, Eccles. x. 20, " For a bird
of the air shall carry the voice," etc.

" For a bird of the air shall carry the voice." This text hath
a difficult (meaning). And now (for so much is expressed)
whence is the voice?

For in the beginning of the verse it is written: " Curse not the
King even in thy thought." Where it is written concerning

even the (unexpressed) thought, and concerning the secret thoughts of thy couch.

Wherefore? Because "a bird of the air shall carry the voice." Which (voice) as yet is unexpressed.

Assuredly this is the true meaning. Whatsoever a man thinketh and meditateth in his heart, he maketh not a word until he bringeth it forth with his lips. (What the text intendeth is) if any man attendeth not hereunto.

For that voice sent forward (from inconsiderate thought) cleaveth the air, and it goeth forth and ascendeth, and is carried around through the universe; and therefore is the voice.

And the Lords of Wings receive the voice and bear it on unto the King (Microprosopus), so that it may enter into His ears.

This is that which standeth written, Deut. v. 28, "And Tetragrammaton hath heard the voice of your words." Again, Num. xi. 1, "And Tetragrammaton heard, and His wrath was kindled."

Hence every prayer and petition which a man poureth forth before God the Most Holy One—blessed be He!—requireth this, that he pronounce the words with his lips.

For if he pronounce them not, his prayer is no prayer, and his petition is no petition.

But as far as the words go forth, they cleave the air asunder, and ascend, and fly on, and from them is the voice made; and that which receiveth the one receiveth also the other, and beareth it into the Holy Place in the head of the King (otherwise, beneath Kether, the Crown).

From the three cavities (of the brain of Microprosopus) distilleth a certain distillation, and it is called the Brook. As it is said in 1 Kings xvii. 3, "The brook Kherith," as it were an excavation or channel of the ears.

And the voice entereth into that curved passage, and remaineth in that brook of that distillation.

And then is it therein detained, and examined, whether it be good or whether it be evil. This is the same which is said, Job xxxiv. 3, "Because the ear examineth the words."

For what cause doth the ear examine the words? Because the voice is detained in that brook distilling into the curved passage of the ears, and doth not swiftly enter into the body, and thereunto is an examination instituted between the good and the evil.

" As the palate tasteth meat." Wherefore can the palate taste meat? Because in the same manner it causeth it to delay, and (the meat) doth not enter so rapidly into the body. And hence (the palate) proveth and tasteth it (to discern) whether it be sweet and pleasant.

From this opening of the ears depend other openings, (namely) the opening of the eye, the opening of the mouth, the opening of the nose.

From that voice which entereth into the opening of the ears, if it be necessary (a certain part) entereth into the opening of the eyes, and these pour forth tears.

From that voice, if it be necessary (a certain part) entereth into the opening of the nose, and from that voice it produceth smoke and fire.

This is that which is written, Num. xi. 1, " And Tetragrammaton heard, and His wrath was kindled, and the fire of Tetragrammaton turned against them."

And if it be necessary that voice goeth forth into the opening of the mouth, and it speaketh, and determineth certain things.

From that voice are all things; from that voice (a certain part) entereth into the whole body, and by it are all things affected. Whence doth this matter depend? From that ear.

Blessed is he who observeth his words. Therefore is it written, Ps. xxxiv. 13, " Keep thy tongue from evil, and thy lips from speaking guile."

Unto this ear is attributed hearing, and under (the idea of) hearing are those brains comprehended.[1]

Chokmah is contained therein, as it is written, 1 Kings iii. 9, " And wilt Thou give unto Thy servant a hearing heart."

Binah also, as it is written, 1 Sam. iii. 9, " Speak, for Thy servant heareth." Also 2 Kings xviii. 26, " Because we have heard." And hencefrom all things depend.

Däath also, as it is said, Prov. iv. 10, " Hear, O my son, and receive My sayings." And again, *ibid.* ii. 1, " Thou shalt hide My sayings with thee." And thereunto all things depend from the ears.

From these ears depend prayers and petitions, and the opening of the eyes.

This is the same which standeth written, 2 Kings xix. 16,

[1] The three divisions of the Brain of Microprosopus.

" Incline, O Tetragrammaton, Thine ear, and hear; open Thine eyes, and see." Thus all things depend hencefrom.

From this ear depend the highest Arcana, which go not forth without, and therefore is (this ear) curved in the interior parts, and the Arcana of Arcana are concealed therein. Woe unto him who revealeth the Arcana!

And because the Arcana come into contact with this ear, and follow the curvings of that region, hence the Arcana are not revealed unto those who walk in crooked paths, but unto those (who walk in) those which are not crooked.

Hence is it written, Ps. xxv. 14, " The SVD IHVH, *Sod Tetragrammaton,* Secret of Tetragrammaton, is with them that fear Him, and He will show them His covenant " ; namely, unto such as keep their path and thus receive His words.

But they who are perverse in their ways receive certain words, and quickly introduce the same into themselves, but in them is no place where they can be detained (for examination).

And all the other openings are opened therein, until those words can issue forth from the opening of the mouth.

And such men are called the sinners of their generation, hating God the Most Holy One—blessed be He.

In Mischna, or our tradition, we have taught that such men are like unto murderers and idolaters.

And all these things are contained in one saying, where it is written, Lev. xix. 16, " Thou shalt not go up and down as a tale-bearer among thy people, neither shalt thou stand against the blood of thy neighbor: ANI IHVH, I am Tetragrammaton."

Therefore he who transgresseth the first part of that verse doth the same as if he were to transgress the whole.

Blessed is the portion of the just, concerning whom it is said, Prov. xi. 13, " A tale-bearer revealeth secrets, but he that is of a faithful spirit concealeth the matter."

" Spirit, RVCh, *Ruach,*" properly (is used here) for the Ruach of such is extracted from the Supernal Holy Place.

Now we have said that this is a symbol. Whosoever revealeth Arcana with fixed purpose of mind, he is not of the body of the Most Holy King.

And therefore to such a man nothing is an Arcanum, neither is from the place of the Arcanum.

And whensoever his soul departeth, the same adhereth not unto the body of the King, for it is not his place. Woe unto that man! woe unto himself! woe unto his Neschamah![2]

But blessed is the portion of the just who conceal secrets, and much more the Supernal Arcana of God the Most Holy One—blessed be He!—the highest Arcana of the Most Holy King.

Concerning them it is written, Isa. lx. 21, " Thy people also shall be all righteous; they shall inherit the land forever."

CHAPTER XVII

Concerning the Countenance of Microprosopus

His countenance is as two abodes of fragrance, and all that I have before said is His testimony.

For the testimony, SHDVThA, *Sahedutha,* dependeth from Him, and in all His testimony dependeth.

But these places of fragrance are white and red; the testimony of Ab the Father, and Aima the Mother; the testimony of the inheritance which He hath taken by right and obtained.

And in our tradition we have also established by how many thousand degrees the whiteness differeth from the redness.

But yet at once they agree together in Him in one,[1] under the general form of the whiteness; for whensoever it is illuminated from the light of the white brilliance of the Ancient One, then that white brilliance overcloudeth the redness, and all things are found to be in light.

But whensoever judgments ascend (otherwise, threaten) in the universe, and sinners are many, leprosy is found in all things (otherwise, throughout the universe), and the redness spreadeth over the countenance, and overcloudeth all the whiteness.

And then all things are found in judgment, and then (He putteth on) the vestments of zeal, which are called "the garments of vengeance " (Isa. lix. 17), and all things depend herefrom.

And because the testimony existeth in all things, hence so many Lords of Shields are enshrouded by those colors, and attend upon those colors.

[2] See Introduction concerning the names of the parts of the Soul.

[1] I.e., the various degrees of the whiteness.

When those colors are resplendent, the worlds all and singular exist in joy.

In that time when the white brilliance shineth all things appear in this color; and when He appeareth in redness, similarly all things appear in that color.

CHAPTER XVIII

CONCERNING THE BEARD OF MICROPROSOPUS

In those abodes (otherwise forms) of fragrance the beard beginneth to appear from the top of the ears, and it descendeth and ascendeth in the place of fragrance.

The hairs of the beard are black, and beautiful in form as in (that of) a robust youth.

The oil of dignity of the supernal beard of the Ancient One (floweth down) in this beard of Microprosopus.

The beautiful arrangement of this beard is divided into nine parts. But when the most holy oil of dignity of the Most Holy Ancient One sendeth down rays into this beard, its parts are found to be twenty-two.[2]

And then all things exist in benediction, and thence Israel the patriarch (*i.e.,* Jacob) took his blessing. And the symbol of this is to be found in these words, Gen. xlviii. 20, " BK, with the twenty-two shall Israel bless." (The real translation of BK is " in thee," but the numerical value of BK is twenty-two; hence the symbolism here rendered.)

We have described the conformations of the beard already, in the Conclave of the Assembly. Here also I desire to enter upon this matter in all humility.

Now we thus examined all the parts of the beard, that in the Conclave of the Assembly (we found) that they were all disposed from the parts of the beard of the Most Holy Ancient One.

Six there are; nine they are called. For the first conformation goeth forth through that Spark of the most refulgent Lightbearer,[3] and goeth down beneath the hair of the head, assuredly beneath those locks which overhang the ears.

---

[2] Answering to the number of the letters of the Hebrew alphabet, which together with the ten Sephiroth form the thirty-two paths of wisdom of the " Sepher Yetzirah."

[3] See " Book of Concealed Mystery," chap. ii. §§ 31, 40, etc.

And it descendeth before the opening of the ears unto the beginning of the mouth.

But this arrangement is not found in the Most Holy Ancient One. But when that fountain of Wisdom, CнKMTнA, *Chokmatha,* floweth down from MZLA, *Mezla,* the Influence of the Most Holy Ancient One, and dependeth from Him, and when Aima, the Mother, ariseth, and is included in that subtle ether, then She, Aima, assumeth that white brilliance.[4]

And the Scintilla entereth and departeth, and together mutually are They bound, and thence cometh the One Form.

And when there is need, One ariseth above the Other, and the Other again is concealed in the presence of Its Companion.

And therefore there is need of all things; of one thing for performing vengeance, of another for showing forth mercy.

And therefore David the king hath sought out this beard, as we have shown already.

In this beard nine conformations are found, (among which are) six myriads which depend among them, and are extended throughout the whole body.

And those six which depend hang in the locks which are beneath the abodes of fragrance, three on this side and three on that.

And in the ornamentation of the beard hang the three remaining (conformations); one above the lips, and two in those locks which hang down upon the chest.

And all those six (other conformations), three on this side and three on that side, go forth, and all depend from those locks which hang down, and they are extended throughout the whole body.

But on account of those three (conformations), which are more connected with the ornament of the beard than all the others, the Holy Name is written in its purity.

When it is written thus, Ps. cxviii. 5: " I invoked IH, *Yah,* in my trouble: IH, *Yah,* heard me at large: Tetragrammaton is with me, therefore I will not fear."

But that which we have already laid down in the Conclave of

---

[4] In the "Book of Concealed Mystery," chap. i. § 31, HVA and ALHIM are shown to be interchangeable, and they both are feminine. And now we come to the "Three Mothers," of the "Sepher Yetzirah," the Great Supernal Feminine Triad, which is even before the triune father. I may say no more here; in fact, I have almost revealed too much. Let the reader carefully meditate on § 651, for there the indicible Arcanum is shadowed.

the Assembly concerning these words, "In my trouble I invoked IH, *Yah*," that this is to be referred to that place where the beard beginneth to be extended, which place is more remote, and before the ears, is also correct.

And in the book of the dissertation of the school of Rav Yeyeva the Elder it is thus said and established, that the beginning of the beard cometh from the supernal CHSD, *Chesed*, Mercy.

Concerning which it is written, "LK IHVH HGDVLH VHGBVRH VHThPARTh, *Leka, Tetragrammaton; Ha-Gedulah, Ve-Ha-Geburah, Ve-Ha-Tiphereth*, Thine, O Tetragrammaton, Gedulah (another name for Chesed), Geburah, and Tiphereth (the names of the fourth, fifth, and sixth Sephiroth, which Protestants usually add to the end of the Lord's Prayer, substituting, however, Malkuth for Gedulah), Thine, O Tetragrammaton, are the Mercy, the Power, and the Glory (or Beauty)." And all these are so, and thus it (the beard) commenceth.

Therefore the nine (conformations) arise from and depend from the beard; and thus it commenceth from before the ears. But (the conformations) remain not in permanence save through another cause, as we have before laid down.

For whensoever the universe hath need of mercy, the Influence, Mezla, of the Ancient One is uncovered; and all those conformations which exist in the most adorned beard of Microprosopus are found to be entirely mercies, yet so that they can exercise vengeance against the haters of the Israelites, and against those who afflict them.

But the whole ornament of the beard consisteth in those locks which hang down, because all things depend thencefrom.

All those hairs which are in the beard of Microprosopus are hard and rigid, because they all subject the judgments when the Most Holy Influence is manifested.

And when there is to be contention, then He appeareth like unto a brave hero, victorious in war. And then that becometh bare of hair which is bare of hair, and that becometh bald which is bald.

Moses commemorated these nine conformations a second time, Num. xiv. 17, when there was need to convert them all into mercy.

For although he recite not now the thirteen conformations (of the beard of Macroprosopus), yet from this idea the thing depended; for he did not allow himself to enter into those conformations simply that he might enumerate them.

But unto the Influence directed he his meditation, and made mention thereof. As it is written, Num. xiv. 17, "And now, I beseech thee, let KCH, *Kach,* the Power of Tetragrammaton, be great!"

What is to be understood by KCH, IHVH, *Kach Tetragrammaton,* the Power of Tetragrammaton? Thus is MZLA QDISHA, *Mezla, Qadisha,* the Holy Influence, called, even the Concealed with all Concealments. And from the Influence that Strength and that Light depend.

And since of this (Influence) Moses was speaking, and this (Influence) he was commemorating, and concerning this (Influence) he was meditating, he then immediately recited those nine conformations which belong unto Microprosopus.

So that they all might exist in light, and that judgment might not be found therein. And therefore this whole judgment (otherwise, this whole beard) dependeth from the Influence.

When the hairs begin to be restrained He Himself is as the hero of an army victorious in war.

In this beard (of Microprosopus) floweth down the oil of dignity from the Concealed Ancient One, as it is said, Ps. cxxxiii. 2, " Like excellent oil upon the head, descending upon the beard, the beard of Aaron."

CHAPTER XIX

CONCERNING THE LIPS AND MOUTH OF MICROPROSOPUS

Those hairs cover not the lips, and the entire lips are red and rosy. As it is written, Cant. v. 13, " His lips as roses." (In the ordinary version *SHVSHNIM, Shushanim,* is translated " lilies," not " roses."

His lips murmur Geburah, Severity, but they also murmur *Chokmah,* Wisdom.

From those lips alike depend good and evil, life and death.

From these lips depend the Lord of Vigilance. For when those lips murmur, they all are excited to bring forth secret things, as well as the Lords of Judgment in all the tribunals wherein they have their abiding-place.

And therefore are these called the Watchers; as it is written, Dan. iv. 17, " This matter is by the decree of the Watchers, and the demand by the word of the Holy Ones."

What is a Watcher? In the book of the dissertation that is explained from this passage, 1 Sam. xxviii. 16, " And is become thine enemy."

Seeing that judgments are stirred up against those who obtain not mercy from the Supernals.

Hence are those stirred up who are the lords of the enmity of all things.

And, nevertheless, in each case are there mercy and judgment. And therefore is it said, Dan. iv. 13, " A watcher and a holy one "; judgment and mercy.

And between those lips when they are opened is the mouth disclosed.

By that RVCH, *Ruach*, breath, which goeth forth from His mouth, many thousands and myriads are enshrouded; and when it is extended by the same are the true prophets enfolded, and all are called the mouth of Tetragrammaton.

When forth from His mouth the words proceed through His lips, the same are muttered through the whole circuit of 18,000 worlds,[1] until they are all bound together at once in the twelve paths and the known ways. And one thing ever expecteth another.

By the tongue is the vocal expression of the sublime spoken, in the middle nexus of the utterance.

And therefore is it written, Cant. v. 16, " His mouth is most sweet." And this same palate of His conveyeth a sweet taste; wherefore He smileth when He tasteth food (which is pleasant).[2]

[1] That is the number 18 on the plane of Asiah. And 18 is the fourth part of 72. And 72 is the number of the Schemahamphorasch (see ante), and the number of the Quinaries or sets of five degrees in the 360 degrees of the Zodiac. And there are six such sets in the thirty degrees of each sign. And thus we return to the twelve signs of the Zodiac, and these are operated on from the ten Sephiroth through the " seven paths of the Queen," and these again depend from the first three Sephiroth, and these again from Kether, and Kether is Macroprosopus, from whom backward depend the Negative Existences in their Veils; and Macroprosopus is called HVA, Hoa, which = 12, and finds its expression in " Aima Elohim." Thus rusheth through the Universe the Flux and Reflux of the Eternal Word.

[2] I am doubtful as to whether this is the best translation of the last clause; Rosenroth has not translated it at all. The Chaldee is MMThQIM VDAI MAI ChKV KDA VChIK ITOVM LAKVL, Mamthaqim Vadeai Maai Chiko Kedea Vecheik Yitauom Leakol.

"And He is altogether the desirablenesses (or delights)"
(of the powers of) fire and (the powers of) water, because
the fire and water are counterchanged with each other mutually (otherwise, are conformed together), and are beautiful in
his conformation.[3]

For the colors are mutually associated together.

In His palate are the (guttural) letters (of the Hebrew
Alphabet—namely, A, H, Cн, O) formed and constructed; in
the circuit of His (mouth) are they condensed (into the palatals
G, I, K, Q).[4]

The letter A, *Aleph,* which cast forth the kings and constituted the kings [5] (*i.e.,* that guttural letter which is referred to
the First Sephira, Kether, the Crown, becometh the palatal
letter G, *Ghimel*).

The letter Cн, *Cheth,* which goeth forth and descendeth and
ascendeth, and is crowned in the head (referring to the Second
Sephira, *Chokmah,* Wisdom), and is fire condensed in ether
(*i.e.,* developeth in the palatal letter I, *Yod*).

The letter H, *He,* the golden-yellow color (otherwise, ger-
minating power) of the Mother, Aima, having been connected
with the Female Power, is extended in the Greater Female Po-
tency into the desire of the Holy City, which two (otherwise,
for these places) are mutually bound together the one unto the
other (these two are Aima, the supernal H of IHVH, and the
Holy City, the Bride, as She is called in the Apocalypse, the final

---

[3] This whole section requires com-
ment. I must first observe that Knorr
de Rosenroth in his Latin version has
supposed that in the word "MChM-
DIM," Machemadim, fire and water
(ASh and MIM) are hidden as in a sort
of anagram. Now while it is true that
"MIM" can be thus extracted, "ASh"
cannot, for the remaining letters,
ChMD, will by no exegetical rule I
know of form a word signifying fire.
The following I take to be the real
meaning of the passage. Chokmah is
the fire, I, and Binah is the water, H,
the Father and Mother Who, conjoined,
produce the Son. Now the fire is symbolized by a triangle with the apex
uppermost, and water by a triangle with
the apex reversed; these two together
united form the sign of the Macrocosm,
the external symbol of Vau, V, Microprosopus. And He inherits the double
qualities of the Father and the Mother,
shown by the word "delights"
("Machemadim") being written in the
plural.

[4] The letters of the Hebrew alphabet
are usually classed in the following
manner:
Gutturals = A, H, Ch, O (R by
some).
Palatals = G, I, K, Q.
Linguals = D, Th, T, L, N.
Dentals = Z, S, Sh, Tz (R by others).
Labials = B, V, M, P.
The "Sepher Yetzirah" further classes
them as—
3 Mothers (Primitives) = A, M, Sh.
7 Duplicated = B, G, D, K, P, R, Th.
12 Simples = H, V, Z, Ch, T, I, L, N,
S, O, Tz, Q.
In the above classification it classes R
as a dental.
[5] This section contains references to
the Edomite kings and their symbology;
namely, as denoting the primal worlds
which were destroyed. (See "The
Book of Concealed Mystery," chap. i;
§ 3; "The Greater Holy Assembly,"
chap. ii. and chap. xxvi.; and "The
Lesser Holy Assembly," chap. x.)

H of IHVH). (And the guttural letter H, *He,* formeth the palatal letter *K, Kaph,* which is referred unto the Queen.) As it is written, Cant. iv. 6, " Unto the mountain of myrrh, unto the hill of frankincense."

The letter O, *Ayin* (which denoteth the seven Inferiors which were destroyed) is the medium of splendor of mediation (*i.e.,* the internal Light of the broken vessels), hath been formed forth in His lips by revolution therein (and it hath been condensed in Q, *Qoph,* which goeth forth from the middle of the palate unto the lips). For the branches (of the Tree of Life, namely) are connected in Him (Microprosopus) in the spirits (such as they were in the prior world) formed forth (such as they are in the restored world).

For in the mysteries of the letters of Solomon the King, those four letters, A, H, Ch, O, are surrounded by GIKQ.

But it is written in Job. vi. 6, " Can that which is unsavory be eaten without salt? " etc.

Also it is written, Is. xxxii. 17, " And the work of TzDQ, *Tzedeq,* Righteousness (or Justice), shall be peace." Also, Ps. xix. 10, " More to be desired are they than gold, yea, than much fine gold," etc.

But King David saith, *ibid.* 11, " Also by them is thy servant warned."

I affirm concerning myself, that I have been every day cautious concerning them, so that concerning them I might not err (*i.e.,* concerning the judgments, Meshephath, referred to in verse 9).

Excepting a certain day when I was binding together the Crowns of the King [6] in the Cave of Maranæa, I beheld a Splendor of devouring Fire flashing from His wrathful Countenance of Flame, and with terror I trembled at the sight.

From that day forth I ever acted with caution in my meditations concerning them, neither have I omitted that all the days of my life.

Blessed is his portion who is prudent regarding Him who is more ancient than (otherwise, concerning the gentleness of) the King, so that he may taste thereof, as is fitting.

---

[6] I.e., tracing out the properties, etc., of the Sephiroth which form the King, Microprosopus, and, as appears from the latter part of this section, those only in their aspect of Judgment and Wrath.

Therefore is it written, Ps. xxxiv. 9, "Taste and see that Tetragrammaton is good," etc.

Also it is written, Prov. ix. 5, "Come, eat of my bread," etc.

CHAPTER XX

Concerning the Body of Microprosopus

The masculine power is extended through Däath; and the Assemblies and Conclaves are filled.

It commenceth from the beginning of the skull, and it is extended throughout the whole body, through the breast, and through the arms, and through all the other parts.

CHAPTER XXI

Concerning the Bride of Microprosopus

Unto His back adhereth closely a Ray of most vehement Splendor, and it flameth forth and formeth a certain skull, concealed on every side.

And thus descendeth the Light of the two brains, and is figured forth therein.

And She (the Bride) adhereth unto the side of the Male; wherefore also She is called, Cant. v. 2, "My dove, my perfect one." Read not, "ThMThI, *Thamathi*, My perfect one"; but "ThAVMThI, *Theomathi*, My twin sister," more applicably.

The hairs of the Woman contain colors upon colors, as it is written, Cant. vii. 5, "The hair of Thy head like purple."

But herewith is Geburah, Severity, connected in the five Severities (*i.e.*, which are symbolized in the numerical value, 5, of the letter H final of IHVH, which is the Bride), and the Woman is extended on Her side, and is applied unto the side of the Male.

Until She is separated from His side, and cometh unto Him so that She may be conjoined with Him, face to face.

And when They are conjoined together, They appear to be only one body.

Hence we learn that the Masculine, taken alone appeareth to

be only half the body, so that all the mercies are half; and thus also is it with the Feminine.

But when They are joined together, the (two together) appear to form only one whole body. And it is so.

So also here. When the Male is joined with the Female, They both constitute one complete body, and all the Universe is in a state of happiness, because all things receive blessing from Their perfect body. And this is an Arcanum.

And therefore it is said, Gen. ii. 3, "Tetragrammaton blessed the seventh day and hallowed it." For then all things are found (to exist) in the one perfect Body, for MTRVNIThA, *Matronitha,* the Mother (*i.e.,* the Inferior Mother) is joined unto the King, and is found to form the one Body with Him.

And therefore are there found to be blessings upon this day.

And hence that which is not both Male and Female together is called half a body. Now, no blessing can rest upon a mutilated and defective being, but only upon a perfect place and upon a perfect being, and not at all in an incomplete being.[1]

And a semi-complete being cannot live forever, neither can it receive blessing forever.

The Beauty of the Female is completed by the Beauty of the Male. And now have we established these facts (concerning the perfect equality of Male and Female), and they are made known unto the Companions.

With this Woman (the inferior H) are connected all those things which are below; from Her do they receive their nourishment, and from Her do they receive blessing; and She is called the Mother of them all.

.   .   .   .

It is written, Prov. vii. 4, "Say unto Chokmah, Thou art my sister."[2] For there is given one Chokmah (Male), and there is also given another Chokmah (Female).

And this Woman is called the Lesser Chokmah in respect of the other.

---

[1] This section is another all-sufficient proof of the teachings maintained throughout the Qabalah, namely, that Man and Woman are from the creation coequal and coexistent, perfectly equal one with the other. This fact the translators of the Bible have been at great pains to conceal by carefully suppressing every reference to the Feminine portion of the Deity, and by constantly translating feminine nouns by masculine. And this is the work of so-called religious men!

[2] Chokmah, Wisdom, the second Sephirah, is Male in respect of Binah, but Female in respect of Kether. This is somewhat analogous to the Greek idea of the birth of Athené, Wisdom, from the brain of Zeus.

And therefore is it written, Cant. viii. 8, " We have a little sister and she hath no breasts."

For in this exile (*i.e.*, separated from the King) She appeareth unto us to be " our little sister." At first, indeed, she is small, but she becometh great and greater, until she becometh the Spouse whom the King taketh unto Himself.

As it is written, Cant. viii. 10, " I am a wall, and my breasts are like towers."

" And my breasts," etc., since they are full with the nourishment of all things; [3] " like towers," because they are the great rivers which flow forth from Aima the Supernal.

[3] Compare the symbolism of the many breasts of the Ephesian Diana.

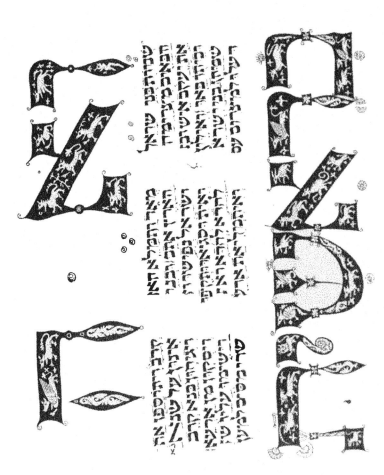

HEBREW MELODIES

—

[*Translated by Mrs. Henry Lucas*]

HEBREW MELODIES

ODE TO ZION

Art thou not, Zion, fain
To send forth greetings from thy sacred rock
Unto thy captive train,
Who greet thee as the remnants of thy flock?
Take thou on every side—
East, west, and south, and north—their greetings multiplied.
Sadly he greets thee still,
The prisoner of hope, who, day and night,
Sheds ceaseless tears, like dew on Hermon's hill—
Would that they fell upon thy mountain's height!

Harsh is my voice when I bewail thy woes,
But when in fancy's dream
I see thy freedom, forth its cadence flows
Sweet as the harps that hung by Babel's stream.
My heart is sore distressed
For Bethel ever blessed,
For Peniel, and each ancient, sacred place.
The holy presence there
To thee is present where
Thy Maker opes thy gates, the gates of heaven to face.

The glory of the Lord will ever be
Thy sole and perfect light;
No need hast thou, then, to illumine thee,
Of sun by day, or moon and stars by night.
I would that, where God's Spirit was of yore
Poured out unto thy holy ones, I might
There too my soul outpour!
The house of kings and throne of God wert thou,
How comes it then that now
Slaves fill the throne where sat thy kings before?

365

Oh! who will lead me on
To seek the posts where, in far-distant years,
The angels in their glory dawned upon
Thy messengers and seers?
Oh! who will give me wings
That I may fly away,
And there, at rest from all my wanderings,
The ruins of my heart among thy ruins lay?
I'll bend my face unto thy soil, and hold
Thy stones as precious gold.
And when in Hebron I have stood beside
My fathers' tombs, then will I pass in turn
Thy plains and forest wide,
Until I stand on Gilead and discern
Mount Hor and Mount Abarim, 'neath whose crest
Thy luminaries twain, thy guides and beacons rest.

Thy air is life unto my soul, thy grains
Of dust are myrrh, thy streams with honey flow;
Naked and barefoot, to thy ruined fanes
How gladly would I go;
To where the ark was treasured, and in dim
Recesses dwelt the holy cherubim.

I rend the beauty of my locks, and cry
In bitter wrath against the cruel fate
That bids thy holy Nazarites to lie
In earth contaminate.
How can I make or meat or drink my care,
How can mine eyes enjoy
The light of day, when I see ravens tear
Thy eagles' flesh, and dogs thy lions' whelps destroy?
Away! thou cup of sorrow's poisoned gall!
Scarce can my soul thy bitterness sustain.
When I Ahola unto mind recall,
I taste thy venom; and when once again
Upon Aholiba I muse, thy dregs I drain.

Perfect in beauty, Zion! how in thee
Do love and grace unite!

The souls of thy companions tenderly
Turn unto thee; thy joy was their delight,
And, weeping, they lament thy ruin now.
In distant exile, for thy sacred height
They long, and toward thy gates in prayer they bow.
Thy flocks are scattered o'er the barren waste,
Yet do they not forget thy sheltering fold,
Unto thy garments' fringe they cling, and haste
The branches of thy palms to seize and hold.
Shinar and Pathros! come they near to thee?
Naught are they by thy Light and Right divine.
To what can be compared the majesty
Of thy anointed line?
To what the singers, seers, and Levites thine?
The rule of idols fails and is cast down,
Thy power eternal is, from age to age thy crown.

The Lord desires thee for his dwelling-place
Eternally; and blest
Is he whom God has chosen for the grace
Within thy courts to rest.
Happy is he that watches, drawing near, ·
Until he sees thy glorious lights arise,
And over whom thy dawn breaks full and clear
Set in the orient skies.
But happiest he, who, with exultant eyes,
The bliss of thy redeemed ones shall behold,
And see thy youth renewed as in the days of old.

JEHUDA HALEVI.

"GOD, WHOM SHALL I COMPARE TO THEE?"

God! whom shall I compare to Thee,
When Thou to none canst likened be?
Under what image shall I dare
To picture Thee, when ev'rywhere
All Nature's forms Thine impress bear?

Greater, O Lord! Thy glories are
Than all the heavenly chariot far.

Whose mind can grasp Thy world's design?
Whose word can fitly Thee define?
Whose tongue set forth Thy powers divine?

Can heart approach, can eye behold
Thee in Thy righteousness untold?
Whom didst Thou to Thy counsel call,
When there was none to speak withal
Since Thou wast first and Lord of all?

Thy world eternal witness bears
That none its Maker's glory shares.
Thy wisdom is made manifest
In all things formed by Thy behest,
All with Thy seal's clear mark imprest.

Before the pillars of the sky
Were raised, before the mountains high
Were wrought, ere hills and dales were known,
Thou in Thy majesty alone
Didst sit, O God! upon Thy throne!

Hearts, seeking Thee, from search refrain,
And weary tongues their praise restrain.
Thyself unbound by time and place,
Thou dost pervade, support, embrace
The world and all created space.

The sages' minds bewildered grow,
The lightning speed of thought is slow.
"Awful in praises" art Thou named;
Thou fillest, strong in strength proclaimed,
This universe Thy hand has framed.

Deep, deep beyond all fathoming,
Far, far beyond all measuring,
We can but seek Thy deeds alone;
When bow Thy saints before Thy throne
Then is Thy faithfulness made known.

Thy righteousness we can discern,
Thy holy law proclaim and learn.

Is not Thy presence near alway
To them who penitently pray,
But far from those who sinning stray?

Pure souls behold Thee, and no need
Have they of light: they hear and heed
Thee with the mind's keen ear, although
The ear of flesh be dull and slow.
Their voices answer to and fro.

Thy holiness forever they proclaim:
The Lord of Hosts! thrice holy is His name!

JEHUDA HALEVI.

SERVANT OF GOD

Oh! would that I might be
A servant unto Thee,
Thou God by all adored:
Then, though by friends out-cast,
Thy hand would hold me fast,
And draw me near to Thee, my King and Lord!

Spirit and flesh are Thine,
O Heavenly Shepherd mine!
My hopes, my thoughts, my fears, Thou seest all,
Thou measurest my path, my steps dost know.
When Thou upholdest, who can make me fall?
When Thou restrainest, who can bid me go?
Oh! would that I might be
A servant unto Thee,
Thou God, by all adored.
Then, though by friends out-cast,
Thy hand would hold me fast,
And draw me near to Thee, my King and Lord!

Fain would my heart come nigh
To Thee, O God! on high,
But evil thoughts have led me far astray
From the pure path of righteous government.

24

Guide Thou me back into Thy holy way,
And count me not as one impenitent.
Oh! would that I might be
A servant unto Thee,
Thou God, by all adored.
Then, though by friends out-cast,
Thy hand would hold me fast,
And draw me near to Thee, my King and Lord!

If in my youth I still
Fail to perform Thy will,
What can I hope when age shall chill my breast?
Heal me, O Lord! with Thee is healing found—
Cast me not off, by weight of years opprest,
Forsake me not when age my strength has bound.
Oh! would that I might be
A servant unto Thee,
Thou God, by all adored.
Then, though by friends out-cast,
Thy hand would hold me fast,
And draw me near to Thee, my King and Lord!

Contrite and full of dread,
I mourn each moment fled
Midst idle follies roaming desolate;
I sink beneath transgressions manifold,
That from Thy presence keep me separate;
Nor can sin-darkened eyes Thy light behold.
Oh! would that I might be
A servant unto Thee,
Thou God, by all adored.
Then, though by friends out-cast,
Thy hand would hold me fast,
And draw me near to Thee, my King and Lord!

So lead me that I may
Thy sovereign will obey.
Make pure my heart to seek Thy truth divine;
When burns my wound, be Thou with healing near!
Answer me, Lord! for sore distress is mine,
And say unto Thy servant, I am here!

Oh! would that I might be
A servant unto Thee,
Thou God, by all adored!
Then, though by friends out-cast,
Thy hand would hold me fast,
And draw me near to Thee, my King and Lord!

JEHUDA HALEVI.

MY KING

Ere time began, ere age to age had thrilled,
I waited in His storehouse, as He willed;
He gave me being, but, my years fulfilled,
　I shall be summoned back before the King.

He called the hidden to the light of day,
To right and left, each side the fountain lay,
From out the stream and down the steps, the way
　That led me to the garden of the King.

Thou gavest me a light my path to guide,
To prove my heart's recesses still untried;
And as I went, Thy voice in warning cried:
　"Child! fear thou Him Who is Thy God and King!"

True weight and measure learned my heart from Thee;
If blessings follow, then what joy for me!
If naught but sin, all mine the shame must be,
　For that was not determined by the King.

I hasten, trembling, to confess the whole
Of my transgressions, ere I reach the goal
Where mine own words must witness 'gainst my soul,
　And who dares doubt the writing of the King?

Erring, I wandered in the wilderness,
In passion's grave nigh sinking powerless:
Now deeply I repent, in sore distress,
　That I kept not the statutes of the King!

With worldly longings was my bosom fraught,
Earth's idle toys and follies all I sought;
Ah! when He judges joys so dearly bought,
    How greatly shall I fear my Lord and King!

Now conscience-stricken, humbled to the dust,
Doubting himself, in Thee alone his trust,
He shrinks in terror back, for God is just—
    How can a sinner hope to reach the King?

Oh! be Thy mercy in the balance laid,
To hold Thy servant's sins more lightly weighed,
When, his confession penitently made,
    He answers for his guilt before the King.

Thine is the love, O God! and Thine the grace,
That folds the sinner in its mild embrace;
Thine the forgiveness bridging o'er the space
    'Twixt man's works and the task set by the King.

Unheeding all my sins, I cling to Thee!
I know that mercy will Thy footstool be:
Before I call, oh! do Thou answer me,
    For nothing dare I claim of Thee, my King!

O Thou Who makest guilt to disappear,
My help, my hope, my rock, I will not fear;
Though Thou the body hold in dungeon drear,
    The soul has found the palace of the King.
                                MOSES b. NACHMAN.

TO THE SOUL

O thou, who springest gloriously
    From thy Creator's fountain blest,
    Arise, depart, for this is not thy rest!
The way is long, thou must preparèd be,
    Thy Maker bids thee seek thy goal—
    Return then to thy rest, my soul,
For bountifully has God dealt with thee.

Behold! I am a stranger here,
  My days like fleeting shadows seem.
  When wilt thou, if not now, thy life redeem?
And when thou seek'st thy Maker have no fear,
  For if thou have but purified
  Thy heart from stain of sin and pride,
Thy righteous deeds to Him shall draw thee near.

O thou in strength who treadest, learn
  To know thyself, cast dreams away!
  The goal is distant far, and short the day.
What canst thou plead th' Almighty's grace to earn?
  Would thou the glory of the Lord
  Behold, O soul? With prompt accord
Then to thy Father's house return, return!

JEHUDA HALEVI.

SABBATH HYMN

Come forth, my friend, the bride to meet,
Come, O my friend, the Sabbath greet!

"Observe ye" and "remember" still
The Sabbath—thus His holy will
God in one utterance did proclaim.
The Lord is one, and one His name
To His renown and praise and fame.
    Come forth, my friend, the bride to meet,
    Come, O my friend, the Sabbath greet!

Greet we the Sabbath at our door,
Well-spring of blessing evermore,
With everlasting gladness fraught,
Of old ordained, divinely taught,
Last in creation, first in thought.
    Come forth, my friend, the bride to meet,
    Come, O my friend, the Sabbath greet!

Arouse thyself, awake and shine,
For, lo! it comes, the light divine.
Give forth a song, for over thee

The glory of the Lord shall be
Revealed in beauty speedily.
　　Come forth, my friend, the bride to meet,
　　Come, O my friend, the Sabbath greet!

Crown of thy husband, come in peace,
Come, bidding toil and trouble cease.
With joy and cheerfulness abide
Among thy people true and tried,
Thy faithful people—come, O bride!
　　Come forth, my friend, the bride to meet,
　　Come. O my friend, the Sabbath greet!

SHELOMO HALEVI.

O SLEEPER! WAKE, ARISE!

O sleeper! wake, arise!
　Delusive follies shun,
Keep from the ways of men and raise thine eyes
　To the exalted One.
Hasten as haste the starry orbs of gold
　To serve the Rock of old.
O sleeper! rise and call upon thy God!

Behold the firmament
　His hands have wrought on high,
See how His mighty arms uphold the tent
　Of His ethereal sky,
And mark the host of stars that heaven reveals—
His graven rings and seals.
Tremble before His majesty and hope
　For His salvation still,
Lest, when for thee the gates of fortune ope,
　False pride thy spirit fill.
O sleeper! rise and call upon thy God!

Go seek at night abroad
　Their footsteps, who erewhile
Were saints on earth, whose lips with hymns o'erflowed,
　Whose hearts were free from guilt.
Their nights were spent in ceaseless prayer and praise,
　In pious fast their days.

Their souls were paths to God, and by His throne
  Their place is set anigh.
Their road through life was but a stepping-stone
  Unto the Lord on high.
O sleeper! rise and call upon thy God!

Weep for thy sins, and pause
  In wrongful deeds, to implore
God's pardoning grace, nor fret thyself because
  Of evildoers more.
Cleave to the right, and of thy substance bring
  To honor Him, thy King
When saviours then Mount Zion joyfully
  Ascend with eager feet,
And nations shout for gladness, thou wilt be
  Prepared thy God to meet.
O sleeper! rise and call upon thy God!

Whence does man's wisdom flow—
  Man, who of dust is wrought,
Whose poor pre-eminence on earth does show
  Over the beast as naught?
Only those gazing with the inward eye
  Behold God's majesty:
They have the well-spring of their being found,
  More precious far than wine.
Thou also thus, though by earth's fetters bound,
  Mayst find thy Rock divine.
O sleeper! rise and call upon thy God!

The Lord is Lord of all,
  His hands hold life and death,
He bids the lowly rise, the lofty fall,
  The world obeys His breath.
Keep judgment, then, and live and cast aside
  False and rebellious pride,
That asketh when and where, and all below
  And all above would know;
But be thou perfect with the Lord thy God!
O sleeper! rise and call upon thy God!
                         JEHUDA HALEVI

THE LAND OF PEACE

Whose works, O Lord, like Thine can be,
  Who 'neath Thy throne of grace,
For those pure souls from earth set free,
  Hast made a dwelling-place?

There are the sinless spirits bound
  Up in the bond of life,
The weary there new strength have found,
  The weak have rest from strife.

Sweet peace and calm their spirits bless,
  Who reach that heavenly home,
And never-ending pleasantness—
  Such is the world to come.

There glorious visions manifold
  Those happy ones delight,
And in God's presence they behold
  Themselves and Him aright.

In the King's palace they abide,
  And at His table eat,
With kingly dainties satisfied,
  Spiritual food most sweet.

This is the rest forever sure,
  This is the heritage,
Whose goodness and whose bliss endure
  Unchanged from age to age.

This is the land the spirit knows
  That everlastingly
With milk and honey overflows—
  And such its fruit shall be.

                    SOLOMON IBN GEBIROL.

THE HEART'S DESIRE

Lord! unto Thee are ever manifest
My inmost heart's desires, though unexprest
In spoken words. Thy mercy I implore
Even for a moment—then to die were blest.

Oh! if I might but win that grace divine,
Into Thy hand, O Lord, I would resign
My spirit then, and lay me down in peace
To my repose, and sweetest sleep were mine.

Afar from Thee in midst of life I die,
And life in death I find, when Thou art nigh.
Alas! I know not how to seek Thy face,
Nor how to serve and worship Thee, Most High.

Oh! lead me in Thy path, and turn again
My heart's captivity, and break in twain
The yoke of folly: teach me to afflict
My soul, the while I yet life's strength retain.

Despise not Thou my lowly penitence,
Ere comes the day, when, deadened every sense,
My limbs too feeble grown to bear my weight,
A burden to myself, I journey hence.

When to the all-consuming moth a prey,
My wasted form sinks slowly to decay,
And I shall seek the place my fathers sought,
And find my rest there where at rest are they.

I am on earth a sojourner, a guest,
And my inheritance is in her breast,
My youth has sought as yet its own desires,
When will my soul's true welfare be my quest?

The world is too much with me, and its din
Prevents my search eternal peace to win.
How can I serve my Maker when my heart
Is passion's captive, is a slave to sin?

But should I strive to scale ambition's height,
Who with the worm may sleep ere fall of night?
Or can I joy in happiness to-day
Who know not what may chance by morning's light?

My days and nights will soon, with restless speed,
Consume life's remnant yet to me decreed;
Then half my body shall the winds disperse,
Half will return to dust, as dust indeed.

What more can I allege? From youth to age
Passion pursues me still at every stage.
If Thou art not my portion, what is mine?
Lacking Thy favor, what my heritage?

Bare of good deeds, scorched by temptation's fire,
Yet to Thy mercy dares my soul aspire;
But wherefore speech prolong, since unto Thee,
O Lord, is manifest my heart's desire?

JEHUDA HALEVI.

O SOUL, WITH STORMS BESET!

O soul, with storms beset!
Thy griefs and cares forget.
Why dread earth's transient woe,
When soon thy body in the grave unseen
    Shall be laid low,
And all will be forgotten then, as though
    It had not been?

Wherefore, my soul, be still!
Adore God's holy will,
Fear death's supreme decree.
Thus mayst thou save thyself, and win high aid
    To profit thee,
When thou, returning to thy Lord, shalt see
    Thy deeds repaid.

Why muse, O troubled soul,
O'er life's poor earthly goal?

When thou hast fled, the clay
Lies mute, nor bear'st thou aught of wealth, or might
With thee that day,
But, like a bird, unto thy nest away,
Thou wilt take flight.

Why for a land lament
In which a lifetime spent
Is as a hurried breath?
Where splendor turns to gloom, and honors show
A faded wreath,
Where health and healing soon must sink beneath
The fatal bow?

What seemeth good and fair
Is often falsehood there.
Gold melts like shifting sands,
Thy hoarded riches pass to other men
And strangers' hands,
And what will all thy treasured wealth and lands
Avail thee then?

Life is a vine, whose crown
The reaper Death cuts down.
His ever-watchful eyes
Mark every step until night's shadows fall,
And swiftly flies
The passing day, and ah! how distant lies
The goal of all.

Therefore, rebellious soul,
Thy base desires control;
With scantly given bread
Content thyself, nor let thy memory stray
To splendors fled,
But call to mind affliction's weight, and dread
The judgment-day.

Prostrate and humbled go,
Like to the dove laid low,

Remember evermore
The peace of heaven, the Lord's eternal rest.
When burdened sore
With sorrow's load, at every step implore
His succor blest.

Before God's mercy-seat
His pardoning love entreat.
Make pure thy thoughts from sin,
And bring a contrite heart as sacrifice
His grace to win—
Then will His angels come and lead thee in
To Paradise.

SOLOMON IBN GEBIROL.

SANCTIFICATION

The sixfold wingèd angels cry
To Him, Who hates iniquity:
    Holy art Thou, O Lord!
    Holy art Thou!

The mighty ones of earth do call
To Him, Who has created all:
    Blessed art Thou, O Lord!
    Blessed art Thou!

They, who in radiance shine, proclaim
Of Him, Who wrought them out of flame:
    Holy art Thou, O Lord!
    Holy art Thou!

Those doubly tried by flood and fire
United chant in frequent choir:
    Blessed art Thou, O Lord!
    Holy and blest!

Pure spheres celestial echoing round,
With voice of sweetest song resound:
    Holy art Thou, O Lord!
    Holy art Thou!

All those redeemèd not by gold,
Repeat in faith and joy untold:
  Blessed art Thou, O Lord!
    Blessed art Thou!

They who pass swiftly to and fro
Make answer, as they come and go:
  Holy art Thou, O Lord!
    Holy art Thou!

Who seek His law, and testify
That there is none beside Him, cry:
  Blessed art Thou, O Lord!
    Holy and blest!

The hosts of radiant seraphs call
To Him, most glorious of them all:
  Holy art Thou, O Lord!
    Holy art Thou!

The sons of mighty men declare
His majesty beyond compare:
  Blessed art Thou, O Lord!
    Blessed art Thou!

All they who glorify His name,
With every morn anew proclaim:
  Holy art Thou, O Lord!
    Holy art Thou!

Israel, His people, ceaselessly
Cry as they bend and bow the knee:
  Blessed art Thou, O Lord!
    Holy and blest.

Those shining as a crystal spring,
Chant in the presence of their King:
  Holy art Thou, O Lord!
    Holy art Thou!

The stranger's children evermore
The mighty Lord of lords adore.
  Blessed art Thou, O Lord!
    Blessed art Thou!

Those who of fire are fashioned, crowd
On crowd unnumbered, chant aloud:
　　Holy art Thou, O Lord!
　　　Holy art Thou!

They cry, whom He has freed from thrall,
And His inheritance does call:
　　Blessed art Thou, O Lord!
　　　Holy and blest.

Pure visions, bathed in endless light,
Declare 'midst radiance infinite:
　　Holy art Thou, O Lord!
　　　Holy art Thou!

Who to the covenant adhere,
The remnant saved, cry loud and clear:
　　Blessed art Thou, O Lord!
　　　Blessed art Thou!

'Neath folded wings, in cadence meet,
The glorious ones each hour repeat:
　　Holy art Thou, O Lord!
　　　Holy art Thou!

She, who among the nations dwells,
Chosen, apart, His glory tells:
　　Holy art Thou, O Lord!
　　　Holy and blest!

The high exalted ones make known
Of Him, Who fills the heavenly throne:
　　Holy art Thou, O Lord!
　　　Holy art Thou!

They who their God each day proclaim
" Awful in deeds," exalt His name:
　　Blessed art Thou, O Lord!
　　　Blessed art Thou!

Those who are awe-inspiring say
Of Him more awful far than they:
　　Holy art Thou, O Lord!
　　　Holy art Thou!

To all creation's King of kings,
From earth, from heaven, responsive rings:
  Holy art Thou, O Lord!
    Holy and blest!

                JOSEPH IBN ABITUR.

HYMN OF PRAISE

O God of earth and heaven,
  Spirit and flesh are Thine!
Thou hast in wisdom given
  Man's inward light divine,
And unto him Thy grace accords
  The gift of spoken words.
The world was fashioned by Thy will,
Nor didst Thou toil at it, for still
Thy breath did Thy design fulfil.

My times are in Thy hand,
  Thou knowest what is best,
And where I fear to stand
  Thy strength brings succor blest.
Thy loving-kindness, as within
  A mantle, hides my sin.
Thy mercies are my sure defence,
And for Thy bounteous providence
Thou dost demand no recompense.

For all the sons of men
  Thou hast a book prepared,
Where, without hand or pen,
  Their deeds are all declared:
Yet for the pure in heart shall be
  A pardon found with Thee.
The life and soul Thou didst create
Thou hast redeemed from evil strait,
Thou hast not left me desolate.

The heavens Thou badest be,
  Thy bright, celestial throne,

Are witnesses to Thee,
  O Thou the Lord alone.
One, indivisible, Thy name
  Upholds creation's frame.
Thou madest all—the depth, the height,
Thou rulest all in power and might,
Supreme, eternal, infinite!

ABRAHAM IBN EZRA.

PASSOVER HYMN

When as a wall the sea
  In heaps uplifted lay,
A new song unto Thee
  Sang the redeemed that day.

Thou didst in his deceit
  O'erwhelm the Egyptian's feet,
While Israel's footsteps fleet
  How beautiful were they!

Jeshurun! all who see
  Thy glory cry to thee:
" Who like thy God can be? "
  Thus even our foes did say.

Oh! let thy banner soar
  The scattered remnant o'er,
And gather them once more
  Like corn on harvest-day.

Who bear through all their line
  Thy covenant's holy sign,
And to Thy name divine
  Are sanctified alway.

Let all the world behold
  Their token, prized of old,
Who on their garment's fold
  The thread of blue display.

Be then the truth made known
  For whom, and whom alone,
The twisted fringe is shown,
  The covenant kept this day.

Oh! let them, sanctified,
  Once more with Thee abide,
Their sun shine far and wide,
  And chase the clouds away.

The well-beloved declare
  Thy praise in song and prayer:
"Who can with Thee compare,
  O Lord of Hosts?" they say.

When as a wall the sea
  In heaps uplifted lay,
A new song unto Thee
  Sang the redeemed that day.

JEHUDA HALEVI.

MORNING PRAYER

O Lord! my life was known to Thee
Ere Thou hadst caused me yet to be,
Thy Spirit ever dwells in me.

Could I, cast down by Thee, have gained
A standing place, or, if restrained
By Thee, go forth with feet unchained?

Hear me, Almighty, while I pray,
My thoughts are in Thy hand alway,
Be to my helplessness a stay!

Oh! may this hour Thy favor yield,
And may I tread life's battle-field
Encompassed by Thy mercy's shield.

Wake me at dawn Thy name to bless,
And in Thy sanctuary's recess
To praise and laud Thy holiness.

JEHUDA HALEVI.

25

JUDGMENT AND MERCY

By the faithful of His children in their conclaves
  Shall His name be sanctified,
Awe-inspiring are the praises of His angels,
And the voices in His temple spread His glory
  Far and wide.

Those who keep His law shall yet again be gathered
  To the stronghold of His might,
Those who fear Him commune, praying, with each other—
He will hear and in the book of their memorial
  He will write.

Let your deeds be fair and righteous—then unbroken
  He the covenant will hold.
He who maketh bright the heavens, He will heed you
And will count your prayers more precious than the off'rings
  Brought of old.

May the tribes of those who worship and proclaim Him
  Be uplifted as of yore,
When He pruneth, may He cut the straggling branches,
For to Him belong the sov'reignty and kingdom
  Evermore.

May He lead us once again unto the mountain
  Of His sanctuary's shrine,
There to glorify Him ever in His temple,
For our God will not forget His word, the holy
  And divine.

At His name shall heaven and earth break forth in praises
  With a joy that shall not cease,
And the woods shall shout and clap their hands in gladness,
For the Lord our God has visited His people,
  Bringing peace.

From each band of angels mighty in their splendor,
  From each shining, circling star,

Hymns and praises evermore declare His glory,
Saying, " Praise Him with the sound of joyful trumpets,
    The Shophar ! "

All the creatures of the universe together,
    Heaven above and earth below,
Shall proclaim, " The Lord in all His works is mighty,
He is king o'er all the earth, and His salvation
    All shall know."

ANON.

GRACE AFTER MEALS

Our Rock with loving care,
    According to His word,
Bids all His bounty share,
    Then let us bless the Lord.

His flock our Shepherd feeds
With graciousness divine,
He satisfies our needs
With gifts of bread and wine.
Therefore with one accord
We will His name adore,
Proclaiming evermore
None holy as the Lord.
    Our Rock, etc.

The land desired so long,
Our fathers' heritage,
Inspires our grateful song
To God from age to age;
His bounteous gifts afford
Us sustenance each day,
His mercy is our stay,
For faithful is the Lord.
    Our Rock, etc.

Oh! be Thy mercy moved,
Our Rock, to dwell with us,

With Zion, Thy beloved,
Our temple glorious.
May we, redeemed, restored,
Be led there every one,
By David's holy son,
The anointed of the Lord.
  Our Rock, etc.

Thy city fill once more,
Thy temple-walls upraise,
There will we Thee adore
With joyful songs of praise,
Thee, merciful, adored,
We bless and sanctify,
With wine-cups filled up high,
By blessings of the Lord.
  Our Rock, etc.

      ANON.

"LORD OF THE UNIVERSE"

Lord of the universe, Who reigned
 Ere earth and heaven's fashioning,
When to create the world He deigned,
 Then was His name proclaimèd King.

And at the end of days shall He,
 The Dreaded One, still reign alone,
Who was, Who is, and still will be
 Unchanged upon His glorious throne.

And He is one, His powers transcend,
 Supreme, unfathomed, depth and height,
Without beginning, without end,
 His are dominion, power, and might.

My God and my Redeemer He,
 My rock in sorrow's darkest day,
A help and refuge unto me,
 My cup's full portion, when I pray.

My soul into His hand divine
  Do I commend: I will not fear,
My body with it I resign,
  I dread no evil: God is near.

ANON.

HYMN FOR THE CONCLUSION OF THE SABBATH

May He Who sets the holy and profane
Apart, blot out our sins before His sight,
And make our numbers as the sand again,
  And as the stars of night.

The day declineth like the palm-tree's shade,
I call on God, Who leadeth me aright,
The morning cometh—thus the watchman said—
  Although it now be night.

Thy righteousness is like Mount Tabor vast,
Oh! let my sins be wholly put to flight,
Be they as yesterday, forever past,
  And as a watch at night.

The peaceful season of my prayers is o'er,
Would that again had rest my soul contrite,
Weary am I of groaning evermore,
  I melt in tears each night.

Hear Thou my voice: be it not vainly sped,
Open to me the gates of lofty height,
For with the evening dew is filled my head,
  My locks with drops of night.

Oh! grant me Thy redemption, while I pray,
Be Thou entreated, Lord of power and might,
In twilight, in the evening of the day,
  Yea, in the gloom of night.

Save me, O Lord my God! I call on Thee:
Make me to know the path of life aright,

From sore and wasting sickness snatch Thou me,
　　Lead me from day to night.

We are like clay within Thy hand, O Lord!
Forgive us all our sins, both grave and light,
And day shall unto day pour forth the word
　　And night declare to night.

May He Who sets the holy and profane
Apart, blot out our sins before His sight,
And make our numbers as the sand again,
　　And as the stars of night.

ANON.

GOD AND MAN

O Lord! I will declare
Thy holy name, Thy glories past compare:
My tongue shall not conceal, O Lord!
Thy righteousness made known to me:
I heard and I believed Thy word,
I will not ask presumptuously.
For should the vase of clay
" What doest thou? " unto its maker say?
Him have I sought and known,
A rock of strength, a tower of might,
Resplendent as the glorious light,
Without or veil or covering, radiant shown:
Exalted, magnified,
　　　　　　Extolled and glorified.

The heavens from hour to hour
Declare Thy wondrous works, proclaim Thy power;
Sunrise and sunset, still the same,
Prostrate in awe eternally.
The angels pass through flood and flame
'As unto Thee they testify;
Thy praise they celebrate,
O Thou, the fruit of lips who dost create.

For Thou uphold'st alone,
Unwearied and invisible,
The depths, the heights, where move and dwell
The living creatures and the heavenly throne:
Exalted, magnified,
> Extolled and glorified.

Who has the glory praised
Fitly of Him, Whose word the heavens upraised?
The Eternal One, Who dwells concealed
In His exalted heights, but yet
In Zion's temple, full revealed,
Did erst His glorious presence set,
And He showed visions then
To cause His image to be seen of men;
Yet past all measuring
His wisdom is, past depth and height
He flashes on His prophet's sight
In visions only as the heavenly king·
Exalted, magnified,
> Extolled and glorified.

His power, exceeding great,
Is without end: who can His praise narrate?
Happy the man, who testifies
Unto His greatness manifold,
Whose faith in God unshaken lies,
In God, whose arms the world uphold,
Who, fearing God, can trust
In Him, acknowledging His deeds are just,
That for himself has He
Made all His works, His creatures all,
And that His awful day will call
All men, the judgment of their deeds to see:
Exalted, magnified,
> Extolled and glorified.

Do thou then heed and learn,
Prepare thyself thy nature to discern.
See whence thou comest, what thou art,
And who created thee and taught

Thee knowledge, and in every part
Of thee the power of motion wrought.
Mark then God's might untold,
And rouse thyself His wonders to behold.
But to Himself concealed
Dare not to stretch thy hand, for then
Thou seekest, with presumptuous ken,
The first and last, the hidden and revealed:
Exalted, magnified,
   Extolled and glorified.

JEHUDA HALEVI.

HYMN FOR TABERNACLES

Thy praise, O Lord! will I proclaim
In hymns unto Thy glorious name.
O thou Redeemer, Lord and King,
Redemption to Thy faithful bring!
Before Thine altar they rejoice
With branch of palm and myrtle stem,
To Thee they raise the prayful voice—
Have mercy, save and prosper them.

Mayst Thou, in mercy manifold,
Dear unto Thee Thy people hold,
When at Thy gate they bend the knee,
And worship and acknowledge Thee.
Do Thou their heart's desire fulfil,
Rejoice with them in love this day,
Forgive their sins and thoughts of ill,
And their transgressions cast away.

They overflow with prayer and praise
To Him, Who knows the future days.
Have mercy Thou, and hear the prayer
Of those who palms and myrtles bear.
Thee day and night they sanctify,
And in perpetual song adore;
Like to the heavenly hosts they cry:
" Blessed art Thou for evermore."

ELEAZAR b. JACOB KALIR.

HYMN FOR PENTECOST

When Thou didst descend upon Sinai's mountain,
It trembled and shook 'neath Thy mighty hand,
And the rocks were moved by Thy power and splendor;
How then can my spirit before Thee stand
On the day when darkness o'erspread the heavens,
And the sun was hidden at Thy command?
The angels of God for Thy great name's worship,
Are ranged before Thee, a shining band,
And the children of men are waiting ever
Thy mercies unnumbered as grains of sand;
The law they received from the mouth of Thy glory,
They learn and consider and understand.
Oh! accept Thou their song and rejoice in their gladness,
Who proclaim Thy glory in every land.

JEHUDA HALEVI.

HYMN OF GLORY

Sweet hymns and songs will I indite
To sing of Thee by day and night,
Of Thee, Who art my soul's delight.

How doth my soul within me yearn
Beneath Thy shadow to return,
Thy secret mysteries to learn.

And even while yet Thy glory fires
My words, and hymns of praise inspires,
Thy love it is my heart desires.

Therefore I will of Thee relate
All glorious things, and celebrate
In songs of love Thy name most great.

Thy glory shall my discourse be,
In images I picture Thee,
Although Thyself I cannot see.

In mystic utterances alone,
By prophet and by seer made known,
Hast Thou Thy radiant glory shown.

Thy might and greatness they portrayed,
According to the power displayed
In all the works Thy hand has made.

In images of Thee they told
Of Thy great wonders wrought of old,
Thy essence they could not behold.

In signs and visions seen of yore
They pictured Thee in ancient lore,
But Thou art One for evermore.

They saw in Thee both youth and age,
The man of war, the hoary sage,
But ever Israel's heritage.

O Thou Whose word is truth alway
Thy people seek Thy face this day,
Oh! be Thou near them when they pray.

May these, my songs and musings, be
Acceptable, O Lord, to Thee,
And do Thou hear them graciously.

Oh! let my praises, heavenward sped,
Be as a crown unto Thy head,
My prayer as incense offerèd.

Oh! may my words of blessing rise
To Thee, Who, throned above the skies,
Art just and mighty, great and wise.

And when Thy glory I declare,
Do Thou incline Thee to my prayer,
As though sweet spice my offering were.

My meditation day and night
May it be pleasant in Thy sight,
For Thou art all my soul's delight.

HYMN OF UNITY FOR THE SEVEN DAYS OF THE WEEK [1]

I

Eternal King, the heavens and earth are Thine,
Thine are the seas and every living thing.
Thy hand upholds creation's vast design,
   Eternal King!

The mighty waters with Thy glory ring,
Unnumbered lands to chant Thy praise combine,
And Kings of earth to Thee their worship bring.

Thy people Israel, for Thy love benign,
Blesses Thy name and joys Thy praise to sing.
Thou art the God of truth, the one, divine,
   Eternal King!

II

I worship Thee for all Thy boundless store
Of righteousness and mercy shown to me,
And for Thy holy book of sacred lore
   I worship Thee.

To Thee alone our fathers bent the knee,
And Thee alone do we this day adore,
Bearing our witness to Thy unity.

Thou art our God, Thy favor we implore,
Thou art our shepherd, and Thy flock are we.
Therefore I bless Thy name and evermore
   I worship Thee.

III

I know it well: Thou art all-good, all-wise.
Thou slayest, but Thy touch death's power can quell;
Thou woundest, but Thy hand the balm supplies:
   I know it well.

---

[1] The original of the "Hymn of Unity" is in seven very long parts. These short ones merely give the leading idea in each of the original parts.

Nor sin nor grief can in Thy presence dwell,
Slumber and sleep come not unto Thine eyes,
Great God, eternal and unchangeable!

The soul of all mankind before Thee lies;
Thou searchest all their hearts, their thoughts canst tell;
Thou hearest graciously their prayerful cries:
            I know it well.

IV

We will extol the Lord of lords, whose name
Is evermore and everywhere adored.
In songs and hymns our lips His praise shall frame,
            We will extol the Lord!

He is the hope of Israel, His word
A lamp unto our feet, a guiding flame
To those who trust in Him with full accord.

He is through countless ages still the same,
The shield of our salvation and our sword,
And generations, each to each, proclaim:
            We will extol the Lord!

v

Who shall narrate Thy wonders wrought of old?
The utterance of the lips Thou didst create,
But all Thy majesty and power untold
            Who shall narrate?

Thy ways on earth in song we celebrate.
Though none may Thy similitude behold,
Yet know we by Thy works that Thou are great.

Thousands of angels, by Thy word controlled,
To do Thy bidding Thy commands await:
Yet of them all, Thy wonders manifold
            Who shall narrate?

VI

Alone didst Thou, O Lord, the heaven's wide tent
Uprear, and bid the earth beneath be shown ;
Thy word the oceans in their boundaries pent
    Alone.

No aid or counsel hadst Thou save Thine own
When Thou with lights didst hang the firmament
And call the hosts celestial round Thy throne.

Thy works, in universal cadence blent,
Give praise to Thee, and make Thy glory known.
Thou madest all, great God beneficent,
    Alone!

VII

Of old Thou didst the Sabbath bless and praise,
Because thereon Thou didst Thy work behold
Completed in the sun's new-kindled rays
    Of old.

Bless Thou, this day, with mercies manifold
Thy people, that in love and awe obeys
Thy word, and chants Thy righteousness untold.

Lord, we desire to do Thy will always!
Make pure our hearts like thrice-refinèd gold,
And these, our prayers, accept as in the days
    Of old.

ANON.

PENITENTIAL PRAYER

Forth flies my soul, upborne by hope untiring,
The land of rest, the spring of life desiring,
Unto the heavenly dwelling-place aspiring,
    To seek its peace by day and night.

My spirit does God's majesty adore,
And without wings shall to His presence soar,
There to behold His glory evermore,
    At dawn, at noonday, and at night.

On all His works mine eye in wonder gazes,
And heavenward an eager look upraises;
Day unto day proclaims its Maker's praises,
   And night declares them unto night.

Thy loving-kindness is my lifelong guide,
But often from Thy path I've turned aside.
O Lord, how hast Thou searched my heart and tried
   My inmost thoughts at dead of night!

Sleepless upon my bed the hours I number,
And, rising, seek the house of God, while slumber
Lies heavy on men's eyes, and dreams encumber
   Their souls in visions of the night.

In sin and folly passed my early years,
Wherefore I am ashamed, and life's arrears
Now strive to pay, the while my bitter tears
   Have been my food by day and night.

Pent in the body's cage, pure child of heaven,
Bethink thee, life but as a bridge is given.
Awake, arise, to praise God gladly, even
   In the first hours of the night.

Haste then, pure heart, to break sin's deadly sway,
And seek the path of righteousness alway;
For all our years are but as yesterday—
   Soon past, and as a watch at night.

Short is man's life, and full of care and sorrow,
This way and that he turns some ease to borrow,
Like to a flower he blooms, and on the morrow
   Is gone—a vision of the night.

How does the weight of sin my soul oppress!
Because God's law too often I transgress;
I mourn and sigh: with tears of bitterness
   My bed I water all the night.

I rise at dawn and still the salt stream flows,
My heart's blood would I shed to find repose;

But when my soul is downcast with my woes,
  I will recall my prayer at night.

My youth wanes like a shadow that is cast,
Swifter than eagles' wings my years fly fast,
And I remember not my gladness past,
  Either by day or yet by night.

Proclaim we then a fast, a holy day,
Make pure our hearts from sin, God's will obey,
And unto Him, with humble spirits, pray
  Unceasingly, by day and night.

May we yet hear His words: " Thou art my own,
My grace is thine, the shelter of My throne,
For I am thy Redeemer, I alone!
  Endure but patiently this night."

MOSES IBN EZRA.

THE LIVING GOD WE PRAISE

The living God we praise, exalt, adore!
He was, He is, He will be evermore.

No unity like unto His can be,
Eternal, inconceivable, is He.

No form or shape has th' Incorporeal One,
Most holy beyond all comparison.

He was, ere aught was made in heaven or earth,
But His existence has no date or birth.

Lord of the Universe is He proclaimed,
Teaching His power to all His hand has framed.

He gave His gift of prophecy to those
In whom He gloried, whom He loved and chose.

No prophet ever yet has filled the place
Of Moses, who beheld God face to face.

Through him (the faithful in his house) the Lord
The law of truth to Israel did accord.

This law God will not alter, will not change
For any other through time's utmost range.

He knows and heeds the secret thoughts of man,
He saw the end of all ere aught began.

With love and grace doth He the righteous bless,
He metes out evil unto wickedness.

He at the last will His anointed send,
Those to redeem, who hope and wait the end.

God will the dead to life again restore,
Praised be His glorious name for evermore.

ANON.

CPSIA information can be obtained
at www.ICGtesting.com
Printed in the USA
BVOW06s1508230217
476872BV00011B/320/P